FITZWILLIAM MUSEUM CAMBRIDGE

CATALOGUE OF PAINTINGS

VOLUME III

BRITISH SCHOOL

BY

J. W. GOODISON

Emeritus Fellow of
Darwin College, Cambridge

CAMBRIDGE UNIVERSITY PRESS

CAMBRIDGE

LONDON · NEW YORK · MELBOURNE

FOR THE FITZWILLIAM MUSEUM, CAMBRIDGE

Published by the Syndics of the Cambridge University Press
The Pitt Building, Trumpington Street, Cambridge CB2 1RP
Bentley House, 200 Euston Road, London NW1 2DB
32 East 57th Street, New York, NY 10022, USA
296 Beaconsfield Parade, Middle Park, Melbourne 3206, Australia

ISBN 0 521 21638 9 Volume I
ISBN 0 521 21637 0 Volume II
ISBN 0 521 21620 6 Volume III
ISBN 0 521 21639 7 Set

Vol. I First published by the Fitzwilliam Museum 1960
Vol. II First published by the Fitzwilliam Museum 1967
Vol. III First published by Cambridge University Press 1977
The set First issued by Cambridge University Press 1977

Printed in Great Britain at the
University Press, Cambridge

Library of Congress Cataloguing in Publication Data (Revised)

Cambridge. University. Fitzwilliam Museum.
Catalogue of paintings.

CONTENTS: v. 1. Dutch and Flemish, by H. Gerson & J. W. Goodison. French, German, Spanish, by J. W. Goodison & D. Sutton.–v. 3. British School, by J. W. Goodison
1. Paintings – England – Cambridge – Catalogues.
2. Cambridge. University. Fitzwilliam Museum.
N1217.A55 750'.74'02659 61–19559
ISBN 0 521 21620 6 (v. 3)

CATALOGUE OF PAINTINGS IN THE FITZWILLIAM MUSEUM CAMBRIDGE

CONTENTS

PREFACE

The initial volume of the current *Catalogue of paintings in the Fitzwilliam Museum* was published in 1960. In it the Dutch and Flemish Schools were dealt with by Dr (now Professor) Horst Gerson and by Mr J. W. Goodison; the French, German and Spanish Schools by Mr J. W. Goodison and Mr Denys Sutton. Seven years later a second volume appeared, devoted to the Italian Schools; again a work of collaboration, but in this instance between Mr Goodison and Mr (now Professor) Giles Robertson, who took on the responsibility for it after the untimely death in 1951 of Dr Hans Gronau. Volume I, complete up to 1958, carried a general note on the history of the whole collection of paintings in the Museum since the founder, Richard, 7th Viscount Fitzwilliam of Merrion, combined his inheritance from the Fitzwilliam and the Decker families; and this account need not be repeated here. Volume II was complete to the end of 1965, including six Italian paintings acquired since the text of the previous volume was written.

Now Volume III, devoted to what has become the most numerous section of the painting collection, 350 works of the British School, has been made ready by Mr Goodison. With it he has discharged his undertaking as general editor of the long-awaited series which was first projected in 1949 to replace, after almost half a century, Earp's *A descriptive catalogue of the pictures in the Fitzwilliam Museum*. What is offered in the new volume is complete up to the end of 1975. The Museum is grateful to Mr Goodison for continuing during the opening decade of his retirement from its service the large and happily ever-growing task which he had begun as Keeper of Paintings and Deputy Director.

The new acquisitions, since Mr Goodison's series of catalogues began, include not only several paintings by British contemporaries bought in the four years from 1971, during which period the Fitzwilliam was one of the museums in this country to benefit by a Calouste Gulbenkian Foundation grant of £1,000 a year towards buying works of art by living artists (providing that this sum was matched annually from the Museum's own purchase funds); but also a larger number, all landscapes and none by living painters, bought with the Fairhaven Fund. Indeed the first quarter century of buying such landscapes for the Museum with this fund provided by Huttleston, 1st Lord Fairhaven, is being celebrated by a full exhibition in our Adeane

Gallery of all that has been chosen by the Syndicate to date, drawings as well as paintings; and this exhibition has been timed to coincide with the readiness of Volume III to go to press. In the most recent years the British collection has grown also through other benefactions: three paintings by Wilson Steer from the late Mrs G. John Scaramanga, two by Sickert from Keith Baynes, who has been generous also with his own works, and a *Self-portrait* by George Richmond allocated to the Museum by the Lords Commissioners of the Treasury from the Kerrison Preston estate, are of notable importance. Outstanding among gifts from the Friends of the Fitzwilliam has been Alfred Elmore's *On the brink*, his masterpiece on a 'modern life' subject; and from the Contemporary Art Society, Paul Nash's *November moon*.

The Fitzwilliam Museum Syndicate wish to thank also the Syndics of the University Press for their valuable collaboration in the production of this final volume of the *Catalogue of paintings*.

November 1976 MICHAEL JAFFÉ

EXPLANATIONS

Right and *left* refer to the point of view of the spectator, unless otherwise indicated by the context.

In the dimensions, height precedes width; the measurements are those of the painted surface.

Notes on condition are restricted to those paintings whose impaired state might affect their estimation.

ABBREVIATIONS

A.R.A.	Associate of the Royal Academy
b.	born
Bart	Baronet
Bef. or bef.	before
B.I.	British Institution
Bros.	Brothers
bt	bought
C.B.E.	Commander of the Order of the British Empire
C.M.G.	Commander of the Order of St Michael and St George
coll.	collection
Constable	W. G. Constable, *Catalogue of the pictures in the Marlay Bequest, Fitzwilliam Museum, Cambridge* (1927)
d.	died
D.S.O.	Distinguished Service Order
Earp	F. R. Earp, *A descriptive catalogue of the pictures in the Fitzwilliam Museum* (1902)
ed.	editor, edited
edn	edition
exbn	exhibition
exh.	exhibited
F.B.A.	Fellow of the British Academy
F.R.S.	Fellow of the Royal Society

Hazlitt, 1974	Hazlitt, Gooden & Fox, London, exhibition, 'Landscapes from the Fitzwilliam', 1974
K.B.E.	Knight Commander of the Order of the British Empire
K.C.B.	Knight Commander of the Order of the Bath
K.C.V.O.	Knight Commander of the Royal Victorian Order
K.G.	Knight of the Order of the Garter
kt	knight, knighted
Ltd	Limited
M.C.	Military Cross
MS	manuscript
no.	number
O.M.	Order of Merit
p.	page
P.C.	Privy Councillor
pl.	plate
P.R.A.	President of the Royal Academy
Principal pictures	*The principal pictures in the Fitzwilliam Museum, Cambridge*
R.A.	Royal Academy, Royal Academician
rep.	reproduced
R.S.A.	Royal Scottish Academy
Rt Hon.	Right Honourable
suc.	succeeded

CATALOGUE

ALMA-TADEMA, Sir Lawrence

1836–1912. Of Dutch birth; trained at Antwerp. Settled in London, 1870; naturalised, and became A.R.A., 1876; R.A., 1879; kt, 1899; O.M., 1907. A prolific painter, best known for his historical subjects.

1012 SIR HENRY THOMPSON, BART (1878)

Wood, $11\frac{1}{16} \times 8\frac{1}{4}$ in (28·1 × 20·9 cm).[1] Head and shoulders, turned towards the right; moustache and whiskers. Wears brownish jacket and grey waistcoat, with stiff wing collar and black bow tie. Signed lower left, 'LAT'. On the back is a MS label: 'A sketch of the Owner, made on board the "Gipsy", Thames House Boat, by Alma Tadema, when he stayed with me & Herbert on the boat for a little sketching visit in the year 1878; made on the panel of the cabin sleeping room door. Henry Thompson "Owner"!'

Given by Sir H. F. Herbert Thompson, Bart, 1920. Painted for Sir Henry Thompson, Bart, father of the donor, 1878; exh. London, Grosvenor Gallery, 1882–3, Winter Exhibition (237).

A sketch painted directly onto the wood, in the form of a vignette. Sir Henry Thompson (1820–1904), surgeon, kt, 1867, Bart, 1899; a gifted amateur painter, and pupil of Alma-Tadema.

NOTE. [1] Dimensions of the panel; the sketch is framed within an oval mount.

1013 SIR HERBERT THOMPSON, BART (1877)

Wood, $11\frac{1}{8} \times 8\frac{7}{8}$ in (28·3 × 22·6 cm).[1] Head and shoulders turned towards the left. Wears grey clothes with a red smoking cap, a tassel falling over forehead. Signed lower right, 'L Alma Tadema'. On the back is a MS label: 'A sketch of Herbert, made on board the Gipsey, on the cabin door, by Alma Tadema, when he staid with us for a sketching visit in the year 1877. Henry Thompson.'

Given by Sir H. F. Herbert Thompson, Bart, 1920. Painted for Sir Henry Thompson, Bart, father of the donor, 1877; exh. London, Grosvenor Gallery, 1882–3, Winter Exhibition (238).

A sketch painted directly onto the wood, in the form of a vignette. Sir (Henry Francis) Herbert Thompson (1859–1944), barrister, succeeded his father, Sir Henry Thompson, as 2nd baronet in 1904; he was a fellow of

University College, London, and became F.B.A. in 1933. The *Gipsy* was his father's house-boat on the Thames.

NOTE. [1] Dimensions of the panel; the sketch is framed within an oval mount.

1014 94° IN THE SHADE (1876)

Canvas,[1] $13\frac{7}{8} \times 8\frac{1}{2}$ in (35·3 × 21·6 cm). In the foreground of a harvest field, lies a man in a white suit and sun helmet poring over a book, a butterfly net before him. Signed and inscribed lower right, 'L Alma Tadema op CLXIV'.

Given by Sir H. F. Herbert Thompson, Bart, 1920. Coll. Sir Henry Thompson, Bart, father of the donor; exh. London, Grosvenor Gallery, 1882–3, Winter Exhibition (64); Whitechapel Art Gallery, 1908, Spring Exhibition (451); Bermondsey Settlement Fine Arts Exhibition (date unknown);[2] R.A., 1913, 'Works by the late Sir Lawrence Alma-Tadema' (39); Hazlitt, 1974 (1).

Painted in 1876.[3] The scene shows a cornfield at Godstone, Surrey, with the donor, at that date aged seventeen, lying in the foreground.

REPRODUCED. Exhibition catalogue, Hazlitt, 1974, pl. 66.

NOTES. [1] Laid down on a mahogany panel. [2] The Bermondsey Settlement exhibitions were held annually at Whitsun from 1896 to 1912. [3] So dated in the catalogue of the Grosvenor Gallery exhibition, 1882–3, and by Rudolf Dircks, 'The later works of Sir Lawrence Alma-Tadema, O.M., R.A.', *The Art Journal* (1910), Christmas, p. 28, in his 'List of works'.

ASHFORD, William

1746–1824. Born in Birmingham. Settled in Dublin 1764, where he exhibited at the Society of Artists from 1767; in London exhibited at the R.A. from 1775, at the Society of Artists from 1777, and at the B.I. President of the Irish Society of Artists, 1813; of the Royal Hibernian Academy on its foundation in 1823. Landscape painter.

445 VIEW IN MOUNT MERRION PARK

Canvas, $25\frac{1}{4} \times 44\frac{3}{4}$ in (64·1 × 111·1 cm). A greensward enclosed by trees, with a herd of deer at right, and others beside a tall tree left; Dublin Bay in the distance to right with one end of the Hill of Howth. Cloudy sky. Foliage and ground ochre-greens and ochre-browns, water and sky pale blue-grey; creamy clouds.

Pendant to no. 447.

447 VIEW IN MOUNT MERRION PARK

Canvas, $25\frac{3}{8} \times 44\frac{3}{4}$ in ($61{\cdot}9 \times 111{\cdot}1$ cm). To left open parkland with cattle, deer and sheep, slopes away towards trees, beyond which is Dublin Bay with the Hill of Howth in the distance. In the right foreground, emerging obliquely from a wood, is a terraced walk on which are two men in conversation. Colour as for no. 445. Signed towards lower right, 'W. Ashford'.

The view is towards the north. The terraced walk is the North Terrace[1] and the two figures in conversation are said to be 'Lord Fitzwilliam giving orders to his steward'.[2] Pendant to no. 445. Another version was in an anonymous sale at Christie's, 17 April 1964 (46), rep., bought by the Earl of Pembroke.

462 VIEW IN MOUNT MERRION PARK (1804)

Canvas, $37\frac{3}{4} \times 50\frac{3}{4}$ in ($95{\cdot}9 \times 131{\cdot}5$ cm). In the left foreground stands a large classical portico, and at the right are two tall trees, on the open ground between are figures and dogs. On a lower level beyond is open parkland, bordered by a belt of trees, two square towers showing above them at the left. The portico is brown, the foliage and ground are in ochre-greens and ochre-browns. In the distance stretches a panorama of Dublin, with the bay to the right and a glimpse of Booterstown.[3] Grey and cream clouds in a pale sky. Signed and dated lower left, 'W. Ashford. 1804'.

The view is towards the north. The two towers are part of Roebuck Castle.[4] Another version was in an anonymous sale at Christie's, 17 April 1964 (45), rep., the catalogue states that the portico was 'part of the now-demolished summer-house'; bought by the Hon. Desmond Guinness, Leixlip Castle, Co. Kildare.

464 VIEW IN MOUNT MERRION PARK

Canvas, $25\frac{1}{2} \times 30$ in ($64{\cdot}8 \times 76{\cdot}2$ cm). Across a greensward, dotted with figures and sheep and closed in with trees to right and left, a white house is seen towards the centre, with another building to left of it and part of a third at the right, beside which is the end of an avenue, with a carriage and horses. The foliage and ground are in ochre-greens. Pale sky with cream and grey clouds.

The white house, referred to as 'The Lodge', is presumably Lord Fitzwilliam's residence; the building at the right is the stables, and the avenue between them is the Eastern Avenue.[5] Perhaps one of a set, with nos. 466, 467.

466 VIEW IN MOUNT MERRION PARK

Canvas, 25½ × 30⅛ in (64·8 × 76·6 cm). A pool among rocks, which rise to a bluff at the right; on the far side of the pool are deer, with a wood beyond and a distant glimpse of the sea. The rocks are in tones of brown, the foliage in ochre-greens. Pale sky with grey and cream clouds.

The view is near Mountanville Gate, in the south-western part of the park.[6] Perhaps one of a set, with nos. 464 and 467.

467 VIEW IN MOUNT MERRION PARK

Canvas, 25¼ × 30 in (62·2 × 76·2 cm). A greensward surrounded by trees, with two isolated trees in the middle, and some sheep. At the far side part of The Lodge and part of the stables (see no. 464) are seen to the left; to the right two columns. Foliage and ground ochre-greens and ochre-browns. Pale sky with grey and cream clouds. Signed lower left, 'W. Ashford'.

The two columns were on the axis of the Eastern Avenue, at the entrance to a ride in a plantation.[7] Perhaps one of a set, with nos. 464, 466.

Founder's Bequest, 1816.

Mount Merrion was Lord Fitzwilliam's residence in Ireland. It was situated to the south of Dublin, near Booterstown, in a district of residential estates. The area of the park was 259 acres.[8] The style of The Lodge (see no. 464) is late eighteenth or early nineteenth century, but the house near it and the stables are in a fairly early eighteenth-century style. No. 462 is dated 1804, but it cannot be assumed that this is the date of the remaining five paintings. These are all considerably smaller than no. 462, and are related by size to form two groups: a pair of pendants, nos. 445, 447; and a set of three, nos. 464, 466, 467. No. 462 thus stands alone. In addition, the drawings in the Fitzwilliam Museum show that Ashford was working in Mount Merrion Park in 1806,[9] though none of the drawings corresponds with the paintings.

NOTES. [1] From a ground plan preceding a series of twenty-four views of the park, plus a title-page dated 1806, in Indian ink wash and line, by William Ashford, in the Fitzwilliam Museum, Founder's Bequest, 1816 (no. 3933).

[2] William Key, *A catalogue of paintings and drawings bequeathed...by... Viscount Fitzwilliam* (n.d.; perhaps 1817), p. 14. Key was for many years Lord Fitzwilliam's 'head and most confidential servant'. [3] Key, *op. cit.*, p. 10. [4] Key, *loc. cit.*, n. 3. [5] The Lodge and the stables are identified from Ashford's drawings referred to in n. [1], the avenue from the ground plan. [6] Identified from another view of the same place among Ashford's drawings referred to in n. [1]. [7] Identified from Ashford's drawings referred to in n. [1]. [8] Ground plan preceding Ashford's drawings referred to in n. [1]. [9] See n. [1].

BAYNES, Keith Stuart

1887–1977. Born near Reigate, Surrey. Slade School of Art, London, 1912–15; influenced by the Post-Impressionists, member of the London Group. Landscape painter.

PD. 106–1975 SELF-PORTRAIT (1923)

Canvas, $16\frac{1}{4} \times 13\frac{1}{8}$ in ($41{\cdot}3 \times 33{\cdot}3$ cm). Head and shoulders, slightly to right. Bare-headed, clean-shaven; dark hair in tones of dark brown and grey-brown; the face in tones of dark brown, light brown and orange, with very pale brown lights. Blue jacket. The background mainly in tones of ochre. Signed and dated lower right, 'Keith Baynes 1923'.

PD. 107–1975 ST JEAN-DE-LUZ (1911)

Canvas board, $7\frac{1}{2} \times 10\frac{1}{8}$ in ($19{\cdot}0 \times 25{\cdot}7$ cm). Across a small harbour at low tide, with a harbour wall at the right, rises a group of buildings with a tower at the left, cream with grey-brown shadows, the roofs orange and green; at the foot of them is a strip of light blue water with a small ship beached at the right. The bed of the empty harbour is in tones of ochre, mauve and grey, with the orange-brown roof of a small building to the left; the harbour wall is in tones of grey-blue and ochre. Light blue sky. Signed lower right, 'Keith Baynes'.

St Jean-de-Luz, where Baynes spent the winter of 1911–12, is in the extreme south-west corner of France, in the *département* of Basses Pyrénées. The picture is dated 1911 on a label at the back.

PD. 109–1975 THE ALFAMA, LISBON (1966)

Canvas board, $20 \times 24\frac{1}{8}$ in ($50{\cdot}8 \times 61{\cdot}3$ cm). Seen from an elevated viewpoint, the mass of a large building, with a pediment, and a cupola to the right, rises from an expanse of low buildings in the foreground, all in tones of yellow, pink, grey, blue, green, orange and mauve. To right and in the distance stretches open water, green, orange and blue, on which are some ships and boats. Blue, green and mauve sky. Signed and dated lower left, 'Keith Baynes 1966'.

Exh. Colchester, The Minories, 1969, 'Keith Baynes' (93).

PD. 110–1975 LISBON (1971)

Canvas, 18 × 14 in (45·7 × 35·5 cm). View down a straight street, with buildings at the end; the buildings of the street are in green, mauve, blue, red and white, those at the end in yellow and orange; figures in the street echo the colours of the buildings. Blue sky with white cumulus clouds. Signed lower left, 'Keith Baynes'.

The picture is dated 1971 in an inscription on a label at the back, seemingly by the artist.

PD. 111–1975 ANTOINE GILI AT VERNET-LES-BAINS (1955)

Canvas board, $13\frac{1}{2} \times 11\frac{1}{2}$ in (34·3 × 29·2 cm). He is seated, at whole-length, turned half to the left, playing a 'cello. Bare-headed, clean-shaven; pink face and light brown hair; he wears a grey suit; the 'cello is orange in colour, with grey lights and brown shadows. Behind are two walls of a room, in tones of green; a jacket and hat, buff and light brown, hang on the wall to the left; ochre, brown and grey floor. Signed and dated lower right, 'Keith Baynes 1955'.

Exh. Colchester, The Minories, 1969, 'Keith Baynes' (114).

Vernet-les-Bains, in south-eastern France, is in the *département* of Pyrénées Orientales. Gili is probably to be identified from two other paintings in the 1969 exhibition at Colchester, nos. 108 and 109, entitled respectively *Catalan cellist I* and *Catalan cellist II*.

REPRODUCED. Exh. catalogue, *Keith Baynes* (1969), The Minories, Colchester.

PD. 112–1975 LIBOURNE (1950)

Canvas, 20 × 24 in (50·8 × 60·9 cm). A river, blue, white, green, yellow and orange in colour, with brown reeds at the right, fills the foreground; its low, further bank, orange and green, runs diagonally across from the right to the upper left; above it are the buildings of a town, dominated by a round pointed tower, with trees to the right, the buildings in tones of orange, grey, blue and white; projecting at the left is a small promontory of the nearer river bank, with green and yellow trees. Sky of blue, green, yellow and pink. Signed lower left, 'Keith Baynes'.

Exh. Colchester, The Minories, 1969, 'Keith Baynes' (60).

Libourne lies on the river Dordogne in the Gironde *département* of France. In the catalogue of the 1969 exhibition at Colchester the picture is dated 1950.

PD. 113–1975 CHAMBOLLE-MUSIGNY (1950)

Canvas, $20\frac{1}{8} \times 24\frac{1}{8}$ in (51·1 × 61·2 cm). Across a bright green field lying diagonally in the centre, with a mass of shrubs in the left foreground in tones of green, brown and grey, lies a village dominated by a square, yellow church tower with a blue cupola, the houses with brown or dark orange roofs, and walls of orange or cream. Hills covered with woods and meadows rise behind the village, mainly in orange, greens and browns. Blue sky with white, grey and pink clouds. Signed lower right, 'Keith Baynes'.

Exh. Colchester, The Minories, 1969, 'Keith Baynes' (59).

Chambolle-Musigny is in the Côte d'Or *département* of France. The catalogue of the 1969 exhibition at Colchester dates the picture 1950.

PD. 114–1975 DAHLIAS (1955)

Canvas, 24 × 20 in (60·9 × 50·8 cm). A bunch of single dahlias in a globular vase stands on a square table. The dahlias are white, yellow, red, mauve and orange, with green foliage; the vase is grey with a blue-grey highlight; the table top is in tones of light brownish grey, with a brown linear pattern. Tomato red background. Signed and dated lower right, 'Keith Baynes 1955'.

Given by Keith Stuart Baynes, 1975.

BEALE, Charles

b. 1660. Son of the portrait painter Mary Beale, with whom he worked as an assistant; pupil of Thomas Flatman. Best known as a portrait miniaturist.

643 UNKNOWN MAN (1693) PLATE 4

Canvas, $29\frac{3}{4} \times 24\frac{3}{4}$ in (75·5 × 62·8 cm).[1] Nearly half-length, turned towards the left, eyes looking front. Clean-shaven; bare-headed, long periwig.

Wears a copper-coloured silk gown and a lace cravat. Within a painted masonry oval, on which is the signature and date lower right, 'Carolus Beale fecit. 1693'.

Given by Charles Fairfax Murray, 1908. With Paul & Dominic Colnaghi & Co., London, 1863; C. F. Huth sale, Christie's, 19 March 1904 (40), bt Agnew; exh. London, Geffrye Museum, Eastbourne, Towner Art Gallery, 1975–6, 'The excellent Mrs Mary Beale' (41).

When with Colnaghi's in 1863, and in the Huth sale of 1904, described as a portrait of the poet John Dryden (1631–1700). But, despite some general resemblance of feature, the identification does not survive a comparison with authentic portraits of him at or about the same time of life, which show a much older-looking man. The portrait by Kneller in the National Portrait Gallery (no. 2083), for example, of the same date, 1693, depicts a man with a worn and lined face very different from the plump, smooth countenance of the man in this painting. Nor is it likely to be a copy of an earlier portrait of Dryden, since the costume is characteristic of the period around 1693.[2]

REPRODUCED. *Principal pictures* (1912 edn) p. 8, (1929 edn) p. 9; exhibition catalogue, E. Walsh and R. Jeffree, *The excellent Mrs Mary Beale* (1975), Geffrye Museum, p. 41.

NOTES. [1] Lined; dimensions of the painted surface. [2] It may be noted that in their enumeration of portraits of Dryden, no portrait by Charles Beale is mentioned either by E. Malone, *Prose works of John Dryden*, 3 vols. (1800), I, part i, pp. 432–7, or by Robert Bell, *Poetical works of John Dryden*, 3 vols. (1854), I, pp. 97–8.

BEAUMONT, Sir George Howland, Bart

1753–1827. Connoisseur, art collector, patron and amateur landscape painter; closely connected with the foundation of the National Gallery, 1824. Suc. father as 7th Baronet, 1762; exh. R.A., 1779–1825.

PD. 23–1952 LANDSCAPE

Canvas, $17\frac{3}{4} \times 14\frac{3}{4}$ in ($45{\cdot}1 \times 37{\cdot}5$ cm).[1] A broken bluff, with trees at the right, in tones of brown, rises in the foreground above a pool. Through an opening to left of centre, predominantly light orange-yellow, is seen a level river-valley, grey-green, pale yellow and light blue. Beyond are dark grey-blue mountains. The sky is light blue with clouds of grey and cream.

Bought from the Fairhaven Fund, 1952. With P. & D. Colnaghi & Co. Ltd, London, from whom bought.

NOTE. [1] Lined; dimensions of the painted surface.

BEECHEY, Sir William PLATE 22

1753–1839. Born at Burford, Oxfordshire. Entered the R.A. schools, 1772; exh. R.A., 1776–1839; in Norwich, 1782–7; became A.R.A. and Portrait Painter to Queen Charlotte, 1793; R.A. and kt, 1798.

628 HEBE FEEDING JUPITER'S EAGLE

Canvas, $26\frac{7}{8} \times 18\frac{5}{8}$ in ($68{\cdot}2 \times 47{\cdot}2$ cm).[1] Hebe, a whole-length figure, in a pink, draped dress caught at the shoulders to leave the arms bare, with golden hair bound with a blue ribbon, is seated on clouds, turned to left, a dark grey drapery passing over her right shoulder and floating above the figure. A gold bracelet encircles her left upper arm. With her right arm she embraces the head of Jupiter's eagle, which is feeding out of a golden dish she holds across in her left hand.

Given by H. J. Pfungst, 1904. Probably coll. G. E. Worthington of Beckenham, Kent; sold privately by 'Mrs Worthington' of Ealing, London, 1903;[2] anon. sale, Robinson & Fisher, London, 21 May 1903 (120);[3] bt from an unknown dealer by H. J. Pfungst.

Painted in a broad, loose style, differing from that of Beechey's portraits, but found in others of his subject pictures. Beechey painted a number of pictures on the subject of Hebe. The earliest is said to date from 1803,[4] and others were exhibited between 1804 (R.A., no. 6) and 1831 (Society of Artists, no. 33). Of these, two large paintings, exhibited at the B.I. in 1811 (no. 43) and in 1816 (no. 4), both represented Hebe feeding Jupiter's eagle, as in the present picture. The figure of Hebe has been described in the acquisition records of the Fitzwilliam Museum both as a portrait of Lady Beechey, the painter's second wife, and of his daughter, Charlotte, Lady Grantley, but neither identification seems at all likely. Lady Beechey was twenty-nine when she married in 1793, as against the apparent age of at most twenty of the girl in the picture; Charlotte, born in 1801, is more possible on grounds of age, but her features, particularly her snub nose, are quite different from those of the conventionally 'classical' type of countenance of the picture.[5] In addition, both seem to have had dark hair. In classical mythology Hebe, the daughter of Jupiter and

Juno, is the goddess of youth and was cupbearer to the immortals. The subject of Hebe, sometimes in the rôle depicted here, is a recurring theme in English neo-classical painting.

NOTES [1] Lined; dimensions of painted surface. [2] From inscriptions at the back of the picture. In 1822 Beechey was paid by 'Mr Worthington' for a portrait of 'Mrs W.', and in 1823 for frames (W. Roberts, *Sir William Beechey, R.A.* (1907), pp. 255, 256). [3] Described as 'A Portrait of Lady Beechey as "Hebe". From the Beechey Family.' This corresponds with a pencil inscription on the stretcher of no. 628. A label at the back referring to the purchase from 'Mrs Worthington' in 1903 describes her as a descendant of the painter and as having inherited the picture. [4] Roberts, *op. cit.*, gives an account of some of the *Hebe* pictures on pp. 82–4. [5] Cf. an engraving of her by H. Meyer after a painting by G. D. Beechey, a plate to *La Belle Assemblée* (1827).

BEETON, ALAN EDMUND

1880–1942. Born in London. Studied in London and Paris; exh. R.A. from 1923, and elsewhere; A.R.A., 1938. Painter of figure subjects and portraits.

1202 THE GIPSY

Canvas, $36\frac{1}{4} \times 22\frac{1}{2}$ in ($92{\cdot}7 \times 57{\cdot}1$ cm). A young woman with black hair, turned towards the front, is seated behind a square basket, her right elbow resting on its handle, chin on her hand; she wears a light green blouse with yellow scarf and coral beads, and a plaid skirt of grey-yellow and black. Her left hand is placed on the handle of the basket, which is partly covered towards the left with a patterned carpet, predominantly pink in colour. Dark brown background.

Given by Harold, 1st Viscount Rothermere, 1927. Exh. R.A., 1927 (717); bt there from the artist by Lord Rothermere for the Fitzwilliam Museum; exh. London and elsewhere, Art Exhibitions Bureau, 1963–4, 'A painter's choice' (19).

The choice of paintings for the exhibition of The Art Exhibitions Bureau was made by Sir Gerald Kelly, P.R.A.

2338 POSING

Canvas, $11\frac{3}{8} \times 12\frac{1}{4}$ in ($28{\cdot}9 \times 31{\cdot}2$ cm).[1] A cream-coloured lay-figure stands, turned towards the right, in the middle of a room, the right foot placed on a green cushion lying upon a book; to the left is a draped, green brocade curtain; behind the figure stands a large cupboard, mainly black and red in colour, to the right of it a wooden-framed sofa upholstered in greyish cream. Brown plank floor.

Given by Huttleston, 1st Lord Fairhaven, 1938. Bt by him, with no. 2339 below, from the French Gallery, London, 1931; exh. there, 1931, 'An anthology of English painting, 1900–1931' (3, 4); anon. sale (= Fairhaven), Christie's, 1 May 1936 (153, 154), bt in; exh. London and elsewhere, Art Exhibitions Bureau, 1963–4, 'A painter's choice' (20, 21).

This and no. 2339 below come from a series of three paintings of lay-figures, the third of which is entitled *Composing* and belonged at one time to Miss Isabel Jeans. An earlier series of four similar paintings, slightly larger, added a subject named *Decomposing* (now Tate Gallery, London, no. 4668), which, with *Posing* from the same series, was exhibited at the R.A. in 1929.[2]

NOTES. [1] Dimensions of the painted surface; the canvas measures 12¼ × 13 in (31·1 × 33·0 cm). [2] See Tate Gallery Catalogues, *The modern British paintings, drawings and sculpture*, 2 vols., by Mary Chamot, Dennis Farr and Martin Butlin (1964), II, p. 17.

2339 REPOSING

Canvas, 11⅜ × 12⅛ in (28·9 × 30·8 cm).[1] A cream-coloured lay-figure reclines in a pink-upholstered chair turned towards the left in the middle of a room, a pale grey wrap lying across the knees; behind the figure is a large cupboard, mainly black and red in colour, and to the left stands a wooden-framed sofa upholstered in greyish cream; in the foreground to the right hangs a draped, green brocade curtain. Brown plank floor.

Given by Huttleston, 1st Lord Fairhaven, 1938. See above, no. 2338.

NOTE. [1] Dimensions of the painted surface, the canvas measures 12⅛ × 13 in (30·8 × 33·0 cm).

BELL, Vanessa

1879–1961. Born in London, daughter of Sir Leslie Stephen. Trained in the R.A. schools, but developed under the influence of the Post-Impressionists. Worked mainly in London, Sussex, Paris and the South of France. Painter and decorative designer.

2375 ON THE SEINE (1921)

Wood, 10$\frac{5}{8}$ × 16$\frac{1}{8}$ in (27·0 × 46·0 cm). Beyond a group of leaning trees in the right foreground, their trunks light brown and green, growing from a sloping river bank (grey), is seen an arch of a bridge (light brown) which spans the river to the left; part of a farther, metal bridge is seen through the arch. Signed and dated lower right, 'VB 1921'.

Bequeathed by Frank Hindley Smith, 1939. With the Independent Gallery, London, 1922.

The bridges appear to be the Pont Royal in Paris, with the Pont du Carrousel beyond.

REPRODUCED. *Burlington Magazine* (1922), CCXXXII, p. 35.

2376 PORTRAIT OF MRS M. (1919)

Canvas, 26$\frac{7}{8}$ × 22$\frac{3}{8}$ in (68·2 × 56·8 cm). Half-length, seated, slightly to right, her hands clasped in her lap. She wears a black jacket and skirt, with a cream-coloured blouse; small black hat with a square crown; a dark brown fur round her shoulders. Warm grey background. Signed and dated lower left, 'VB/1919'.

Bequeathed by Frank Hindley Smith, 1939.[1] With the Independent Gallery, London, 1922; exh. Bristol, City Art Gallery, 1931, exhibition of contemporary British painting, lent F. Hindley Smith.[2]

REPRODUCED. *Burlington Magazine* (1922), CCXXXII, p. 32.[3]

NOTES. [1] With the title, *Woman with furs.* [2] Information from W. W. Maxwell, then Director of the Bristol City Art Gallery (letter of 9 May 1952, Fitzwilliam Museum). [3] With the title *Portrait of Mrs M.*

BEVAN, Robert Polhill

1865–1925. Born in Hove. Westminster School of Art, London, and Académie Julian, Paris; 1893–4 at Pont Aven, Brittany, where he knew Gauguin. After 1897, for some years regularly visited Poland; settled in Hampstead, London, 1900. Member of the Camden Town Group, the London Group and the New English Art Club. Painted landscapes and scenes with horses.

PD. 10–1969 THE POLISH TAVERN

Canvas, 15$\frac{1}{8}$ × 22$\frac{1}{8}$ in (38·3 × 56·2 cm). A one-storey thatched building, placed diagonally, fills the centre of the composition; at the end of it, to the left, is a projecting, gabled entrance, and at the side, near another gabled projection, stands a cart. Flat, open land stretches beyond, with a distant, low line of trees. Painted in bright, broken colour: the thatch and the ground near the building mainly in reds, yellows and blues, the shadowed end of the building mainly red and a deeper blue, the grass in the foreground and beyond the building in bright greens, reds and yellows. A bluish green sky, pink towards the horizon.

Bought from the Fairhaven Fund, 1969. Coll. Robert Alexander Polhill Bevan, C.B.E., son of the artist; sold to the d'Offay Couper Gallery, London; their exhibition, 1969, 'Robert Bevan, early paintings, 1895–1908' (10), where it was bought.

In the exhibition at the d'Offay Couper Gallery, this was one of three versions of the subject. It was described in the catalogue as 'second sketch', and dated *c.* 1903, the date given also to no. 11, described as 'final picture', of virtually the same dimensions, to which it is very close in every respect. The third version, a smaller 'first sketch' ($5\frac{5}{8} \times 9$ in; $14{\cdot}3 \times 22{\cdot}8$ cm), no. 7, broadly handled in a manner quite different from the other two, was dated *c.* 1901. All three are described as painted in Poland.[1] As Bevan worked there in 1901 and again in 1903,[2] the approximate form of dating adopted in the exhibition catalogue presumably indicates a degree of uncertainty as between one year and the other. This is encountered again in another Polish subject, *Return to the village*, similar in style to the present painting, which has been dated *c.* 1903 with the reservation that it might be as early as 1901.[3] It seems, therefore, that the present painting should be regarded as of 1903, though possibly of 1901.[4] The date in either case indicates that the subject must be in the region of Szeliwy, the childhood's home of Bevan's Polish wife, Stanislawa de Karlowska.[5] A preliminary drawing for the composition[6] in black chalk belongs to the Fitzwilliam Museum (no. PD. 11–1969).

REPRODUCED. Catalogue of the d'Offay Couper Gallery exhibition, 'Robert Bevan, early paintings, 1895–1908', no. 10 (colour).

NOTES. [1] These catalogue notes are derived from information supplied by Mr R. A. P. Bevan. [2] R. A. P. Bevan, *Robert Bevan, 1865–1925, a memoir by his son* (1965), p. 12. [3] Bevan, *op. cit.*, pl. 16. [4] Mr R. A. P. Bevan agrees with the possibility of an alternative date of 1901 (letter of 19 December 1971, Fitzwilliam Museum). [5] Introduction to the catalogue of the d'Offay Couper Gallery exhibition of 1969. [6] Bevan, *op. cit.*, p. 13.

BLAKE, William

1757–1827. Born in London, where, but for one short interval, he spent his life. Apprenticed as an engraver; student at the R.A., 1778; made his living by engraving for the book-sellers. Painter (mainly in water-colours), poet and pictorial designer.

PD. 27–1949 AN ALLEGORY OF THE SPIRITUAL CONDITION OF MAN (181(1?)) PLATE 23

Tempera[1] on canvas, $59\frac{3}{4} \times 47\frac{5}{8}$ in ($151{\cdot}8 \times 120{\cdot}9$ cm).[2] The general colour is buff, with restrained local colour applied thinly in certain areas; the figures are linear in treatment. Faith (left-hand figure at the bottom) is in light blue with a pink girdle, Charity (in the centre) was presumably originally in white, Hope (at the right) is in light red. The figure above Faith was originally in yellow, or perhaps light brown, the centre figure is in pink, the figure above Hope was presumaby in white, which was also the colour of the figures in the top row. The same colours recur in the small scenes at either side. In the landscape are passages of green and blue in stronger tones. The subjects of the small scenes, all but two of them biblical, are as follows. (Top left) the Creation; Adam and Eve; the Ark; the Rainbow; Jehovah's covenant with Abraham, and the Destruction of the Egyptians in the Red Sea; the Judgment of Solomon; the Captivity; the Crucifixion. (Bottom right) the three Maries at the Sepulchre; Pentecost; a martyrdom by burning, and a scene of liberation (?) from prison; the casting-down of the seven-headed dragon; the Last Trump; the Last Judgment and the Redeemer. Inscribed, signed and dated (in gold) lower left, 'P.....d in /...o by / Wm Blake / 181(1?)'[3] (i.e. 'Painted in Fresco' etc.).[4]

Given by the executors of Walford Graham Robertson (1867–1948), through the National Art-Collections Fund, 1949. Coll. Thomas Butts (1759–1846);[5] his son, Thomas Butts jr (d. 1862) and grandson, Captain F. J. Butts (d. 1905); bt from the widow of Captain Butts, through the Carfax Gallery, London, by W. Graham Robertson, 1906;[6] Robertson sale, Christie's, 22 July 1949 (52), bt in by his executors; exh. Bournemouth Arts Club, Southampton Art Gallery, and Brighton Art Gallery and Museum, 1949, 'Original works by William Blake...from the Graham Robertson Collection' (1); London, Arts Council, 1951, 'The tempera paintings of William Blake' (1).

Much damaged through former rising and flaking of the paint, and abrasion of the surface; cleaned and restored, 1950. This is Blake's largest extant picture. The title is taken from the 'Annotated lists of Blake's paintings, drawings and engravings' drawn up by W. M. Rossetti for the first edition of Gilchrist's *Life of William Blake* (1863).[7] It has been assumed that this title was given it by Rossetti,[8] but in view of the tentative nature of his remarks in explanation of the subject,[9] this seems unlikely. More probably it is the title by which the picture was known to the Butts family, in whose possession it was in 1863. It may therefore be Blake's own title for it, and if so it is significant for the understanding of his symbolism.[10] A detailed study of the picture made by Kerrison Preston[11] interprets its theme as the attainment by the soul of man of a spiritual state leading to unity with God.[12] This mystical achievement is based on the Christian virtues of Faith, Hope and Charity, symbolised by three figures standing on the earth. The three figures above them are identified as the Spirit of Love, who soars upwards between Wantonness on the one hand and Abstinence (or Repression) on the other. At the top, the soul of man,[13] filled with humility and peace by the Holy Spirit above, and borne towards heaven by two angels, is attended by Poetry (Blake's hero, Los), at the right, and Inspiration (Blake's Enitharmon), at the left. The small surrounding Bible scenes illustrate the mystical way to unity with God, running downwards on the left from Creation to the Crucifixion (the dark night of the soul), and upwards on the right from the empty sepulchre to the Last Judgment and the Redeemer. Among points of detail, Preston suggests (p. 12) that certain features indicate the influence of Indian mysticism, with which Blake was familiar. It has also been suggested that the picture illustrates the doctrines of the Kabbala, an ancient Jewish system of theology and magic, in a Christianised version.[14] Some general similarity is to be found between three of the small Bible scenes and other paintings of the same subjects by Blake. The Judgment of Solomon is related to an undated tempera painting in the Fitzwilliam Museum (no. PD. 28–1949), see p. 18 below, the Captivity to a water-colour dated 1806, belonging to the Fogg Museum of Art, Harvard University, U.S.A., the Crucifixion to *The soldiers casting lots for Christ's garments*, a water-colour dated 1800, in the Fitzwilliam Museum (no. PD. 30–1949).

REPRODUCED. Kerrison Preston, *Notes on Blake's large painting in tempera, The spiritual condition of man* (1949), pp. 4, 11, 13; *William Blake, catalogue of the collection in the Fitzwilliam Museum, Cambridge*, ed. David Bindman (1970), pls. 16–22.

NOTES. [1] The term commonly used for the technique of Blake's paintings, which he himself described as 'fresco', as in the signature on this picture. It is different from the technique properly described by either of these terms, and according to John Linnell consisted in painting in water-colour 'tempered with common carpenter's glue' on a wet gesso ground (Alexander Gilchrist, *Life of William Blake* (1863 edn), I, pp. 368–9, (1880 edn), I, pp. 413–14, (ed. W. Graham Robertson, 1907), p. 388, (ed. Ruthven Todd, 1945), p. 359). See also J. T. Smith, *Nollekens and his times* (1829 edn), p. 487. Dr Johann Hell, who cleaned and restored the picture in 1950, described the medium used as 'mainly glue' (letter of 5 June 1952, Fitzwilliam Museum). [2] Lined; dimensions of the painted surface. [3] Not 'William Blake' as sometimes stated. The last figure of the date is doubtful, but seems most likely to be a '1'. [4] *William Blake, catalogue of the collection in the Fitzwilliam Museum, Cambridge*, ed. David Bindman, (1970), p. 32, no. 32. [5] So affirmed by W. M. Rossetti in his 'Annotated lists of Blake's paintings, drawings and engravings' (Gilchrist, *op. cit.* (1863 edn), II, p. 231, no. 199, (1880 edn), II, p. 245, no. 224, (1907 edn), p. 453, no. 199), in accordance with his declaration in the foreword, 'The interest attaching to the great collection of Blake's works formed by his almost solitary purchaser, Mr. Butts, has induced me to specify which were once his.' In the 1863 edition he also, in many instances, gives the names of other owners. [6] *The Blake collection of W. Graham Robertson*, ed. Kerrison Preston (1952), pp. 10, 96. [7] Gilchrist, *loc. cit.*, n. 3. [8] E.g., in *The Blake collection of W. Graham Robertson*, p. 96. [9] *Loc. cit.*, n. 3, where he says 'The conception of the subject seems to approach that of a Last Judgment, though not recognisable distinctly as such', etc.... [10] The customary abbreviation of the title to 'The spiritual condition of man' may therefore be misleading. [11] *Notes on Blake's large painting in tempera, The spiritual condition of man* (1949). [12] Speaking of Blake's poetry, Joseph Wicksteed, *Blake's vision of the Book of Job* (1910), p. 24, says 'Blake's dominant theme in all his later work is the reconciliation of the individual life with the universal life of humanity (Christ); and the re-discovery in that reconciliation of a lost God and Heaven'. [13] Identified as the Virgin Mary by W. Graham Robertson, who considered the picture to 'symbolise the Immaculate Conception' (his edn of Gilchrist's *Life* (1907), p. 453, no. 199); similarly identified by A. G. B. Russell, 'The Graham Robertson collection', *Burlington Magazine* (1920), XXXVII, 34. [14] By Désirée Hirst, *Country Life* (1950), CVII, 456.

PD. 28–1949 THE JUDGMENT OF SOLOMON PLATE 23

Tempera[1] on copper, $10\frac{1}{2} \times 15$ in ($26{\cdot}7 \times 38{\cdot}1$ cm). Solomon, seated on a blue throne, wears a red tunic and a blue cloak; the angels behind him are in orange-brown touched with red. The kneeling woman is in white, the other in pale pink. The groups at left and right are in pale blue, except for the executioner who wears a blue tunic and a red cloak. The steps are grey, the background brown.[2]

Given by the executors of Walford Graham Robertson (1867–1948), through the National Art-Collections Fund, 1949. Coll. Thomas Butts (1759–1846);[3] his son, Thomas Butts jr (d. 1862) and grandson, Captain F. J. Butts (d. 1905); bt from the widow of Captain Butts, through the Carfax Gallery, London, by W. Graham Robertson, 1906;[4] exh. London, Tate Gallery, 1947, 'William Blake' (51); Robertson sale, Christie's, 22 July 1949 (16), bt in by his executors; exh. Bournemouth Arts Club, Southampton Art Gallery, and Brighton Art Gallery and Museum, 1949, 'Original works by William Blake...from the Graham Robertson Collection' (3).

Much damaged through loss of paint and surface wear; in the heads, the face of the man at the extreme left is renewed, as is Solomon's left cheek, but restoration of the other heads is confined to occasional strengthening in the outlines, which also occurs elsewhere, notably in the hands. Restored in 1906, when the missing areas were repainted, in part from the small painting of the same subject in no. PD. 27–1949 above (p. 16);[5] loose paint secured in 1965. The subject is taken from I Kings, iii. 25, 26. One of a series of biblical subjects in tempera executed by Blake for Thomas Butts, several of which are dated either 1799 or 1800.[6]

REPRODUCED. *The Blake collection of W. Graham Robertson*, ed. Kerrison Preston (1952), pl. 30; Geoffrey Keynes, *William Blake's illustrations to the Bible* (1957), pl. 62; *William Blake, catalogue of the collection in the Fitzwilliam Museum, Cambridge*, ed. David Bindman (1970), pl. 9.

NOTES. [1] See n. [1] to no. PD. 27–1949 above, p. 18. [2] *William Blake, catalogue of the collection in the Fitzwilliam Museum, Cambridge*, ed. David Bindman (1970), p. 22, no. 21. [3] See n. [3] to no. PD. 27–1949, p. 18 above; listed by W. M. Rossetti in Alexander Gilchrist, *Life of William Blake* (1863 edn), II, p. 225, no. 128, (1880 edn), II, p. 237, no. 154, (ed. W. Graham Robertson, 1907), p. 445, no. 128. [4] *The Blake collection of W. Graham Robertson*, ed. Kerrison Preston (1952), p. 99, no. 30. [5] Details of the restoration of 1906 are given in Preston, *op. cit.*, pp. 100–1. [6] A list of them is given by Anthony Blunt, *The art of William Blake* (1959), pp. 104–5. Blake mentions that he is busy on this commission, which consisted of 'Fifty small Pictures at One Guinea each', in a letter of 26 August 1799 to George Cumberland, printed in *The writings of William Blake* (1925), II, p. 178, and in *The letters of William Blake* (1956 edn), pp. 38–9, (1968 edn), p. 32, no. 7, both ed. Geoffrey Keynes.

BOARD, Ernest

1877–1934. Born at Worcester. Studied at the Royal College of Art, London, in the R.A. schools, and in the studio of E. A. Abbey, R.A.; exh. R.A. from 1902. Subject painter.

2485 BLUE AND GOLD (1918)

Canvas board, 10 × 14 in (25·9 × 35·5 cm). To the left, on a terrace, a lady stands in a blue and gold crinoline dress, behind her a tree in autumn leaves; to the right, steps descend into a pool, from which three bathing figures emerge towards her. Signed top right, 'BOARD'.

Given by Claude Dickason Rotch, 1942.

A two-hour evening sketch painted at the Bristol Savages, 1918.[1]

NOTE. [1] From an inscription at the back.

BOGDANI, Jacob

1660–1724. Of Hungarian origin. Settled in London by 1691; much employed by William III and Queen Anne. A prolific painter of bird pictures and still-life.

361 BIRDS IN A LANDSCAPE PLATE 5

Canvas, 36 × 35 in (91·4 × 88·9 cm). To the left of the cock pheasant is a grey partridge, to the right two Barbary partridges, one of them nearly white; at the extreme right is a reed-hen. Above, a green parrot pecks at some yellow grapes; nearby a bullfinch and a blue tit. The ground and the tree-trunk are brown, the foliage a dull, lightish green; the distance is grey-green. A sky of warm grey clouds with areas of pale blue. Signed lower centre, 'J. Bogdani'.

Bequeathed by Daniel Mesman, 1834.

Cleaned 1953. A characteristic example of one type of his bird pictures, of which there are a number of others larger in size, in the Royal collection.[1]

REPRODUCED. Andor Pigler, *Bogdany Jacab* (1941), pl. XXXII.

NOTE. [1] See Oliver Millar, *The Tudor, Stuart and early Georgian pictures in the collection of Her Majesty the Queen* (1963), pp. 164–6, nos. 472–86, rep. pl. 171, 172, 174.

BONINGTON, Richard Parkes

1802–1828. Born near Nottingham; the family moved to Calais probably in 1817, and soon afterwards to Paris. Pupil of Francia in Calais; joined the Ecole des Beaux-Arts, Paris, under Gros, 1819. Friend of Delacroix. Revisited England 1825, 1827, 1828; visited Italy, 1826.

PD. 11–1955 LANDSCAPE WITH A POND PLATE 40

Canvas, $10\frac{1}{4} \times 13\frac{3}{4}$ in (26·0 × 34·9 cm). The rising ground at the right, and the darker areas of the water, are brown, the lighter areas of the water grey. The tall trees are in tones of grey-greens, with warm grey palings below; the trees at the right are ochre. The cottage is dark brown with a red chimney. The distance at the left, with a brown cow in the foreground, is brown-green with grey-green beyond, and blue in the distance. In the cream-coloured sky there is a passage of strong blue in the upper left corner.

Given by the National Art-Collections Fund, from the Ernest Edward Cook Collection, 1955. Coll. Mrs Worthington, Cullompton, Devon;[1] with Gooden & Fox, London, from whom it was bought by E. E. Cook (d. 1955), 1933; exh. Hazlitt, 1974 (3).

From the similarity of their themes, it appears probable that the source of this composition may be traced to Rembrandt's etching, *Cottage with a white paling*;[2] the likelihood that it is thus basically an invented subject is quite in conformity with the somewhat artificial character of the whole picture. From the highly conventionalised treatment, and the technique employed in the foreground, making use of a glazed brown under-painting, the picture must date from the middle or late years of Bonington's brief career. An exact repetition of the composition is known in a picture by his friend, the painter Paul Huet,[3] and a water-colour version of it, possibly by Bonington, belongs to the Rhode Island School of Design, Providence, U.S.A. Though Bonington frequently borrowed from other compositions for his figure-subjects, this is the only known example of the practice among his landscapes.

REPRODUCED. *Fifty-second Annual Report of the National Art-Collections Fund, 1955* (1956), opp. p. 33; *The Ernest Cook Collection*, n.d. (1957), p. 30; Hazlitt, 1974, pl. 20.

NOTES. [1] Information kindly supplied by Messrs Gooden & Fox, who add that it is understood 'that the picture had never been in the market' (letter of 17 October 1955, Fitzwilliam Museum). [2] A. M. Hind, *A catalogue of*

Rembrandt's etchings, 2nd edn (1923), I, p. 94, no. 203; suggested by Dr Marion Spencer in a letter of 30 April 1965 (Fitzwilliam Museum). [3] Information from Dr Spencer, *ibid.* n. 2, whose help in cataloguing this picture is gratefully acknowledged.

BOUGHTON, George Henry

1833–1905. Born near Norwich. In 1834 taken to America; student in New York, and in 1860 in Paris; settled in London, 1862; exh. R.A. from 1863; R.A., 1896.

637 WINTER SCENE IN HOLLAND

Canvas, $16\frac{1}{8} \times 23\frac{7}{8}$ in ($41{\cdot}0 \times 60{\cdot}6$ cm). In a snow-covered landscape, bluish in colour, a few figures are skating in the dim evening light on a pond in the foreground, willow-trees to right. In a cloudy sky the sun is setting over a distant town. Signed lower left, 'G. H. Boughton'.

Given by H. J. Pfungst, 1906.

Painted for the donor two years before the artist's death, to form a pendant to a *River scene* by Jan van Goyen.[1]

NOTE. [1] Letter from H. J. Pfungst, 30 November 1906 (Fitzwilliam Museum).

BRETT, John

1831–1902. Born at Bletchingley, Surrey. Entered the R.A. Schools, 1854. Influenced by the Pre-Raphaelites; exh. R.A. 1856 onwards. A.R.A., 1881. Painted mainly landscapes and marine subjects.

PD. 19–1968 LANDSCAPE (1852)

Millboard, 7×10 in ($17{\cdot}8 \times 25{\cdot}4$ cm). A line of trees rising from the further bank of a stream runs diagonally into the background from left to right. The stream flows centrally through the foreground, where its course broadens out, some cattle to the left. On the right, the open ground of the nearer bank is crossed by a path, on which stands a woman; small shrubs, grasses and fencing fill the immediate right foreground. Trees and herbage predominantly in tones of light yellow-green. Pale sky of cream and blue. Signed and dated lower right, 'John Brett 1852'.

Bought from the Fairhaven Fund, 1968. With P. & D. Colnaghi & Co. Ltd, London, from whom it was bought.

An early work, before his style of painting was influenced by the Pre-Raphaelites.

REPRODUCED. Allen Staley, *The Pre-Raphaelite landscape* (1973), pl. 69a.

PD. 55–1973 ROCKY COAST SCENE (1872)

Millboard, 9⅞ × 14 in (25·0 × 35·6 cm). The nearer shore of a bay running in to the right is filled with rounded brown rocks, with a few which are dull red, extending across the width of the foreground. Beyond them is a narrow strip of blue sea, with some white breakers, backed by a line of cliffs of a lighter brown, ending in a headland at the left. Pale blue sky with a few cream clouds. Dated lower right, 'Oct 24 72'.

Bought from the Fairhaven Fund, 1973. Anon. sale, Christie's, 5 March 1971 (159), bt Colnaghi; exh. London, P. & D. Colnaghi & Co. Ltd, 1973, 'English drawings, watercolours and paintings' (182); bt from Colnaghi's; exh. Hazlitt, 1974 (5).

Sea and coast scenes predominate in Brett's later work, the subjects being found round the coasts of Britain or on the Channel coast of France. This interest is first evident in paintings made during a visit to the Bay of Naples in the winter of 1863–4, and from 1870 he spent his summers sailing in British waters. Small oil sketches such as the present one were painted from nature on these cruises in a single session of a few hours.[1]

REPRODUCED. Fitzwilliam Museum, *Annual Report* for 1973, pl. IV; exhibition catalogue, Hazlitt, 1974, pl. 36.

NOTE. [1] Allen Staley, *The Pre-Raphaelite landscape* (1973), p. 136.

BRIDGE, JOSEPH

1845–1894. Born and worked in Shrewsbury. Student at the R.A. schools, 1863; exh. R.A., 1867–72, and at Birmingham until 1891.

609* EDWARD, 3RD EARL OF POWIS

Canvas, 27½ × 22½ in (69·2 × 57·1 cm). Nearly half-length, slightly to right. Bald, white hair, beard and slight moustache. Wears dark jacket with a yellow waistcoat; dark grey, spotted bow-tie. Signed lower left, 'J B', in a monogram.

Bought from J. J. R. Bridge, son of the painter, 1897.

Edward James Herbert, 3rd Earl of Powis, of the third creation (1818–1891); High Steward of the University of Cambridge, 1863 to his death. The portrait was painted posthumously from a photograph, 1891–2.[1]

NOTE. [1] Information from J. J. R. Bridge (undated letter, about 1902, Fitzwilliam Museum).

BRITISH SCHOOL, *c.* 1300

736 (?) ST DOROTHY

Distemper on stone, $14\frac{1}{4} \times 8\frac{1}{2}$ in ($36{\cdot}2 \times 21{\cdot}6$ cm). Nearly whole-length standing under an octofoil gothic arch, turned slightly left, the haloed head inclined forward, the right hand raised holding an implement, the left holding a small tub-shaped vessel. Light-coloured hair bound with a fillet falls over the shoulders; over a dull purplish robe she wears a light blue mantle with red lining, one end draped over the left arm. Background (originally pink) sown with black fleurons.

Given by Thomas Hacke Naylor, 1882. From the parish church of St Andrew, Old Chesterton, Cambridge, where it was found about 1871 at the restoration of the church;[1] exh. London, Society of Antiquaries, 1896, 'English medieval paintings and illuminated manuscripts' (11).

The paint is laid directly upon the stone, and though much of it has been lost the design remains clear, its main lines incised into the stone. From the appearance of the edges and back, it seems probable that the stone slab is the sliced-off face of one section of a slender column. The earliest surviving parts of the church go back to about 1260. Although doubtful, the identification of the figure as St Dorothy is the most probable. Her usual emblem is a basket of roses and apples, with which the small vessel in her left hand, with an indication of contents, may be taken to correspond; figures of St Dorothy thus depicted are well known on rood-screens in East Anglia. But the implement in her right hand, which is like a small pick, cannot be paralleled, and is unexplained.

REPRODUCED. *Principal pictures* (1912 edn), p. 222, (1929 edn), p. 256.

NOTE. [1] T. H. Naylor, 'On a fresco in Chesterton church', *Cambridge Antiquarian Society. Communications* (1881), XXII, 3–5.

BRITISH SCHOOL, EARLY FIFTEENTH CENTURY

706 CHRIST BEFORE PILATE

Wood,[1] $13\frac{1}{8} \times 11\frac{7}{8}$ in ($33{\cdot}3 \times 30{\cdot}2$ cm). Pilate, with dark brown hair and beard and a gold crown, wears a blue mantle (*houppelande*) lined with ermine over a black garment patterned in red, and has a red shoe; a man to the left of him has fair hair with a black skull-cap and is dressed in pale pink; Christ, with dark brown hair, beard and moustache, and a gilt halo, wears a white mantle over a blue robe; a man below him has fair hair and an embossed red robe. To left of Pilate's crown is a small portion of gilt background; to the right of Pilate is a background of black with a red pattern. The cap of a man in the lower right corner is blue. The back of the panel has a thin layer of gesso, painted over.

707 CHRIST BEARING THE CROSS

Wood,[1] $13\frac{1}{8} \times 11\frac{3}{4}$ in (33·3 × 29·9 cm). The soldier at the top is swathed in pale pink, with a dark grey helmet; Christ's robe is blue, his hair, beard and moustache dark brown, with a gilt halo; a soldier behind him has dark grey chain mail, helmet and gauntlet, and a buff garment; the cross is light brown; the mantle of the Virgin Mary to the left is light blue, St John beside her has fair hair and a red garment, the haloes of both are gilt. The back of the panel has a thin layer of gesso, painted over.

Given by the Friends of the Fitzwilliam Museum, 1910. Said to have been found in taking down a cottage in Huby's Yard, St Saviour's, Norwich;[2] coll. George E. Fox (1833–1908); exh. London, Society of Antiquaries, 1896, 'English medieval paintings and illuminated manuscripts' (22); bequeathed to Mill Stephenson, 1908; bought from him by the Friends of the Fitzwilliam Museum, 1910; exh. London, R.A., 1923, 'British primitives' (36, 37); Victoria and Albert Museum, 1930, 'English medieval art' (352, 353); Norwich, Castle Museum, 1973, 'Medieval art in East Anglia, 1300–1520' (54).

Much defaced by loss of paint and by surface damage; restored 1941, 1950 and 1974. As examples of the international gothic style of painting in a late phase, these paintings recall in some respects German work of the School of Cologne. Beyond the tradition that they were discovered in Norwich at a date unknown but, presumably, from their earliest known ownership by George E. Fox, in the latter part of the nineteenth century, there is no known evidence for attributing them to a local East Anglian school.[3] From the armour and from the *houppelande* worn by Pilate, they may be dated to a period of *c.* 1400–20/25. At the base of no. 706 the scene of *Christ before Pilate* runs into a mutilated *Christ presented to the people*, surviving in a strip from the top of the painting with two labels reading 'Crucifige, crucifige'. The full series of scenes of the Passion thus appears to have been arranged in a vertical sequence on one or more panels, in which the episodes merged one into another. From the fact that

Christ is crowned with thorns in his appearance before Pilate, it is evident that the series must have been taken from the gospel of St John, the only version in which the crowning with thorns takes place at this stage.[4]

REPRODUCED. Friends of the Fitzwilliam Museum, *Annual Report* for 1910; *Principal pictures* (1912 edn), pp. 223, 224, (1929 edn), pp. 254, 255; catalogue of the exhibition, 'British primitives', R.A., 1923, illustrated 1924 edn, pl. xx; Margaret Rickert, *Painting in Britain in the middle ages* (1954 edn), pl. 159 (B), (1965 edn), pl. 157 (B) (no. 706); catalogue of the exhibition, 'Medieval art in East Anglia, 1300–1520', p. 38, no. 54.

NOTES. [1] Top and bottom edges rough sawn, side edges smooth; apparently carried out in solid oil paint, without glazing, though an emulsion of oil and size may have been used. [2] Attempts to trace the site of Huby's Yard have been unsuccessful. [3] They differ strikingly in both style and conception from the late-fourteenth-century paintings of the Passion in Norwich Cathedral (retable in St Luke's Chapel, and two panels from St Michael-at-Plea in the Lady Chapel), with which there has been in the past a tendency to associate them, see T. Borenius and E. W. Tristram, *English medieval painting* (1927), p. 40, Joan Evans, *English art, 1307–1461* (1949), p. 101, Margaret Rickert, *Painting in Britain in the middle ages* (1954 edn), p. 177, (1965 edn), p. 162; Rickert, *op. cit.* (1965 edn), pp. 163–5, puts forward a stylistic analysis which is hardly convincing. [4] The subject of no. 706 is identified as *Christ before Herod*, on account of the gold crown, by A. H. R. Martindale in the catalogue of the exhibition 'Medieval art in East Anglia, 1300–1520', Castle Museum, Norwich, 1973, p. 38, no. 54; but this seems impossible as Christ is wearing the crown of thorns, a feature of the gospel story not referred to by St Luke, in whose account alone the Herod episode occurs.

BRITISH SCHOOL, 1598

1773 UNKNOWN LADY

Wood, $20\frac{1}{4} \times 15\frac{3}{4}$ in (51·4 × 40·0 cm). Nearly half-length, slightly to left, the left hand across in front holding gloves. Dark brown hair. Wears a black dress with a frontal panel of black and gold embroidery on grey, which includes the figure of a talbot-dog; pale blue-grey ruff, open in front, a locket attached to it at the right. From a double necklace, hangs on the bosom a gold enamelled pendant with the device of an eagle displayed; a long, double gold chain enamelled in black runs around the outside of the ruff, a gold jewel with gems, with the device of an eagle displayed, hanging from it at her left shoulder. Deep Venetian red background. Inscribed upper right, '·A°; 1590 / ·Æ^{TIS}·SVÆ, 31'; upper left a grey talbot-dog differenced with a black crescent.

Given by the Friends of the Fitzwilliam Museum, 1936. Coll. Captain Norman Colville,[1] from whom it was acquired by Messrs Frank Partridge, London; bt from Partridge's.

The face is a falsification; X-ray examination shows that the original face has been scraped away and replaced by the present one painted upon a fresh ground. It also reveals that the date originally read 1598 and the age 30, and that the talbot-dog in the upper left corner is an addition, alterations which were evidently contemporaneous with one another, from the similar liquid handling of the paint in both. The date of these changes cannot be accurately assessed, but they could well be relatively recent. The talbot-dog is evidently taken from the one embroidered on the dress, being virtually identical in design as well as repeating the heraldic charge of a crescent. Presumably on this account, the portrait when puchased was doubtfully described as depicting a Countess of Shrewsbury, a talbot-dog being the cognizance of the Talbots, Earls of Shrewsbury. But the original portrait can have had no connection with the Earls of Shrewsbury. The crescent on the dog is the mark of cadency of a second son, and although the 7th Earl was the second son of the 6th Earl, he succeeded his father in 1590, eight years before the date of the portrait. Both the original and the altered date and age are in any case out of the question for a Countess of Shrewsbury, as the only one possible, Mary Cavendish, wife of the 7th Earl, was born in 1556. The original portrait must have been connected in some respect with the Talbot family, and no doubt this was the intention with the falsified one also, but the available evidence leads to no more positive conclusion. The significance of the device on the two jewels of an eagle displayed is more probably emblematic than heraldic.

REPRODUCED. Friends of the Fitzwilliam Museum, *Annual Report* for 1936.

NOTE. [1] Bought from a *marchand amateur* in London.

BRITISH SCHOOL, *c.* 1595–1600

2051 UNKNOWN MAN

Wood, 30¼ × 24½ in (76·8 × 62·2 cm). Nearly half-length, turned towards the right and looking upwards, his arms folded, showing the left hand. Wears black dress and black, tall-crowned hat. To right a view of the Thames with part of the City of London, and the Tower of London.

Bequeathed by Charles Haslewood Shannon, R.A., 1937. Coll. Reginald Cholmondeley, Condover Hall, Shropshire;[1] exh. London, 1866, 'Exhibition of national portraits' (188); late R. Cholmondely sale, Christie's, 6 March 1897 (9); sale of Sir Frederick de la Pole, Bart, Christie's, 24 February 1922 (4), bt Martin; coll. Charles Ricketts, R.A. and C. H. Shannon, R.A.; exh. Cambridge, Fitzwilliam Museum, 1933–7.

The face, hands and the landscape to the right of the head are basically original, but injured by over-cleaning, the face and hands much repaired; the rest of the background and the sky repainted. The costume, with the hairdressing, moustache and lower lip tuft, indicate a date of *c.* 1595–1600. The young man in the portrait exemplifies the cult of the 'humour' of melancholy in late Elizabethan and Jacobean times, affected particularly by those with scholarly and artistic pretensions, and by lovers. He seems most likely to belong to the latter class, characteristically dressed in black, wearing a hat, and with his arms folded in the classic pose of afflicted lovers, his gaze fixed on some vision of delight.[2] Such portraits were typically situated out of doors, but usually in a situation more solitary than the one here, which appears, despite great discrepancies, to be intended for the Tower of London, part of the City, and the Thames, with the Palace of Placentia, perhaps, in the distance. The discrepancies may be partly due to repainting. At least from the 1866 Exhibition of national portraits, the portrait has been identified, for reasons unknown, as of Sir Henry Pole, Baron Montacute (1492(?)–1538), but dates alone, not to mention the melancholic humour of the portrait, rule this out. In style, the portrait has affinities with the miniatures of Isaac Oliver.

REPRODUCED. John Woodward, *A picture history of British painting* (1962), p. 24; *Apollo* (1964), LXXIX, 269.

NOTES. [1] Condover Hall was built by Thomas Owen (d. 1598), and descended by inheritance to the Cholmondeleys; the collection of pictures was chiefly made by Nicholas Owen Smythe, d. 1814 (L. P. Neale, *Views of the seats of noblemen and gentlemen*, 2nd series (1825), II. [2] See Roy Strong, 'The Elizabethan malady', *Apollo* (1964), LXXIX, 264–9, reprinted in his *The English Icon* (1969), pp. 352–4.

BRITISH SCHOOL, *c.* 1660–5

2548 THE YOUNG STUDENT

Canvas, $28\frac{3}{4} \times 24\frac{1}{2}$ in ($73{\cdot}0 \times 62{\cdot}2$ cm).[1] Half-length to right, the right hand across the body holding a book. Bare-headed, curly dark brown hair to shoulders; clean-shaven. Over a brown doublet, unbuttoned from the chest, with short sleeves revealing full shirt-sleeves, and a deep, lace-bordered falling-band, he wears a gold-laced, black academical gown with a gold-embroidered red shoulder knot. Dark brown background.

Given by Mrs Sigismund Goetze, 1943. Coll. Judge George Evans; his sale, Christie's, 29 November 1918 (112).

The gown seems probably to be that of a fellow-commoner of the University of Cambridge.[2] A date of *c.* 1660–5 may be deduced from the costume, in particular from the style of hairdressing, the falling-band and the shoulder knot. The picture, which is undistinguished in quality, is in style independent of both van Dyck on the one hand and of Lely on the other, but is faintly reminiscent of Dobson in the character of the head and in the general presentation. Very similar in design and motive, but by a rather better hand, is a *Portrait of a student* in the Walker Art Gallery, Liverpool, acquired in 1971.

NOTES. [1] Lined; dimensions of the painted surface. [2] Cf. the gown of the 'Sociorum Commensalis' engraved in D. Loggan's *Cantabrigia illustrata* (1688), pl. VII, no. 4.

BRITISH SCHOOL, *c.* 1670–80

161 ELEANOR, COUNTESS OF TYRCONNEL

Canvas, $30\frac{1}{8} \times 25\frac{1}{4}$ in ($76{\cdot}5 \times 64{\cdot}1$ cm).[1] Half-length to right. Bare-headed, dark brown hair in ringlets, parted in the middle, a long curl falling in front of each shoulder; pearl ear-drops, close pearl necklace. Low décolletage, bordered by a white chemise frill; brownish bodice with jewelled clasps down the front; short, blue, tabbed shoulder-sleeves, over full, white, elbow-length chemise sleeves held with a jewelled clasp; a greenish cloak falls from the shoulders and is draped over the left arm; a dark buff and gold scarf caught at the right shoulder with a jewlled clasp is carried across the bodice. Dark background.

Founder's Bequest, 1816.

Lady Eleanor Holles, daughter of John, 1st Earl of Clare (d. 1637), and third wife of Oliver, 2nd Viscount Fitzwilliam and Earl of Tyrconnel; she was still living in 1677, her will proved 1681. The 2nd Viscount Fitzwilliam was the great-great-great-great uncle of the Founder of the Fitzwilliam Museum; his earldom of Tyrconnel became extinct on his death in 1667. The painting of the face, which is well drawn and of a dense, even paint texture, is in strong contrast with the treatment of the costume, superficially rendered in a loosely handled, fluid technique. Stylistically, the portrait is not without affinities with the work of Jacob Huysmans, who died in London in 1696.

NOTE. [1] Lined; dimensions of the painted surface.

BRITISH SCHOOL, 1723

446 FRANCES, VISCOUNTESS FITZWILLIAM

Canvas, 27¼ × 21½ in (69·2 × 54·6 cm).[1] Half-length, slightly right, the head slightly left. Brown hair, dressed with pearls, a jewel in front. Wears a blue dress with a low, round décolletage, edged with a frill of lace, jewelled clasps down the front of the bodice; full sleeves caught at the elbow, with white under-sleeves; an ermine-lined red mantle round her shoulders. On a table right, stands the coronet of a Viscountess. Mauve-brown background. Inscribed to left, 'Frances Daughter of Sr J^n^ Shelley Bar^t^ of Mitchel grove Sussex: Wife of R^d^ Ld Visc^t^ Fitzwilliam 1723'.

Founder's Bequest, 1816.

Frances, daughter of Sir John Shelley, Bart, in 1704 married Richard, 5th Viscount Fitzwilliam (see below, no. 440), and died in 1771, aged ninety-nine; see also under van Somer, no. 442, p. 236 below. On the evidence of the costume, the date '1723' in the inscription may be accepted as the date of the painting, though the portrait appears flattering for a woman aged about fifty-one.

NOTE. [1] Lined; dimensions of the painted surface.

BRITISH SCHOOL, EARLY EIGHTEENTH CENTURY

440 RICHARD, 5TH VISCOUNT FITZWILLIAM OF MERRION

Canvas, 30¼ × 25¼ in (76·8 × 64·2 cm). Half-length, seated, to right, leaning somewhat forward, the right arm held across the body, the hand extended. Bare-headed, light-coloured periwig; clean-shaven; wears red-pink velvet coat. Brown background, the back of a chair behind him to the left.

Founder's Bequest, 1816.

Richard, 5th Viscount Fitzwilliam of Merrion (*c.* 1677–1743), succeeded his father in 1704, and sat in the Irish House of Lords; Whig Member of

Parliament for Fowey, Cornwall, 1727–34. The pose of the figure and its proportion to the size of the canvas suggest that the picture has been cut down, possibly from a three-quarter-length portrait. His apparent age is about thirty-five, giving an approximate date of *c.* 1710–15 for the portrait, which is broadly similar in type to the work of Kneller.

BRITISH SCHOOL, EARLY EIGHTEENTH CENTURY

444 LADY DECKER

Canvas, 29⅞ × 26 in (75·9 × 66·1 cm). Half-length, to front, the head inclined to her right. Brown hair falling in curling locks; she wears a blue dress with a gold lining, which hangs loosely from the shoulders, open over a low-cut white chemise. Dark brown background. Within a painted oval of carved moulding.

Founder's Bequest, 1816.

Henrietta, daughter of the Rev. Richard Watkins, D.D., rector of Whichford, Warwickshire, married Sir Matthew Decker, Bart, before 1717; she died in 1759, aged eighty. Decker, a wealthy London merchant, came to England from Amsterdam in 1702, and was created a baronet in 1716. Their daughter, Catherine, married the 6th Viscount Fitzwilliam, and became the mother of the founder of the Fitzwilliam Museum. Lady Decker appears to be aged about twenty-five, giving a date of about 1715 for the portrait, which is of a type associated with the style of Jonathan Richardson.

BRITISH SCHOOL, EARLY EIGHTEENTH CENTURY

926 UNKNOWN MAN

Canvas, 23¾ × 19¾ in (60·3 × 50·2 cm).[1] Bust-length, turned in profile left, head half left. Clean-shaven, wearing a bright blue, loose cap, with a gilt tassel at the back, collarless grey-brown coat and white shirt buttoned at the neck. Dark brown background.

Given by F. A. White, 1918. Coll. C. E. Newton-Robinson; his executors' sale, Christie's, 3 April 1914 (121), bt Agnew; Thos Agnew & Sons Ltd sale, Christie's, 7 June 1918 (62), bt F. A. White.

In the Newton-Robinson sale, and subsequently, described as a self-portrait of Jonathan Richardson senior (1665–1745), but neither attribution nor identification can be accepted.[2] The picture is, rather, in the Kneller tradition of portraiture, with its baroque sense of movement and liveliness of expression, though technically it is distinct from Kneller. It has much the appearance of being a self-portrait, though there is a not inconsiderable resemblance to Kneller himself.[3] The costume could be of a date towards the end of the seventeenth century, but the earlier eighteenth century is more probable.

NOTES. [1] Lined; dimensions of the painted surface. [2] An identification as Jonathan Richardson the younger (1694–1771), suggested by W. K. Wimsatt, *The portraits of Alexander Pope* (1965), p. 75, is no more acceptable. [3] Compare, for example, the features in the self-portrait of 1685 in the National Portrait Gallery, no. 3794.

BRITISH SCHOOL (?), FIRST HALF OF THE EIGHTEENTH CENTURY

9 A MUSICIAN

Canvas, 40¼ × 34½ in (102.2 × 87·7 cm).[1] Three-quarter-length to right, looking front, seated at a keyboard instrument on which he is playing. Clean-shaven, wearing a loose red cap; green coat open down the front showing the jabot of a white shirt. He sits on a high-backed wooden chair, a brown curtain behind it.

Given by Adam Lodge, 1875. Coll. 'Mr. Hallitt';[2] Richard Clark (1780–1856), London, by 1830;[3] his sale, London, Puttick's, 25–8 June 1853 (577), bt Ellerton; John Lodge Ellerton (1810–1873);[4] exh. London, 1885, 'International inventions loan exhibition' (65).

This picture, datable from costume to the first half of the eighteenth century, was claimed by its owner Richard Clark, in 1830, as a portrait of G. F. Handel when young, painted by Sir James Thornhill when both were in the service of the Duke of Chandos at Cannons, his house in Middlesex.[5] Clark apparently had reason to believe that the portrait came from Cannons, and had been assured (by the painter William Etty, among others!) that it was the work of Thornhill. The notice he wrote about the picture is not very clearly expressed, but it distinctly reads as though, in the light of these considerations, he himself had originated the identification of the portrait as Handel. On grounds of both style and quality, an attribution to Thornhill is out of the question; as regards identification, as a portrait of Handel it could not have been painted at Cannons, for he did not arrive there until 1717 when he was aged thirty-two, while the man in the picture is a youth aged about twenty at the most.[6] The Cannons provenance of the portrait is given in the catalogue of the Clark sale of 1853, where it is described as having been purchased from Cannons by 'Mr. Hallitt'. There cannot be much doubt that this refers to William Hallett (d. 1782), who bought a quantity of material after the demolition of Cannons for the construction of his new house on the same site, Cannons Park.[7] The portrait may, therefore, have belonged to the Duke of Chandos (1673–1744), who was deeply interested in music, but nothing resembling it appears in the sale of the Chandos pictures at Cock's, London, on 6–8 May 1747.[8] The Clark sale catalogue is silent on the question of whether or not Hallett believed the portrait to depict Handel. The problem of the origins of the painting is to some extent clarified by an unattributed and unidentified miniature, in 1970 belonging to Mr Ove Pontoppidan in Denmark, which corresponds with it but is of much better quality; perhaps, therefore, both go back to an original of some merit. The present version may possibly be English, as the ladder-back chair in which he sits, different from that in the miniature, is at this date probably of English make. In his printed notice of 1830, Clark argues for the correctness of his identification of the portrait as Handel when young, by comparison with authentic later portraits, but none can be said to afford any confirmation. Whom it may represent remains an open question.

REPRODUCED. *Magazine of Art* (1885), VIII, 312; Earp, p. 194; *Principal pictures* (1912 edn), p. 175, (1929 edn), p. 206; C. R. L. Fletcher and Emery Walker, *Historical portraits*, (1919), III, p. 80.[9]

NOTES. [1] Lined; dimensions of the painted surface. [2] Catalogue of the Clark sale, 25–8 June 1853 (577); for his identity see below. [3] From a long printed notice dated 1830 at the back of the picture, evidently written by Richard Clark. [4] Brother of the donor, he was born John Lodge, and assumed the additional name of Ellerton about 1845. [5] From the printed notice referred to in n. [3]. Some of the decorations at Cannons were painted by Thornhill between 1715 and 1725; Handel was in residence between 1717 and 1719 (O. E. Deutsch, *Handel* (1955), p. 78). The picture, which has become known as the 'Chandos' portrait, was given and was formerly catalogued as of Handel by Thornhill. [6] For Clark's proneness to the invention of myths, see *Dictionary of National Biography* (1887), X, p. 404. [7] C. H. Collins Baker and Muriel I. Baker, *The life and circumstances of James Brydges, first Duke of Chandos* (1949), pp. xix, 437–8, 444–7. [8] Reprinted in J. R. Robinson, *The princely Chandos* (1893), pp. 213–19. [9] Always as Handel by Thornhill. Listed as such by J. M. Coopersmith, *Music and Letters* (1932), XIII, 160.

BRITISH SCHOOL, MID EIGHTEENTH CENTURY

M.53 A LADY

Canvas, 23⅝ × 19⅝ in (60·0 × 49·9 cm).[1] Half-length, to right. Bare-headed, dark brown hair dressed with pearls; fresh complexion; triple collar of pearls round the throat; wears a grey silk dress with pearl clasps down front of bodice, short sleeves caught with a pearl, with full, white under-sleeves; white fichu edged with lace borders the deep décolletage; pink and yellow flowers with green leaves at the bosom. Dark brown background.

Bequeathed by Charles Brinsley Marlay, 1912. Bt by C. B. Marlay from P. & D. Colnaghi & Co. Ltd, London; exh. London, South Kensington Museum, 1867, 'National portraits' (240); R.A., 1878, 'Old masters' (265); Grosvenor Gallery, 1888, 'Century of British art' (116); R.A., 1908, Winter Exhibition (103).

In all the four exhibitions to which it was lent between 1867 and 1908, described as a portrait of Lavinia Fenton, Duchess of Bolton, by William Hogarth, but neither identification can be upheld; subsequently catalogued as by George Knapton,[2] but, although with a certain stylistic resemblance, it is much inferior to him in quality. The portrait may be dated from the costume *c.* 1745–50, and bears traces, in the general conception, of the influence of Hogarth, in the treatment of the face, of Highmore, and, in the handling of the dress, of Vanderbank.

REPRODUCED. Constable, pl. XXX.

NOTES. [1] Lined; dimensions of the painted surface. All four corners are made up. [2] Constable, pp. 41–2.

BRITISH SCHOOL, 1767

PD. 22–1951 A YOUNG DRAUGHTSMAN (1767)

Canvas, 22⅝ × 17⅝ in (57·5 × 44·8 cm).[1] Whole-length, standing in a landscape, turned front, the head half right; he leans with his left elbow on rocks at the right, the hand holding a roll of paper, a *porte-crayon* in the other hand, the left leg crossed over the right; bare-headed, chestnut hair, clean-shaven. His clothes are blue, with ribbed white stockings and black shoes. To left, in the background, across a stretch of water, a cliff rises crowned with trees; a town lies beyond, with a hill in the distance. Lower right, the letters 'W W', with the date, '1767', below.

Bequeathed by Roger Francis Lambe, 1951.

Cleaned 1952; made up for a width of about ½ in (1·2 cm) down each side. The two Ws in the lower right corner, which, together with the date, have more the appearance of an inscription than of a signature, have caused William Williams to be suggested as the painter. But his work is quite different, and inferior, in style, and his signature also is different, in both form and calligraphy. From the youth's features, and from the whole feeling of the figure, both subject and painter seem unmistakably British, though the landscape background looks distinctly Italian. Of average quality, freely handled in a painterly style, the figure superior to the landscape; in age he appears to be about eighteen.

NOTE. [1] Lined; dimensions of the painted surface.

BRITISH SCHOOL, 1760s

652 PORTRAIT OF A LIBRARIAN

Canvas, 36 × 27⅞ in (91·4 × 70·8 cm).[1] His clothes are dull crimson, with white stockings and black shoes. The bookcase is brown, the walls grey, the carpet deep red and deep green, the upholstery green.

Given by Charles Fairfax Murray, 1908.

When given, described as by Sir Joshua Reynolds, and subsequently re-attributed doubtfully to Zoffany; but neither ascription is satisfactory, though in treatment and feeling the figure has some analogy with early portraits by Reynolds. The costume and wig are of a form found in the 1750s, but a rather later date for the painting is indicated by the table at the left, which is of a type only introduced during the 1760s.

REPRODUCED. *Principal pictures* (1912 edn), p. 135 (as Reynolds), (1929 edn), p. 250 (as Zoffany).

NOTE. [1] Lined; dimensions of the painted surface.

BRITISH SCHOOL, EIGHTEENTH CENTURY

438 MARY, VISCOUNTESS FITZWILLIAM

Canvas, 23⅞ × 18¼ in (60·7 × 46·4 cm).[1] Bust, to right. Auburn hair in falling ringlets; collar of pearls; blue dress opening down the front, with a low décolletage edged with a white chemise frill; a red drapery over her left shoulder. Dark brown background. Inscribed along the top, 'Mary Stapyleton Wiffe of Thomas L$^{d.}$ Visc^{t} Fitzwilliam 1679'.

Founder's Bequest, 1816.

The paint repaired and flaking. Mary, daughter of Sir Philip Stapleton, of Wighill, Yorkshire, married Thomas, 4th Viscount Fitzwilliam (see below, no. 439) as his first wife; he married again in 1699. Mother of the 5th Viscount (see p. 30, no. 440). From its unusual size and very poor quality, this must be a copy, which the character of the lettering in the inscription suggests is of the eighteenth century; in both these respects and in the framing, it corresponds with the portrait of her husband, no. 439 below, and seems to be by the same hand. From the evidence of the costume, the '1679' of the inscription could be the date of the original, which has not been traced.

NOTE. [1] Lined; dimensions of the old canvas.

BRITISH SCHOOL, EIGHTEENTH CENTURY

439 THOMAS, 4TH VISCOUNT FITZWILLIAM OF MERRION

Canvas, $23\frac{7}{8} \times 18\frac{1}{4}$ in ($60{\cdot}7 \times 46{\cdot}4$ cm).[1] Bust, to left. Bare-headed, brown periwig; clean-shaven. Wears a blue coat lined with red; long cravat. Dark brown background. Inscribed along the top, 'Thomas Ld Visc^{t} Fitzwilliam 1700'.

Founder's Bequest, 1816.

Extensive flaking and repair of the paint. Thomas, 4th Viscount Fitzwilliam of Merrion (d. 1704), succeeded his father on the latter's death in (?)1673; he was outlawed in 1689 for his devotion to James II, but was soon restored. From its unusual size and very poor quality, the portrait must be a copy, which the character of the lettering in the inscription suggests is of the eighteenth century; in both these respects and in the framing, it corresponds with the portrait of his first wife, no. 438 above, and seems to be by the same hand. From the evidence of the costume, the '1700' of the inscription could be the date of the original, which has not been traced.

NOTE. [1] Lined; dimensions of the old canvas.

BRITISH SCHOOL, EIGHTEENTH CENTURY

465 MEMORIAL TO THOMAS AND JOHN FITZWILLIAM

Canvas, 33¼ × 45¼ in (84·4 × 114·9 cm). In front of the two rectangular recesses of a monument, lying on a projecting base, recline two figures of dead men in armour, one at either side, their feet towards the centre. Both are bare-headed; the figure at the left has black hair and a dark brown beard, a sword pierces his chest; the figure at the right has brown hair, the broken shaft of a lance pierces his chest; both wear a tabard of the Fitzwilliam arms.[1] Beside his feet, each has his helm, and in the recess behind each stands an oval shield. White labels on the walls of the recesses read, at the left '·THOMAS FFITZ·/WILLYAM'; at the right 'IHOAN, FFITZ,/WILLIAM'. At the top, two grotesques back to back in the centre flank a roundel of a white-barred trefoil on a blue ground; a similar grotesque is at each extreme outer corner. On the front of the projecting base a panel with a blue ground is inscribed, 'IN DOYNG THEIR DUETIES AGAINST THE SCOTS / AT FLODDON FIELD UPON FRIDAY 9th SEPTEMr 1513'. The architecture of the monument is reddish brown in colour, with a lighter-coloured moulding around each recess.

Founder's Bequest, 1816. Coll. Viscounts Montague at Cowdray House, Sussex, until after 1793, when it passed at a date unknown to Richard, Viscount Fitzwilliam, founder of the Fitzwilliam Museum.

Thomas and John Fitzwilliam were sons of Sir Thomas Fitzwilliam of Aldwark, Yorkshire, and brothers of William Fitzwilliam, Earl of Southampton (see p. 115, no. 164); upon the death of the latter in 1542 his estates at Cowdray in Sussex passed to his half-brother Sir Anthony Browne, forbear of the Viscounts Montague. This painting of the two brothers, killed at the battle of Flodden Field in 1513, is one of two versions which were at Cowdray House, described as the original and a copy;[2] it is one of the few paintings saved when the house was destroyed by fire in 1793, and is identified as the copy.[3] The earliest known record of the original goes back to 1730, when George Vertue saw it on a visit to Cowdray.[4] This picture may well have been inspired by the series of sixteenth-century paintings at Cowdray House of historical events in the reign of Henry VIII, in some of which the Earl of Southampton and Sir Anthony Browne played a leading part.[5] In date it appears to have been probably of the earlier seventeenth century. Its form recalls the type of church wall-monument known from this period, with a 'speaking' effigy against an architectural setting in two divisions, inscriptions on each and another below. In the process of adaptation as a pictorial motive, the monumental effigy has given way to the realistic corpse-figures still bleeding from their wounds, which yet retain the formality of arrangement of the prototype. The grotesques along the top can be paralleled in the use of similar motives in the decorative painting of this period.[6] The barred trefoil argent was a badge of the Fitzwilliams. The Fitzwilliam Museum copy is of no more than journeyman quality, though it has been ascribed to Thomas Hudson,[7] and may, therefore, be of the earlier eighteenth century. A version is at Oxburgh Hall (National Trust); a copy of the Fitzwilliam Museum picture by Miss Lucas was, in 1905, at Kirkham Abbey, Yorkshire (Lord Liverpool).

REPRODUCED. Earp, p. 102.

NOTES. [1] The Fitzwilliam quartering, lozengy argent and gules, on the tabard of John Fitzwilliam at the right, is differenced with a crescent, the mark of cadency of a younger son; Thomas was the eldest. [2] Sir William H. St John Hope, *Cowdray and Easebourne Priory* (1919), pp. 37, 38, 61 (no. 90), 63 (no. 199), 64 (n. 8). For another painting saved from the fire, see p. 115, no. 164. [3] Inventory by W. Seguier, March 1816, of the pictures in the Founder's Bequest (Fitzwilliam Museum). [4] *Walpole Society* (1932), XX, Vertue Note Books II, p. 82, giving the form of the inscription as 'doing their duti against the Scots', as against the longer inscription on the present copy. [5] Hope, *op. cit.*, pp. 38, 39–44. [6] Cf. Edward Croft-Murray, *Decorative painting in England, 1537–1837* (1962), I, pls. 70, 74, 75, 78. [7] Seguier, *loc. cit.* The *Catalogue of the pictures at Cowdray House* (1777; reprinted in Hope, *op. cit.*, pp. 59–63) lists the two versions of this painting under nos. 90 and 199, but with no painter's name to either. It includes, however, a number of copies of pictures in the house by C. Lucy, a portrait painter born in 1692, who might thus have been responsible for the Fitzwilliam Museum copy also.

BRITISH SCHOOL, EARLY NINETEENTH CENTURY

1100 HOLY FAMILY WITH ST JOHN THE BAPTIST

Canvas, 29 × 24 in (73·7 × 60·9 cm).[1] The Virgin Mary, in a pink dress with a light blue drapery over her knees, the naked Christ Child asleep in her lap, sits at the right looking towards St Joseph, blocked in in pinkish brown, who stands at the left beside a donkey in brown under-painting; between them is the child St John, sketched in, who gazes at the Christ Child. A brown bank rises at the right beside the Virgin Mary, and trees in blue-grey fill the background, all uncompleted; a grid for the transfer of the design is visible in some areas.

Bequeathed by Samuel Sandars (1837–1904), with a life-interest to his widow, received 1923.

Unfinished. Bequeathed as 'ascribed to Sir Joshua Reynolds', but in style it is manifestly of the earlier years of the nineteenth century. The figure of the Virgin Mary, which alone is partially completed, shows a close general relationship in style to the work of Sir Thomas Lawrence. In subject the picture is ostensibly a *Rest on the flight into Egypt*, but with the iconographically curious introduction of the child St John. This, with the individualised character of the head of the Virgin and the contemporary fashion of her high-waisted dress, suggests the possibility of its being a family group.

NOTE. [1] Lined; dimensions of the painted surface.

BRITISH SCHOOL, *c.* 1852

2729 J. M. W. TURNER, R.A.

Canvas, 13½ × 11½ in (34·3 × 29·2 cm).[1] Whole-length, standing, almost in profile to right, a palette in his left hand, a paint-brush in his right, at an easel on which is a large sea-piece. Bare-headed, grey hair, clean-shaven; wears a dark brown coat and fawn trousers. Behind the easel and to the left of it, the dark walls of a room hung with pictures; a fireplace in the wall to the left with a brown wooden chair beside it.

Given by Howard Bliss, 1945.

Joseph Mallord William Turner (1775–1851), celebrated landscape painter. A crudely painted invention based on a wood-engraving by W. J. Linton, after a drawing by Sir John Gilbert,[2] showing Turner at three-quarter-length; the engraving was published in the *Illustrated Exhibitor and Magazine of Art* (1852), I, 216. Though Gilbert's sketch was made in 1841, the sea-piece shown on the easel is of a type which Turner was painting about 1810.

NOTES. [1] Lined; dimensions of the painted surface. [2] Walter Thornbury, *The life of J. M. W. Turner, R.A.* (1862), II, pp. 321–2.

BROWN, Ford Madox

1821–1893. Born in Calais. Student in Bruges, Ghent and Antwerp; worked in Paris; visited Italy, 1845; settled in London, 1846. Exh. R.A., 1841–52, and elsewhere both in London and the provinces. Subject painter, sympathetic towards the outlook of the Pre-Raphaelites.

PD. 9–1950 CORDELIA'S PORTION PLATE 45

Canvas on wood, $22 \times 30\frac{3}{8}$ in ($55{\cdot}9 \times 77{\cdot}2$ cm).[1] Lear is in white against a yellow hanging; Cordelia, in light green, stands beside the King of France wearing pale blue over brown; to the left stand Goneril and Regan, one dark, in dark grey, the other with red hair, in deep red over light grey, their husbands Albany and Cornwall kneeling in front, one in dark brown, the other with an orange cloak.

Bequeathed by Thomas Henry Riches, 1935, with a life-interest to his widow, who died 1950. Exh. Nottingham, University Art Gallery, 1961, 'Shakespeare in art' (71); Liverpool, Walker Art Gallery, 1964, 'Ford Madox Brown' (41); London, Arts Council, 1964, 'Shakespeare in art' (57).

The subject is taken from Act I, Scene I, of Shakespeare's *King Lear*, at the moment when the King of France takes the disinherited Cordelia for his wife. Madox Brown executed in Paris in 1844 a series of sixteen pen and ink outline drawings of subjects from *King Lear*,[2] now at Manchester (Whitworth Art Gallery), two of which, both on the theme of Cordelia's portion, are closely connected with this composition (nos. D.51 and 52. 1927). In 1863 the subject was in his mind again,[3] and two years later, in November 1865, a large water-colour commissioned by Frederick Craven was begun[4] (Lady Lever Art Gallery, Port Sunlight), for which a chalk cartoon in monochrome was executed[5] (Manchester City Art Gallery). Two years later again, in 1867, an oil-painting, slightly larger in size, was started,[6] but it was only finished, for Albert Wood,[7] in 1875[8] (Southampton Art Gallery, no. S/97). Two other versions are known, both oil-paintings: the present one in the Fitzwilliam Museum, and a second which was among the contents of Madox Brown's studio sold after his death,[9] whereabouts now unknown. All five versions exhibit minor differences one from another; the present one, which is rather smaller than those at Manchester, Port Sunlight and Southampton,[10] is somewhat sketchy in treatment.

NOTES. [1] Dimensions of the painted surface. [2] Ford M. Hueffer, *Ford Madox Brown* (1896), pp. 37, 434. [3] Included in a list of 'works in contemplation' sent to George Rae, Hueffer, *op. cit.*, p. 197. (4) Hueffer, *op. cit.*, pp. 207, 441; it was finished in November 1866, *ibid.*, p. 221, though from the fact that it is dated '"66–72"' it appears that some work was done on it subsequently, as was not unusual with Madox Brown. [5] Hueffer, *op. cit.*, pp. 207, 441. [6] Hueffer, *op. cit.*, pp. 232, 441. [7] Letter of 31 December 1874 to James Leathart (private ownership). [8] Hueffer, *op. cit.*, p. 300. [9] At his house, 1 St Edmund's Terrace, Regent's Park, London, by T. G. Wharton, 29–31 May 1894 (150), rep. [10] No size is given in the catalogue for the version in the Madox Brown sale.

M.Add. 3 THE LAST OF ENGLAND (1860) PLATE 45

Canvas, $18\frac{1}{4} \times 16\frac{5}{8}$ in ($46{\cdot}4 \times 42{\cdot}3$ cm), oval.[1] The man's coat and hat brown; the woman's shawl red and black, her bonnet grey with madder ribbons, the tarpaulin over her knees deep red. Pale green sea. Signed and dated lower right, 'F MADOX BROWN 1860'.

Bought from the Marlay Fund, 1917. Bt from the painter by Col. W. J. Gillum (d. 1910), 1860;[2] exh. London, Leicester Galleries, 1909, 'Works by Ford Madox Brown' (4), lent Miss Mary Slater;[3] bt from Miss Slater; exh. Manchester, City Art Gallery, 1968, 'Art and the Industrial Revolution' (11).

Reduced repetition of the original ($32\frac{1}{2} \times 29\frac{1}{2}$ in; $82{\cdot}5 \times 74{\cdot}9$ cm), painted 1852–5, at Birmingham (City Museum and Art Gallery, no. 24'91), with some variation in the colouring. A finished cartoon in pencil, and a study in chalk for the woman's head, both dated 1852, are also at Birmingham (nos. 791'06, and 795'06). A second repetition in water-colour, smaller still (circular, 13 in (33·0 cm) diameter), dating from 1864–6,[4] is in the Tate Gallery, London (no. 3064). A first water-colour sketch for the picture, 1852–64,[5] which belonged in 1865 to B. G. Windus, is now untraced.[6] The subject 'treats of the great emigration movement [of the last century], which attained its culminating point in 1852';[7] Madox Brown was inspired to paint it by the departure of his friend the sculptor Thomas Woolner for the Australian gold-fields in that year. The emigrant couple are portraits of the painter and his second wife, Emma Hill. True to Pre-Raphaelite principles, the original version, 'To ensure the peculiar look of *light all round*, which objects have on a dull day at sea...was painted for the most part in the open air on dull days, and when the flesh was being painted, on cold days'.[8]

REPRODUCED. Exhibition catalogue, '*Works by Ford Madox Brown*' (1909), Leicester Galleries, p. 19; Constable, pl. XXX.

NOTES. [1] Dimensions of the painted surface; on a rectangular canvas, 18½ × 17¼ in. (47·7 × 43·9 cm). [2] F. M. Hueffer, *Ford Madox Brown* (1896), pp. 169, 438, probably a commission; for Col. Gillum, see N. Pevsner, *Burlington Magazine* (1935), xcv, 78. [3] As Col. Gillum employed a London agent of the name of Slater, the picture may have passed more or less directly from him to Miss Mary Slater (information kindly communicated by Mr J. R. Gillum and Lt-Col. W. W. Gillum, 1952). [4] Hueffer, *op. cit.*, p. 438. [5] Hueffer, *op. cit.*, p. 438 (also mentioning a 'Photograph worked over', but 1860 is surprisingly early for a photographic print, if this is what is meant), and *Preraphaelite diaries and letters*, ed. W. M. Rossetti (1900), p. 112. [6] Lent by Windus to Madox Brown's 1865 exhibition (no. 46) at 191 Piccadilly, London. At the posthumous Windus sale, Christie's 14 February 1868, lot 315 may have been this sketch. [7] Quoted by Hueffer, *op. cit.*, p. 100, from Madox Brown's catalogue note to his 1865 exhibition, no. 14. [8] *Loc. cit.*, n. 7.

BROWN, Sir John Alfred Arnesby

1866–1955. Born at Nottingham. Studied under Andrew McCallum, and at the Herkomer School, Bushey; exh. R.A. from 1890; R.A., 1915; kt, 1938. Landscape painter.

1073 THE YACHT RACE

Canvas, 16 × 19⅞ in (40·6 × 50·5 cm).[1] In an extensive flat landscape with pale green and yellow lights and bluish shadows, the sails of several yachts appear in the middle distance above trees to the right; in the foreground to the left are farm buildings and trees. Above is a large expanse of sky, almost filled with grey and white clouds. Signed lower left, 'Arnesby Brown'.

Given by the artist, 1922

This is the study for a larger painting with the same title, formerly in the collection of the Rt Hon. Sir Leslie Scott, K.C., which was exhibited at the R.A. in 1922.[2] A high proportion of Arnesby Brown's work was painted in Norfolk, where he lived for much of his life; this picture is probably of a subject on the Norfolk broads.

REPRODUCED. *Principal pictures* (1929), p. 27.

NOTES. [1] Dimensions of the painting; the canvas measures 16½ × 20½ in (41·9 × 52·1 cm). [2] Rep. *Royal Academy Illustrated* (1922), 33.

CAMERON, Sir David Young

1865–1945. Born in Glasgow. Glasgow School of Art, and, in 1885, the Royal Scottish Academy, Edinburgh. Painter in oils and water-colours, draughtsman and etcher; influenced mainly by Rembrandt, and by nineteenth-century French and Dutch landscape painters. R.A., 1920; kt, 1924; H. M. Painter and Limner in Scotland, 1933. Landscape and architectural subjects.

1078 A LITTLE TOWN OF PROVENCE (1922)

Canvas, 26⅛ × 26 in (66·4 × 66·1 cm). At the foot of a line of blue hills, a small scattered town lies in an expanse of broken, undulating ground, painted in tones of warm brown, an isolated dwelling on a knoll in the foreground. A deep sky of turquoise blue above is partly veiled by warm cream clouds. Signed lower right, 'D. Y. Cameron'.

Given by the artist, 1922. Exh. Huddersfield Art Gallery, 1946, 'Two hundred years of British painting' (271); Edinburgh (Arts Council), 1965–6, 'Sir D. Y. Cameron, centenary exhibition' (40).

Painted expressly for the Fitzwilliam Museum during 1922; described by the painter as the town of Fréjus somewhat freely treated.

REPRODUCED. *Principal pictures* (1929), p. 35.

CLAUSEN, SIR GEORGE

1852–1944. Studied at the South Kensington Schools (later Royal College of Art), 1867–73, and in Paris; exh. R.A. and New English Art Club, London; R.A., 1908; kt, 1927. Figure-painting and landscape.

923 SELF-PORTRAIT (1918)

Canvas, 24¾ × 20⅛ in (62·9 × 51·1 cm). Nearly half-length, slightly to the right, holding a paint-brush in his right hand. Bare-headed, bald, white hair; white beard and moustache; spectacles. Wears khaki-coloured jacket and waistcoat, with white shirt and blue tie. Grey background to the left, to the right a rectangular canvas in lighter greys with a passage of pale blue. Signed and dated upper right, 'G. CLAUSEN. 1918'.

Given by the artist, 1918. Exh. Colchester, The Minories, Clausen exhibition, 1963.

The first of a series of self-portraits contributed by living painters to the Fitzwilliam Museum at the invitation of the then Director, (Sir) Sydney Cockerell. The others consist of portraits of Orpen, Steer, Strang and Walton.

REPRODUCED. *Principal pictures* (1929), p. 40.

1118 HENRY FESTING JONES (1923)

Canvas, $18\frac{1}{4} \times 15\frac{1}{4}$ in ($46{\cdot}4 \times 38{\cdot}7$ cm). Head and shoulders, to left, looking front. Bare-headed, grey hair; grey beard and moustache; spectacles. Wears grey jacket and waistcoat, with a blue and red tie. Dark grey background. Signed and dated lower right, 'G. CLAUSEN. 1923'.

Given by Henry Festing Jones, 1923. Exh. London, R.A., 1923 (520).

Henry Festing Jones (1851–1928), author, is probably best known as the biographer of Samuel Butler, to whom he was literary executor.

COLEMAN, JAMES

Known from two portraits of the Fuller family of Birmingham, one dated to 1786, in the Birmingham City Museum and Art Gallery (nos. 38'30, 39'30). Father of Edward Coleman, of Birmingham, portrait and still-life painter; active from about 1813.

503** THOMAS, 9TH VISCOUNT FITZWILLIAM OF MERRION

Canvas, $29\frac{3}{4} \times 24\frac{5}{8}$ in ($75{\cdot}6 \times 62{\cdot}6$ cm). Half-length to left. Bare-headed, bald, grey hair, clean-shaven. Wears black jacket and high-collared waistcoat, with jabot. Dark brown background.

Given by the Rev. Hereford Brooke George, 1895. Given or bequeathed by the 9th Viscount Fitzwilliam to Richard Francis George, father of the donor.[1]

Thomas, 9th Viscount Fitzwilliam of Merrion (1755–1832), succeeded his brother in the peerage in 1830; both were younger brothers of the 7th Viscount, the founder of the Fitzwilliam Museum, and on the death of Thomas Fitzwilliam without heirs the peerage became extinct. The donor of the portrait believed 'the artist's name to be Coleman',[2] and a comparison with the two portraits by James Coleman at Birmingham serves to identify it as by the same hand.[3]

REPRODUCED. Earp, p. 102.

NOTES. [1] Towards the end of his life, Viscount Fitzwilliam was a patient of Richard Francis George, a surgeon at Bath (letter of 30 January 1895 from the donor, Fitzwilliam Museum). [2] Letter of 30 January 1895 (Fitzwilliam Museum). [3] Letter of 22 April 1953 from Dr Mary Woodall (Fitzwilliam Museum).

COLLINS, Charles Allston

1828–1873. Born in London. Student at the R.A.; about 1850 became a follower of the Pre-Raphaelites. Later abandoned painting for literature.

676 WILKIE COLLINS (1853) PLATE 46

Wood, 11¾ × 9½ in (29·9 × 24·1 cm).[1] Dark brown hair; black coat, grey waistcoat, black tie. Red-brown desk; green background. Signed and dated on the desk, 'CAC [in a monogram] 1853'.

Given by Charles Fairfax Murray, 1909. Coll. Sir J. E. Millais, Bart, P.R.A. (1829–1896); Millais sale, Christie's, 2 July 1897 (7), bt Murray; exh. Manchester, City Art Gallery, 1911, 'Loan exhibition of the works of Ford Madox Brown and the Pre-Raphaelites' (301); Birmingham, City Museum and Art Gallery, 1947, 'The Pre-Raphaelite Brotherhood' (15); Bournemouth, Russell-Cotes Art Gallery, 1951, 'Paintings and drawings by the Pre-Raphaelites and their followers' (37); London, R.A., 1956–7, 'British portraits' (438); London, Victoria and Albert Museum, 1970, 'Charles Dickens' (P32).

(William) Wilkie Collins (1824–1889), son of William Collins, R.A., and brother of Charles Allston Collins, was a writer of highly dramatic novels; he was a friend of Charles Dickens, with whom he collaborated. The portrait may well have been a gift from the painter to Millais, who was a close friend of the Collins family and, more particularly, at the period of this painting, of Charles.

REPRODUCED. Exhibition catalogue *Charles Dickens* (1970), Victoria and Albert Museum, pl. 42.

NOTE. [1] The painted surface, which is of the same dimensions as the rectangular panel, has an arched, pointed top.

CONSTABLE, John

1776–1837. Born at East Bergholt, Suffolk. Student at the R.A. schools, but mainly self-taught; lived in London from 1799; exh. R.A. and elsewhere from 1802; R.A., 1829. Landscape painter.

2291 PARHAM'S MILL, GILLINGHAM (1824) PLATE 34

Canvas, 9¾ × 11⅞ in (24·8 × 30·2 cm).[1] The tiles of the roof and porch are a brownish red; the planks of the end wall are grey-brown; the wall beside the porch is buff-cream; the mill wheel is deep grey. The bank to the left and the herbage on it are in browns and subdued greens; the nearer willow has a grey stem, the further one a buff-cream stem, the foliage of both is light green. The water is grey and brown, white where it runs from the wheel. The meadow and distance are in subdued greens, with trees of darker and richer greens; the little stream is light blue. Sky of light blue with cream and grey clouds.

Bequeathed by the Rev. Osmond Fisher (d. 1914), with a life-interest to his son, the Rev. O. P. Fisher; received 1937. Coll. Archdeacon John Fisher (d. 1832), father of the Rev. Osmond Fisher, who bought it from the painter; exh. London, Wildenstein's, 1937, 'A centenary memorial exhibition of John Constable, R.A.' (55); Auckland, N.Z., City Art Gallery (and Sydney and Melbourne, Australia), 1973–4, 'John Constable, the natural painter' (34).

Cleaned and lined, 1937. The original canvas was inscribed on the back, 'John Fisher / 1824', and, in another hand, 'J. Constable R.A. / fecit', 'property of his son Osmond Fisher'; the old (original) stretcher was inscribed, 'London June 7th 1824 / John Constable fecit'.[2] Painted for Archdeacon Fisher in London in June 1824.[3] Constable first visited Gillingham in Dorset in 1820, and stayed there with Archdeacon Fisher in 1823, when he 'made one or two attacks on the old mill'.[4] In anticipation of a visit in London from Fisher, who had already paid him for the picture, he records in his journal for part of 1824 that he began work on the present *Parham's Mill* in the first days of June, and that it was finished on the 7th, though more work on it is recorded on the 17th; it was taken away by Fisher on the 20th.[5] Two other examples of this composition are known, in the possession respectively of Mr and Mrs Paul Mellon, U.S.A.,[6] and of the Earl of Haddington.[7] Another painting of the mill, upright and from a different point of view, is in the Victoria and Albert Museum (no. 1632–1888).[8] At the time of Constable's paintings, the mill was in the ownership of Matthew Parham, though it was also known as 'Perne's Mill', by which name the present structure on the site is still known. Parham's mill was burnt down in 1825.[9]

REPRODUCED. C. R. Leslie, *Memoirs of the life of John Constable, R.A.*, ed. Hon. Andrew Shirley (1937), pl. 72; R. B. Beckett, *John Constable and the Fishers* (1952), p. 112; *John Constable's Correspondence*, VI (1968), p. 163, pl. 11; exhibition catalogue, *John Constable, the natural painter* (1973), Auckland, N.Z., p. 79.

NOTES. [1] Lined; dimensions of the painted surface. [2] The note on the stretcher does not seem to be in either Constable's or Archdeacon Fisher's hand, and was probably written by the Rev. Osmond Fisher. [3] *John Constable's Correspondence*, ed. R. B. Beckett (1968), VI, pp. 163–5 (also printed in R. B. Beckett, *John Constable and the Fishers* (1952), pp. 173–5); C. R. Leslie, *Memoirs of the life of John Constable, R.A.*, ed. Hon. Andrew Shirley (1937), p. 166. [4] Beckett, *op. cit.*, p. 130. [5] Beckett, *op. cit.*, pp. 162, 163–5. Mr R. B. Beckett kindly supplied a note of the unpublished entry for 7 June from the original journal in the possession of the Earl of Plymouth. [6] This may be identified with the picture painted for Mrs Hand of Salisbury in 1826, which was probably the one exhibited in the same year at the R.A. (122), see Beckett, *op. cit.*, pp. 166, 212–13, 218, 230; it was formerly in the collections of Francis Gibson (d. 1859), Lewis Fry, C. A. Barton, S. P. Joel, Sir Bernard Eckstein, Bart, and W. L. Lewis, New York. [7] This may be the 'Undershot mill at Gillingham' in the C. F. Huth sale at Christie's, 19 March 1904 (45); Lord Haddington's picture descended to him from George Salting who bought it from Messrs Gooden & Fox. [8] Presumably Constable sale, Foster's, second day, 16 May 1838 (57), bt in; bequeathed to the Museum by Miss Isabel Constable, 1888. See Graham Reynolds, *Victoria and Albert Museum. Catalogue of the Constable collection* (1960), p. 175, no. 288. [9] Beckett, *op. cit.*, p. 206.

2383 SALISBURY PLATE 34

Canvas, 24 × 20⅜ in (61·0 × 51·8 cm). The greens are mostly yellowish or bluish, the wall greyish pink in the lights and warm grey in the shadows, the masonry of the culvert brownish grey, the spire a warm silver-grey.

Bequeathed by Frank Hindley Smith, 1939. Bt in a miscellaneous local sale at Hereford, 1925; sold Christie's, anon. (= Russell Ward & Sons), 31 March 1926 (92), bt Permain; bt from him by Leggatt Bros., London, who sold it in the trade to Howard Young, U.S.A.; bt back and sold to the Independent Gallery, London (P. M. Turner), 1927; exh. London, Wildenstein's, 1937, 'A centenary memorial exhibition of John Constable, R.A.' (51), lent F. Hindley Smith[1]; Auckland, N.Z., City Art Gallery (and Melbourne and Sydney, Australia), 1973–4, 'John Constable, the natural painter' (36).

From its manner of handling, the picture appears to have been painted for the most part on the spot.[2] It has been referred to Constable's visit to Archdeacon Fisher at Salisbury in 1821,[3] but this is unlikely as the visit took place in November. Summer visits were paid in 1820, 1823 and 1829. The painting may most probably be assigned, on grounds of style, to the latest of these dates; compare, for example, two Salisbury sketches in the Victoria and Albert Museum (nos. 153–1888 and 334–1888), both dated 1829.[4] The picture may have been painted in Lower Marsh Close, near Fisher's house, thus showing the wall of the Bishop's garden and the stream which ran from his fish-pond;[5] or perhaps alternatively, as the spire of the Cathedral appears so close, inside the garden, which was separated from the cathedral by a wall with tall trees beyond it.[6]

REPRODUCED. *Burlington Magazine* (1927), LI, December, no. 19 of 'Notable works of art now on the market'; C. R. Leslie, *Memoirs of the life of John Constable, R.A.*, ed. Hon. Andrew Shirley (1937), pl. 64; exhibition catalogue, *John Constable, the natural painter* (1973), Auckland, N.Z., p. 83.

NOTES. [1] Probably bought by him from the Independent Gallery (P. M. Turner). [2] Unusual for Constable with a canvas of this size, but the proximity of Archdeacon Fisher's house in the Close could account for the exception. [3] C. R. Leslie, *Memoirs of the life of John Constable, R.A.*, ed. Hon. Andrew Shirley (1937), p. 122, and the catalogue of Wildenstein's 'Centenary memorial exhibition of John Constable, R.A.', 1937, p. 31, no. 51. [4] Graham Reynolds, *Victoria and Albert Museum. Catalogue of the Constable collection* (1960), pp. 185, 186, nos. 311, 312, rep. pl. 230, 231. [5] Suggested by R. B. Beckett, 1953. [6] Cf. *Salisbury Cathedral and the Close*, Victoria and Albert Museum (no. 318–1888), Reynolds, *op. cit.*, p. 127, no. 196, pl. 156, which is probably taken from the Bishop's garden.

PD. 207–1948 HAMPSTEAD HEATH PLATE 32

Canvas, 21¼ × 30¼ in (54·0 × 76·9 cm).[1] The immediate foreground is brown and green, with light brownish buff beyond it; the cart is grey with brown horses; one man (to left) has a red waistcoat, the other yellow; the nearer donkey is dark grey, the further one light grey. The middle distance is in quiet, yellowish greens, with passages of brownish buff; the path at the right is buff, the house beyond it white. In the distance, the darker greens are of a bluish tint, the lighter slightly yellowish. Cream clouds with mauve shadows in a light blue sky.

Bought from the Marlay Fund, with a contribution from the National Art-Collections Fund, 1948. Coll. William Sharp, of Handsworth, near Birmingham (d. 1881, aged 86); sale by his executors, Christie's, 9 July 1881 (72),[2] bt Agnew; sold by Thos Agnew & Sons Ltd, London, 1881, to Walter Holland of Liverpool (d. 1915); sold with the contents of his house by Ellis & Sons, Liverpool, 15–21 November 1932 (1000), bt in; sold by Miss A. E. Holland, of Liverpool, through the Fine Art Society Ltd, London, to Leggatt Bros., London, who sold it to Vicars Bros., London, 1933; sold by Vicars to Sir Bernard Eckstein, Bart, 1933; sale by his executors, Sotheby's, 8 December 1948 (64), bt in; bt from his trustees; exh. London, R.A., 1968–9, 'Royal Academy of Arts, bicentenary exhibition' (70); Tate Gallery, 1973, 'Landscape in Britain, *c.* 1750–1850' (225); Hazlitt, 1974 (10); Tate Gallery, 1976, 'Constable' (187).

Cleaned 1963. Stylistically this takes its place with the pictures painted by Constable between about 1815 and the early 1820s; among dated examples it resembles in particular the *Flatford Mill* of 1817 in the Tate Gallery (no. 1273). Constable is not certainly known to have painted at Hampstead before 1819,[3] when he first went to live there, and no Hampstead subject was exhibited until 1821.[4] The present picture seems probably to date from about 1820,[5] or perhaps a little later. It is very close sylistically to a *Hampstead Heath* in the Victoria and Albert Museum (no. F.A. 36), which has been assigned to about this year,[6] or alternatively to about 1821–2,[7] and which is so nearly the same in dimensions (21 × 30½ in., 53·3 × 77·6 cm) as to suggest that the two may have been intended as companion pieces. It also has much in common with *The salt box* in the National Gallery (no. 1236), which may be dated on C. R. Leslie's authority around 1820,[8] though it has also been dated about 1821,[9] and in which one of the figures in the Fitzwilliam Museum picture reappears. A pencil drawing by Constable corresponding in some detail with the right-hand half of the picture, measuring 7¼ × 9⅞ in (18·4 × 25·1 cm), which seems to be a sketch made on the spot, is in the Fitzwilliam Museum (no. PD. 208–1948); it may be noted that in the painting the distance has been somewhat rearranged and the whole landscape has been endowed with greater depth and sweep. The view appears to be taken from near Whitestone Pond, looking towards the north-west; the distant church with a square tower on the hill almost in the centre is probably St Mary's, Hendon. Maintenance work on the Heath supplies the motive for the narrative episode characteristically introduced into the foreground.

REPRODUCED. *Illustrated London News*, 26 February 1949, CCXIV, 283; *Winkler prins*, Amsterdam (1952), XII (under 'Landschapschilderkunst ix'); C. R. Leslie, *Memoirs of the life of John Constable*, ed. Jonathan Mayne (1951), pl. 24; C. Winter, *The Fitzwilliam Museum* (1958), pl. 100; Graham Reynolds, *Constable, the natural painter* (1965), pl. 31; exhibition catalogue, Hazlitt, 1974, pl. 21.

NOTES. [1] Lined; dimensions of the painted surface. [2] The catalogue describes the contents of the sale as 'The very choice collection of modern pictures formed during the last half century with great taste and judgment by William Sharp Esq.'. [3] In November of this year he showed two Hampstead paintings to Joseph Farington, see *The Farington diary*, ed. James Greig (1928), VIII, p. 234. See also n. [8]. [4] R.A., no. 89, *Hampstead Heath.* [5] So dated by Jonathan Mayne in his edition of C. R. Leslie, *Memoirs of the life of John Constable* (1951), pl. 24, and by Graham Reynolds, *Constable, the natural painter* (1965), pl. 31. [6] Reynolds, *op. cit.*, pl. 30, though in his earlier *Victoria and Albert Museum. Catalogue of the Constable collection* (1960), p. 191, no. 323, it is included in a small group, approximately dated on grounds of style to about 1820–30 (p. 8), but the reasons for so including it are not made very clear. [7] C. J. Holmes, *Constable and his influence on landscape painting* (1902), p. 248. [8] Leslie, ed. Mayne, *op. cit.*, p. 72, writes of it as a picture he has known for twenty-five years; as this passage first occurs in the edition of 1845, it would refer the picture to about 1820, though the context implies a date of about 1818. The latter date is adopted by Martin Davies, *National Gallery Catalogues. The British School* (1959), p. 16. [9] Holmes, *op. cit.*, pp. xii, 120, 245, where he speculates that it may be the *Hampstead Heath* exhibited in that year at the R.A., no. 89.

PD. 7–1951 SKY STUDY, SUNSET

Oils on paper, $5\frac{3}{4} \times 9\frac{1}{8}$ in ($14{\cdot}6 \times 23{\cdot}2$ cm). Across the centre and top are bars of dark grey cloud against a blue sky, both flecked with small yellow clouds. The distant sky below is barred with bright sunset colours.

Bought from the Fairhaven Fund, 1951. Probably coll. Mrs Ella Mackinnon;[1] bought by Henry Newson-Smith about 1890, probably from Leggatt's Gallery, London;[2] inherited by his son, Sir Frank Newson-Smith, Bart, 1898; his sale, Christie's, 26 January 1951, lot 18 (with no. PD. 8–1951, below, mounted together), bt Agnew; bt from Thos Agnew & Sons Ltd, London, together with no. PD. 8–1951; exh. Colchester, The Minories, 1958, 'First loan exhibition' (45).

The majority of Constable's sky studies date from 1821 and 1822.[3] It appears from his letters that he was then concentrating on such studies both to improve his skies and to increase his mastery of the pictorial relationship between sky and land.[4] His studies of this kind, painted in oils on paper, appear to have been very numerous.[5] They are frequently inscribed on the back with details of date and weather conditions, but no inscriptions are now to be seen on this sketch, or on nos. PD. 8–1951 and PD. 222–1961. Studies consisting of clouds only, such as these three, date mainly from 1822[6] rather than 1821.

NOTES. [1] Daughter of Constable's son, Captain C. G. Constable, who d. 1879. [2] Information from Sir Frank Newson-Smith, Bart (letter of 28 June 1955, Fitzwilliam Museum), which enables Mrs Mackinnon to be identified as the probable earlier owner, and from Oscar E. Johnson (letter of 1 July 1955, Fitzwilliam Museum). [3] C. R. Leslie, *Memoirs of the life of John Constable, R.A.*, ed. Hon. Andrew Shirley (1937), pp. 116 (letter of 20 September 1821), 117–18 (letter of 23 October 1821), 131 (letter of 7 October 1822). [4] See particularly the letter of 23 October 1821. [5] Leslie, ed. Shirley, *loc. cit.*, n. 3. [6] Graham Reynolds, *Victoria and Albert Museum. Catalogue of the Constable collection* (1960), p. 26.

PD. 8–1951 SKY STUDY WITH MAUVE CLOUDS

Oils on paper, $5\frac{5}{8} \times 8\frac{3}{4}$ in ($14{\cdot}2 \times 22{\cdot}2$ cm). Across the centre are massive dark clouds, mainly mauve-grey. Above is a blue sky, and below a distant layer of light, cream-coloured clouds.

Bought from the Fairhaven Fund, 1951. For provenance, see no. PD.7–1951 above; exh. Colchester, The Minories, 1958, 'First loan exhibition' (37).

See no. PD. 7–1951 above.

PD. 79–1959 AT HAMPSTEAD, LOOKING TOWARDS HARROW

PLATE 34

Paper laid down on wood, $6\frac{7}{8} \times 9\frac{3}{16}$ in ($17{\cdot}5 \times 23{\cdot}4$ cm). The foreground is a warm yellowish brown, with green-brown beyond towards the deep blue trees. The darker clouds are in tones of blue interspersed with warmer passages; along the horizon the sky is warm cream at the left, changing towards the right to orange-cream, which is the colouring of the light clouds.

Bought from the Fairhaven Fund, 1959. Coll. Hugh Constable (grandson of the painter); bt from him by Leggatt Bros., London;[1] exh. Leggatt's Gallery (77 Cornhill, London), 1899, 'Pictures and water-colour drawings by John Constable, R.A.' (27);[2] Darell Brown sale, Christie's, 23 May 1924 (7), bt Agnew; sold by Thos Agnew & Sons Ltd to Arthur Jackson, Manchester, 1925; sale by Arthur Jackson's executors, Christie's, 30 November 1928 (60), bt Leggatt; sold by Leggatt Bros. to H. L. Fison, 1928; exh. London, Leggatt's, 1958, 'Autumn Exhibition' (34), lent H. L. Fison; sale by H. L. Fison's executors, Christies, 6 November 1959 (13), bt Thos Agnew & Sons Ltd, from whom it was purchased.

Cleaned 1960. A strip along the bottom about $\frac{3}{4}$ in ($1{\cdot}9$ cm) wide is of a different paper from the rest, but this seems to be an original addition. Small studies of transient sky effects of this type first occur in Constable's work in 1820.[3] The present sketch must be of a date rather later than this, to judge from its similarities with sketches of 1821 and 1822. Compare, for example, a *Hampstead* in the Manchester City Art Galleries (see their *English painting, 1800–1870* (1951), no. 7, rep.) inscribed by Constable on the back with the date 1821, and a *View at Hampstead: evening* in the Victoria and Albert Museum (no. 337–1888), similarly inscribed with the date 1822.[4] Distant views from Hampstead towards Harrow, lying to the north-west, are not infrequent in this series of Constable's sketches.

NOTES. [1] From labels at the back, and information kindly supplied by Mr Hugh Leggatt, 1967. [2] The catalogue states that they were 'purchased direct from the Constable Family'. [3] Graham Reynolds *Victoria and Albert Museum. Catalogue of the Constable collection* (1960), p. 26. [4] *Ibid.*, p. 148, no. 247, pl. 186.

PD. 222–1961 SKY STUDY WITH A SHAFT OF SUNLIGHT

Oils on paper, 5¼ × 5⅞ in (13·3 × 14·9 cm).[1] From small, cream-coloured clouds above a dark, blue-grey cloud mass in the centre, a shaft of sunlight falls obliquely to the left.

Bequeathed by John Eric Bullard, 1961. Provenance the same as for no. PD. 7–1951, above, down to the Newson-Smith sale of 1951, in which it was lot 21 (with two others, on one mount), bt Agnew; bt from Thos Agnew & Sons Ltd, London, by J. E. Bullard, 1951.

See no. PD. 7–1951 above.

NOTES. [1] Outside dimensions of the irregular rectangle of the paper.

PD. 15–1968 EAST BERGHOLT (1808)

Millboard, 6⅜ × 9⅞ in (16·2 × 25·1 cm). Across an open, level stretch of grass, bounded by a hedge at the right and with a tall tree at the left, a dense mass of trees, with the red roofs of a house at the right, rises beyond a grey wall. Towards the left, in a space between the wall and a low hedge, is a group of small trees, one of them an autumnal, light orange-brown in colour. The green of the trees and the hedges is mainly dark in tone, the grass considerably lighter. Grey sky with white clouds, a line of blue along the top. Painted on a brown ground. Inscribed on the back in ink, 'E B.', and, twice, '1808'.

Bequeathed by Sidney Ernest Prestige, d. 1965, with a life-interest to his widow; received upon her death, 1968. With P. M. Turner, the Independent Gallery, London; exh. London, Tate Gallery, 1976, 'Constable' (83).

The inscription on the back is recognisable as probably in Constable's own hand, with which its details are consistent. It is known that he was in Suffolk during the late summer and autumn of 1808.[1] He would then have been with his family at East Bergholt, for which the initials E.B. are found as an abbreviation in inscriptions elsewhere in his work.[2] The date of 1808 for the painting is confirmed by its similarity in style with the small *View at Epsom* (Tate Gallery, no. 1818, 11 × 13½ in, 27·9 ×

33·7 cm), also on millboard, which is dated on the back by Constable 'June 1809'.[3] From the mass of trees in the centre and the red roofs to the right of it, the scene is identifiable as a view towards East Bergholt Rectory, the adjacent trees and Rectory being known from other views of East Bergholt by Constable.[4]

REPRODUCED. Exhibition catalogue, *Constable* (1976), Tate Gallery, p. 70.

NOTES. [1] Historical Manuscripts Commission JP3, *John Constable's correspondence, the family at East Bergholt*, ed. R. B. Beckett (1962), p. 28. [2] Cf. Graham Reynolds, *Victoria and Albert Museum. Catalogue of the Constable collection* (1960), p. 113, no. 157, and p. 136. [3] Beckett, *op. cit.*, p. 31, n. (3). [4] In particular from *Golding Constable's kitchen garden* (Christchurch Mansion Museum, Ipswich) and a drawing, *View at East Bergholt over the kitchen garden of Golding Constable's house* (Victoria and Albert Museum, London, no. 623–1888). See also L. Parris, I. Fleming-Williams and C. Shields, exhibition catalogue, *Constable, paintings, watercolours and drawings* (1976), Tate Gallery, nos. 26, 83, 93, 120, 128, 135.

PD. 16–1968 HOVE BEACH

Canvas, 13 × 20 in (33·0 × 50·8 cm).[1] A calm sea, light, greenish blue with white wavelets, extends on the left, with a low point of land in the distance. At the right are low, sloping cliffs covered with green herbage, surmounted by buildings, some white, some light brown. The beach runs diagonally between the two from the lower left corner, warm buff in colour, with two black boats drawn up from the water, and dotted with figures. Grey sky with white clouds.

Bequeathed by Sidney Ernest Prestige, d. 1965, with a life-interest to his widow, d. 1968, when the picture was received.

Some rubbing in the darks; cleaned 1968. Formerly described as *Brighton beach*, but the topography identifies it as Hove.[2] This appears, from its character, to be a picture painted from the subject, and could belong in date to any of Constable's known visits to Brighton in 1824, 1825, 1826 and 1828. Already in 1824 he had accepted an order for a 'Brighton seapiece' from the Paris dealer, J. Arrowsmith.[3]

REPRODUCED. Fitzwilliam Museum, *Annual Report* for 1968, pl. XI.

NOTES. [1] Laid down on panel 1968. [2] See Graham Reynolds, *Victoria and Albert Museum. Catalogue of the Constable collection* (1960), p. 166, no. 270, rep. pl. 206. [3] *John Constable's correspondence*, ed. R. B. Beckett (1966), IV, p. 194.

PD. 21–1969 SHOREHAM BAY, NEAR BRIGHTON (1824)

Paper laid down on canvas, $5\frac{7}{8} \times 9\frac{3}{4}$ in ($14{\cdot}9 \times 24{\cdot}8$ cm).[1] The low sandy shore of the bay at the left curves round to a distant point of land, beyond which is higher ground sloping up at the right to low hills in the distance; an undulating green foreground rises to a hillock at the right, both edged with a fringe of darker green bushes, beyond which lower, flat land stretches away to the distant hills. A deep expanse of hazy blue sky is filled with cream-coloured clouds; light blue sea.

Given by Miss Gertrude Caton-Thompson, Litt.D., F.B.A., 1969. Coll. Captain Charles Golding Constable (d. 1879);[2] his widow, Mrs A. M. Constable (d. 1889); exh. London, Victoria and Albert Museum, 1880–3 (no. 31);[3] Edinburgh, Museum of Science and Art, 1883–6 (no. 101); sold Christie's, 23 June 1890 (85), bt William Caton-Thompson (d. 1893); his widow, Mrs George E. Moore, from whom inherited by their daughter, the donor, 1934.

A label attached to the stretcher is inscribed 'Shoreham bay. The walk to the Chalybeate/wells Brighton. Tuesday 20th July 1824'. This is not in Constable's own hand, but no doubt perpetuates his original inscription written on the back of the sketch, as was his wont, concealed when the latter was laid down on canvas.[4] In May 1824, for the sake of his wife's health, Constable took his family to Brighton, where they remained until November,[5] he himself paying periodical visits from London. He left for one such visit on 17 July.[6] Though Brighton and its surroundings held little appeal for Constable, he made many small oil sketches there, 'done in the lid of my box on my knees as usual', as he wrote to his friend Archdeacon Fisher.[7] Shoreham-by-sea, at the mouth of the river Adur, lies six miles to the west of Brighton; the chalybeate springs, famous for the tonic properties of their waters, lie in Hove, almost on the boundary with Brighton, in what is now St Ann's Well Gardens. A similar coastal view, though from a different view-point, appears in no. 303 of the Constable collection at the Victoria and Albert Museum.[8]

REPRODUCED. Fitzwilliam Museum, *Annual Report* for 1969, pl. x.

NOTES. [1] Dimensions of the sheet of paper; the dimensions of the stretcher are $6\frac{3}{8} \times 10\frac{1}{4}$ in ($16{\cdot}2 \times 26{\cdot}1$ cm). [2] Constable's second son, captain in the mercantile marine. [3] Included in the loan from his widow of Captain Constable's collection of his father's work; see Graham Reynolds, *Victoria and Albert Museum. Catalogue of the Constable collection* (1960), p. 2. Thanks are due to Mr Reynolds for kindly providing detailed information about the exhibition of this painting. [4] In the printed loan register of the Victoria and Albert Museum, it is noted that the sketch is dated 1824. [5] *John Constable's correspondence*, ed. R. B. Beckett (1968), VI, pp. 159–60, 175. [6] *Op. cit.*, n. 5, p. 166. [7] *Op. cit.*, n. 5, p. 189. [8] Reynolds, *op. cit.*, p. 183, pl. 228.

PD. 44–1972 ARCHDEACON JOHN FISHER PLATE 33

Canvas, 14 × 11⅞ in (35·9 × 30·3 cm).[1] Brown hair, fresh complexion; dressed in black. Brown background.

Bought with funds from the G. F. Webb bequest, with a Grant-in-Aid from the Victoria and Albert Museum, 1972. Exh. R.A., 1817 (216); coll. the Venerable John Fisher, Archdeacon of Berkshire (d. 1832); his son, the Rev. Osmond Fisher (d. 1914); his son, the Rev. Osmond Philip Fisher (d. 1937), who bequeathed it, with a life-interest to his widow (d. 1957), to his nephew, John P. Fisher; exh. Manchester, City Art Gallery, 1956, 'John Constable' (24); bt from John P. Fisher;[2] exh. London, Tate Gallery, 1976, 'Constable' (152).

Cleaned 1972. John Fisher (1788–1832), who became Archdeacon of Berkshire in 1827, was the intimate friend of Constable and owner of a number of his paintings. When Constable and Maria Bicknell married in October 1816, they spent six weeks of their honeymoon with Fisher and his wife (married in the previous July) in their vicarage at Osmington in Dorset. This portrait and the one following of Mary Fisher (no. PD. 45–1972) were apparently painted during this visit as a present to the Fishers.[3]

REPRODUCED. C. R. Leslie, *Memoirs of the life of John Constable, R.A.*, ed. Hon. Andrew Shirley (1937), p. lxix; Andrew Shirley, *John Constable, R.A.* (1944), pl. 129; R. B. Beckett, *John Constable and the Fishers* (1952), p. 16; *John Constable's correspondence*, ed. R. B. Beckett (1968), VI, frontispiece; Fitzwilliam Museum, *Annual Report* for 1972, pl. VIII; *Burlington Magazine* (1973), CXV, 251, pl. 90; Leslie Parris, Ian Fleming-Williams and Conal Shields, exhibition catalogue, *Constable, paintings, watercolours and drawings* (1976), Tate Gallery, pp. 103, (no. 152), 112 (colour).

NOTES. [1] Lined; dimensions of the painted surface. [2] In *John Constable and the Fishers* (1952), p. 35, n. 2, and in *John Constable's correspondence* (1968), VI, p. 31, n. 2, R. B. Beckett states that this portrait and that of Fisher's wife below (no. PD. 45–1972) passed to Archdeacon Fisher's 'grandson Edward Fisher'. Some confusion is indicated here, as John P. Fisher describes them as bequeathed to him by his uncle the Rev. O. P. Fisher (letter of 31 October 1971, Fitzwilliam Museum). [3] See *John Constable's correspondence*, ed. R. B. Beckett (1962), I, pp. 144, 146; these two letters from Constable's sister Ann evidently relate to letters of his referring to the portraits, now missing. See also vol. VI (1968), p. 31, n. 2 and p. 34.

PD. 45–1972 MRS MARY FISHER PLATE 33

Canvas, 14⅛ × 12 in (35·9 × 30·5 cm).[1] Dark brown hair; pale grey dress. Grey background.

Bought with funds from the G. F. Webb bequest, with a Grant-in-Aid from the Victoria and Albert Museum, 1972. Coll. the Venerable John Fisher, Archdeacon of Berkshire (d. 1832); descended through the Fisher family (see no. PD. 44–1972 above), to John P. Fisher, from whom it was bought.

Cleaned and restored 1972. Mary Cookson, wife of John Fisher, Archdeacon of Berkshire, whom she married in July 1816. See no. PD. 44–1972 above.

REPRODUCED. R. B. Beckett, *John Constable and the Fishers* (1952), p. 32; *John Constable's correspondence*, ed. R. B. Beckett (1968), VI, p. 28; Fitzwilliam Museum, *Annual Report* for 1972, pl. VIII; *Burlington Magazine* (1973), CXV, 251, pl. 91.

NOTE. [1] Lined; dimensions of the painted surface.

COOPER, Thomas Sidney

1803–1902. Born at Canterbury. Self-taught, but largely formed through his friendship with E. J. Verbockhoven in Brussels, 1827–31; settled in London; exh. R.A., 1833 to his death, at the B.I. and elsewhere; R.A., 1867; C.V.O., 1901. Animal painter.

469 CATTLE BY A RIVER (1835) PLATE 40

Wood, 6 × 10⅜ in (15·2 × 26·4 cm). The herbage is red-brown, the cattle creamy, red-brown and warm grey, the water cold grey. The clouds are a very pale mauve-grey, with a little blue sky. Signed and dated lower right, 'T S Cooper/1835'.

Given by Mrs Richard Ellison, 1862.

492 CATTLE REPOSING (1846) PLATE 41

Canvas, 44 × 62¼ in (111·7 × 158·1 cm). Before an open, thatched shed at the right, with trees behind it, stands a brown bull, with a recumbent brown and white cow at his feet and sheep to the right. Under the shed a black and white cow stands by a brown calf. To the left is an open landscape, with a scattered flock of sheep and one cow, in pallid local colours. The sky is light blue, with warm grey clouds. Signed and dated lower left, 'T Sid^{y} Cooper/1846'.

Given by Mrs Richard Ellison, 1862. Perhaps exh. R.A., 1846 (456).[1]

REPRODUCED. *Bryan's dictionary of painters and engravers*, ed. G. C. Williamson (1903), I, p. 326.

NOTE. [1] Entitled *Cattle reposing*, which is the title on an old manuscript label at the back of the picture, though in the Ellison gift of 1862 it was called simply *Landscape with cattle*.

COX, DAVID

1783–1859. Pupil of Joseph Barber in Birmingham, where he was born. Principally a painter in water-colours; began to paint seriously in oils in 1840, when he had some instruction from W. J. Müller; first exhibited in London, 1805; member of the Old Water-colour Society, 1813. Lived successively in London (1804–14), Hereford (1814–27), London (1827–41) and Birmingham (1841–59). Landscape painter.

1339* COAST SCENE NEAR HASTINGS

Oils on paper,[1] $5\frac{1}{4} \times 8\frac{1}{2}$ in ($13{\cdot}4 \times 21{\cdot}6$ cm). Cliffs recede into the picture from the left, where there is a group of houses, the sea to the right. On the beach in the foreground are a small boat with sails set, and a string of figures, one mounted. Painted in grey and white.

Bequeathed by J. R. Holliday, 1927. (?) Coll. G. Wills Ingram.[2]

If the place is correctly identified, this must date from 1812, when Cox visited Hastings and painted some small sketches in oils.[3]

NOTES. [1] Laid down on millboard. [2] From a much-defaced label on the back of the frame. [3] N. Neal Solly, *Memoir of the life of David Cox* (1873), pp. 25–6. A second fragmentary old label at the back identifies the subject as 'Scene on the South Coast near Hastings'.

1788 THE VALE OF CLWYD (1849) PLATE 35

Canvas, $36\frac{5}{8} \times 56$ in ($90{\cdot}5 \times 142{\cdot}3$ cm). The foliage is of a somewhat greyish tone of green, the grass yellower and warmer; the sheep are of a pinkish tone of light grey, which is also the colour of the distant hills, with passages of light blue. The sky is blue with cream clouds. Signed and dated lower left, 'David Cox. 1849'.

Bequeathed by Arthur William Young, 1936. Coll. George Briscoe, of Wolverhampton;[1] his sale, Christie's, 12 May 1860 (34), bt Frederick Timmins; sold by Timmins, 1872;[2] Mariano de Murrieta, by 1873;[3] Messrs Murrieta sale, Christie's, 30 April 1892 (69), bt Agnew; exh.

London, Guildhall, 1897, 'Loan collection' (69), lent T. J. Barratt;[4] R.A., 1903, Winter Exhibition (117); Barratt sale, Christie's, 11 May 1916 (44), bt Robson.

Painted for George Briscoe.[5] This is a second version, with certain modifications, of the original of the same size, painted in 1846.[6] The earlier version was Cox's first large work in oils,[7] but the second was regarded in his own day as the better of the two, and as one of the finest of his works in this medium.[8] These two, together with *Collecting the flocks*,[9] also of the same size, are said to be the only oils as large as this which he painted.[10] The river Clwyd runs through Denbighshire and Flint, emerging into the sea near Rhyl, and Cox made many drawings of the scenery of its valley. This *Vale of Clwyd* subject is based on sketches he made in 1844 'from Sir John Williams's park at Bodelwyddan near St. Asaph'.[11]

REPRODUCED. B. Webber, *James Orrock, R.I.* (1903), II, p. 66:[12] Barratt sale catalogue, 1916.[13]

NOTES. [1] N. Neal Solly, *Memoir of the life of David Cox* (1873), pp. 155, 190. [2] Solly, *op. cit.*, pp. 190, 201. [3] Solly, *op. cit.*, p. 190. [4] Perhaps bought at the Murrieta sale by Agnew for Barratt; see B. Webber, *James Orrock, R.I.* (1903), II, pp. 67–8. [5] Solly, *op. cit.*, pp. 155, 190, where he mistakenly gives its date as 1848; W. Hall, *A biography of David Cox* (1881), p. 118. [6] Solly, *op. cit.*, p. 141; it last appeared in the sale of the John Clark collection, Christie's, 8 June 1895 (93), bt Tooth, London, who sold it to Maclean, London. [7] Solly, *op. cit.*, p. 141. [8] Solly, *op. cit.*, p. 190; Hall, *op. cit.*, p. 118. [9] Last recorded in the sale of the collection of Thomas Walker, deceased, Christie's, 2 June 1888 (58), bt Henson, £2362.10.0. [10] Solly, *op. cit.*, p. 190. [11] Hall, *op. cit.*, p. 70; Solly, *op. cit.*, p. 189, describes it as 'near St. Asaph, about halfway between Rhyl and Denbigh'. [12] It is not stated which of the two versions is reproduced, but by implication it appears that it is the one then in the Barratt collection, i.e. the present one, and this seems to be borne out by comparison with the photogravure. [13] Hall, *op. cit.*, p. 258, refers circumstantially to the publication in 1879 of an etching of the first, 1846, version by L. A. Brunet-Debaines, though the Murrieta and the Barratt sale catalogues refer this to the second, present version; it has not been possible to find an impression of the print for verification.

PD. 10–1950 LANDSCAPE WITH CATTLE BY A POOL (1850) PLATE 35

Wood, $8\frac{3}{4} \times 10\frac{1}{2}$ in ($22{\cdot}2 \times 26{\cdot}7$ cm). A row of tall trees, ochre-green in colour, recedes into the picture from the left, with a herd of black, white and brown cattle in front of it, some of them standing in a pool at the left, which is light grey-green. Pinkish ground extends to the right, with two figures, and behind is a blue-grey distance; light blue-grey sky with cream clouds. Signed and dated lower left, 'David Cox 1850'.

Bequeathed by Thomas Henry Riches, 1935, with a life-interest to his widow, who died 1950. Coll. Edwin Bullock; sold Christie's, 8 May 1887 (35), bt Agnew; James Orrock, by 1890, when he lent it to the Birmingham City Museum and Art Gallery, David Cox Exhibition (159).

From its small size, this may have been painted direct from nature.[1] Another, larger version on canvas, 13¾ × 17¾ in (34·9 × 45·1 cm), with minor variations, not signed or dated, belongs to F. T. Bacon, Little Shelford, Cambridge. Cox would often supply a repetition of a painting if asked to do so, but always with some degree of variation.[2]

NOTES. [1] W. Hall, *A biography of David Cox* (1881), p. 152. [2] N. Neal Solly, *Memoir of the life of David Cox* (1873), p. 187.

CRESWICK, Thomas

1811–1869. Born in Sheffield. Studied under J. V. Barber, Birmingham; in London from 1828, when he first exh. at the R.A.; exh. also at the B.I. and the Society of Artists, Suffolk Street; R.A., 1851. Landscape painter; his figures and animals sometimes painted by other artists.

480 CROSSING THE STREAM (1849) PLATE 41

Canvas, 32 × 44⅞ in (81·3 × 113·6 cm). A placid stream, filling the entire foreground, runs into the distance between wooded banks; at the right, a view of distant hills, with a glimpse of a castle. In the foreground a girl, in a white blouse and red skirt, and a small boy in brown with grey breeches, wade across the stream towards the right along a line of stones, a dog at the right. The feathery trees are of an ochre-green, reflected in a greyer tone in the water; the distance is painted in pale opalescent tones; the sky is light blue with pale cream clouds. Signed and dated lower left, 'THO^S^ CRESWICK/1849'.

Given by Mrs Richard Ellison, 1862. (?) Exh. London, B.I., 1849 (299);[1] London, International Exhibition, 1862 (601); placed on loan to the City of Cambridge, 1972.

NOTE. [1] A possible identification from the date and the title in the exhibition catalogue, *The stepping stones*, though the dimensions of the frame are against it. These are given in the catalogue as 39 × 49 in (99·0 × 124·5 cm), which are improbably small for a canvas of this size; the present frame, measuring 45¼ × 58¾ in (114·9 × 149·2 cm), could well be the original.

CROME, John

1768–1821. Born in Norwich. Apprenticed to a coach, house and sign painter; the chief influences in his formation Wilson and Hobbema. Lived in Norwich, and painted mainly Norfolk scenes; visited Paris, Holland and Belgium, 1814. Exh. principally with the Norwich Society (from 1805), but also at the R.A. and B.I. Landscape painter.

PD. 49–1949 MATLOCK HIGH TOR PLATE 29

Canvas, $15\frac{1}{8} \times 23\frac{3}{8}$ in ($38{\cdot}1 \times 59{\cdot}4$ cm).[1] The herbage is greyish green; the water light, bluish grey; clouds warm cream or silver-grey, with a quiet, light blue sky.

Bought from the Fairhaven Fund, 1949. Possibly coll. Joseph Gillott (1799–1872), see his executors' sale, Christie's, 26 April 1872 (205), bt Grundy & Smith;[2] John Heugh, sold Christie's 24 April 1874 (166), bt Agnew, Manchester; exh. London, R.A., Winter, 1876 (17), lent Sir W. G. Armstrong; sold Armstrong Heirlooms, Christie's, 24 June 1910 (58), bt Vicars, London; 1st Viscount Mackintosh of Halifax by 1949; with Gooden & Fox, London, who sold it to Leggatt Bros, London, from whom it was purchased.

The scene has been described both as a Welsh subject and as High Tor, Matlock, but comparison with approximately contemporary engravings shows the latter identification to be the correct one.[3] Crome visited Derbyshire in 1811, and in view of the scene represented the present picture may be dated to this year, or soon after; at the exhibition of the Norwich Society in 1811 he showed a *Drawing of rocks near Matlock* (no. 146). This dating is in conformity with general stylistic considerations, and is borne out by the close resemblance of style with a *Trowse Bridge* in the Castle Museum, Norwich, given this approximate date,[4] which may possibly be the painting with this title in the same exhibition of the Norwich Society. The figures have been considered as undoubtedly the work of Crome's son, John Berney Crome (1794–1843),[5] who precociously exhibited at the R.A. in 1811. A striking example of the influence on Crome of Richard Wilson. The same scene, from almost the same viewpoint, was painted several times by Joseph Wright of Derby, see no. PD. 8–1848, p. 294 below.

REPRODUCED. *Country Life* (1949), CV, 1064.

NOTES. [1] Lined; dimensions of the painted surface. [2] Entitled *A rocky river scene*; dimensions given as $15\frac{1}{2} \times 24$ in. [3] As Welsh in the Heugh sale, 1874, when lent to the R.A. by Sir W. G. Armstrong, 1876, when in Viscount Mackintosh's collection, and when purchased; but as High Tor in the Armstrong sale, 1910. In a letter to *Country Life* ((1949), CV, 1064), seeking identification of the subject, Viscount Mackintosh remarks that the high cliffs look like the limestone of Derbyshire; the Editor replies that it 'looks as though it might be the valley of the Derwent below High Tor near Matlock'. [4] C. H. Collins Baker, *Crome* (1921), p. 167. [5] By Dr Norman Goldberg, 1960, who otherwise confirmed Crome's authorship of the painting (Fitzwilliam Museum records).

PD. 1–1966 A SANDY HOLLOW

Canvas, $15\frac{1}{8} \times 20\frac{1}{8}$ in (38·4 × 51·1 cm).[1] In the foreground is a deep hollow with water at the bottom; the steep sandy bank at the far side rises to the sky-line, and at its summit are several stunted trees on a low knoll, with others to the left. Overhead is a grey, cloudy sky with cream lights towards the horizon. The bank is a brownish ochre, grey-green in the shadows; the herbage is olive-green and brownish green.

Bequeathed by Guy John Fenton Knowles (d. 1959), with a life-interest to Lady Vera Murray Morrison, who d. 1966. Coll. D. Gurney;[2] bt from his family by the 1st Lord Wimborne (1853–1914), 1867;[3] exh. London, R.A., 1881, 'Old Masters' (22); his son, 1st Viscount Wimborne; his sale, Christie's, 2 March 1923 (64),[4] bt Colnaghi.

Much damaged by over-cleaning and repainting, and by compression of the impasto in lining. Despite this, the large massing, the simplicity and unity of the pictorial motives, and what can still be gauged of the original atmospheric effect, relate it to such works of Crome's middle period as *Mousehold Heath, boy keeping sheep* (London, Victoria and Albert Museum, no. 232–'79), *Return of the flock* (1st Viscount Mackintosh of Halifax, d. 1964), and *Road with pollards* (Norwich, Castle Museum, Colman Collection). The dating of these pictures remains somewhat conjectural, but they may probably be assigned to a period of approximately 1812 to 1815, the present one with them.[5] Another version belongs (1968) to Mr Christopher Norris;[6] but though of the same subject, its differences make of it a separate composition, and neither picture can therefore be considered a replica of the other.

REPRODUCED. Derek Clifford and Timothy Clifford, *John Crome* (1968), pl. 90a.

NOTES. [1] Lined; dimensions of the painted surface. [2] This is probably Daniel Gurney (1791–1880), of North Runcton Hall, Norfolk. [3] *A catalogue of the pictures at Canford Manor* (1888), no. 46. [4] As 'From the Collection of D. Gurney, Esq.'. Derek Clifford and Timothy Clifford, *John Crome* (1968), p. 209, no. P57, take the ownership a stage further back to C. Steward, presumably on the speculative identification of the present picture with a *Sand-bank* by Crome, lent by C. Steward to an exhibition at Norwich, Free Library, 1860, 'Deceased local artists', no. 194; they also speculate that the Fitzwilliam Museum picture is possibly the same as a *Mulbarton gravel pit* by Crome, lent to the B.I. in 1848, no. 142, by Thomas Turton, Bishop of Ely. [5] W. F. Dickes, *The Norwich school of painting* (1905), C. H. Collins Baker, *Crome* (1921), and the Cliffords, *op. cit.*, differ among themselves on the question of dating. For the present picture, Collins Baker, *op. cit.*, lists it on p. 162, without a date, as a picture he had not seen (see also p. 94); the Cliffords, *op. cit.*, catalogue it on p. 209, no. P57, dating it *c.* 1810 by comparison with *The beaters*, which bears this date upon it, but the analogy is not convincing. [6] Bought 1957 from Leggatt Bros., who bought it from a Mrs Christopher.

DALL, Nicholas Thomas

d. 1777. Of Danish origin. Established himself in London about 1760; exh. at the Incorporated Society of Artists, and later at the R.A., 1761–76; A.R.A., 1771. Landscape painter.

26 ASHBY LODGE, NORTHAMPTONSHIRE

Canvas, 32 × 48⅛ in (81·3 × 122·2 cm).[1] The three-storied, square, stone house, light brown in colour, occupies the centre of the middle distance, a straight line of trees running down to it from the right; in front is a paddock, in which are four horses, with groups of trees to the left. A meadow in the foreground, in which are three cattle, two light brown and one dark brown, is separated from the paddock by a dark hedge, with several tall trees to the right and shorter ones to the left. Beyond the house to the left are some low buildings among trees, with trees receding into the distance. The nearer foliage is dark green tinged with brown, further away it is a clearer olive-green, and pale in the distance; the foreground meadow is an even, dark olive-green, the paddock lighter. Light blue sky with cream and grey clouds.

Bequeathed by the Rev. James William Arnold, D.D. (d. 1865), received 1873.[2] Coll. George Arnold, of Ashby Lodge, Northamptonshire (1683–1766);[3] descended to his great-great-grand-daughter, Georgeana Coape (d. 1849);[4] sale by Phillips (of London) at Ashby Lodge, 20–2 April 1854 (69),[5] bt Rev. J. W. Arnold, D.D.; exh. London, R.A., 1879, 'Old Masters' (26); on loan to the City of Cambridge, 1972–6.

Bequeathed, and originally catalogued, as by William Hogarth,[6] who painted the portraits of George Arnold, of Ashby Lodge, and his daughter

Frances, about 1738–40, reputedly while on a visit to the house, where the portraits remained until sold in 1854 (see pp. 108–9, nos. 21, 24). But the picture bears no resemblance to the landscapes which occur in the background of some of Hogarth's paintings, and an alternative attribution to George Barret,[7] if less impossible, is also wide of the mark for so purely topographical a picture. The attribution to Dall, first put forward in 1918,[8] is confirmed not only by this general quality but by individual points of style, such as the distribution and deadness of the lighting, the character of the foliage masses and the way they are handled, the baldness of the architecture, the use of the animal staffage, and the characteristic clouds. Points of comparison are offered by a series of topographical paintings by Dall of Shugborough, belonging to the Earl of Lichfield, one of which was exhibited at the Incorporated Society of Artists in 1769. Ashby Lodge was built by George Arnold as his residence in 1722,[9] and from the size of the trees near the house it seems likely that the picture was painted before his death in 1766, giving an approximate date for the picture during the first half of the 1760s.

ENGRAVED. Woodcut in *The Magazine of Art* (1885), VIII, 43.

REPRODUCED. M. H. Grant, *The old English landscape painters*, 2 vols. (n.d.; (?) 1932), I, pl. 20.

NOTES. [1] Lined; dimensions of the painted surface. [2] Bequeathed with a life-interest to his widow. [3] On the likely assumption that it was painted during his lifetime, see below. [4] Daughter and heiress of George Henry Arnold; she married James Coape in 1840. [5] Presumably by James Coape, though no seller is specified in the sale catalogue; his eldest son, Henry Fraser James, took the name of Coape-Arnold. [6] Earp, p. 96. [7] Catalogue of the sale by Phillips at Ashby Lodge in 1854, and W. G. Constable, *Richard Wilson* (1953), p. 104. [8] By Sir Alec Martin. [9] George Baker, *The history and antiquities of the county of Northampton* (1822–30), I, p. 247.

DANDRIDGE, BARTHOLOMEW

1691–*post* 1754. Student at Kneller's academy, London, 1712; known work from about 1728; popular as a painter of both full-scale portraits and small conversation-pieces.

658 PORTRAIT OF A PAINTER PLATE II

Canvas, $50\frac{1}{4} \times 40\frac{3}{8}$ in ($128{\cdot}3 \times 102{\cdot}5$ cm).[1] Rosy complexion; fawn-coloured coat with ochre button-frogs; dull crimson drapery; dark brown background.

Given by Charles Fairfax Murray, 1908. With the Galerie Sedelmayer, Paris.

Cleaned and restored, 1936. Given by Fairfax Murray as a possible self-portrait of Richard Wilson,[2] as which it was formerly catalogued; subsequently rejected as a portrait of Wilson,[3] to whom it cannot either be attributed. The portrait belongs in style with the succession to Kneller, and is attributable to Dandridge from the design, the animation of the pose, the vitality of the head, the pictorial treatment of the features, and the handling of such details as the cap and the linen. Among portraits affording a close comparison, two signed examples in the National Portrait Gallery may be referred to, *Nathaniel Hooke* (no. 68) and the *Unknown man* (no. 1557, formerly called *William Kent*). The painting may well be a self-portrait, possibly the very one recorded by George Vertue in 1729,[4] when Dandridge was thirty-eight, but no self-portraits, painted or engraved, appear to be extant for purposes of comparison.

REPRODUCED. *Principal pictures* (1912 edn), p. 212 (1929 edn), p. 242; *Burlington Magazine* (1948),XC, 117, fig. 27.

NOTES. [1] Lined; dimensions of the painted surface. [2] Letter of 28 April 1908 (Fitzwilliam Museum). [3] Douglas Cooper, 'The iconography of Richard Wilson', *Burlington Magazine* (1948), XC, 116. [4] *Walpole Society* (1934), XXII, Vertue III, 39, 'his own picture painted by himself half fig. a pallet by him a sprightly good Air'.

Copy after B. Dandridge

693 'G. F. HANDEL'

Canvas, $46\frac{5}{8} \times 37$ in ($118{\cdot}4 \times 94{\cdot}0$ cm).[1] Three-quarter-length standing, to left, eyes looking front, the right arm brought round to the front, the hand holding a scroll of music, the left placed against the body in front. Clean-shaven, wears a dark green cap; grey coat with strips of gold braid in pairs down the front; a red drapery taken from behind over the right shoulder falls inside the right arm; white shirt, part of the sleeve exposed at the wrist, with ruffles.[2]

Bequeathed by Felix Thornley Cobbold, 1909. Coll. W. Hobson, London; anon. sale, Christie's, 23 July 1909 (98), bt Cobbold.[3]

Restored 1951. George Frederick Handel (1685–1759), famous musical composer; in 1710 left his native Germany for England, where he spent the rest of his life. In common with a number of other supposed portraits of Handel, this identification is not convincing. The picture is a weak version, presumably a copy, of a painting now in the Musikbibliothek of the city of Leipzig, which was engraved in 1821 by Charles Turner as of Handel by W. Hogarth,[4] but is probably by Bartholomew Dandridge.[5] If the head in that painting is not impossible as a conventionalised likeness of Handel, it quite lacks the general energy of expression, conveyed particularly by the determined mouth, characteristic of all the undoubted portraits, such as that by Mercier (Lord Malmesbury), the anonymous portrait, no. 1976 in the National Portrait Gallery, both *c.* 1730, and the Hudson of 1756 (National Portrait Gallery, no. 3970). No closer date for the portrait is indicated by the costume than the period of Dandridge's known activity.

REPRODUCED. *Principal pictures* (1912 edn), p. 42, (1929 edn), p. 50.

NOTES. [1] Lined; dimensions of the painted surface. [2] Listed by J. M. Coopersmith, *Music and Letters* (1932), XIII, 157. [3] Catalogued as 'Hogarth' (i.e. doubtfully), representing Handel. [4] Alfred Whitman, *Charles Turner* (1907), p. 105, no. 247. [5] The Fitzwilliam Museum painting is listed as by Dandridge, and doubtfully dated *c.* 1740, by C. H. Collins Baker, 'The Price family', *Burlington Magazine* (1938), LXXII, 136. The pose is closely similar to that of the *Portrait of a painter* by Dandridge, no. 658 above.

DANIELL, William

1769–1837. Voyaged with his uncle Thomas Daniell, R.A., to India and back, via China, 1784/5–94; exh. R.A. and B.I., from 1795; student at the R.A., 1799; R.A., 1822. Landscape painter, and engraver.

948 COAST SCENE

Paper, 6 × 8 in (15·2 × 20·3 cm). To the right, at the foot of a massive cliff rising from the sea, is a beach with a group of buildings, upon the beach some boats with raised ends and figures; other buildings crown the cliff. To left is a distant view of a mountainous coast-line with a small town at the water's edge; above are white clouds in a blue sky. The cliff is in tones of dull green and light ochre; the buildings in tones of grey and light brown; the distance is grey-green and blue-grey; the water is grey and grey-blue.

Bequeathed by Joseph Prior, 1909.

Bequeathed with the title *A mediterranean scene*, but Daniell is not known to have visited that region, and none of his exhibited work is drawn from it. Unless the painting is taken from a sketch by someone else, it seem more likely to be of a scene on the coast of Madeira, with the precipitous landscape and the peculiar form of the boats. A Madeira coast scene is included among the plates of *A picturesque voyage to India by way of China* by William Daniell and his uncle Thomas Daniell, 1810, showing that they touched at the island. The architecture and the type of trees make it unlikely to be an oriental scene, though some of the plates in the *Picturesque voyage* show boats of a similar form.

DAVIE, ALAN

b. 1920. Living artist.

PD. 46–1973 ENTRY OF THE FETISH (1955)

Hardboard, 48⅛ × 60⅛ in (122·2 × 152·4 cm). In the innermost of three concentric rectangles, is a series of forms centring upon a circle, one of which passes through the rectangles to the upper left of the composition. The colours are yellow, black, cream, dull red, brown, a lighter and a deeper blue. Signed and dated lower right, 'Alan Davie 55'.

Bought from the Gulbenkian and University Purchase Funds, 1973. Coll. Martin Richmond, to whom it was given by the artist; exh. London, Arthur Tooth & Sons, 1958, 'Critic's Choice' (21), lent Martin Richmond, from whom it was bought.

Though dated, apparently incorrectly, to 1954 by Alan Bowness, he points out that in many cases Davie has worked on his pictures over a period of time.[1]

REPRODUCED. *Alan Davie*, ed. Alan Bowness (1967), no. 75.

NOTE. [1] *Alan Davie*, ed. Alan Bowness (1967), pp. 134, 136.

DEVERELL, WALTER HOWELL

1827–1854. Born in the U.S.A. of English parents. At Sass's Drawing School, London, from 1843; R.A. schools, 1846; taught at the Government School of Design from 1848. Close friend of Rossetti, Millais and Holman Hunt, but not a member of the Pre-Raphaelite Brotherhood. Subject painter.

774 SELF-PORTRAIT PLATE 46

Canvas, 10⅛ × 8 in (25·7 × 20·3 cm). Dark brown hair, black jacket, light blue waistcoat, crimson tie. The wall is brown and grey-green; bluish green foliage.

Given by Charles Fairfax Murray, 1915. Given by the artist to his cousin, Harriet Hogarth;[1] coll. W. T. Deverell, London;[2] exh. Birmingham, City Museum and Art Gallery, 1947, 'The Pre-Raphaelite Brotherhood' (19); Bournemouth, Russell-Cotes Art Gallery, 1951, 'Paintings and drawings by the Pre-Raphaelites and their followers' (46).

An inscription written on the stretcher dates the picture 'about 1849'.

NOTES. [1] Label at the back of the picture, which describes her as the daughter of J. R. Hogarth, of Heston Hall, Middlesex. [2] Label formerly at the back of the picture. A loan in 1912 is recorded at the Tate Gallery, London, of a *Portrait of W. Deverell* from Wykeham Deverell, surviving brother of the artist, which might have been this painting; an exhibition of pictures by W. H. Deverell, announced in *The Times* of 23 March 1912, p. 11, to be held at the National Gallery of British Art (Tate Gallery) for two or three months from April, does not appear to have materialised, at least no catalogue of it is now traceable.

DEVIS, Arthur

1711–1787. Born at Preston, Lancashire. Said to have been a pupil of P. Tillemans; in London by 1742; exh. Free Society of Artists, 1761–80; retired to Brighton, 1781. Painter almost exclusively of full-length portraits on a small scale.

1113 FRANCIS PAGE OF NEWBURY — PLATE 12

Canvas, $29\frac{3}{4} \times 25$ in ($75{\cdot}6 \times 63{\cdot}5$ cm).[1] His clothes are blue, with grey stockings and black shoes. The pedestal and urn are orange-buff, the trees behind them in tones of olive-green and pale brown; the willow on the left pale green; the ground is brown, with a reduced olive-green in the foreground; the sky is grey and cream.

Bequeathed by Professor Frederick Fuller (1819–1909), received 1923.[2]

Francis Page (d. 1785, aged sixty-five), who amassed a large fortune, lived at Goldwell House near Newbury, Berkshire and was a man of some celebrity in his day, known to his contemporaries as 'Mr Page of Newbury'.[3] The painting, which was formerly attributed to Zoffany, can confidently be ascribed to Arthur Devis on the basis of comparison with such authentic works as the *Edward Travers* (coll. Arthur Davis, U.S.A., 1950) and *Sir George and Lady Strickland* (coll. J. E. Strickland, 1950), both of 1751.[4] From the costume and his apparent age, the portrait may be dated *c.* 1760. The reliefs on the urn and pedestal show respectively the Three Graces, and Justice with her scales confronting a warrior.

REPRODUCED. *Principal pictures* (1929), p. 251 (as Zoffany).

NOTES. [1] Lined; dimensions of the painted surface. [2] It may be supposed that the painting was originally at Goldwell House, Berkshire (see below), but no details of a dispersal of its contents have been discoverable. [3] *Gentleman's Magazine* (1785), LV, part II, 676, 749. [4] Sydney H. Paviere, *The Devis family of painters* (1950), nos. 133, 128, rep. pl. II, 28.

DULAC, EDMUND

1882–1953. Of French origin; naturalised 1912. Studied at the Toulouse Art School, and briefly at the Académie Julian, Paris; exh. in London from 1907. Portrait painter, illustrator and theatrical designer.

PD. 51–1966 CHARLES RICKETTS AND CHARLES SHANNON AS MEDIEVAL SAINTS (1920)

Tempera on linen-covered panel, $15\frac{1}{4} \times 12$ in ($38{\cdot}7 \times 30{\cdot}5$ cm), curved top. Two whole-length figures standing side by side, the taller Shannon at the left, with gilt haloes; Shannon is clean-shaven, Ricketts has a fair moustache and beard, and is bald. Both are dressed in black and white Dominican habits, both are bare-footed; Shannon holds his right hand across in front, a kingfisher perched on his forefinger, Ricketts holds both hands in front, a peacock's feather held in the right, the left held vertically. They stand on a rounded hillock covered with grass and flowers, a rabbit to the left, a bird by Shannon's feet. In the background is an open, light green landscape, with dark green trees and hedges, low, distant blue hills. Pale blue sky; a bat wheels above their heads. Signed and dated lower left, 'Edmund/Dulac/1920'.

Bequeathed by Eric George Millar, D.Litt., 1966. Coll. Sir Edmund Davis, Chilham Castle, Kent (d. 1939); Davis sale, Christie's, 15 May 1942 (47), bt Abbot.

Charles de Sousy Ricketts, R.A. (1866–1931), and Charles Haslewood Shannon, R.A. (1863–1937), artists and lifelong friends, formed an outstanding collection of works of art which the latter bequeathed to the Fitzwilliam Museum. As the friend and patron of both of them, Sir Edmund Davis, who had bought Chilham Castle near Canterbury in 1918, a year later gave them the use of the keep as a residence. This painting of the following year was no doubt commissioned by Sir Edmund, who was a patron also of Dulac.

VAN DYCK, SIR ANTHONY

1599–1641. Born at Antwerp. Pupil and assistant of Rubens, *c.* 1617–20; in Italy, *c.* 1621–7; in England 1620–1, and, with interruptions, from 1632 until his death; official painter to Charles I; kt, 1632. Subject and portrait painter.

British school of van Dyck[1]

2312 UNKNOWN MAN

Canvas, $30\frac{1}{8} \times 25\frac{1}{8}$ in (76·5 × 63·8 cm). Nearly half-length, turned in profile right, head half right, the left hand placed on his right shoulder. Bareheaded, fair hair curling to the shoulders; fair moustache and small imperial. A dull crimson cloak is draped over the right shoulder; deep white collar with tasselled strings. Brown background.

Bequeathed by Leonard Daneham Cunliffe, 1937. Late J. E. Reiss sale, Christie's, 6 February 1914 (111), bt Pawsey & Payne (London).

The portrait may be dated from the costume *c.* 1740. In style, and in the use and form of the hand, derived directly from van Dyck.

NOTE. [1] For another painting, see H. Gerson, J. W. Goodison and Denys Sutton, *Fitzwilliam Museum, Cambridge, catalogue of paintings* (1960), I, p. 37, no. 2043.

EDWARDS, EDWIN

1823–1879. Abandoned a successful legal career in 1860 to devote himself to art; exh. R.A., 1861–79. Painter and etcher of landscape.

2465 HIGH STREET, WHITECHAPEL

Millboard, $9\frac{7}{8} \times 13\frac{1}{8}$ in (25·1 × 33·3 cm). The street runs diagonally into the picture from left to right, bordered on both sides by stalls, with traffic between. Rather heavy local colouring, with a predominance of greys and browns.

Given by Philip H. G. Gosse, M.D., 1942. Coll. Mrs Edwin Edwards; her executors' sale, Christie's, 15 July 1907 (126), with another painting by Edwards, bt Bain for Sir Edmund Gosse (d. 1928), who gave it to his son, the donor.[1]

In the 1907 sale, entitled *A street scene*; identified by Sir Edmund Gosse, who dated the picture about 1869.[2]

NOTES. [1] From an inscription on the back; see n. [2]. [2] MS inscription on the back: 'This picture, by Edwin Edwards (1813–1879) (*sic*), represents High

Street, Whitechapel, and was painted about the year 1869. I bought it at the sale of Mrs Edwin Edwards's effects July 1907. Edwin Edwards made a great study of vanishing London; he was mainly an etcher. E. G. Philip has this picture at Castlemead.'

ELMORE, Alfred

1815–1881. Born in Co. Cork, Ireland. Entered R.A. schools, 1832; exh. R.A., B.I. and Suffolk Street (Society of British Artists) from 1834; visited France, Germany and Italy; returned to London, 1844; R.A., 1857. History and genre painter.

PD. 108–1975 ON THE BRINK (1865) PLATE 43

Canvas on wood, 45 × 32¾ in (114·3 × 83·2 cm). Cold lighting on the figure of the woman contrasts with the warmth of the interior. The woman's cloak is green-grey, her dress a muted pink, the flesh-tones greyish; the leaves at the right are deep green, against the window-frame which echoes the colours of the cloak and dress; the shadows are in tones of deep brown, which is the colour worn by the man. The walls of the room are red, the gilt of the frames ochre, the globes of the chandelier buff. The figures at the green-covered table are in pink, brown, grey, cream and black; the standing man and woman are respectively in brown and pale pink. Signed and dated lower left, 'A. Elmore. 1865'.

Given by the Friends of the Fitzwilliam Museum in memory of Dr A. N. L. Munby, with a contribution from the Victoria and Albert Museum Grant-in-Aid, 1975. Exh. R.A., 1865 (138);[1] coll. E. J. Coleman; exh. Paris, 1867, Universal Exhibition, British Section, Group 1 (30 B); coll. Randall Davies (1866–1946); sale by his executors, Sotheby's, 10–11 February 1947 (168), bt Munby; coll. A. N. L. Munby, Litt.D.; exh. London, Thos Agnew & Sons Ltd, 1961, 'Victorian painting, 1837–1887' (3); Arts Council, Aldeburgh and elsewhere, 1962, 'Victorian paintings' (17); Ottawa, National Gallery of Canada, 1965, 'Paintings and drawings by Victorian artists in England' (37); Sheffield, Mappin Art Gallery, 1968, 'Victorian paintings, 1837–1890' (76); London, R.A., 1968–9, 'Bicentenary exhibition' (397); bought from Dr Munby's executors.

Cleaned 1975. The picture is inscribed at the back 'Homburg', and from the time of its exhibition at the R.A. in 1865, the subject has been described as referring to the gaming-tables at the fashionable German resort of that name (correctly Homburg-vor-der-Höhe) in Hesse-Nassau.[2]

Whether Elmore was ever there is unknown, though he had visited Germany on the continental tour from which he returned in 1844. This was Elmore's first essay in genre, his previous work having been confined to history-painting.[3] If more were needed than the picture itself, Elmore's title indicates that the subject of it is a situation of moral crisis, still unresolved. Honour is at stake, a concern with virtue and temptation which relates the subject to the recurring themes in Victorian genre painting of adultery and prostitution.[4]

REPRODUCED. Exhibition catalogue, *Victorian paintings* (1962), Arts Council, pl. 3; Graham Reynolds, *Victorian painting* (1966), pl. 61 (colour); *Burlington Magazine* (1975), CXVII, 759, fig. 86; Fitzwilliam Museum, *Annual Report* for 1975, pl. IV.

NOTES. [1] With the title *On the brink.* [2] *The Art Journal* (1865), N.S. IV, 166. [3] Graham Reynolds, *Victorian painting* (1966), p. 110. [4] Reynolds, *loc. cit.*

ETTY, WILLIAM

1787–1849. Born at York. Entered the R.A. schools, 1807; pupil of Lawrence. Exh. at the R.A. and the B.I., from 1811; in Italy, 1816 and 1822–3; in Paris, 1830; R.A., 1828. Figure painter.

641 DR JOHN CAMIDGE PLATE 36

Millboard, $12\frac{1}{2} \times 9\frac{5}{8}$ in ($30{\cdot}8 \times 24{\cdot}5$ cm). Half-length, turned, facing and looking front. Bare-headed, curly black hair; dark side-whiskers; spectacles. Wears black coat with high collar; high shirt collar with dark blue cravat. Background a draped red curtain, with gilt organ pipes at right.

Bequeathed by Mrs Hustwick, Dr Camidge's only daughter, 1907. Exh. York, 1911, 'Pictures by the late William Etty, R.A.' (128); York, 1949. Etty centenary exhibition (36).

Cleaned 1907. John Camidge (1790–1859), who took the degree of Doctor of Music at Cambridge in 1819, was organist of York Minster from 1842 to 1858, and was a composer of cathedral music. He was the son of another John, also organist of York Minster. A probable date of *c.* 1825 has been put forward for the painting,[1] after Etty's return from Italy, but the apparent age of the sitter suggests a date some years earlier, before this visit took place. Painted with something of the freedom of an oil sketch.[2]

REPRODUCED. *Principal pictures*, (1912 edn), p. 51, (1929 edn), p. 61.

NOTES. [1] Dennis Farr, *William Etty* (1958), p. 164, no. 146. [2] As might be expected in a family so closely identified with York Minster, of which Etty was so proud, the Camidges and Etty appear to have been on terms of personal intimacy (see A. Gilchrist, *Life of William Etty, R.A.*, 2 vols. (1855), preface to I, p. viii).

2052 TWO MALE NUDE STUDIES

Paper backed on canvas, 21⅛ × 24½ in (53·6 × 62·2 cm).[1] Male nude seated in profile to the left, the trunk turned round to the right and seen from the back, the right arm stretched out horizontally to the right; the left leg, seen to the knee, is extended, the right knee is bent and raised. At the right is a study of a complete left leg, in a similar position to the left leg of the figure. Light brown monochrome.

Bequeathed by Charles Haslewood Shannon, R.A., 1937. Coll. Sir Herbert Thompson, Bart; his (anon.) sale, Christie's, 16 July 1904 (27), bt Ricketts; Charles Ricketts, R.A., and C. H. Shannon, R.A.; on loan to the Fitzwilliam Museum, 1933–7.

A life-study, presumably made in the R.A. schools, where Etty worked constantly throughout his career. It has been dated *c.* 1818–20.[2]

NOTES. [1] Including a strip added along the top, 1⅝ in (4·2 cm) wide. [2] Dennis Farr, *William Etty* (1958), p. 173, no. 206.

EWORTH, Hans

Fl. 1540–74. Of Netherlandish origin. Freeman of the Antwerp Guild of St Luke, 1540; possibly to be recognised under varying forms of name as resident in London, 1549–71; employed on court entertainments, 1572–4. Identified with the painter signing H E, who was court painter to Mary I.[1]

PD. 1–1963 UNKNOWN LADY, FORMERLY CALLED MARY I WHEN PRINCESS PLATE 2

Wood, 43¼ × 31½ in (109·9 × 80·0 cm). The dress is of black silk and black velvet, with underskirt and undersleeves of a muted red, which reappears in the head-dress. The standing collar is lined with white and edged with gold lace; the chemise frill, edged with black, round her neck, is enclosed by a collar with gold and black embroidery on white; the undersleeves are edged with gold lace, which encircles the wrists above an embroidered ruffle edged with black; the aiglets are enamelled black on gold. The circular jewel at her breast depicts Esther kneeling before Ahasuerus, who stretches out his sceptre towards her; the cover of the small book hanging by a gold chain from her waist has a possible letter D on it. Grey background.

Bequeathed by Sir Bruce Stirling Ingram, O.B.E., M.C., 1963. Coll. Francis Barchard (d. 1856), of Horsted Place, Uckfield, Sussex, who bought it in 1854;[2] Mrs Maude Barchard, the widow of his great-grandson; bt from her by P. & D. Colnaghi & Co. Ltd, London; exh. Colnaghi's, 1949, when it was bought by Sir Bruce Ingram; exh. London, R.A., 1950–1, 'Works by Holbein and other masters' (28).[3]

Exhibited at the R.A. in 1950–1 as the work of a 'close follower of Hans Holbein the Younger'; first published as by Eworth in 1953,[4] an attribution confirmed by subsequent study.[5] It was formerly considered to be a portrait of Mary I (b. 1516) as princess, that is, before 1553 when she came to the throne. Though this is in general accord with the approximate date of the costume, *c.* 1550–5,[6] the woman appears too young for such an identification. There is little resemblance of feature, either, to authentic portraits of Mary, such as those by Master John, dated 1544 (National Portrait Gallery, no. 428), and by Eworth (Society of Antiquaries, London) and Anthonis Mor (Marquess of Northampton, one of three known original versions), both dated 1554. The jewel at her breast illustrates the biblical story of King Ahasuerus and his queen, Esther (Book of Esther, ch. 3–8), which is the typological parallel in the Old Testament for the coronation of the Virgin Mary as Queen of Heaven. This has been cited as confirmation of the supposed identity of the lady as Mary I when a princess,[7] but not very logically since it would have no relevance before she became queen. If the jewel can be taken as having a personal significance, it may simply indicate that the lady's name was Mary. With her rich costume, she was evidently of high rank, and thus probably an aristocratic young lady at the court of Edward VI or Mary I. From her rings it appears that she was unmarried.

REPRODUCED. *Illustrated London News* (1950), CCXVII, Supplement, p. II (colour); *Souvenir* of the R.A. exhibition, 'Works by Holbein and other masters', 1950–1, p. 11; Ellis Waterhouse, *Painting in Britain, 1530–1790* (1953), pl. 10b; *Country Life* (1963), CXXXIII, 1383; Fitzwilliam Museum, *Annual Report* for 1963, pl. VII; exhibition catalogue, *Hans Eworth* (1965–6), Leicester Museums and Art Gallery, and National Portrait Gallery, pl. 4; Roy Strong, *The English Icon* (1969), pl. 51.

NOTES. [1] Roy Strong, *The English Icon* (1969), pp. 9–10, 83–4. [2] From 'Webb', presumably John Webb, of 13 George Street, Hanover Square, London, who was employed for the decorating and furnishing of Horsted Place from 1852. Information kindly supplied by Mr Mark Girouard (letter of 23 July 1974, Fitzwilliam Museum), and see his 'Horsted Place, Sussex', *Country Life*

(1958), CXXIV, 276, 320. [3] Included in the catalogue (by Roy Strong) of the exhibition 'Hans Eworth', held at Leicester, Museums and Art Gallery, and in London, National Portrait Gallery, 1965–6, no. 28, but not actually shown. [4] Ellis Waterhouse, *Painting in Britain, 1530–1790* (1953), p. 16, pointing out the debt to Holbein. [5] Strong, *op. cit.*, p. 105, no. 51. [6] The costume has been dated as early as *c.* 1545 (C. Willis and P. Cunnington, *Handbook of English costume in the sixteenth century* (1954), p. 154), but this seems too early. Tree-ring measurements of the panel by Dr J. M. Fletcher indicate a 'Likely period of use of the panel' of 1547–56 (letter of 22 January 1976, Fitzwilliam Museum). [7] Ellis Waterhouse, catalogue of the 'Exhibition of works by Holbein and other masters', R.A., 1950–1, p. 25, no. 28.

FIELDING, Anthony Vandyke Copley

1787–1855. Born near Halifax, Yorkshire. Pupil of John Varley. A prolific water-colourist, who worked occasionally in oils, which were exh. R.A. from 1811, and B.I. from 1812; exh. Society of Painters in Water-colours from 1813, President from 1831. Landscape and marine painter.

1797 A HEATH NEAR THE COAST — PLATE 37

Canvas, 12⅝ × 18½ in (32.1 × 47·0 cm). Broken, sandy ground, with sparse brown and green herbage and an occasional rocky outcrop, traversed in the foreground by a track, extends to a low, distant horizon of sea, with hills in the distance to right and left; grey, cloudy sky.

Bequeathed by Arthur William Young, 1936. Coll. William Dell, of Brixton, London; his posthumous sale, Christie's, 21 April 1899 (59),[1] bt Radley.

Thin oil paint resembling water-colour in its manner of use. Landscape subjects of this type, similarly treated, are known in Copley Fielding's work, in both water-colour and oils, from about the middle 1830s to the end of his career. Though the later ones seem generally to be lower in tone than this picture, he did not, at this period, employ a consistent style in his painting.

NOTE. [1] With the title *Sand hills by the sea-shore*, dimensions 12¼ × 18 in (31·2 × 45·7 cm).

FREEDMAN, Barnett

1901–1958. Born in London of Polish immigrant parents. Mainly trained at the Royal College of Art, London; official War Artist, 1940–5; C.B.E., 1946. Painter of landscape, genre and still-life, and graphic artist.

PD. 4–1953 THE BARN AT FINGEST, BUCKINGHAMSHIRE (1933)

Canvas, 19 × 26½ in (48·3 × 67·3 cm). The interior of an old barn, looking towards the partly opened doors, through which is seen part of a house. Mid-way down the barn stands a farm cart. The colouring, which is mainly in browns, ranges through reds to orange and yellow, relieved with greys and grey-greens. Signed and dated lower left, 'Barnett Freedman 33'.

Given anonymously by friends of the artist, who bought it from him for presentation to the Fitzwilliam Museum, 1953. Exh. London and elsewhere, Arts Council, 1958–9, 'Barnett Freedman' (22); placed on loan to the City of Cambridge, 1972.

FRITH, William Powell

1819–1909. Born at Aldfield, Yorkshire. Henry Sass's School of Art, London, 1835–7; entered the R.A. schools, 1837. Exh. B.I. from 1838, and R.A. from 1840. R.A., 1853; C.V.O., 1908. Travelled in northern Europe and Italy. Subject and genre painter.

498 OTHELLO AND DESDEMONA (1856)

Canvas, 22 × 19 in (55·9 × 48·3 cm). Desdemona, at three-quarter-length, wearing a dress of warm cream brocade and black, sits in a red chair turned half to the left, with Othello, in armour with a brown cloak, at her right turned towards her. To right two columns rise; to left, beyond a balustrade, are seen some houses. Blue sky. Signed and dated lower right, 'W. P. Frith 1856'.

Given by Mrs Richard Ellison, 1862. Exh. London, B.I., 1840 (306); again in the possession of the artist, 1856; exh. Harrogate, Corporation Art Gallery, 1951, 'William Powell Frith' (5).

Some areas of paint wrinkled and pulled. One of Frith's earliest subject-pictures, dating from 1840, which he states he subsequently much reduced in size[1] and repainted, evidently in 1856, shortening the legs of the figures in the process. Desdemona was painted from his sister, and Othello from 'an East Indian crossing-sweeper'.[2] The moment depicted is taken from Othello's speech in Act I, Scene III, recounting how he won Desdemona.

NOTES. [1] In the catalogue of the exhibition at the B.I. in 1840, the outside dimensions of the frame are given as 45 × 37 in (114·3 × 94·0 cm). [2] W. P. Frith, *My autobiography and reminiscences*, 3rd edn (1887), I, pp. 78, 81.

FRY, Roger

1866–1934. Born in London. After a scientific education, turned to the practice and critical study of painting. Director of the Metropolitan Museum of Art, New York, 1905–10; editor of the *Burlington Magazine*, 1910–19; from about 1910 turned his attention mainly to modern art; Slade Professor of Fine Art, Cambridge, 1933. Mainly painter of landscape.

1754 STILL-LIFE OF FISH (1928)

Canvas, 18⅜ × 21¾ in (46·7 × 55·3 cm). Five fish lie on a piece of crumpled and folded white paper, beneath which is some brown paper. Seen rather from above. Signed and dated lower right, 'Roger Fry. '28'.

Given by Miss Sara Margery Fry, his sister, in accordance with the artist's wishes, 1935. With the London Artists' Association (date unknown).[1]

NOTE. [1] From a label at the back, which does not appear to relate to an exhibition.

2392 THE CLOISTER (1924)

Oil on millboard, 13 × 16⅛ in (33·0 × 40·9 cm). Internal view along one side of a cloister; at the left, a tall main wall of the building, pierced by Gothic windows and a door, at the right a lower arcade through which the light falls. Statues are ranged along the base of the main wall. The walls and floor are in greenish ochres, the stone window- and door-frames are pink; the wooden roof overhead is a deep pinkish brown. Signed and dated lower left, 'Roger Fry 24'. On the back, the upright way of the millboard, is a painting in oils of a woman seated to the left in a deck chair, on a kind of terrace in a garden.

Bequeathed by Frank Hindley Smith, 1939.

The building of which the cloister forms part has not been identified; but because of the date of the picture, 1924, there is a probability that it was in France.

PD. 73–1972 THE PORT OF CASSIS (1925)

Wood, 12⅝ × 16⅛ in (32·1 × 40·9 cm). The water, with wavelets of dark and light green, recedes from the foreground towards a small steamship, with a dark grey and dull red hull, beside a wharf on the left, on which is a row of pale buildings, mainly cream, pink, grey and green in colour. An edge of the wharf, pale buff, runs diagonally across the left foreground, with a blue and light green rowing boat at the right, a second one, grey, green and pink, towards the steamer. Low hills, with rocks of grey and grey-brown, and grey-green vegetation, rise close behind the port, Inscribed, signed and dated at the back, 'The port of Cassis/Roger Fry. 1925'.

Bequeathed by Mrs M. E. L. Brownlow, 1972.

Cassis is a village on the Mediterranean coast of France between Marseilles and Toulon.

PD. 74–1972 THE CHURCH OF ST ETIENNE, TOULOUSE (1929)

Millboard, 13 × 16⅛ in (33·1 × 40·9 cm). Across a work-yard, with two small huts in it and a number of blocks of stone, rises the high wall of the church, in red-browns and greys; at the right lower buildings join it to the lower part of a tower, similar in colouring. In the centre is some light brown scaffolding against the wall of the church. Light blue sky. Signed and dated lower right, 'Roger Fry 1929'.[1]

Bequeathed by Mrs M. E. L. Brownlow, 1972.

NOTE. [1] The last figure is probably to be read as a '9', but could be a '4'.

GAINSBOROUGH, Thomas

1727–1788. Born at Sudbury, Suffolk. The details of his training are uncertain. Went to London about 1740, where he received some instruction from Hubert Gravelot (returned to France 1745); influenced by Dutch seventeenth-century landscape painting, and by Francis Hayman. Thought to have returned to Suffolk about 1748; established in Ipswich before 1750; moved to Bath, 1759; to London, 1774. Founder member of the R.A., 1768. Painter of portraits, landscape and fancy subjects.

18 THE HON. WILLIAM FITZWILLIAM (1775) PLATE 19

Canvas, 30 × 25 in (76·2 × 63·5 cm). Brown coat and waistcoat; chair upholstery brown, faded from crimson. At the back, label inscribed 'The Honble Wm Fitzwilliam/AEtat 64./T. Gainsborough Pinxit/1775'.[1]

Founder's Bequest, 1816.

Cleaned 1904. William Fitzwilliam (1712–1797), brother of the 6th Viscount Fitzwilliam of Merrion, and thus uncle of the founder of the Fitzwilliam Museum; appointed Usher of the Black Rod in Ireland, 1747. Said to have been engraved in mezzotint by J. Dean,[2] but no such engraving can now be traced.

REPRODUCED. *Principal pictures* (1912 edn), p. 54, (1929 edn), p. 69; J. W. Goodison, *Catalogue of Cambridge portraits* (1955), I, pl. X; Ellis Waterhouse, *Gainsborough* (1958), pl. 160.

NOTES. [1] Ellis Waterhouse, *Gainsborough* (1958), p. 67, no. 257. [2] G. W. Fulcher, *Life of Thomas Gainsborough* (1865), p. 215.

644 JOHN KIRBY PLATE 18

Canvas, $29\frac{7}{8} \times 25$ in ($75\cdot9 \times 63\cdot5$ cm).[1] White hair, dark blue jacket; brown background.

Given by Charles Fairfax Murray, 1908. Coll. Rev. Kirby Trimmer[2] (d. 1887); exh. London, 1868, 'National portraits' (752); anon. sale (= W. Forster, executor of the Rev. Kirby Trimmer), Christie's, 12 May 1888 (lot 61, with no. 645 below), bt Murray.

John Kirby (1690–1753) is known as the author of the first topographical work on the county of Suffolk, *The Suffolk traveller*, published in 1735. This and the portrait of his wife (no. 645 below) are among the earliest of Gainsborough's known portrait paintings. When he began painting portraits on the scale of life, such as these, is unknown. The earliest datable example is the *Admiral Vernon* (National Portrait Gallery, no. 881) of about 1753; but the two Fitzwilliam Museum portraits are painted in a different and manifestly earlier style, which has analogies with the small painting of the dog *Bumper* of 1745 (Sir Edmund Bacon, Bart).[3] As John Kirby's son, John Joshua Kirby (see no. 709 below), was a close friend of Gainsborough in Ipswich, the guess might be hazarded that these portraits are possibly some of the first which Gainsborough painted after he settled in Suffolk in about 1748.[4]

REPRODUCED. *Principal pictures* (1912 edn), p. 55, (1929 edn), p. 66; Ellis Waterhouse, *Gainsborough* (1958), pl. 2.

NOTES. [1] Lined; dimensions of the painted surface. [2] Grandson of Mrs Sarah Trimmer, the grand-daughter of John Kirby and daughter of his eldest son John Joshua Kirby (see no. 709 below). This and nos. 645 and 709 were said by Fairfax Murray, when he gave no. 709 in 1911, to have come 'direct from the heirs through the daughter Mrs. Trimmer' (letter of 5 January 1911, Fitzwilliam Museum), all three thus, by implication, having belonged to John Joshua Kirby and passed from him to Mrs Trimmer. [3] For a view placing the portrait in the same period as the *Admiral Vernon*, the early to mid 1750s, see John Hayes, 'Some unknown Gainsborough portraits', *Burlington Magazine* (1965), CVII, 65. [4] Ellis Waterhouse, *Gainsborough* (1958), p. 77, no. 416, as, 'probably before 1750'.

645 MRS JOHN KIRBY

Canvas, $29\frac{7}{8} \times 24\frac{3}{4}$ in ($75{\cdot}8 \times 62{\cdot}9$ cm).[1] Half-length, turned and facing front. White cap, tied under the chin; grey dress with plain white fichu. Within a feigned oval.

Given by Charles Fairfax Murray, 1908. Coll. Rev. Kirby Trimmer[2] (d. 1887); anon. sale, Christie's (= W. Forster, executor of the Rev. Kirby Trimmer), 12 May 1888 (61, with no. 644), bt Murray; exh. London, Tate Gallery (Arts Council), 1953, 'Thomas Gainsborough' (3).

Alice Brown, who married John Kirby in 1714. For Gainsborough's portrait of her husband, see no. 644 above, with which it shares similar stylistic and technical characteristics.[3]

REPRODUCED. *Principal pictures* (1912 edn), p. 56, (1929 edn), p. 67; Oliver Millar, *Thomas Gainsborough* (1949), p. 12 (colour); Ellis Waterhouse, *Gainsborough* (1958), pl. 2; *Burlington Magazine* (1965), CVII, 64 (head only); Royal Society of Arts, *Journal* (1965), CXIII, 329 (head only).

NOTES. [1] Lined; dimensions of the painted surface. [2] See note [2] to no. 644 above. [3] Ellis Waterhouse, *Gainsborough* (1958), p. 77, no. 417.

709 JOHN JOSHUA KIRBY

Canvas, $29\frac{3}{4} \times 24\frac{7}{8}$ in ($75{\cdot}6 \times 63{\cdot}2$ cm).[1] Nearly half-length, turned half left, looking almost half left, eyes front. Bare-headed, wig; clean-shaven. Wears maroon jacket and waistcoat, both with gilt buttons; plain white neck-cloth. Within a feigned oval. Signed lower right, 'T G'.

Given by Charles Fairfax Murray, 1911. Coll. Rev. Kirby Trimmer[2] (d. 1887); anon. sale (= W. Forster, executor of the Rev. Kirby Trimmer) Christie's, 12 May 1888 (62), bt Murray; lent to the Fitzwilliam Museum, 1910.

John Joshua Kirby (1716–1774) was the eldest son of John Kirby (see no. 644 above), and a close friend of Gainsborough; he became clerk of the works at Kew Palace, and was the father of the authoress, Mrs Sarah Trimmer. If the *Portrait of a gentleman* exhibited as no. 37 at the Society of Artists in 1764[3] was indeed of John Joshua Kirby,[4] it is probably to be identified with this painting.[5] His apparent age does not disagree with this date for the portrait.[6]

ENGRAVED. Mezzotint by John Dixon.[7]

REPRODUCED. *Principal pictures* (1912 edn), p. 57, (1929 edn), p. 68.

NOTES. [1] Lined; dimensions of the painted surface. [2] See note [2] to no. 644 above. [3] A. Graves, *The Society of Artists...dictionary of contributors and their work* (1907), p. 98; the size, 'three-quarters', corresponds with the dimensions of no. 709. [4] W. T. Whitley, *Thomas Gainsborough* (1915), p. 43, 'said to have been' of Kirby, but no source is given. [5] In W. Thornbury, *The life of J. M. W. Turner, R.A.*, 2 vols. (1862), II, p. 58, Turner's friend, 'the Rev. Mr. Trimmer of Heston, near Brentford' (p. 37; probably the Rev. Henry Scott Trimmer), is quoted as stating that Gainsborough painted John Joshua Kirby twice. The other known portrait of him, in the Victoria and Albert Museum (Dyce 16), shows him as a young man and is too small ($16\frac{1}{2} \times 11\frac{1}{2}$ in, $41{\cdot}9 \times 29{\cdot}2$ cm, cf. n. 3) to have been the one exhibited. [6] Ellis Waterhouse, *Gainsborough* (1958), p. 77, no. 419. [7] John Chaloner Smith, *British mezzotinto portraits* (1878), part I, p. 212, no. 21. Dixon moved to London about 1765.

710 'HENEAGE LLOYD AND HIS SISTER' PLATE 17

Canvas, $25\frac{1}{4} \times 31\frac{7}{8}$ in ($64{\cdot}1 \times 81{\cdot}0$ cm).[1] Landscape and sky are in atmospheric tones of green, brown and grey; the girl is in white; the boy has red breeches and a buff coat, with white shirt, waistcoat and stockings. Signed on the stone beneath the boy's foot, 'T.G.'

Given by Charles Fairfax Murray, 1911. Possibly inherited with Hintlesham Hall and estate, Suffolk, from Miss Henrietta Lloyd,[2] by Captain James Hamilton Lloyd-Anstruther (d. 1882), 1837; his eldest son, Lt-Col. Robert Hamilton Lloyd-Anstruther, who lent it to an exhibition of the work of Suffolk artists, Ipswich, Fine Art Club, 1887 (130); sold to P. & D. Colnaghi & Co. Ltd, London, 1895, who sold it to Gooden & Fox Ltd, London, 1904; lent to the Fitzwilliam Museum by C. Fairfax Murray, 1910; exh. Ipswich Museum, 1927, 'Bicentenary memorial exhibition of Thomas Gainsborough, R.A.' (19); London, R.A., 1934, 'British Art' (263); London, Goldsmiths' Hall, 1959, 'Treasures of Cambridge' (33).

One of a number of small paintings with full-length portrait-figures in a landscape, painted in Suffolk during the early years of Gainsborough's career. It may be dated about 1750, by comparison with the *Mr and Mrs Andrews* (National Gallery, no. 6301) close to this date, with which there is much similarity in the painting of the figures,[3] and the costume points also to this approximate date.[4] The sophisticated, park-like setting is unusual in Gainsborough's pictures of this kind, though not unknown;[5] its treatment and lighting find a parallel in the trees of the *John Plampin* (National Gallery, no. 5984), dated by Waterhouse (*op. cit.*, p. 85, no. 546) to the earlier 1750s, and by the National Gallery, from costume, *c.* 1755. The identification of the boy as Heneage Lloyd is open to doubt. He was the second son of Sir Richard Lloyd, became a captain in the Coldstream Guards, and died in December 1776, aged thirty-three.[6] As his earliest date of birth is thus 1742, he would be about eight years of age at the date of the picture, and the boy in the painting looks distinctly more than this.[7] Nor can it be his elder brother Richard Savage Lloyd, who was born about 1730. If it is, therefore, not a Lloyd portrait, the provenance to the Lloyd family of Hintlesham Hall cannot be regarded as more than a probability, since the first certain owner is Lt-Col. Lloyd-Anstruther.[8]

REPRODUCED. *Principal pictures* (1912 edn.), p. 58, (1929 edn), p. 65; *Commemorative catalogue of the exhibition of British art...1934* (1935), pl. LV; *The Listener* (1947), XXXVIII, 383; Carl Winter, *The Fitzwilliam Museum* (1958), p. 348, pl. 86; Ellis Waterhouse, *Gainsborough* (1958), pl. 15; Goldsmiths' Hall exhibition, 1959, 'Treasures of Cambridge', *Illustrations*, pl. 42; *Worcester Art Museum Annual* (1959), VII, p. 5; P. Cunnington and A. Buck, *Children's costume in England* (1965), p. 17 (figures only).

NOTES. [1] Lined; dimensions of the painted surface. [2] She was the granddaughter of Sir Richard Lloyd, Solicitor-General 1754–9, who bought the Hintlesham estate in 1747. [3] The Fitzwilliam Museum picture is also given this date by Ellis Waterhouse, *Gainsborough* (1958), p. 79, no. 452. On p. 52, no. 18, he says of the *Mr and Mrs Andrews*, 'Probably painted soon after marriage of sitters in 1748'; but in *The National Gallery, January 1960–May 1962* (1962), p. 26, it is stated that the 'style of the costume points rather precisely to the year 1750'. [4] P. Cunnington and A. Buck, *Children's costume in England* (1965), pl. 17, date it '*c.* 1750'. [5] E.g., the *Girl seated in a park*, ex Cook Collection, Richmond, Surrey (Waterhouse, *op. cit.*, p. 99, no. 754). It suggests the possibility of a scene in the park of Hintlesham Hall, but no such scene can now be recognised. [6] The inscription on his monument in Hintlesham church reads, 'Heneage Lloyd, Esq., Captain of the Coldstream Regiment of Guards, 22nd December 1776, aged 33' (from a transcription by Charles Partridge in *The East Anglian*, New Series (1905–6), XI, 254, no. 165). [7] The identification has come about in stages. When exhibited at Ipswich in 1887, the picture was entitled 'Portraits in a landscape – Boy and Girl'; when bought by Colnaghi's in 1895 it was described as 'Lloyd Portraits', and while still with Colnaghi's the description was changed to 'Heneage Lloyd and his sister' (information kindly supplied by Mr J. Byam Shaw, who examined Colnaghi's stock book in 1956), identifications presumably due to the seller, Lt-Col. Lloyd-Anstruther. [8] Two Lloyd portraits by Gainsborough were included in his sale at Hintlesham Hall on 16 June 1909 (see Waterhouse, *op. cit.*, p. 79, nos. 453, 454).

915 PHILIP DUPONT PLATE 19

Canvas, $30 \times 24\frac{5}{8}$ in ($76{\cdot}2 \times 62{\cdot}5$ cm).[1] Jacket and waistcoat light brown, with greyer highlights. Ruddy complexion; neutral-coloured hair. Warm brown background.

Given by Charles Fairfax Murray, 1918. Coll. Richard Gainsborough Dupont (1789–1874) of Sudbury, Suffolk, grandson of Philip Dupont, by 1856;[2] his posthumous sale, Sudbury, Wheeler & Westoby, 29 May 1874 (126), bt Page or Chance;[3] presumably the picture exh. Ipswich Fine Art Club, 1887, 'Works by Suffolk artists', no. 140, lent J. H. Chance;[4] Cambridge, Fitzwilliam Museum, 1910, lent Charles Fairfax Murray.

Cleaned 1954. Philip Dupont married Gainsborough's sister Sarah at Sudbury, Suffolk, in 1745. He died in 1788, and since his tombstone gives his age as sixty-six,[5] he was born about 1722. From his appearance in the painting, his age may be estimated at about forty-five to fifty, probably nearer the latter, giving an approximate date for the portrait of around 1770. Stylistic comparisons bear out this date; for example with the *Countess of Sefton* (Earl of Sefton), exh. R.A. 1769, and *Margaret Gainsborough* (National Gallery, no. 1482), assigned to a date of *c.* 1772.[6]

NOTES. [1] Lined; dimensions of the painted surface. [2] G. W. Fulcher, *Life of T. Gainsborough*, 2nd edn (1856), p. 120. [3] The *Ipswich Journal and Suffolk, Norfolk, Essex and Cambridgeshire Advertiser* for 6 June 1874, in an account of the sale, gives the buyer of lot 126, as also of lot 127, a portrait of Mrs Philip Dupont, as 'Mr Page'; Algernon Graves, *Art sales* (1908), I, p. 328, gives the buyer of lot 126 as 'Page', but of lot 127 as 'Chance'; Ellis Waterhouse, *Gainsborough* (1958), p. 65, no. 223, *Philip Dupont*, gives the buyer as 'Chance', deriving the information from a 'MS notebook of Gainsborough sales in my possession, which belonged to Graves', in which the buyer of lot 127 is also given as Chance, who is described as having both pictures still in October 1885 (letter of 9 December 1969, Fitzwilliam Museum). As the name of Page is not known to occur subsequently as the owner of either of these two paintings, it seems likely that, substantially speaking, they were acquired at the 1874 sale by Chance, even if in some way through Page as an intermediary. [4] Chance lent also to the exhibition, no. 139, a portrait of Mrs Philip Dupont, presumably the picture which was lot 127 in the 1874 sale. [5] The information about the Dupont family has been most kindly supplied by Mr L. H. Haydon Whitehead (letters of June, July and November 1969, Fitzwilliam Museum). [6] Martin Davies, National Gallery Catalogues, *The British School*, 2nd edn (1959), pp. 37–8. Waterhouse, *loc. cit.*, surprisingly describes the Fitzwilliam Museum portrait as 'Suffolk period'.

1654 A FOREST ROAD

Canvas, 24¾ × 29¾ in (62·8 × 75·5 cm).[1] A rough track runs over broken ground round the edge of a dense wood at the left, curving from the centre foreground until it dips out of sight below some trees on a slope at the right, beyond which opens a vista of distance, with a square tower to left, and bright clouds. A dead tree rises in the extreme right foreground. Blue sky with heavy white and grey clouds. The trees are in greens and browns, the ground is brown. Under the trees to the left is a group of three figures beside a fence, beyond stands an animal; where the track dips there is a horseman.

Given by the Friends of the Fitzwilliam Museum, 1933. With Edward Noyes, Chester; coll. Edmund Peel (1826–1903);[2] his son Major Hugh E. E. Peel (1871–1950); anon. sale (= Major Peel), Christie's, 28 July 1933 (49), bt for the Friends of the Fitzwilliam Museum.

Severely over-cleaned everywhere. Cleaned 1952. A painting of Gainsborough's Suffolk period, similar in general character to *Gainsborough's forest* (National Gallery, no. 925) of 1748, though its poor condition precludes any precise comparison with other paintings. It may be approximately dated *c.* 1750.[3] A landscape drawing with much similarity of composition, in 1969 with the Sabin Galleries, London, has been dated to the early 1750s.[4]

REPRODUCED. Friends of the Fitzwilliam Museum, *Annual Report* for 1933.

NOTES. [1] Lined; dimensions of the painted surface. [2] From information at the back of the canvas. [3] Ellis Waterhouse, *Gainsborough* (1958), p. 110, no. 860. [4] John Hayes, *The drawings of Thomas Gainsborough* (1970), p. 137, no. 96, rep. pl. 23.

PD. 3–1966 LANDSCAPE WITH A POOL PLATE 18

Canvas, 13¾ × 11¾ in (34·9 × 29·8 cm).[1] The central tree is autumnal in colour, as is some of the foliage elsewhere; the herbage otherwise is mainly in sallow greens. The sandy track and bank of the pool are in part painted in grey. The clouds are grey and cream against a very pale blue sky. General light tone, with local colour in the shadows.

Bequeathed by Percy Moore Turner (d. 1950), with a life-interest to his widow, relinquished 1966. Coll. J. E. Fordham (1799–1881), Melbourn Bury, by 1856;[2] exh. London, R.A., 1878, 'Old Masters' (103); descended to A. R. Fordham (grandson); his sale, Sotheby's, 21 November 1934 (90), bt Colnaghi; exh. London, 45 Park Lane, 1936, 'Gainsborough loan exhibition' (88), lent P. M. Turner; Hazlitt, 1974 (25).

A painting of the early, Suffolk, period of Gainsborough's career. It has been dated to the middle 1750s,[3] but it may be questioned whether it is not rather earlier than this. In character it stands apart from such rather contrived landscapes as the pair belonging to the Duke of Bedford (Woburn Abbey), which were bought in 1755, while it is strikingly similar to *Gainsborough's forest* (National Gallery, no. 925), which is accepted as of 1748.[4] In its directness, also, it has a kinship with the landscape in *Mr and Mrs Andrews* (National Gallery, no. 6301), dated to about 1750.

REPRODUCED. 'Gainsborough loan exhibition', London, 1936, vol. of illustrations, p. 19; M. Woodall, *Gainsborough's landscape drawings* (1939), pl. 15; Fitzwilliam Museum, *Annual Report* for 1966, pl. VI; exhibition catalogue, Hazlitt, 1974, pl. 10.

NOTES. [1] Lined; dimensions of the painted surface. [2] G. W. Fulcher, *Life of Thomas Gainsborough, R.A.*, 2nd edn (1856), p. 236; he gives the owner as J. G. Fordham, but in view of the date this must be a slip for J. E. Fordham. [3] Ellis Waterhouse, *Gainsborough* (1958), p. 111, no. 875. [4] For a detailed comparison, see M. Woodall, *Gainsborough's landscape drawings* (1939), p. 29.

GERTLER, Mark

1891–1939. Born in London of Polish immigrant parents. Trained in London, mainly at the Slade School, and worked mainly in London; member of the New English Art Club, and then of the London Group. Painted figure subjects, portraits, landscape and still-life.

2728 SEA-SHELLS (1907)

Canvas, 11 × 15 in (27·9 × 38·1 cm). Three mother-of-pearl shells lie in a row on a brown wooden table, with a fourth, larger one standing upright behind them. Signed and dated upper right, 'Mark Gertler/1907'.

Given by Howard Bliss, 1945. With the Goupil Gallery, London.[1]

Probably painted when he was fifteen, as his date of birth was 9 December. It was at this age that Gertler had 'briefly attended classes at the Regent Street Polytechnic', London.[2]

NOTES. [1] From a printed trade label at the back of the picture. [2] John Rothenstein, *Modern English painters* (1956), II, p. 207.

PD. 6–1968 VIOLIN AND BUST

Millboard, 14½ × 18⅛ in (36·8 × 46·3 cm). A plaster bust of a woman stands on a brown table in front of a violin lying with some music in an open violin-case lined with blue; some yellow fabric passes across the bust from its right shoulder to the violin-case at the right. To the left is a white fruit-dish, containing grapes and pears, behind it an obliquely-placed brown, panelled door. In the background are rectangles of colour – blue across the top, ochre at the right and dull pink in the centre.

Bequeathed by Thomas Balston, O.B.E., M.C., through the National Art-Collections Fund, 1968. Exh. London, Leicester Galleries, 1934, 'Paintings and pastels by Mark Gertler' (85), bt Thomas Balston; London, Whitechapel Art Gallery, 1949, 'Mark Gertler memorial exhibition' (61).

Thick, palette knife paint. The Leicester Galleries state that most of the paintings in their exhibition of 1934 'would have come straight from' the artist.[1] It thus seems probable that this year, or slightly before it, is the likely date for the painting.

NOTE. [1] Letter of 10 April 1968 (Fitzwilliam Museum).

PD. 7–1968 THE PIGEON HOUSE (1920)

Canvas, 24 × 17⅞ in (60.9 × 45·4 cm). The square pigeon house, with buff walls and a pink roof, stands in a walled enclosure with a black barn to the left. In the extreme foreground is a light blue gate in a wall, two bushy trees growing to the left of it, and two more in the walled enclosure. Beyond the pigeon house are slightly rolling fields, light yellow or pink or blue, divided by dark green hedges and trees. Light grey sky. Signed and dated lower left, 'Mark Gertler/Sep 1920'.

Bequeathed by Thomas Balston, O.B.E., M.C., through the National Art-Collections Fund, 1968. Exh. London, Goupil Gallery, 1921, 'Mark Gertler' (4); Whitechapel Art Gallery, 1949, 'Mark Gertler memorial exhibition' (29), lent T. Balston.

REPRODUCED. Hubert Wellington, *Mark Gertler*, British Artists of To-day Series (1925), pl. 2.

GILL, William

Active 1826–69. Exhibited in London between these dates, mainly at the Society of British Artists, Suffolk Street, but also at the R.A. and the B.I., from addresses first in London, then in Warwick and Leamington, and finally in London again. Genre painter.

499 LEAP-FROG **PLATE 39**

Wood, 18 × 25⅛ in (46·0 × 63·7 cm). The figures are in somewhat muted colours in which creamy whites, greys and browns predominate, with a red cap on the central boy, a pink waistcoat on the one holding up his hat, and a pink-red jacket on the one lying on his back. Variegated grey-browns in the ground. The deeply shadowed buildings are in warm greys and grey-greens, the timbered building in buff-creams. Grey clouds.

Given by Mrs Richard Ellison, 1862. Exh. London, Society of British Artists, 1852 (43); coll. G. Roake, London, sold Christie's 2 May 1857 (38), bt Morant or Villiers.

This picture, typical of the genre painting of the middle decades of the nineteenth century, may presumably be dated to 1852, the year in which it was shown at the annual exhibition of the Society of British Artists.[1] It seems to have been admired in its day, as Christie's catalogue of the sale in 1857 describes it as 'a beautiful specimen'.

NOTE. (1) A much despised body (see A. Paul Oppé, *Early Victorian England*, ed. G. M. Young (1934), pp. 106–7), of which Gill was a member.

GILMAN, Harold

1876–1919. Born at Road, Somerset. Studied at the Slade School, London, 1897–1900; influenced by Sickert, and later by the Post-Impressionists. Founder member of the Camden Town Group, 1911, and of its successor, the London Group, 1913. Painter of interiors, landscapes and portraits.

PD. 29–1948 STILL-LIFE

Canvas, 12⅜ × 16⅜ in (31·4 × 41·6 cm). In the centre of a mahogany table running across the base of the picture, with a dark brown chair back to the left, stand a vase of foliage and one of flowers, a small bowl, and a few apricots, reflected in a rectangular, dark-framed mirror on the dark buff wall behind. To the left are a glass jar half full of a red-brown liquid and a small picture, to the right a silver dish. Signed lower right, 'H. Gilman'.

Given by Captain Stanley William Sykes, O.B.E., M.C., 1948. Coll. the mother of the artist, Mrs John Gilman; bought from her by Alex Reid & Lefevre Ltd, London; exh. London, Lefevre Gallery, 1948, 'Paintings and drawings by Harold Gilman' (12), where it was bought by Captain Sykes for the Fitzwilliam Museum.

The low-toned, golden brown key of this painting is characteristic of Gilman's earlier work before the transformation of his style, especially as regards the use of colour, in 1910 through his study of the Post-Impressionists. In the catalogue of the Lefevre Gallery exhibition it was dated 1910, but it seems likely to be earlier than this. Compare, for example, a *Self-portrait*, formerly in the Edward Le Bas collection, which is assigned to a date of *c.* 1907, and to which the palette of the present picture is very similar.[1]

NOTES. [1] See B. Fairfax Hall, *Paintings and drawings by Harold Gilman and Charles Ginner in the collection of Edward Le Bas* (1965), p. 47, rep. pl. 1. Gilman's later use of colour is seen in pl. 2, *Woman on a sofa*, which was exhibited in 1910.

PD. 3–1967 NUDE ON A BED PLATE 59

Canvas, $24\frac{1}{8} \times 18\frac{3}{8}$ in ($61{\cdot}4 \times 46{\cdot}7$ cm). The figure and the bed-clothes are painted in a broken mosaic of individual colours of much variety; the girl has brown hair, the foot of the bedstead is black. The carpet pattern is dull green and red against dull ochre; the chimney-piece is mainly in tones of warm grey, above it a horizontal band of red; the wall to the right of it is light green.

Given by Benjamin Fairfax Hall, in memory of Edward Le Bas, 1967. Coll. Edward Le Bas, C.B.E., R.A. (1904–1966) by 1939, when he lent it to an exhibition at the Redfern Gallery, London, 'The Camden Town Group' (31); exh. London, R.A., 1963, 'A painter's collection' (35); Edinburgh, Scottish National Gallery of Modern Art, 1963, 'From a painter's collection' (4); London, Reid Gallery, 1964, 'Paintings and drawings by Harold Gilman' (19); bequeathed to B. Fairfax Hall, 1966; exh. Colchester, The Minories, Oxford, Ashmolean Museum, Sheffield, Graves Art Gallery, 1969, 'Harold Gilman' (27).

The picture may be dated *c.* 1914.[1] In the use of clear colour applied in separate touches, it is characteristic of the changed methods adopted by Gilman from about 1910.

REPRODUCED. B. Fairfax Hall, *Paintings and drawings by Harold Gilman and Charles Ginner in the collection of Edward Le Bas* (1965), pl. 6 (in colour); Fitzwilliam Museum, *Annual Report* for 1967, pl. XII.

NOTES. [1] The picture has been precisely dated to 1914 by H. Wood Palmer (catalogues of the two exhibitions of 1963 in London and Edinburgh). As this date, however, is given without supporting justification, the less precise '*c.* 1914' given subsequently by B. Fairfax Hall (*Paintings and drawings by Harold Gilman and Charles Ginner in the collection of Edward Le Bas* (1965), p. 47) seems preferable.

GILPIN, Sawrey

1733–1807. Born at Carlisle. Pupil of Samuel Scott in London; from 1758 devoted himself to painting animals, especially horses. President of the Incorporated Society of Artists; R.A., 1797.

2751 A GREY ARAB

Canvas, 28 × 35⅞ in (71·1 × 91·2 cm). A grey horse, with darker legs and hind-quarters, a black mane and dark grey tail, stands in profile to the right facing a bay horse which stretches out its head across a fence. Background of moorland, with a castle in the distance to the left. Stormy sky, clearing at the left; the horses brightly illuminated against a dark landscape.

Bought from the Coppinger Prichard fund, with a contribution from the Friends of the Fitzwilliam Museum, 1945. Coll. Lord Rossmore, sold Christie's, 27 July 1945 (67), bt Laughton.

In the Rossmore sale, catalogued as *The Godolphin Arabian*, but this was a bay brown horse. The same motive and composition occur in a large painting by Gilpin of a horse named Jupiter, exhibited at the R.A. in 1792.[1] Gilpin is known to have painted, on occasion, 'cabinet versions' of his large pictures,[2] of which no. 2751 might be an example. H. B. Chalon (1770–1849) borrowed the motive of this picture on at least two occasions, one in a painting from the series of the Seven Passions of the Horse (with Leger, London, 1949), the other a painting of *Delphini* (coll. Lt-Col. G. H. Vere-Laurie, 1950).[3] Benjamin Marshall's painting of *Lop* (Royal Collection)[4] of about 1794, is very similar in the view and the action of the horse, and in the stormy setting.

REPRODUCED. Friends of the Fitzwilliam Museum, *Annual Report* for 1945; Basil Taylor, *Animal painting in England* (1955), pl. 35, and *Stubbs* (1971), fig. 7.

NOTES. [1] Rep. Walter Shaw Sparrow, *A book of sporting painters* (1931), p. 41. [2] Sparrow, *op. cit.*, p. 40. [3] Rep. *Country Life* (1950), CVII, 1301. [4] Oliver Millar, *The later Georgian pictures in the collection of Her Majesty the Queen*, 2 vols. (1969), I, p. 82, no. 938, rep. II, pl. 183.

GINNER, Charles

1878–1952. Born and trained in France; settled in London, 1910. Influenced by the Post-Impressionists. Original member of the Camden Town Group, 1911, and of the London Group, 1913; member of the New English Art Club. A.R.A., 1942. Painter of urban scenes and landscape.

PD. 209–1948 THE PUNT IN THE MILL STREAM

Canvas, 24 × 18 in (60·9 × 45·7 cm). The stream runs diagonally into the picture, across the centre, from right to left, where, in the middle distance, it passes under tall, over-arching trees. A grassy bank at the left slopes down to the water where the brown punt is moored; across the water, to the right, are tall, dense shrubs; at the extreme right is part of an open paling fence, dark brown. At the top, to the right of the trees, is a cloudy, light blue sky. The trees are a subdued grey-green, the shrubs yellow-green; both, with the sky, are reflected in the water. Signed lower left, 'C. GINNER'. Thick impasto.

Given by Professor Francis Wormald, C.B.E., Litt. D., F.B.A., 1948. Exh. London, Royal Institute of Oil Painters, 1933, '50th exhibition' (457); bought from the painter by F. Wormald, 1937; exh. Bedford, Cecil Higgins Art Gallery, 1969, 'The Camden Town Group' (18).

When exhibited in 1933, entitled *The lock house*; it depicts part of the garden at Paper Mill House, Standon, Hertfordshire.

PD. 9–1968 DAHLIAS AND CORNFLOWERS

Canvas, 20 × 23⅞ in (50·8 × 61·7 cm). On a grey ledge against an ochre wall, a tubular blue and white Chinese vase, containing a bunch of orange dahlias, stands at the left; at the right, in a large, white earthenware jug with blue and yellow decoration, is a bunch of dark blue cornflowers. In front, and between the two, is a small earthenware jug with blue and red decoration on light brown. Behind the large jug a plate stands against the wall with blue, green and red decoration. Signed lower right, 'C. GINNER'. Thick impasto.

Bequeathed by Thomas Balston, O.B.E., M.C., through the National Art-Collections Fund, 1968. Exh. London, Godfrey Phillips Galleries, 1929,[1] 'Paintings by Charles Ginner' (6); Arts Council, 1951, 'British painting 1925–1950, second anthology' (34), lent T. Balston; placed on loan to the City of Cambridge, 1972.

In the catalogue of the Arts Council exhibition of 1951 the picture is dated 1929.

NOTE. [1] The catalogue bears no date, but the library catalogue of the Victoria and Albert Museum assigns it to 1929.

PD. 75–1972 THE CHURCH OF ALL SOULS, LANGHAM PLACE, LONDON

Canvas, 30 × 21⅞ in (76·2 × 55·6 cm). Beyond an open foreground, in which are a number of pedestrians and a tall lamp standard, with an open-topped red bus and other traffic to the left, the portico of the church rises towards the right, surmounted by its circular tower and pointed spire, grey-buff in colour, with a dark group of statuary on a light yellow pedestal before it. The body of the church extends to the right, yellow with a mauve-grey roof, above which rises the grey roof of a taller building with red chimney stacks. To the left, across the line of traffic, is a square brown building, grey on the shadowed side, and beyond the church is another, grey-ochre in colour. Pale sky with cream clouds against blue. Dense, thick paint. Signed lower left, 'C GINNER'.

Bequeathed by Mrs M. E. L. Brownlow, in memory of Goldsworthy Lowes Dickinson and his family, 1972. Bt by Mrs Brownlow from the Redfern Gallery, London, 1955.

The women's dress indicates a date of about 1916, a period when Ginner frequently chose busy street scenes as his subjects.

REPRODUCED. *Burlington Magazine* (1973), cxv, 769, fig. 91.

GOETZE, Sigismund Christian Humbert

1866–1939. Born in London. Student at the Slade School of Art; entered the R.A. schools, 1885; exh. R.A. from 1888, and at the Paris Salon. Painter of portraits and landscape.

2541 RETURN OF THE SARDINE BOATS, DOUARNENEZ, BRITTANY

Canvas on plywood, 15⅜ × 25¾ in (39·0 × 65·4 cm). A small harbour in the foreground, full of shipping, has, mainly towards the left, several dark grey fishing boats with russet-brown sails; at the extreme left some blue nets hung up to dry. Beyond the harbour the grey waters of a bay recede to a distant shore of grey-green cliffs and hills. Pale blue and grey sky. Signed lower right, 'Sigismund Goetze'.

Most of Goetze's landscapes date from his later years, his earlier work having been mainly portraiture.

2542 FESTA DI SAN GIORGIO, PORTOFINO

Canvas on plywood, 15¼ × 25½ in. (38·7 × 64·8 cm). Buildings along two sides of a small harbour are seen diagonally across it; those towards the right, mainly light yellows, greys, pinks and greens in colour, are in sunlight, those towards the left, greyish-red broken by the red, white and green of the Italian flag, are in shadow. Behind the buildings at the right, which are dominated by the campanile of a church in the background, a steep hillside rises, covered with green trees; along the waterfront are crowds of people. Upper left, a patch of blue-grey sky. Signed lower right, 'Sigismund Goetze'.

2543 TAMARISK TREE, LAKE COMO (1934)

Canvas on plywood, 25¾ × 15¼ in (65·4 × 38·7 cm). In the foreground at the right an ancient tree with a grey-green trunk and light brown foliage, bends towards the left over the blue and grey water of the lake; at its foot a kneeling woman in blue and buff with a red head-scarf, is washing clothes, a basket beside her to the left, beyond which two grey posts project from the water. Across the lake is a line of buildings, behind which rises a high hill, blue-grey in colour, to right and left of it distant white mountain slopes. Sky of grey clouds with some small areas of blue.

Inscribed and signed at the back, 'Old Tamarisk, Lenno, Lago di Como, April 1934. S.G.'

2544 OLD BRIDGE, GLEN MORISTON

Canvas on plywood, 18⅜ × 25⅞ in (46·7 × 65·8 cm). Towards the right the high arch of a pink-grey bridge, dark grey under the arch, spans a stream, mainly brown in colour, which fills the foreground, pink-grey rocks at either side of it. To the left, beyond the bridge, a green embankment runs up to the line of the road, two green trees growing from it; from the rocks at the right rises a conifer. Blue and grey sky.

Inscribed and signed at the back, 'Old Bridge, Glen Moriston, Loch Ness. S. Goetze.'

2545 VANNES, BRITTANY

Canvas on plywood, $15\frac{1}{4} \times 25\frac{3}{8}$ in ($38{\cdot}7 \times 64{\cdot}5$ mc). Seen from above, a watercourse runs round to the left from the right foreground, the buff and grey embankment of a road rising from it at the right, and beside it at the left a cream-coloured house with a grey roof, at its foot figures washing clothes in the water. Behind the house rise some green trees, beyond them the grey-brown turret and walls of a castle. Beside the road at the right runs a copse of trees with brown foliage. Cream and blue-grey sky. Signed lower right, 'Sigismund Goetze'.

Exh. Huddersfield, Corporation Art Gallery, 1923, '14th autumn exhibition of pictures' (5).

A label at the back in the handwriting of the artist, is inscribed, 'Lavoir: from the bridge, Vannes. Brittany'.

Given by Mrs Sigismund Goetze, 1943.

GOLDING, John

b. 1929. Living artist.

PD. 116–1975 D.II (1974)

Acrylic on cotton duck, 65×78 in ($165{\cdot}1 \times 198{\cdot}2$ cm). The surface is divided into three vertical rectangles; the widest, at the right, is predominantly yellow, the narrowest, next to it, is blue, the third, at the left, is orange-yellow. At the left-hand of the painting, along both edges of the blue rectangle, and towards the right in the yellow one, are narrow vertical strips, of varying lengths, in light, variegated colours; similar, horizontal passages occur along the top and bottom edges of the painting.

Bought from the Gulbenkian and University Purchase Funds, 1975. Exh. Cambridge, Kettle's Yard Gallery, 1975, 'John Golding' (5); bt from the artist through the Rowan Gallery, London.

Dated 1974 in an inscription at the back.

GOODALL, Frederick

1822–1904. Born in London. Pupil of his father, the engraver Edward Goodall. His earlier work influenced by Sir David Wilkie's genre painting; after visits to Egypt in 1858/9 and 1870, painted mainly biblical and Egyptian subjects, but also some portraits and English landscape. R.A., 1862.

470 COTTAGE INTERIOR (1844) PLATE 40

Millboard, 13 × $16\frac{7}{8}$ in (33·0 × 42·8 cm). In a dark, timber-framed room, with a cavernous fireplace and a window at the back, a young man is seated at the right with a baby on his lap, beside a young woman turned towards the fireplace, who carries a terracotta dish. He wears a grey coat and buff breeches, the baby a pink skirt, ochre bodice and white cap, the woman a buff skirt, grey apron, purple-brown bodice and black bonnet. At the left of the fireplace stand a wooden chair and cradle. The roof and walls are in deep, transparent brown, the fireplace is a lighter and greyer brown. Signed and dated lower left, 'F. Goodall 1844'.

Given by Mrs Richard Ellison, 1862.

An early genre subject modelled on the work of Sir David Wilkie.

482 THE HEATH-CART (1850)

Wood, $11\frac{7}{8}$ × 16 in (30·2 × 40·6 cm). Among sandy dunes, with hills in the distance, a two-wheeled cart piled with bundles of heath and drawn by a donkey, fills the centre, moving forward towards the left. Seated in it are a woman in a green and blue skirt with red drapery over her head and shoulders, nursing a baby, and a dark-haired young girl in an orange skirt and white shawl. The donkey is led by a bare-footed small boy, wearing a blue jacket. To the right of the cart a man walks, with a stick under his left arm, smoking a clay pipe, dressed in brown coat, breeches and hat, with a blue waistcoat. Signed and dated lower left, 'F Goodall 1850'.

Given by Mrs Richard Ellison, 1862.

In his early years Goodall paid a visit to Ireland, and Irish genre subjects, of which this appears likely to be one, occur occasionally in his work.

REPRODUCED. Earp, p. 80.

GORE, Spencer Frederick

1878–1914. Born at Epsom, Surrey. Trained at the Slade School, London; influenced by W. R. Sickert and the Impressionist painters, later by the Post-Impressionists. Member of the New English Art Club, and a founder member of the Camden Town Group, 1911. Painter of theatrical scenes, domestic interiors and landscapes.

PD. 3–1955 THE GREEN DRESS PLATE 59

Canvas, 18 × 14 in (45·7 × 35·5 cm). The flesh is in tones of grey-pink, the skirt is green; the same green is used on the wall above the bed, which is orange in colour. The furniture is brown. The window glass is painted with touches of light cream on blue-grey.

Bequeathed by James William Freshfield, 1955. Coll. Frank Rutter (d. 1937) by 1935;[1] Mrs Frank Rutter; J. W. Freshfield by 1938;[2] exh. Bedford, Cecil Higgins Art Gallery, 1969, 'The Camden Town Group' (19); Colchester, The Minories,Oxford, Ashmolean Museum, Sheffield, Graves, Art Gallery, 1970, 'Spencer Gore' (17).

Painted under the influence of W. R. Sickert, with whom he formed a close friendship in his later twenties. The theme, the *contre-jour* lighting and the technical treatment can all be closely paralleled in Sickert's work of the period from about 1907 to about 1910; see, for example, *Mornington Crescent* in the National Gallery of South Australia, Adelaide,[3] and *Mornington Crescent, nude* (William E. Wallace).[4] The present picture, which must belong to the same period, has been dated 1908–9.[5]

REPRODUCED. Frank Rutter, *Modern masterpieces* (1935), I, p. 198; Mary Chamot, *Modern painting in England* (1937), p. 42, pl. II (colour); *Connoisseur* (1970), 174, 207.

NOTES. [1] Vol. I of his book *Modern masterpieces*, where it is reproduced, though without a date of publication came out in parts in 1935. [2] Lent by him to the Fitzwilliam Museum in this year. [3] Rep. pl. 29 in *Sickert* (1943), by Lillian Browse, who dates it '*circa* 1907', pl. 179 in *Sickert* (1973), by Wendy Baron, dated '1907'. [4] Rep. Browse, *Sickert* (1960), pl. 56, and dated to 1908, Baron, *op. cit.*, pl. 175, dated to 1907. [5] By John Woodeson in his catalogue of the Gore exhibition at Colchester, etc., 1970. He points out that the picture bears no Gilman label, explaining in a note that 'After Gore's death his widow and Harold Gilman went through all the pictures in her possession, and dated and numbered them. Many of these labels survive'.

GOWER, George

Active by 1573, d. 1596. Serjeant Painter to Elizabeth I, 1581; associate of Nicholas Hilliard, by whom strongly influenced; painter to the navy by 1593.

Follower of George Gower

M. 43 UNKNOWN LADY

Wood, 21⅞ × 17⅜ in (55·6 × 44·2 cm). Bust to front, head turned slightly left. Fair hair in tight curls, a small feathered cap towards the back of the head. Wears an embroidered white dress, with a lace-edged, blue-tinted ruff open across the straight bodice top. Pearls round the neck with a pearl drop; pearl ear-drops; a quadruple rope of pearls hangs outside the ruff; a triangular, jewelled gold pendant or brooch at the top of the bodice. Background of brown oak-tree branches against blue-grey.

Bequeathed by Charles Brinsley Marlay, 1912.

Manifestly cut down from a larger portrait, probably a three-quarter-length; datable from costume *c.* 1595–1600. Formerly catalogued as School of Marcus Gheeraerts the Younger,[1] but closely related to the Hilliardesque later work of George Gower, such, for example, as the *Lettice Knollys, Countess of Leicester* (Marquess of Bath).[2] Seemingly by the same hand are two three-quarter-length portraits of women of the same approximate date, the *Elizabethan lady* at Oxford (Bodelian Library),[3] and *Mary Fitton* (Commander the Hon. F. H. M. FitzRoy Newdegate), which has been described as close to Gower, if not by Gower himself, at a late stage of his career.[4]

REPRODUCED. Constable, XXVII, no. 43.

NOTES. [1] Constable, p. 35, no. 43. [2] Roy Strong, *The English Icon* (1969), p. 180, no. 133. [3] Mrs R. Lane Poole, *Catalogue of portraits in the possession of the University, colleges, city and county of Oxford* (1912), I, p. 23, no. 56; rep. Bodleian Picture Books, *Portraits of the sixteenth and early seventeenth centuries* (1952), no. 8. [4] Strong, *op. cit.*, p. 193, no. 146, and text of no. 145. Dr Strong considers the Fitzwilliam Museum portrait nearer to Robert Peake the Elder than to Gower (letter of 5 September 1974, Fitzwilliam Museum), but this view seems incompatible with the vigour of the drawing and with certain points of stylistic detail, such as the painting of the eye-balls.

GRANT, Duncan James Corrour

b. 1885. Living artist.

2395 MISS MARY COSS (1931)

Canvas covered board, 17⅜ × 13⅞ in (44·2 × 35·3 cm). Bust, turned and facing half right. Bare-headed, dark hair; long earrings. Wears a plain green dress, with a V-shaped neck opening. The shadows and half-tones in the flesh are of a green matching the dress; background in tones of olive-green and brown. Signed and dated upper right, 'D Grant / ·1 31'.

Bequeathed by Frank Hindley Smith, 1939. Exh. London, Thos Agnew & Sons Ltd, 1931, 'Recent pictures by British artists' (47),[1] where it was bought by F. Hindley Smith.

Painted in Rome in the spring of 1931.[2] Miss Coss married first Francis Cooke, and secondly Edward Barnes.

NOTES. [1] As *Head of a girl.* [2] Letters of 8 and 20 January 1948 from Miss Coss's sister, Mrs Margaret Flower (Fitzwilliam Museum).

PD. 81–1974 DESIGN FOR NEEDLEWORK

Card, 9⅜ in diameter (23·8 cm). Within a circle, against a cream background, is a stylised design of flowers and leaves, with stalks at the left; the flowers are orange, reddish mauve, cream, yellow and blue in colour, the stalks are deep mauve. Signed lower left, 'D Grant'.

Given by Keith Baynes, 1974. Exh. London, Thos Agnew & Sons Ltd, 1937, 'Recent work by Duncan Grant' (30).

GRAY, Maurice

1889–1918. Born in London. At Trinity College, Cambridge, 1908–9; student at the Slade School of Art, London; exh. New English Art Club.

2721 LANGDALE PIKES

Canvas, 24⅛ × 36 in (61·3 × 91·4 cm). At the left a dark ridge, brown and green in colour, runs down to the level valley bottom at the right, which is in tones of ochre and grey-green. Across the valley the hills slope steeply upwards, above them in the distance the outline of a moor, with the twin peaks of the Langdale Pikes standing up at the left above the dark ridge, all in tones of grey and ochre-grey. Cloudy sky of ochre-grey, with a break of orange-yellow at the left behind the Langdale Pikes. Signed lower right, 'M. Gray'.

Given by Mrs Alan Gray, the artist's mother, 1943.

The Langdale Pikes in the Lake District of Cumbria lie to the west of Ambleside; the view-point is near Crinkle Crags. Perhaps painted before the outbreak of the 1914–18 war, in which Gray was killed on active service.

GUNN, SIR JAMES

1893–1964. Born at Glasgow. Studied at the Glasgow School of Art, and the Académie Julian, Paris; President, Royal Society of Portrait Painters, 1953; R.A., 1961; kt, 1963. Portrait and landscape painter.

PD. 120–1975 LOUIS COLVILLE GRAY CLARKE (1959)

Canvas on millboard, $12\frac{1}{8} \times 11\frac{3}{8}$ in (30·7 × 28·9 cm). A small half-length in the middle of the rectangle of primed canvas. Seated to front, the fore-arms and hands resting upon a flat surface before him, a wineglass between the fingers of the right hand. Bare-headed, grey hair brushed back; grey moustache; the head held forward, looking down. Wears a black dinner-jacket.

Given by the Friends of the Fitzwilliam Museum, 1975. Bt for the Friends of the Fitzwilliam Museum from Thos Agnew & Sons Ltd, London.

Louis Clarke (1881–1960), archaeologist, anthropologist and connoisseur of art. Fellow of Trinity Hall, Cambridge; Curator of the University Museum of Archaeology and Ethnology, 1922–37; Director of the Fitz-william Museum, 1937–46; hon. LL.D., Cambridge, 1959. The painting, which is inscribed at the back, 'LOUIS CLARKE 1959 / FOR / DILET-TANTE', is a portrait study for the large conversation piece of members of the Society of Dilettanti, painted by Sir James Gunn between 1954 and 1959.[1] It shows fifteen members of the Society seated at a dining-table, or standing beside it, in the St James's Club, London, Dr Clarke being seated towards the end of the table at the left. This small study is an excellent likeness; another version, head only, is in the possession of the Earl Spencer at Althorp Park, Northamptonshire.[2] The conversation piece belongs to the Society of Dilettanti.[3]

REPRODUCED. Fitzwilliam Museum, *Annual Report* for 1975, pl. v.

NOTES. [1] Letter of 1 March 1976, from Mr Brinsley Ford, Secretary of the Society of Dilettanti (Fitzwilliam Museum). [2] K. J. Garlick, 'A catalogue of pictures at Althorp', *Walpole Society* (1976), XLV, 34, no. 253. [3] Exh. R.A., 1959 (376), rep. *The Royal Academy Illustrated* (1959), p. 63.

HARLOW, GEORGE HENRY

1787–1819. Born in London. Pupil of Sir Thomas Lawrence; exh. R.A. from 1805; in Italy, 1818–19. Portrait and history painter.

630 PROFESSOR CHARLES HAGUE PLATE 36

Canvas, 29½ × 24⅛ in (74·9 × 61·3 cm).[1] Wears the cream-coloured academic gown, lined with red, and hood of the same colours, of a Doctor of Music of Cambridge, over dark grey dress, with white choker. Dark brown background.

Purchased, 1904. Coll. R. Hague Ingram, from whom it was bought.

Charles Hague (1769–1821) became Professor of Music in the University of Cambridge in 1799, where he took the degree of Doctor of Music in 1801. The portrait may be presumed to be of about the same date as the mezzotint by Meyer of 1813, since it was published by W. D. Jones of Cambridge. A portrait of Hague offered to the Fitzwilliam Museum by his daughter, Miss Hague, in 1857, and refused, may have been the same as this. A probably contemporary copy of the portrait was in the Arthur F. Hill sale, Sotheby's, 18 June 1947, lot 13, bt Spiller.

ENGRAVED. Mezzotint by H. Meyer, published 1813.

REPRODUCED. J. W. Goodison, *Catalogue of Cambridge portraits* (1955) I, pl. XVIII.

NOTE. [1] Lined; dimensions of the painted surface.

HARRIS, Frederick Leverton

1864–1926. Born near Croydon. Business man, politician and connoisseur; Privy Councillor, 1916. Adopted the practice of painting about 1920, self-taught. Landscape painter.

1120 SOUILLAC (1923)

Wood, 14½ × 17½ in (36·8 × 44·5 cm). View across a small town set amidst low hills; the tall, square tower of a church is prominent to the left, in the right foreground is a diagonal stretch of field, partly plough. The predominating colours are the bright greens of grass and foliage, the reduced reds of tiled roofs, and the variegated buffs and greys of buildings and other roofs. Cloudy, blue summer sky. Signed and dated lower left, 'F. L. HARRIS / 1923'.[1]

Given by the Friends of the Fitzwilliam Museum, 1924. Exh. London, New English Art Club, 1923/4, 'Sixty-ninth Winter Exhibition' (11); bt from the artist.

Souillac is a small manufacturing town in France on the river Dordogne, in the *département* of Lot. To judge from exhibition catalogues, it was a favourite subject with the artist.

REPRODUCED. Friends of the Fitzwilliam Museum, *Annual Report* for 1924.

NOTE. [1] Now almost invisible, but plainly seen in the illustration to the *Annual Report* for 1924 of the Friends of the Fitzwilliam Museum.

PD. 1–1972 GEORGE MOORE (1920)

Canvas, 10 × 8⅛ in (25·4 × 20·6 cm). Seen to the knees, seated, almost in profile to the left, in a wing armchair, his hands held together before him. Bare-headed, white hair; fair moustache. He wears a dark blue suit; the chair is light green. Background of light brown panelling. Inscribed, dated and signed on the back of the canvas, 'Guilford Hill / Sandwich / Sept 1920 / F. J. Harris'.

Given by Peter Harris, the artist's nephew, 1972. Exh. London, Goupil Gallery, 1926, 'Fifty paintings by F. L. Harris' (55).[1]

George Augustus Moore (1852–1933), novelist, of Irish origin; lived principally in London. The identification of Guilford Hill has proved elusive. In 1920 Leverton Harris was living near Dorking, though he subsequently built himself a house at Sandwich called Small Downs House.

NOTE. [1] Unpriced in the catalogue, and thus evidently not for sale.

HAYMAN, Francis

1708–1776. Born in Exeter. Pupil of Robert Browning in London; taught at the St Martin's Lane Academy with Hubert Gravelot; foundation member of the R.A., 1768. His varied work included history paintings and genre, besides portraits and conversation pieces.

PD. 20–1951 GEORGE DANCE PLATE 12

Canvas, 21⅝ × 17 in (53·4 × 43·1 cm).[1] He wears a maroon coat, a gold-braided blue-green waistcoat, black breeches and white stockings; his wig is grey. The chairs are brown with crimson seats. The panelling is grey, the floor grey-buff; the picture has a gold frame.

Bequeathed by Roger Francis Lambe, 1951. Anon. sale (= Mrs Metges), Sotheby's, 6 June 1935 (4), bt Agnew;[2] bt by R. F. Lambe from Thos Agnew & Sons Ltd, London, 1935; exh. London, Geffrye Museum, 1972, 'George Dance' (1).

George Dance the elder (1700–1768), architect, was Surveyer to the City of London; he designed the Mansion House, begun in 1739, and a number of City churches. The portrait is identified as being of Dance in the

Sotheby sale of 1935, and this may be accepted as correct since a family source is suggested by the nature of the accompanying lots. Of three drawings, two are by Dance's son George, the other is by his son Nathaniel depicting his only daughter Hester, and a pair of portraits in oil, painter unidentified, are named as of Hester and her husband Nathaniel Smith. This is one of only two known portraits of Dance, the other, by his son Sir Nathaniel Dance-Holland, is in the Mansion House, London. From the costume, the date of the portrait appears to be about 1750.[3] The chairs, with their interlaced backs, recur in other paintings by Hayman, and it has been suggested that this design is derived from his association with Hubert Gravelot.[4]

REPRODUCED. Dorothy Stroud, *George Dance, architect* (1971), pl. 1; exhibition catalogue, *George Dance* (1972), Geffrye Museum, p. 7.

NOTES. [1] Lined; dimensions of the painted surface. [2] A written label at the back of the picture, not apparently of any great age, giving details of Dance and his children, is signed 'B. F. Scarlett', perhaps a one-time owner, but he remains unidentified. [3] Dated by Dorothy Stroud, *George Dance, architect* (1971), p. 74 and pl. 1, *c.* 1758, but no reason is given for this relatively precise dating. [4] Desmond Fitz-Gerald 'Gravelot and his influence on English furniture', *Apollo* (1969), xc, 140 ff.

HERKOMER, Sir Hubert von

1849–1914. Of Bavarian origin; came to England, 1857. Trained principally at the South Kensington art schools; R.A., 1890; kt, 1907. Drew for the illustrated papers; painter of subject pictures and portraits.

503* PROFESSOR HENRY FAWCETT (1886)

Canvas, $56\frac{1}{8} \times 44\frac{1}{8}$ in ($142{\cdot}5 \times 112{\cdot}0$ cm). To below the knees, seated, turned and facing half left; both arms rest on the chair arms, an academical cap in the right hand. Bare-headed, receding dark brown hair; clean-shaven, blue spectacles, eyes closed. Wears black academical gown over black clothes, dark blue knotted tie. Signed and dated lower left, 'H H 86'.

Given to the University of Cambridge by the subscribers, and placed in the Fitzwilliam Museum, 1887.

Henry Fawcett (1833–1884), fellow of Trinty Hall, who was accidentally blinded in 1858, became Professor of Political Economy at Cambridge in 1863, and Postmaster-General and a Privy Councillor in 1880. Shortly after his death a subscription was set on foot for a memorial to him, to consist of a portrait for presentation to the University,[1] which was accepted in 1887.[2]

REPRODUCED. *Principal pictures* (1912 edn), p. 74, (1929 edn), p. 92.

NOTES. [1] *Cambridge University Reporter* (1884–5), pp. 282–96. [2] *Op. cit.* (1886–7), p. 476.

HIGHMORE, JOSEPH

1692–1780. Born in London. Entered Kneller's academy in Great Queen Street, London, 1713; worked in London from 1715; founder member of the academy in St Martin's Lane, 1720; studied Rubens and van Dyck; influenced by French painting; retired to Canterbury, 1762. Painted portraits and some history subjects.

646 MRS ELIZABETH BIRCH AND HER DAUGHTER (1741) PLATE 8

Canvas, $46\frac{7}{8} \times 38\frac{1}{4}$ in (119·1 × 97·2 cm).[1] Mrs Birch wears a dress of oyster satin, revealing a blue lining at the sleeve and at the bodice opening; black hair. Her daughter wears a blue dress with a pink scarf; dark brown hair, with a pink bow and a white feather. The garland of flowers is yellow, pink and white. The chair is brown, set against foliage of a yellowish brown. Grey-brown architecture in the background, with grey clouds in a blue sky; the trees are blue-green and ochre yellow. Signed and dated on the chair, 'Jos: Highmore. pinx: 1741'.

Given by Charles Fairfax Murray, 1908. With Eugene Benjamin, of New Bond Street, London; posthumous sale of his stock, Christie's, 23 November 1898 (546), bt Agnew.

Cleaned 1966. A manuscript label at the back of the picture describes her as 'the famous Mrs Elizabeth Birch', but the nature of her fame remains obscure.

REPRODUCED. *Principal pictures* (1912 edn), p. 76, (1929 edn), p. 94; *Antiques*, New York (1955), LXVII, 47.

NOTE. [1] Lined; dimensions of the painted surface.

PD. 19–1951 UNKNOWN MAN (1745) PLATE 8

Canvas, 19 × 14 in (48·3 × 35·6 cm). He wears a dark blue coat with silver buttons, a yellow waistcoat with silver lace, red breeches, white stockings and black shoes. The musket is brown and grey. The panelling and door in the background, and the floor, are brown. Signed and dated (indistinctly) lower left, 'Jos: Highmore pinx: 1745'.

Bequeathed by Roger Francis Lambe, 1951. With Williams & Sutch, London; bought from them by Leggatt Bros., who sold it to R. F. Lambe, 1938; exh. London, R.A., 1956–7, 'British portraits' (179); Iveagh Bequest, Kenwood, 1963, 'Paintings by Joseph Highmore' (27).

Perhaps a painting of an actor in a theatrical rôle, and so described when sold by Leggatt's to R. F. Lambe. A characteristic example of the small whole-lengths in a lively rococo style painted by Highmore during the 1740s; compare some of the figures in the *Pamela* paintings of about 1744 below, pp. 102–5, nos. M.Add. 6–9.

REPRODUCED. Catalogue, *Paintings by Joseph Highmore* (1963), Iveagh Bequest, Kenwood, pl. VII; *Apollo* (1963), LXXVIII, 135.

M.Add. 6–9 Four subjects from Samuel Richardson's novel *Pamela*. The references are to the Everyman edition, vol. I, 1965, vol. II, 1963.

M.Add. 6 PAMELA AND MR B. IN THE SUMMER HOUSE (I, pp. 11–12)

PLATE 7

Canvas, $24\frac{3}{4} \times 29\frac{3}{4}$ in ($62{\cdot}9 \times 75{\cdot}6$ cm).[1] Mr B's coat is brown with gold lace, his waistcoat white, his breeches scarlet, with white stockings and black shoes. Pamela's dress is white, shadowed with crimson. The walls are light brown, the floor light brown and grey, the chairs green.

M.Add. 7 PAMELA LEAVES MR B'S HOUSE IN BEDFORDSHIRE (I, p. 85)

Canvas, $24\frac{5}{8} \times 29\frac{3}{4}$ in ($62{\cdot}6 \times 75{\cdot}6$ cm).[1] In front of the lower walls of a large house, warm grey in colour, a small coach (chariot) stands drawn by four dark brown horses, directed towards the left. The coach is black and dark grey, with red wheels, with a coat of arms on the door; in it sits Pamela, looking away from the house, in a white and brown dress, wearing a straw hat; the coachman seated on the box wears a long blue coat with yellow collar and cuffs. A woman (Mrs Jervis) and two men stand at the door of the house; Mr B. watches from an upper window.

M.Add. 8 PAMELA SHOWS MR WILLIAMS A HIDING PLACE FOR THEIR LETTERS (I, p. 104)

Canvas, $24\frac{3}{4} \times 29\frac{5}{8}$ in ($62{\cdot}9 \times 75{\cdot}3$ cm).[1] In a garden with high pink walls and a stone doorway at the right, Pamela in white and Mr Williams in a black cassock and academical gown, with white bands and a black tricorne hat, stand talking together in the centre foreground; Pamela indicates a sunflower growing against the wall at the right to mark the hiding place for their letters. At the left a stout woman (Mrs Jewkes), in a red dress, ochre-coloured in the lights, standing on a blue-green area of lawn, breaks a branch from a shrub; the rest of the ground is in tones of brown. In the background, trees of a bluish-green rise above the garden walls against a blue sky with warm cream clouds.

M.Add. 9 PAMELA TELLS A NURSERY TALE (II, p. 462) PLATE 7

Canvas, $24\frac{5}{8} \times 29\frac{3}{4}$ in (62·6 × 75·6 cm).[1] Pamela is in blue, the seated woman (Miss Goodwin) in yellow, the one sewing in brown, the standing figure at the left in yellow, the woman beyond her in light blue. The boy's coat is scarlet, the two younger of the other children are in white, the third in grey; the cradle is cane yellow. The walls and floor are in tones of brown; the curtains of the bed are green.

Bought from the Marlay Fund, 1920. Joseph Highmore's sale, London, Langford's, 5 March 1762 (24)[2]; coll. Major Dermot McCalmont, Cheveley Park, Cambridgeshire;[3] his sale, Christie's, 26 November 1920 (130),[4] bt A. H. Buttery; purchased from him by the National Gallery, whence acquired by the Fitzwilliam Museum;[5] M.Add. 9, exh. London, R.A., 1934, 'British art' (54); M.Add. 6, 8, 9, London, Iveagh Bequest, Kenwood, 1963, 'Paintings by Joseph Highmore' (16, 20, 26); M.Add. 6, 9, Kenwood, 1968, 'French taste in English painting' (29a, 29b).

The engravings show that all four have been cut laterally, M.Add. 6 and 8 at both sides, M.Add. 7 at the left, M.Add. 9 at the right. Four of the series of twelve paintings, of about 1744, of subjects from Samuel Richardson's novel *Pamela*, which was published in two parts in 1740 and 1741. The novel recounts, in the form of letters mostly written by Pamela, how she was confided by her mistress, upon her death, to the care of her son, 'Mr B.', who, however, sets out to seduce her, but failing in his purpose ends by marrying her. The novel had a great success,[6] and in February 1744 Highmore advertised for subscription, in the *London Daily Post and General Advertiser*, a series of twelve prints 'representing the most remarkable adventures of Pamela'; ten of the paintings could be seen at his house in London.[7] The series was published the following year, with the title, 'The Life of Pamela on twelve engravings with descriptions in French and English'. The descriptions explain the subject of each scene. In his advertisement, Highmore goes on to say that he has 'endeavoured to comprehend her whole story as well as to preserve a connection between the several pictures, which follow each other as parts successive and dependent so as to complete the subject'. The prints were thus designed as a publication extraneous to the novel, conceived as a pictorialised version of it,[8] not as illustrations. Yet Highmore was sufficiently aware of a degree of incompatibility between his purpose of pictorial narration and the ramifications of a novelist's theme, to realise the necessity for the 'descriptions'. It seems a somewhat anomalous undertaking despite the wide popularity of the novel, though it was not unsuccessful, as a second issue of the prints appeared in 1762. After being secured by the National Gallery, the twelve paintings were divided up between the Fitzwilliam Museum, the Tate Gallery, London, and the National Gallery of Victoria, Melbourne, each taking four. The Fitzwilliam Museum paintings are respectively the subjects numbered 2, 5, 6 and 12 in the series of engravings. The remaining eight and their places in the series are as follows: Tate Gallery, no. 3573, *Mr B. finds Pamela writing* (1); no. 3574, *Pamela in the bedroom with Mrs Jewkes* (7); no. 3575, *Pamela is married* (9); no. 3576, *Pamela asks Sir Jacob Swinford's blessing* (10): National Gallery of Victoria, no. 1114/3, *Pamela fainting* (3); no. 1115/3, *Pamela preparing to go home* (4); no. 1116/3, *Pamela greets her father* (8); no. 1117/3, *Pamela and Lady Davers* (10). In these paintings of Highmore's maturity, the stylistic influence of Hubert Gravelot, who worked in England from 1723 to 1746, is noticeable both in the invention of some of the scenes and in some of the individual figures.

ENGRAVED. All in reverse, dated 1 July 1745.

M. Add. 6. By L. Truchy, with text 'Mr. B. expostulating with Pamela in the Summer house after some liberties taken. Mrs. Jewkes (who is seen through the Window) having just left her'.

M. Add. 7. By A. Benoist, with text 'Pamela setting out in the travelling Chariot (for her Father's, as she is made to believe) takes her farewell of Mrs. Jervis; Mr. B. observing her from the window; by whose private order she is carried into Lincolnshire'.

M. Add. 8. By A. Benoist, with text 'Pamela being now in the custody of Mrs. Jewkes, seizes an occasion (as they are walking in the garden) to propose a correspondence with Mr. Williams, in order to contrive an Escape, who agree to hide their letters near the Sunflower'.

M. Add. 9. By A. Benoist, with text 'Pamela with her Children and Miss Goodwin to whom she is telling her nursery tales. This last Piece leaves her in full possession of the peaceable fruits of her Virtue long after having surmounted all the difficulties It had been exposed to'.

REPRODUCED. Constable, pl. XXVIII (M. Add. 6–9); Philip James, *Children's books of yesterday* (1933), p. 18 (M. Add. 9);[9] *Commemorative catalogue of the exhibition of British art, Royal Academy of Arts...1934* (1935), pl. XXII (M. Add. 9); *Kunst og Kultur*, Oslo (1958), 41, p. 239 (M. Add. 7); Ellis Waterhouse, *Painting in Britain, 1530 to 1790* (1953), pl. 106 (M. Add. 9); exhibition catalogue, *Paintings by Joseph Highmore*, Iveagh Bequest, Kenwood (1963), pl. IVA, IVB (M. Add. 6, 8); *Country Life* (1974) CLV, 316 (M. Add. 6).

NOTES. [1] Lined; dimensions of the painted surface. [2] Lot 24 included the complete series of twelve paintings; see below. [3] He was the son of Col. Sir Hugh McCalmont, K.C.B., and inherited the Cheveley estate from his cousin Harry Leslie Blundell McCalmont (1861–1902), who had bought it in 1892. [4] Lot 130 included the complete series of twelve paintings; see below. They were catalogued as illustrations by Cornelis Troost to Samuel Richardson's *Clarissa Harlowe*; the correct identifications were published in the *Times Literary Supplement*, no. 987, 16 December 1920, 864, unsigned but by C. H. Collins Baker. [5] The rest of the series was divided up between, respectively, the Tate Gallery, London, and the National Gallery of Victoria, Melbourne; see below. [6] In 1742 an edition appeared illustrated with engravings by Hubert Gravelot, some after Francis Hayman, some after his own designs, but Highmore's paintings owe nothing to these illustrations. [7] W. T. Whitley, *Artists and their friends in England, 1700–1799*, 2 vols. (1928), I, p. 48, quoted more correctly and more fully, and the source identified, by Elizabeth Johnston in her catalogue of the exhibition at the Iveagh Bequest, Kenwood, London, in 1963, 'Paintings by Joseph Highmore', p. 22. [8] For Highmore's views of the value of the graphic immediacy of pictorial narration, see Johnston, *op. cit.*, p. 23, quoting from *The Gentleman's Magazine* (1766), XXXVI, 353–6. [9] Reproduced from an engraving by L. P. Boitard, forming the frontispiece to *The court of Queen Mab*, London (1752), fairy stories by the Comtesse d'Aulnoi, showing the picture in an upright form with various modifications.

HILTON, Roger

1911–1975. Born in London. Student at the Slade School of Art, London, 1929–31; in Paris and London, 1931–9; first one-man exhibition, 1936; teacher of art; worked in Corwall.

PD. 35–1972 LARGE ORANGE (NEWLYN) JUNE 1959

Canvas, 60 × 54 in (152·4 × 137·2 cm). On the orange-coloured ground is a large circular form of deeper orange; upon its upper part to the left is a square black form, from which two black lines run upwards; towards the top at the right is a rectangular form of blue and black. Four small white dots are spaced along the upper margin of the black form; a broken white line crosses the two black lines, and a similar, double line below crosses the orange and the black form.

Given by the Contemporary Art Society, 1972. Bt from the artist by the Waddington Galleries, London; their exhibition, 1960, 'Roger Hilton' (12); coll. R. Alistair McAlpine; given by him to the Contemporary Art Society, London, 1971; exh. London, Arts Council, Serpentine Gallery, 1974, 'Roger Hilton' (36).

Painted at Newlyn in Cornwall, where the artist had his studio.

REPRODUCED. Exhibition catalogue, *Roger Hilton* (1974), Arts Council, (colour).

HITCHENS, Sydney Ivon

b. 1893. Living artist.

PD. 8–1962 CHESTNUT FOREST

Canvas, $20\frac{1}{4} \times 41\frac{3}{8}$ in ($51{\cdot}4 \times 105{\cdot}1$ cm). The forms make a colour pattern of browns, ochres and greys in varying tones and intensities, with some white passages due to the priming of the canvas. Signed lower left, 'Hitchens'.

Given by the Cambridge Contemporary Art Trust, 1962. Bt from the artist,[1] by the Cambridge Contemporary Art Trust, 1952.

Painted about 1950, in the autumn, in West Sussex where the artist was living.[2]

NOTES. [1] Information kindly supplied by the artist (letter of 6 August 1970, Fitzwilliam Museum). [2] See n. [1]; his residence was at Lavington Common, Petworth.

PD. 2–1968 THE BROWN BOAT (1961)

Canvas, $18\frac{3}{4} \times 56\frac{3}{4}$ in. ($47{\cdot}7 \times 144{\cdot}2$ cm). A rowing boat is at the further side of a small piece of water, which is surrounded by grassy banks and trees. The water is ochre and blue-green, the banks and trees are broadly treated in green, mauve, blue-green and dark grey, with some areas of white due to the priming of the canvas. Signed lower left, 'Hitchens'.

Given by Howard Bliss, 1968. Bt by the donor from the artist, 1961 or 1962.

Painted at the artist's home at Lavington Common, West Sussex, during the summer of 1961.[1]

NOTE. [1] Information from the artist to the donor, January 1970.

PD. 3–1968 THE BOAT HOUSE (1956)

Canvas, 20 × 33⅛ in (50·8 × 84·2 cm). A large boat house, with a gabled roof, stands at the far end of a sheet of water, on which floats a brown boat. To the right of the boat house are dark trees, above them a cloudy blue sky, brown-ochre at the right. The trees and their reflections in the water are dark, warm grey; the boat house and a bank to the right are green. A layer of mist behind the boat house is amethyst, reflected in the water. Indeterminate forms in blue close the composition at the left.

Given by Howard Bliss, 1968. Bt by the donor from the artist, through the Leicester Galleries, London, probably in December 1956.

Painted in Sussex, 1956, in the early morning.[1]

REPRODUCED. Medici Society, London; Fitzwilliam Museum, *Annual Report* for 1968, pl. XII.

NOTE. [1] Information from the artist to the donor, January 1970.

PD. 17–1974 BLUE DOOR, HOUSE AND OUTSIDE (1972)

Canvas, 21 × 51⅞ in (53·3 × 131·7 cm). A design predominantly in long, rectangular areas of pure colour, mauve, orange-brown, light blue and sage-green; the mauve and light blue areas, mainly horizontal in direction, occupy the upper centre and the upper right; the orange-brown, mainly vertical, are at the left and right, and in the centre; the sage-green, in rounded shapes, are in the centre and towards the right. Dated lower right, '72'.

Given anonymously, 1974. With the Waddington Galleries, London; their exhibition, 1973, 'Ivon Hitchens, retrospective exhibition' (34); sold to Dr M. I. A. Hunter.

One of a number of related paintings, the 'Blue Door Series'; it is regarded by the artist, together with three others, as the more important of this group.[1]

REPRODUCED. *Ivon Hitchens*, ed. Alan Bowness (1973), pl. 117 (colour).

NOTE. [1] Letter from the artist, 2 June 1975 (Fitzwilliam Museum); two of the other three are reproduced in *Ivon Hitchens*, ed. Alan Bowness (1973), pl. 115, 116 (colour).

HOGARTH, William

1697–1764. Born in London. Painter and engraver. Apprenticed to an engraver on silver plate; about 1720 began engraving prints, and entered Vanderbank's and Chéron's academy in St Martin's Lane. His early paintings mostly small-scale portrait groups; painted genre subjects, including moralities, which began with *The harlot's progress* about 1731; his full-scale portraits painted principally between 1740 and 1745; aspired to be a history painter; Serjeant Painter to the King, 1757. Lived and worked in London.

21 GEORGE ARNOLD PLATE 10

Canvas, $35\frac{5}{8} \times 27\frac{7}{8}$ in ($90{\cdot}5 \times 70{\cdot}8$ cm).[1] The coat and waistcoat are silvery grey, the wig pale creamish grey with brown shadows; rubicund complexion; brown-grey background.[2]

Bequeathed by the Rev. James William Arnold, D.D. (d. 1865), received 1873.[3] Coll. George Arnold, of Ashby Lodge, Northamptonshire; descended to his great-great-grand-daughter, Georgeana Coape (d. 1849);[4] sale by Phillips (of London) at Ashby Lodge, 20–2 April, 1845 (133),[5] bt Rev. J. W. Arnold, D.D.; exh. London, R.A., 1879, 'Old Masters' (32); Tate Gallery, 1971–2, 'Hogarth' (107).

Cleaned 1971. George Arnold (1683–1766), was the fifth son of George Arnold of St Martin's in the Fields, London, Secretary of War for Scotland 1724. In 1718 he bought an estate at Ashby St Ledgers, Northamptonshire, and there built, in 1722, Ashby Lodge, where he resided.[6] This portrait, and no. 24, of his daughter Frances, are said to have been painted when Hogarth was on a visit to Ashby Lodge.[7] Frances Arnold was born in 1721, and from the costume in both and her apparent age, these two portraits may be dated about 1738–40.[8]

ENGRAVED. Woodcut in *The Magazine of Art* (1885), VIII, 44.

REPRODUCED. *Principal pictures* (1912 edn), p. 79, (1929 end), p. 98; R. B. Beckett, *Hogarth* (1949), pl. 101; Carl Winter, *The Fitzwilliam Museum* (1958), pl. 77; F. Antal, *Hogarth and his place in European art* (1962), pl. 65a; *Burlington Magazine* (1965), CVII, p. 64, fig. 10; G. Baldini, *L'opera completa di Hogarth, pittore* (1967), no. 91; Ronald Paulson, *Hogarth, his life, art and times*, 2 vols. (1971), I, pl. 169b; Lawrence Gowing, exhibition catalogue, *Hogarth* (1971), Tate Gallery, p. 45.

NOTES. [1] Lined; dimensions of the painted surface. [2] R. B. Beckett, *Hogarth* (1949), p. 48, no. 101. [3] Bequeathed with a life-interest to his widow. [4] Daughter and heiress of George Henry Arnold; she married James Coape in 1840. [5] Presumably by James Coape, though no seller is specified in the sale catalogue; his eldest son, Henry Fraser James Coape, took the name of Coape-Arnold. [6] Ronald Paulson, *Hogarth, his life, art and times*, 2 vols. (1971), I, p. 448, describes him as a picture collector, but the catalogue of the sale at Ashby Lodge in 1854 states that the collection of pictures was formed by Lumley Arnold (1723–1781), his son and heir. [7] George Baker, *The history and antiquities of the county of Northamtpon* (1822–30), I, p. 248. [8] Austin Dobson, *William Hogarth* (1902 edn) p. 175, (1907 edn), p. 206, includes this and no. 24 under 'Paintings of uncertain date'; Beckett, *op. cit.*, p. 48, nos. 101 and 100 respectively, dates them 'Possibly *c.* 1738'; Paulson, *op. cit.*, I, p. 449, dates them *c.* 1740.

24 FRANCES ARNOLD PLATE II

Canvas, $35\frac{5}{8} \times 27\frac{3}{4}$ in (90·5 × 70·5 cm).[1] Black hair; pale, grey-yellow dress with white lace, the pearl necklace tied with a blue ribbon. Red chair. Brown-grey background.[2]

Bequeathed by the Rev. James William Arnold. D.D. (d. 1865), received 1873.[3] Coll. George Arnold, of Ashby Lodge, Northamptonshire; descended to his great-great-grand-daughter, Georgeana Coape (d. 1849); sale by Phillips (of London) at Ashby Lodge, 20–2 April 1854 (134), bt Rev. J. W. Arnold, D.D.; exh. London, R.A., 1879, 'Old Masters' (36); Paris, 1909, 'Cent portraits de femmes' (13); London, Tate Gallery, 1971–2, Hogarth' (106).

Cleaned 1971. Frances Arnold, born 1721, was the youngest daughter of George Arnold, of Ashby Lodge, Northamptonshire. See his portrait by Hogarth, no. 21 above.

ENGRAVED. Woodcut in *The Magazine of Art* (1885), VIII, 40.

REPRODUCED. *Principal pictures* (1912 edn), p. 80, (1929 edn), p. 97; Austin Dobson, *William Hogarth* (1902 edn), p. 132, (1907 edn), p. 206; R. B. Beckett, *Hogarth* (1949), pl. 100; G. Baldini and G. Mandel, *L'opera completa di Hogarth, pittore* (1967), no. 94; Ronald Paulson, *Hogarth, his life, art and times*, 2 vols. (1971), I, pl. 196a; Lawrence Gowing, exhibition catalogue, *Hogarth* (1971), Tate Gallery, p. 44, no. 106.

NOTES. [1] Lined; dimensions of the painted surface. [2] R. B. Beckett, *Hogarth* (1949), p. 48, no. 100. [3] Bequeathed with Hogarth no. 21 above; see no. 21 for further details of the provenance.

647 A MUSICAL PARTY, THE MATHIAS FAMILY

Canvas, $24\frac{5}{8} \times 29\frac{3}{4}$ in (62·6 × 75·6 cm).[1] In a panelled room with brown walls and floor, and a chimney-piece in the background surmounted by a picture, a party of six men and two women is grouped round a music-stand in the centre and a tea-table at the right. A seated woman in a pale golden dress pours out tea at the table, a kettle on a stand at her left, and a boy in grey-green kneels in front of the table taking a piece of paper from a cat; at her right sits a man in dark blue, with a seated woman in pink holding a tea-cup beyond him, both turning towards the woman at the table. Beyond the woman in pink, a man in light brown sits beside the music-stand tuning a violin, with a standing man in dark brown beside him, looking to the left towards a seated man in light brown holding a bassoon and another, in golden brown, with a violoncello, both beside the music-stand, in front of which sits a young man in a long blue coat wearing a loose, pink cap, holding a violin under his right arm.[2]

Given by Charles Fairfax Murray, 1908. Coll. Thomas James Mathias (1754(?)–1835); exh. London, B.I., 1817 (158); coll. George, 5th Earl of Essex (1758–1839);[3] exh. London, R.A., 1884, 'Old masters' (22); Grosvenor Gallery, 1887–8, 'A century of British art from 1737 to 1837' (35); Essex sale, Christie's, 22 July 1893 (43), bt Agnew; bt from Thos Agnew & Sons Ltd by Robert Rankin, 1894; his sale, Christie's, 14 May 1898 (40), bt Agnew; coll. C. Fairfax Murray by 1902;[4] exh. London, R.A., 1908, Winter Exhibition (89), lent Murray.

Hogarth's family and conversation pieces mostly belong to the early years of his career as a painter, beginning about the time of his marriage in 1729. From the type of composition and the style of painting, this picture may be dated to the first years of the 1730s, which accords with the apparent date of the costume. When it was lent to the B.I. in 1817 by T. J. Mathias, it was entitled *A musical party, portraits of Mr Mathias's Family*, which must be accepted as correct, though subsequently the persons were identified differently.[5] Little information is available about the Mathias family.[6] T. J. Mathias was the son of Vincent, who died in 1782 aged seventy-two, so that the older people in the picture must be of the generation of Vincent's father. It is known that Vincent Mathias had two brothers, James, who also died in 1782, aged seventy-one, and Gabriel. Perhaps, therefore, the young violinist in the centre depicts one of these three.

REPRODUCED. *Principal pictures* (1912 edn), p. 81, (1929 edn), p. 99; R. B. Beckett, *Hogarth* (1949), pl. 22.

NOTES. [1] Lined; dimensions of the painted surface. [2] R. B. Beckett, *Hogarth* (1949), p. 45, no. 22, dated *c.* 1731. [3] The catalogue of the Essex sale in 1893, comprising nine lots of English pictures, states that the 5th earl had acquired them 'early in the century'. In 1817 T. J. Mathias went to Italy for the sake of his health, where he remained for the rest of his life, but no Mathias sale is recorded. [4] Austin Dobson and Sir W. Armstrong, *William Hogarth* (1902), p. 184. [5] An old label at the back identifies the members of the party as follows. The young man in the centre and the woman pouring out tea, Mr and Mrs Millar, the host and hostess; proceeding round the circle from Mrs Millar, Mr Locke, Mrs Freke, Henry Needler, Mr Freke (standing), Mr Cottle, Mr Detson. 'Mr Millar' was Andrew Millar (1707–1768), publisher; Henry Needler (1685–1760), musical amateur; 'Mr Freke', John Freke (1688–1756), surgeon, 'Mrs Freke' was his wife; 'Mr Cottle' was a King's Council. The ages at the approximate date of the picture of those people whose dates are known are not incompatible with their appearance. At the R.A. in 1884, the Grosvenor Gallery in 1887–8, the Essex and Rankin sales, the names of some of these people are given, but with the interpolation of Hogarth's. [6] See *The early diary of Frances Burney*, ed. A. R. Ellis, 2 vols. (1907), II, 'Some letters and fragments of the journal of Charlotte Ann Burney', pp. 302, 306, 308, 309–10, 312; *The Gentleman's Magazine* (1782), part II, p. 360; *Dictionary of National Biography* (1894), XXXVII, 47.

648 DR BENJAMIN HOADLY PLATE 8

Canvas, $23\frac{7}{8} \times 18\frac{7}{8}$ in ($60{\cdot}7 \times 47{\cdot}9$ cm).[1] His coat and breeches are brown, with black stockings and shoes. The chair has a dark brown frame and tan-brown upholstery. Buff-coloured floor, grey-green panelling, the bust of Newton is brown. Blue sky and blue-green trees.[2]

Given by Charles Fairfax Murray, 1908. Smart sale, London, Foster & Son, 16 January 1850 (32), bt White;[3] William Benoni White sale, Christie's, 24 May 1879 (200), bt Cox; coll. Joseph Prior, Cambridge (1834–1918); C. Fairfax Murray by 1902;[4] exh. London, R.A., 1908, Winter Exhibition (82), lent Murray; Tate Gallery, 1971–2, 'Hogarth' (103).

Cleaned 1971. Benjamin Hoadly (1706–1757), physician, was a Doctor of Medicine of Cambridge, and a Fellow of the Royal Society; from 1742 to 1745 he was physician to the Royal Household. He wrote a successful comedy, *The suspicious husband*, performed in 1747. The portrait belongs to a class of small whole-length portraits, conceived after the manner of a conversation piece, which Hogarth was painting during the 1730s;[5] very similar in conception is the Thomas Western, dated 1736.[6] It is so close in facial appearance, the position and the lighting of the head, to Hogarth's portrait of Hoadly, dated 1740, at Dublin (National Gallery of Ireland, no. 398), that it can hardly be very different in date, and may be assigned to the late 1730s, which is in accordance with the costume.[7] The bust of Isaac Newton in the background corresponds closely with a marble by L. F. Roubiliac at Trinity College, Cambridge; it has been said that Roubiliac gave Hogarth a terracotta similar to this bust.[8]

REPRODUCED. *The masterpieces of Hogarth* (1911), p. 16; *Principal pictures* (1912 edn), p. 83, (1929 edn), p. 102; C. R. L. Fletcher and Emery Walker, *Historical portraits* (1919), III, p. 90; R. B. Beckett, *Hogarth* (1949), pl. 81; Frederick Antal, *Hogarth and his place in European art* (1962), pl. 39b; Ronald Paulson, *Hogarth, his life, art and times*, 2 vols. (1971), I, pl. 159; Lawrence Gowing, exhibition catalogue, *Hogarth* (1971), Tate Gallery, p. 44.

NOTES. [1] Lined; dimensions of the painted surface. [2] R. B. Beckett, *Hogarth* (1949), p. 53, no. 81. [3] One of 'Nineteen lots removed from a mansion near Peterborough' in a mixed sale; in the copy of the sale catalogue in the library of the Victoria and Albert Museum the nineteen lots are endorsed in the margin 'Smart'. [4] Austin Dobson and Sir W. Armstrong, *William Hogarth* (1902), p. 181. [5] Beckett, *op. cit.*, p. 14. [6] Beckett, *op. cit.*, p. 61, no. 80, rep. pl. 80. [7] Beckett, *op. cit.*, p. 53, no. 81, dates it 'Probably of the 1730s'; Ronald Paulson, *Hogarth, his life, art and times*, 2 vols. (1971), dates it '1737 or 1738' (I, p. 430), and 'around 1738' (I, p. 443). [8] Katherine A. Esdaile, *The life and works of Louis François Roubiliac* (1928), p. 100, quoting from a Christie sale catalogue of 1864. According to this account, Hogarth subsequently sold the terracotta; but a terracotta bust of Newton was lot 56 in the sale after her death of Mrs Hogarth's collection, which took place on 24 April 1790.

727 THE BENCH

Canvas backed onto wood, $6\frac{7}{8} \times 7\frac{1}{8}$ in (17·4 × 18·1 cm). Seated in a row are three half-length figures in legal robes and wigs, all turned slightly to the left, the direction of the row receding slightly into the picture from right to left; behind the principal figure at the right-hand end of the row, and to the right of him, stands a fourth man, turned in profile to the left. The robes of the principal figure, who holds a quill pen in his right hand, are scarlet and white; the figure to the left of him, who is dozing and holds a rolled paper in his right hand, wears dark grey robes with deep white cuffs; the end figure, who sleeps against the shoulder of the second man, is in black; the standing figure, who reads a paper, is also in black, with a black wig. In the background a grey-brown column rises at the right, and to left of it, on a dark grey wall, is part of an achievement of arms.[1]

Given by Charles Fairfax Murray, 1911. Coll. Sir George Hay (1715–1778); his executor, S. Edwards, by 1781;[2] Edward Cheney of Badger Hall, Shropshire (1803–1884); descended by family inheritance to Francis Capel-Cure, of Badger Hall (1854–1933); his sale, Christie's, 6 May 1905 (85), bt C. Fairfax Murray; exh. London, R.A., 1908, Winter Exhibition (84); Tate Gallery, 1971–2, 'Hogarth' (206).

Cleaned 1971. The date of Hogarth's first engraving after this picture, 1758, has usually been accepted as the date when it was painted,[3] but a dating as early as 1753–4 has been suggested.[4] It appears from a lengthy inscription attached to this engraving that the picture should be regarded as an exemplification of Hogarth's theories on the pictorial means of expressing character.[5] The painting is said to depict the bench of judges in the Court of Common Pleas, the principal figure in red robes being named as Sir John Willes, Chief Justice of the Common Pleas, on his right Henry Bathurst (later 2nd Earl Bathurst), next to him William Noel, and behind Willes, Sir Edward Clive.[6]

ENGRAVED. By Hogarth, in 1758 and 1764.[7]

REPRODUCED. *Principal pictures* (1912 edn), p. 84, (1929 edn), p. 101; R. B. Beckett, *Hogarth* (1949), pl. 189; Ronald Paulson, *Hogarth, his life, art and times*, 2 vols. (1971), II, pl. 282a; Lawrence Gowing, exhibition catalogue, *Hogarth* (1971), Tate Gallery, p. 85.

NOTES. [1] R. B. Beckett, *Hogarth* (1949), p. 63, no. 189. [2] John Ireland, *Hogarth illustrated*, 2nd edn, 3 vols. (1791), II, p. 321; Austin Dobson, *William Hogarth* (1907), p. 277; J. Nichols, *Biographical anecdotes of William Hogarth*, 1st edn (1781), p. 133. [3] J. B. Nichols, *Anecdotes of William Hogarth* (1833), p. 362. [4] Ronald Paulson, *Hogarth, his life, art and times*, 2 vols. (1971), II, pp. 286–7, by comparison with the four *Election* paintings (Sir John Soane's Museum, London). [5] Paulson, *op. cit.*, II, pp. 286–91. [6] Ireland, *op. cit.*, II, p. 321, referring to the 1758 engraving; Beckett, *op. cit.*, p. 64, considers these identifications as 'probably quite imaginary', but Paulson, *Hogarth's graphic works*, 2 vols. (1965), I, pp. 238–9, no. 205, accepts the figure named Willes as a portrait, though he speaks of the others with doubt. [7] In reverse, both plates show variations from the painting; Paulson, *loc. cit.*, n. 6.

1642 UNKNOWN MAN PLATE II

Canvas, $29\frac{3}{4} \times 24\frac{5}{8}$ in ($75{\cdot}6 \times 62{\cdot}6$ cm).[1] He has a pink complexion. The coat is grey, over a gold-bordered scarlet waistcoat; the stock and jabot are white; the hat under his arm is black. The background and the moulding of the feigned oval are brown.[2]

Bought from the Spencer George Perceval Fund, 1933. Anon. sale, Christie's, 14 July 1930 (139), bt H. A. Buttery, from whom purchased.

Cleaned 1930.[3] Comparable in style with Hogarth's portraits of the early 1740s, such as the *Portrait of a gentleman* in the Dulwich College gallery (no. 580), dated 1741, and the *Graham children* in the Tate Gallery, London (no. 4756), dated 1742. The painting was unknown previous to its appearance at Christie's in 1930.[4]

REPRODUCED. R. B. Beckett, *Hogarth* (1949), pl. 119.

NOTES. [1] Lined; dimensions of the painted surface. [2] R. B. Beckett, *Hogarth* (1949), p. 51, as *A gentleman in grey*. [3] By H. A. Buttery; the date is presumed, this being the year when he bought it. [4] Thought by H. A. Buttery to have come from the neighbourhood of Brighton.

PD. 11–1964 BEFORE PLATE 9

Canvas, 14⅝ × 17⅝ in (37·2 × 44·7 cm).[1] His coat and breeches are blue-grey, with grey stockings; her dress is pink and ochre-yellow; both have dark brown hair and wear black shoes. The foliage is in tones of olive-green and blue-green; the rocks are brown; darkish blue sky.

PD. 12–1964 AFTER PLATE 9

Canvas, 14⅝ × 17¾ in (37·2 × 45·1 cm).[1] Costume and background of the same colours as above; her stockings are light blue with red garters; his flushed face is bright pink.[2]

Bequeathed by Arnold John Hugh Smith, through the National Art-Collections Fund, 1964. Probably the pair of paintings with these titles ordered by 'Mr Thomson', 1730;[3] on the London art market, 1832;[4] coll. H. R. Willett, of Shooter's Hill, London, 1842;[5] Locker-Lampson; Duke of Hamilton by 1907;[6] bought by A. J. Hugh Smith, 1919;[7] exh. Manchester, City Art Gallery, 1954, 'William Hogarth' (11, 12); London, Iveagh Bequest, Kenwood, 1968, 'French taste in English painting' (31a, 31b); Tate Gallery, 1971–2, 'Hogarth' (50, 51).

Cleaned 1971. Hogarth painted two pairs of small pictures on this theme, the present pair and a pair in an indoor setting, which in 1972 belonged to the Fine Arts Corporation. In a list of paintings in hand, 'bespoke for the present year 1731', drawn up by Hogarth in January 1730/1,[8] a pair with the titles *Before* and *After* is recorded as ordered by 'Mr Thomson' on 7 December 1730, which is probably to be identified with the present pair as it is said that the other pair was painted 'at the particular request of a certain vicious nobleman'.[9] The present pair is considered to be the earlier of the two, on account of its 'consciously French' style, and dated 1730–1, the indoor pair being more characteristic of Hogarth's later work.[10]

REPRODUCED. R. B. Beckett, *Hogarth* (1949), pl. 35, 36; John Woodward, *A picture history of British painting* (1962), p. 49; Fitzwilliam Museum, *Annual Report* for 1964, pl. x; *Illustrated London News* (1964), CCXLV, 202; R. Raines, *Marcellus Laroon* (1966), p. 66, fig. 22 (*Before* only); Ronald Paulson, *Hogarth*, *his life, art and times*, 2 vols. (1971), I, p. 231, figs. 87, 88; L. Gowing, exhibition catalogue, *Hogarth* (1971), Tate Gallery, p. 29, nos. 50, 51.

NOTES. [1] Lined; dimensions of the painted surface. [2] R. B. Beckett, *Hogarth* (1949), p. 63, nos. 35–6. [3] John Ireland, *Hogarth illustrated*, 3 vols. (1798), III, p. 23; 'Mr Thomson' was perhaps John Thomson, see Ronald Paulson, *Hogarth, his life, art and times*, 2 vols. (1971), I, pp. 229–30. [4] J. B. Nichols, *Anecdotes of William Hogarth* (1833), p. 352. [5] Austin Dobson, *William Hogarth* (1907), p. 198, under 'Before and After (2)', with incorrect dimensions. [6] Dobson, *loc. cit.*, but see n. 5; 'Locker-Lampson' was probably Frederick Locker-Lampson (d. 1915). [7] Beckett, *loc. cit.* [8] Ireland, *loc. cit.* [9] J. Nichols, *Biographical anecdotes of William Hogarth* (1782 edn), p. 194; the pair could be the same as the 'two little pictures' commissioned by the Duke of Montague, also included in Hogarth's list of January 1730/1, see n. [3]. [10] Paulson, *loc. cit.*

HOLBEIN, HANS, THE YOUNGER

1497/8–1543. Born in Augsburg. Pupil of his father, Hans Holbein the elder, in Augsburg; in Basel by 1519. First came to England, 1526; in Basel, 1528; second visit to England, 1532–43; in the service of Henry VIII by 1536.

After Hans Holbein

164 WILLIAM FITZWILLIAM, EARL OF SOUTHAMPTON PLATE I

Wood, $73\frac{5}{8} \times 39\frac{3}{8}$ in (187·1 × 100·0 cm). Black cap over a black coif; black gown lined with brown fur, which forms the collar; sleeves of the doublet of black brocade; black boots. Brown staff with a gold knob and tip. Red and dark grey pavement, edged with light-coloured stone. The water is light blue and cream, changing to dark blue in the foreground with dark brown rocks; the rocks at the left are light and dark brown; those edging the further bank are pale buff; the trees behind the rocks are dark green and brown, those beyond pale blue and cream, with light blue distant hills; pale clouds, with blue sky above. His coat of arms[1] encircled by the Garter, upper left; an inscription upper right, 'WILLIAM ◆ FFITZ ◆ WILLIAM / ERLE ◆ OF ◆ SOVTHE / HAMPTON / LORDT ◆ PREVISEALE / AND CHAVNCELER / OF ◆ THE ◆ DOVCHE / OF ◆ LANCASTER / ◆1542◆'

Founder's Bequest, 1816. Presumably always at Cowdray House, Sussex, until after 1793, when it passed at a date unknown into the possession of Richard, Viscount Fitzwilliam, founder of the Fitzwilliam Museum.[2]

The head and shoulders correspond with a drawing by Holbein in the royal collection at Windsor Castle, the principal outlines of which have been worked over with a metal point seemingly in the process of transferring the design onto panel for a painting.[3] The landscape covers an earlier architectural background, visible by infra-red photography (and just evident to the naked eye) in the form of the outline of a moulded, semicircular arch behind the head. The landscape is painted in an impastoed technique quite different from the thin painting of the figure, but from style and the form of the ships it appears to be probably of about the middle of the sixteenth century. The coat of arms at the top to the left and the inscription to the right occupy the spandrels at either side of the arch, and both appear to be original. Two smaller versions, both on wood, are known, one a half-length at Milton Park, Northamptonshire (the Earl Fitzwilliam), which is the best in quality of the three and the closest to the Holbein drawing, to which the head corresponds very nearly in size. It appears to be of about the mid sixteenth century. The other, virtually a head only, is at Hardwick Hall, Derbyshire (National Trust), a rather weak version probably of much the same date. No Holbein original is now identifiable, but the numerous examples of Holbein's work possessed by Thomas Howard, Earl of Arundel, included two paintings of the Earl of Southampton,[4] and in the sale of Edward Harley, Earl of Oxford, London, Cock's, 8 March 1742, lot 29 was 'Lord Fitzwilliams, a Profile by Holbein'. The Fitzwilliam Museum portrait can only go back to an original by Holbein, as by the time of his death in 1543 the standing whole-length was still a rarity in England, even in his own work, and it is out of the question that this portrait could have been the invention of the mediocre artist who painted it. The date of 1542 which it bears is not necessarily to be taken as the date of the painting, since this is the date of the Earl of Southampton's death, and as a repetition of an earlier Holbein the portrait could be of a commemorative nature. Supposing the inscription to repeat that on the original, the latter could not have been earlier in date than 1539, when he became Lord Privy Seal. William Fitzwilliam, Earl of Southampton, of a Yorkshire family, was born about 1490, and was brought up with the future King Henry VIII, in whose service he spent his life. Knighted 1513, Knight of the Garter 1526, Chancellor of the Duchy of Lancaster 1529, Lord High Admiral of England 1536–40, he was created Earl of Southampton in 1537, and became Lord Privy Seal in 1539. He died in 1542.

REPRODUCED. Earp, p. 96; *Principal pictures* (1912 edn), p. 85, (1928 edn), p. 103; Sir William H. St John Hope, *Cowdray and Easebourne Priory* (1919), frontispiece (colour); K. T. Parker, *The drawings of Hans Holbein...at Windsor Castle* (1945), p. 54.

NOTES. [1] Blazoned in Sir William H. St John Hope, *Cowdray and Easebourne Priory* (1919), p. 46. [2] William Fitzwilliam, Earl of Southampton, bought the Cowdray estate in 1529. After his death in 1542 it passed to his half-brother Sir Anthony Browne, from whom it descended by family inheritance through the Viscounts Montague to Lady Elizabeth Mary Browne, who in 1794 married William Stephen Poyntz (d. 1840). In 1793 Cowdray House was destroyed by fire, from which this portrait was one of the few paintings saved. In a catalogue of the paintings at Cowdray published in 1777, it is listed as no. 23, together with a copy by 'Lucy', no. 106, presumably C. Lucy, a portrait painter born in 1692, by whom there were a number of other copies at Cowdray. The copy was destroyed in the fire. See Hope, *op, cit.* pp. 20, 22–6, 36–48, 59–61. Richard Gough, in his account in 1793 of the destruction of the house (reprinted in Hope, *op. cit.*, pp. 36ff.), twice describes the portrait (pp. 37–8, 46). For another picture saved from the fire, see p. 37, no. 465. [3] K. T. Parker, *The drawings of Hans Holbein...at Windsor Castle* (1945), p. 54, no. 66. [4] *Burlington Magazine* (1912), XXI, 257–8.

HOLMES, Sir Charles John

1868–1936. Born at Preston, Lancashire. Self-taught as a draughtsman; member of the New English Art Club, 1904; Director of the National Gallery, 1916–28; kt, 1921; K.C.V.O., 1928. Landscape painter.

1139 FARMYARD AT SOBERTON, SURREY (1923)

Canvas, 27 × 30⅛ in (68·6 × 76·5 cm). A large barn with two gabled entrances closes the far side of a farmyard; its planked walls are grey, the tiled roof russet-coloured and green with grey thatch in the middle and at the right, where the gable of an entrance is white; against the barn stands a disc-harrow. In the foreground towards the left a pool is enclosed by a wall curving round to the left, its sides russet and green, the top light blue; in the left corner lies a heap of buff-coloured dead branches in front of a cream-coloured outbuilding, a green tree behind it. The floor of the yard is orange-coloured. Above the barn is a mass of grey and cream clouds in a blue sky. Signed and dated lower left, 'C.J.H. 1923'.

Given by (Sir) Thomas Dalmahoy Barlow, 1924. Exh. London, New English Art Club, 1924, '70th Exhibition' (22); placed on loan to the City of Cambridge, 1972.

In his autobiography, Holmes refers to this painting with a favourable comment.[1]

NOTE. [1] *Self and partners* (1936), p. 357.

HONE, Nathaniel

1718–1784. Born in Dublin. Came to England when young; worked as an itinerant portrait painter; settled in London during the 1740s; in Italy, 1740–2; foundation member of the R.A., 1768. Portrait painter, who also painted miniatures until the late 1760s.

457 GENERAL LLOYD (1773)

Canvas, 30 × 25⅛ in (76·2 × 63·8 cm). Nearly half-length, to right, looking front, both hands resting on the hilt of a sword upright before him. Bareheaded, grey wig; clean-shaven. Wears scarlet coat and yellow-buff waistcoat. Behind him is a brown wall with a stepped end at the right, blue-grey sky beyond.

Founder's Bequest, 1816.

The required information about this portrait is given in an inscription written on the stretcher at the back, 'Major General Humphrey Evans Lloyd, 1773. Died 1783. Painted by Hone'. This is in the handwriting of the Founder of the Fitzwilliam Museum, Richard, Viscount Fitzwilliam, of whom General Lloyd is said to have been an intimate friend.[1] Possibly the portrait may thus have been painted for Lord Fitzwilliam, though the inscription was evidently written after the general's death. Henry, or Henry Humphrey Evans, Lloyd (1720 (?)–1783), of Welsh birth, was a soldier of fortune who served with the French, Prussian, Austrian and Russian armies, rising in the Austrian service to the rank of major-general. In about 1779 he settled in Belgium, where he died. An enamel miniature of the portrait, copied by Nathaniel Hone's son, Horace Hone, in 1804, is in the National Museum of Wales, Cardiff.

NOTE. [1] William Key, *A catalogue of paintings and drawings bequeathed to the University of Cambridge by the late Lord Viscount Fitzwilliam in the year 1816* (n.d.; about 1817), p. 16; William Key had for many years been Lord Fitzwilliam's confidential principal servant. His statement receives some confirmation from the fact that Lord Fitzwilliam's copy, in the Fitzwilliam Museum, of vol. 1 of Lloyd's *History of the late war in Germany* (1766) was a gift from the author in the year of publication.

916 THE HON. MRS NATHANIEL CURZON (1778) PLATE 14

Canvas, 49⅞ × 39½ in (126·7 × 100·3 cm).[1] Her dress is golden yellow, with white round the bodice and at the wrists; she has light brown hair, the bandeau round it pale grey, the scarf white. The pedestal is deep grey, the highlights on the roundel of charity and on the ornaments touched with yellow; the gilt vase is in tones of yellow and yellow-grey; the music scroll is yellow-grey. The paler portion of the wall in the background is grey, the darker portion to the left is deep brown. Signed and dated lower right, 'N. Hone p^t 1778'.

Given by Charles Fairfax Murray, 1918. Coll. Drury-Lowe family, Locko Park, Derby;[2] sold by Captain W. D. Drury-Lowe (1877–1916);[3] exh. Dublin, National Gallery of Ireland, Belfast, Ulster Museum, London, National Portrait Gallery, 1969–70, 'Irish portraits, 1660–1860' (51).

She was Sophia Susanna Noel, daughter of the 1st Viscount Wentworth, b. 1758, d. 1782. In 1777 she married, as his first wife, Nathaniel Curzon, who in 1804 succeeded his father as 2nd Lord Scarsdale. A version of the portrait at Kedleston Hall, Derbyshire, the family seat, must be regarded as the prime original, but the Fitzwilliam Museum example is unmistakably an autograph repetition, and not a copy.[4] The 2nd Lord Scarsdale's youngest child by his second marriage, Caroline Esther, married in 1827 William Drury-Lowe, a family connection which must presumably account for the presence of the portrait at Locko Park, where a copy of a portrait at Kedleston, by Joseph Wright of Derby, of the 2nd Lord Scarsdale as a child, is also recorded.[5]

REPRODUCED. Exhibition catalogue, *Irish portraits, 1660–1860* (1969), no. 51.

NOTES. [1] Lined; dimensions of the painted surface. [2] Jean Paul Richter, *Catalogue of pictures at Locko Park* (1901), no. 188, though the genealogy is confused and she is mistakenly called Lady Scarsdale. [3] Fitzwilliam Museum Syndicate, meeting of 9 March 1920, minute 5. [4] As claimed by the Earl (later Marquess) Curzon in 1919, on the strength of family tradition. [5] Richter, *op. cit.*, p. 4, no. 13.

HOPPNER, John

1758–1810. Born in London. Student at the R.A. schools, 1775; exh. R.A. from 1780; Portrait Painter to the Prince of Wales, 1789; R.A., 1795. Painted portraits and fancy subjects.

1102 BOY WITH A BIRD'S NEST — PLATE 27

Canvas, $30\frac{1}{2} \times 25\frac{1}{2}$ in ($77{\cdot}5 \times 64{\cdot}7$ cm).[1] His clothes are pink, with a white collar; light brown hair. The foliage of the trees is dark green, their trunks brown; brown-green herbage. Blue distant hills; sky and water blue and grey.

Bequeathed by Samuel Sandars (d. 1894), received 1923. With Thos Agnew & Sons Ltd, London.

Much damaged by over-cleaning. Despite the impoverished paint quality and the rubbed condition of the head, the drawing and the character of the technique link this with certain other paintings by Hoppner of children and young people of the last years of the 1790s, such, for example, as the William, Viscount Melbourne of 1796 in the Royal Collection.[2] That this is the approximate date of the picture is indicated by the costume, and the conception is obviously inspired by paintings by Reynolds, by whom Hoppner was influenced throughout his career, such as the *Lesbia, or The dead sparrow* (Baroness Burton) of (?) 1788.[3]

REPRODUCED. *Principal pictures* (1929), p. 106.

NOTES. [1] Lined; dimensions of the painted surface. [2] Rep. Oliver Millar, *The later Georgian pictures in the collection of Her Majesty the Queen* (1969), pl. 181. [3] Rep. Ellis K. Waterhouse, *Reynolds* (1941), pl. 294b.

HOWARD, Henry

1769–1847. Born in London. Pupil of Philip Reinagle; student at the R.A. schools, 1788; in Italy, 1791–4; exh. R.A. from 1795; R.A., 1808; professor of painting at the R.A., 1833. Painted subject pictures and portraits.

Copy after Howard

2 RICHARD, 7TH VISCOUNT FITZWILLIAM OF MERRION

Wood, 15⅛ × 12 in (38·4 × 30·5 cm).[1] To below the knees, seated in an armchair, turned towards a table at the right, looking front; the left leg is crossed over the right, the left hand on an open book resting on the table and on his knee, the right arm on the arm of the chair. Bare-headed, bald, white hair, domed head. Over yellow clothes, with an open shirt collar, he wears a loose robe of dull red edged with fur. Background, an interior wall, with pilasters right and left, a green curtain draped over that at the right.

Founder's Bequest, 1816.

Cleaned 1964. Viscount Fitzwilliam, born in 1745, founded the Fitzwilliam Museum by the bequest in 1816 to his old University of his collections and a sum of money to erect a museum building; see also under Wright of Derby, p. 292, no. 1. In the first printed catalogue of the paintings and drawings in the bequest, by William Key, Lord Fitzwilliam's former confidential, principal servant, the portrait is described as 'an excellent likeness', and as showing him 'in his morning dress'.[2] In this catalogue, and in an inventory of the bequest,[3] it is given to Henry Howard, though subsequently catalogued as by or after him.[4] On grounds of quality, Howard's authorship seems out of the question, but two mezzotints, respectively by Richard Earlom, 1810,[5] and Charles Turner,[6] both lettered as after a painting by Howard of 1809, demonstrate him as the originator of the portrait, when Lord Fitzwilliam was aged sixty-four. The painting is very close in dimensions to both the mezzotints,[7] suggesting the possibility of a copy from one or other of them.[8] No original by Howard has been traceable. An unfinished miniature by Horace Hone, copying part of the composition with variations, is in the Fitzwilliam Museum.[9]

REPRODUCED. Earp, frontispiece.

NOTES. [1] Dimensions of the painted surface, which is surrounded on all four sides by a narrow, unpainted margin. [2] William Key, *A catalogue of the paintings, and drawings bequeathed to the University of Cambridge by the late Lord Viscount Fitzwilliam in the year 1816* (n.d., but probably 1817), p. 20. Key was appointed first Curator of the Fitzwilliam Museum in 1816. [3] Made in accordance with the provisions of Lord Fitzwilliam's will, manuscript volume in the Fitzwilliam Museum, dated March 1816; the list of paintings was drawn up by William Seguier, later first Keeper of the National Gallery. [4] First thus described in Sidney Colvin, *A brief catalogue of the pictures in the Fitzwilliam Museum* (1895), p. 32; Earp, p. 100, adds a note mentioning an attribution to the almost unknown painter, Thomas Howes, in 'the catalogue of 1853', of which no copies now appear to be extant. [5] John Chaloner Smith, *British mezzotinto portraits* (1878), part I, p. 247, no. 13. [6] Alfred Whitman, *Charles Turner* (1903), p. 91, no. 198. [7] Dimensions, exclusive of the inscription space: Earlom, 15¼ × 12½ in (38·7 × 31·8 cm); Turner, 15⅛ × 12⅜ in (38·4 × 31·4 cm). [8] Both mezzotints are in the same direction as the painting. The panel of the latter is nicked on all four sides, indicating squaring up for the transfer of the composition; the superior quality of the head in both mezzotints rules out the possibility that the painting may have been a copy by either Earlom or Turner for puposes of engraving. [9] The liveliness of the completed head contrasts forcibly with the head in the present picture; rep. Earp, p. 100.

HUDSON, Thomas

1701–1779. Born in Devonshire. Pupil of Jonathan Richardson; worked in London. Popular portrait painter, mainly active from the early 1740s to the late 1750s.

Copy after Thomas Hudson

17 GEORGE FREDERICK HANDEL

Canvas, backed onto wood, oval, 8 × 7 in (20·3 × 17·8 cm). Head and shoulders, towards the left, looking front. Bare-headed, white wig; clean-shaven. Wears grey coat with a border of gold embroidery, white jabot. Dark grey background.

Given by the Rev. Arthur Robert Ward, 1870. Coll. William Boyce (1710–1779); at his death passed into the possession of his niece, who bequeathed it to her godson Thomas F. Walmisley (1783–1866); bought from him by the donor about 1852;[1] exh. London, 1885, 'International inventions loan exhibition' (66).

Good condition. G. F. Handel (1685–1759), famous musical composer; in 1710 he left his native Germany for England, where he spent the rest of his life. This corresponds with the head in the large whole-length by Thomas Hudson, dated 1756, formerly at Gopsall Hall, Leicestershire,[2] and now in the National Portrait Gallery, London (no. 3970). Whether copied from this painting, or from a hypothetical preparatory *ad vivum* head and shoulders study for it,[3] it reproduces the technical characteristics of the Gopsall portrait to a degree which suggests that it could well be a reduction made in Hudson's studio. Given in 1870 as by Giuseppe Grisoni, no doubt on account of the inscription at the back of the picture 'Grisoni Pinx$^{t.}$';[4] but Grisoni, who came to England in 1715, returned to Italy in 1728. Another version, also oval but larger and showing more of the figure, is in the royal collection,[5] and an indifferent bust of the same type forms part of the decorations at Heaton Hall, Manchester, built in 1772. A good copy of the Fitzwilliam Museum painting made for Victor Schoelcher between 1852 and 1857,[6] is now in the Musée de l'Opéra, Paris.[7]

REPRODUCED. Gustav Thormälius, *Georg Friedrich Händel*, n.d. (1913), cover (colour); Earp, p. 82; *Principal pictures* (1912 edn), p. 67, (1929 edn), p. 83.

NOTES. [1] Provenance from a label at the back of the picture signed by the donor. Boyce's will shows that the portrait was not a bequest to his niece; he had a brother John, who died in 1755, and a sister Elizabeth, who married Francis Wyndham. [2] Painted for Handel's friend Charles Jennens. [3] See Oliver Millar, *The Tudor, Stuart and early Georgian pictures in the collection of Her Majesty the Queen* (1963), pp. 183–4, nos. 556 and 558. [4] From its calligraphy probably of the eighteenth century. [5] Millar, *loc. cit.*, no. 558. [6] His *Life of*

Handel (1857), p. 357; the copy was made while the portrait was in the posession of the Rev. A. W. Ward. [7] J. M. Coopersmith in *Music and Letters* (1932), XIII, 158, n. 2.

School of Thomas Hudson

PD. 25–1952 MRS SUSANNAH HOPE

Canvas, $29\frac{3}{8} \times 24\frac{3}{4}$ in ($74{\cdot}6 \times 62{\cdot}9$ cm).[1] Half-length to right; bare-headed, dark hair; pearl ear-drops, a pearl necklace round her throat. Light blue silk dress with a low décolletage, which is edged with a white frill and has a pale pink bow in the centre at the front; sleeves caught up at the elbow to reveal white undersleeves; a fold of a golden-brown drapery passing behind the figure falls at either side of it. Grey-brown background within a painted oval, the spandrels grey.

Bequeathed by Lady (May) Hope, in accordance with the wishes of her husband, 1952. Coll. Sir William H. St John Hope (her husband), (?) by family inheritance;[2] bequeathed to his wife, 1919; exh. Cambridge, Fitzwilliam Museum, 1921–4.

Cleaned and restored, 1953. The history of this picture prior to the ownership of Sir William Hope remains unknown, but descent to him through the family seems likely.[3] He regarded it as a portrait of his great-grandmother, Mrs Susannah Hope, and believed it to be by Joseph Wright of Derby. This is stylistically unacceptable, but is no doubt due to a mistaken identification of it with the larger portrait which Wright painted of her about 1760. This portrait is now lost.[4] Susannah Hope, daughter of Benjamin Stead, b. 1744, d. 1807, married the Rev. Charles Hope of Derby in 1760. From the youthful appearance of the woman depicted, and from her costume, the portrait must date from about this time. The hard, smooth style of the head has an unmistakable affinity with the portraiture of Thomas Hudson, though well below his work in quality.

NOTES. [1] Lined; dimensions of the painted surface. [2] He possessed also a portrait by an unknown painter of Susannah Hope's father-in-law, Dr William Hope (1701–1776), suggesting a family history in common for both of them. [3] See n. [2]. [4] Benedict Nicolson, *Joseph Wright of Derby*, 2 vols. (1968), I, pp. 206, 207 (88).

HUGHES, ARTHUR

1832–1915. Born in London. Entered the R.A. schools, 1847; adopted Pre-Raphaelitism about 1850, and participated in the decorations at the Oxford Union, 1857. Painted subject pictures and landscapes; book illustrator.

1145 EDWARD ROBERT HUGHES AS A CHILD

Canvas, 22⅜ × 11½ in (56·8 × 29·2 cm).[1] Whole-length standing, turned slightly left, wearing a nightgown, ochrish in colour, to his feet. Golden hair falling in ringlets to his shoulders; high colour. His left arm hangs down, the hand grasping a fold of the nightgown; the right arm is bent, the hand, which is unfinished, also grasping a fold. Inscribed upper left, 'E R Hughes at / two & a half years / old. Painted by / his uncle / Arthur Hughes'.[2] Signed lower left, 'ARTHUR HUGHES'.

Bequeathed by Mrs Edward Robert Hughes, 1925. Coll. E. R. Hughes; (?) exh. U.S.A. (New York, Philadelphia, Boston), 1857–8;[3] London, Grafton Galleries, 1911, 'Century of art exhibition of the International Society of Sculptors, Painters and Engravers' (51), lent E. R. Hughes; coll. Mrs E. R. Hughes.

Edward Robert Hughes (1851–1914), nephew of Arthur Hughes, was a painter and became President of the Royal Society of Painters in Water-colours. The inscription on the front of the picture dates it about 1853–4.[4]

NOTES. [1] Dimensions of the painted surface, which has a curved, pointed top on a rectangular canvas. [2] Inscribed on the unpainted spandrel of the canvas under a gilt mount. [3] This was a mixed exhibition of English paintings, which included Pre-Raphaelite work. No copy of a catalogue is known, but across the back of the canvas of the present picture is written the word 'America'. [4] It was submitted to the R.A. in 1855, and rejected. D. G. Rossetti, in reporting this, describes it as 'most admirable', and the nightgown as flannel, which perhaps accounts for its ambiguous colour and the dubious quality of the paint (George Birkbeck Hill, *Letters of Dante Gabriel Rossetti to William Allingham* (1897), pp. 123, 130). Thanks are due to Mr Robin Gibson for this reference.

1509 THE KING'S ORCHARD PLATE 47

Paper on wood, 11¼ × 11½ in (28·6 × 29·2 cm).[1] The boy has auburn hair; he wears a yellow-brown tunic with purple sleeves, mauve-grey hose, and black shoes. The reclining girl has golden hair and bright blue eyes; her hat is red with a blue feather, her dress cream with a gold pattern. The little girl also has golden hair and bright blue eyes; her frock is red-brown with a white and ochre skirt, the bib is white. Brown dog. The foliage and herbage are bright local green, bluer in the shadows. The standing woman is in black. Signed lower right, 'A. HUGHES'.

Bequeathed by Lady Courtney of Penwith, 1929. Coll. J. Hamilton Trist, Brighton, who bought it from the artist in 1863;[2] Trist sale, Christie's, 9 April 1892 (75).

This is the sketch for the picture Hughes exhibited at the R.A. in 1859, no. 609,[3] which was seen by Ruskin partly finished in 1858.[4] The sketch must therefore, at the latest, be of this year. The picture was inspired by a passage from Robert Browning's modern Drama of 1841, *Pippa Passes*,[5] which runs:

> And peasants sing how once a certain page
> Pined for the grace of her so far above
> His power of doing good to, 'Kate the Queen –
> 'She never could be wronged, be poor', he sighed,
> 'Need him to help her!'.

The reference is to Caterina Cornaro, Queen of Cyprus (1454–1510), 'Kate the Queen' in a song just sung by Pippa, and the lines form part of some brooding reflections on it by one of the other characters. The concept thus inspired is otherwise unrelated to the poem. The instrument on which the boy plays is a 'harp-lute, a hybrid instrument which had a brief period of popularity in the early nineteenth century', and which 'occurs in many of Hughes's early costume pieces'.[6] In the large version, the children can be recognised as Hughes's own family, Arthur, Agnes and Emily, who were remarkable for their brilliant colouring.[7] The picture seems originally to have borne the title *The King's garden*.[8]

REPRODUCED. *Picture Post* (1948), 40, 16–17 (colour).

NOTES. [1] Roughly cut along the top. A manuscript catalogue of the J. Hamilton Trist collection (see below), in which the picture is no. 65 (Tate Gallery), gives the dimensions as 11½ × 11 in (29·2 × 27·9 cm), presumably sight measurements, showing that as much perhaps as ¾ in (1·9 cm) has been lost at the top. [2] Thanks are due to Mr Robin Gibson for kindly providing this and much other information about the picture. [3] It was later in the collection of Thomas E. Plint, but has disappeared since his sale at Christie's in 1862. [4] Ruskin's Royal Academy Notes for 1859 (*The works of John Ruskin*, ed. E. T. Cook and Alexander Wedderburn (1904), XIV, p. 233). [5] The lines occur towards the end of Part II, lines 275–9. They were quoted in the 1859 R.A. catalogue, but printed in prose. [6] Robin Gibson, 'Arthur Hughes: Arthurian and related subjects of the early 1860's', *Burlington Magazine* (1970), CXII, 455. [7] Albert Goodwin, in his preface to the *Catalogue of the memorial exhibition of some of the works of the late Arthur Hughes*, Walker's Galleries, London, 1916. [8] Ruskin's Royal Academy Notes for 1858 and 1859 (*loc. cit.*, pp. 163, 233). Perhaps turned into an orchard by the addition of apple blossom (although the trees are in full leaf) in obedience to Ruskin's admonition to paint April blossom in his Academy Notes for 1858, which is supposed to have influenced Arthur Hughes, among other artists, in the pictures they exhibited at the R.A. in 1859 (*loc. cit.*, pp. 154, xxiv).

HUNT, William Holman

1827–1910. Born in London. Entered the R.A. schools 1844, where he met J. E. Millais; exh. at the R.A. and elsewhere from 1846; with Millais and D. G. Rossetti founded in 1848 the reforming Pre-Raphaelite Brotherhood; to ensure truth in his biblical paintings, between 1854 and 1892 paid four visits to Egypt and Palestine. O.M., 1905. Painted mainly subject pictures.

868 THE THAMES AT CHELSEA, EVENING (1853)

Wood, 6×8 in (15·2×20·3 cm). The shadowy river stretches from the foreground to dark buildings at the further side, in a group of which towards the right are a number of lights. The grey water is broken by warm, cream-coloured horizontal reflections, with orange-coloured vertical reflections at the right. The buildings are dark brown, with a luminous grey sky above. Inscribed in ink on the back of the panel, 'Sketch from a window in Cheyne Walk, Chelsea, 1853. Given to John Everett Millais by W. Holman-Hunt'.

Given by Charles Fairfax Murray, 1917. Given by the painter to Sir John Everett Millais, Bart (1829–1896); Millais sale, Christie's, 2 July 1898 (8), bt Fairfax Murray; exh. Liverpool, Walker Art Gallery, 1969, 'William Holman Hunt' (26);[1] London, Guildhall Art Gallery, 1971, 'London and the greater painters' (41).

In 1853 Holman Hunt was living in Chelsea (London), where his address was 5 Prospect Place, Cheyne Walk,[2] running along the river Thames. He described his studio as 'overlooking the river'.[3]

REPRODUCED. Allen Staley, *The Pre-Raphaelite landscape* (1973), pl. 27b.

NOTES. [1] The exhibition was transferred later in the same year to the Victoria and Albert Museum, London. [2] R.A. exhibition catalogue. [3] W. Holman Hunt, *Pre-Raphaelitism and the Pre-Raphaelite Brotherhood*, 2 vols. (1905), I, p. 350.

1760 CYRIL BENONI HOLMAN HUNT (1880) PLATE 46

Canvas, 24×20 in (60·9×50·8 cm). Fresh complexion, fair hair with reddish tints; dark chestnut-brown velvet jacket, white shirt collar, crimson tie; a dark blue ribbon on the straw hat. The float is bright red (above) and green, the same green repeated in the grass. The foliage is bluish green, the bridge brown, the water mainly bluish grey. Signed and dated on the float, 'WHH' (in a monogram), and, below, '1880'.

Bequeathed by Cyril Benoni Holman Hunt, 1934. Exh. London, Grosvenor Gallery, 1880, 'Summer exhibition' (89); Bradford, Cartwright Memorial Hall, 1904, 'Exhibition of Fine Arts';[1] Liverpool, Walker Art Gallery, 1907, 'The art of William Holman Hunt' (20); Glasgow, Corporation Art Gallery and Museum, 1907, 'Pictures and drawings by William Holman Hunt' (4);[2] on loan to the Corporation Museum, Bridport, Dorset, 1932–4; on loan to the City Museum and Art Gallery, Birmingham, 1935–59; exh. Liverpool, Walker Art Gallery, and London, Victoria and Albert Museum, 1969, 'William Holman Hunt' (54); Tokyo, National Museum of Western Art, 1975, 'English portraits' (55).

Cyril Benoni[3] Holman Hunt (1866–1934) was the eldest child of the artist, and spent his life in the Colonial Service in Burma and Malaya. From the evidence of Hunt's correspondence, it appears that this is the second portrait he painted of his son Cyril. The earlier one, whereabouts now unknown, was already started in September 1873, and was finished in 1875, before Hunt left for his third visit to Palestine.[4] The present painting was begun after his return in 1878,[5] the portrait itself being completed in 1879[6] and the whole picture in 1880.[7] The picture is in the frame designed for it by Hunt, carved in relief with a naturalistic design of branches bearing leaves, apple blossom and apples, painted in their natural colours, against a punched gilt ground. An inner slip is lettered along the base, to left 'CYRIL·B·HOLMAN·HUNT', to right 'W·HOLMAN·HUNT'. Two drawings for the frame in pen and ink belong to Mr Stanley Pollitt.[8]

REPRODUCED. W. Holman Hunt, *Pre-Raphaelitism and the Pre-Raphaelite Brotherhood*, 2nd edn (1913), II, p. 272; *Connoisseur* (1959), CXLIV, 10; *Liverpool Bulletin, Walker Art Gallery* (1968–70), 13, p. 62; exhibition catalogue, *English portraits* (1975), Tokyo, no. 55.

NOTES. [1] The label of the exhibition, thus entitled, is at the back of the picture, which, however, is not included in the published catalogue. [2] In both the Liverpool and Glasgow exhibitions entitled *The Fisherman: a portrait.* [3] 'Benoni' (sometimes incorrectly spelled 'Benone') is Hebrew for 'Child of distress or sorrow', his mother, William Holman Hunt's first wife, Fanny, having died shortly after his difficult birth. [4] Correspondence with Mr and Mrs F. G. Stephens, in the Bodleian Library, Oxford, MSS Don. e. 66–68, quoted by Mary Bennett in the catalogue of the exhibition 'William Holman

Hunt' (Walker Art Gallery, Liverpool, and Victoria and Albert Museum, London, 1969), and with J. L. Tupper, in the Henry E. Huntington Library and Art Gallery, San Marino, California, U.S.A., with whose permission the extracts in n. [5] and [6] are quoted; Miss Bennett has very kindly provided transcripts from both sets of correspondence. [5] Letter dated 16 October 1878, 'After I wrote last I went down to Shropshire and there...stayed and painted a portrait of Cyril' (Huntington Library). [6] Hunt writes on 21 April 1879, 'I shall have to work on a portrait of Cyril as he will be going back to school and before his next holidays he will be too old' (Huntington Library). Cyril was then almost twelve and a half, having been born in the month of December in 1866. [7] He writes of the final completion of the picture on 10 August 1880, 'I think that tomorrow I shall finish for the Grosvenor Cyril's portrait' (Bodleian Library). [8] See Mary Bennett, 'Footnotes to the Holman Hunt exhibition', *Liverpool Bulletin, Walker Art Gallery* (1968–70), 13, pp. 63–4, rep.

IBBETSON, Julius Caesar

1759–1817. Born near Leeds, Yorkshire. Self-taught. Apprenticed to a ship painter in Hull; to London, 1777; exhibited at the R.A. and the B.I. from 1785. Left London, 1798; resided in the Lake District, and from 1805 at Masham, Yorkshire. Painter mainly of landscape, often with figures or animals.

M. 50 ULLSWATER FROM THE FOOT OF GOWBARROW FELL (1808)

PLATE 27

Canvas, 23 × 34⅞ in (58·4 × 88·6 cm). The herbage is in ochrish greens; the foreground rocks are bluish grey; the water light grey; the sky is pale blue, with cream and grey clouds. Shadowed forms everywhere have a bluish cast. Signed, inscribed and dated lower right, 'J. Ibbetson f Masham Sept 1808'. Inscribed in paint on the back of the canvas, 'Ullswater Cumberland / taken from Gowbarrow / looking up the Lake / painted by Julius C. Ibbetson / Masham Yorks'.[1]

Bequeathed by Charles Brinsley Marlay, 1912.[2] Coll. Mary, Marchioness of Thomond;[3] F. D. Reynolds (of Dublin); his posthumous sale Christie's, 15 July 1893 (23), bt Vokins.

Gowbarrow is on the west side of the lake; the view shows Glenridding on the lakeside in the distance, with Helvellyn beyond and above it. This seems to have been a favourite subject with Ibbetson. The earliest known version, now at Leeds,[4] is dated 1801, when it was exhibited at the R.A. (no. 681), and another was exhibited there in 1806 (no. 379).[5] A third, dated 1803, was formerly with Leggatt Bros., London.[6] The line of the view up the lake is similar, though not exactly the same, in all four, but the foregrounds vary considerably.

REPRODUCED. Constable, pl. XXIX, no. 50.

NOTES. [1] Unlined canvas. Probably Ibbetson's own inscription, see Rotha Mary Clay, *Julius Caesar Ibbetson* (1948), pp. 88, 113. [2] Constable, p. 40, no. 50. [3] Not in either of the sales which included pictures, held by her executors, Christie's, 18, 19 May 1821 and 26 May 1821. [4] Leeds City Art Gallery and Temple Newsam House, no. 2/53, see *Catalogue of paintings*, Part I (1954), p. 41, rep. in volume of illustrations, p. 23. [5] Rep. Clay, *op. cit.*, pl. 82, as coll. J. E. Brennan; at one time with the Mitchell Galleries, London. [6] Said to have been painted for Ibbetson's friend, William Danby, of Swinton.

INCHBOLD, John William

1830–1888. Born in Leeds. Trained in London; student at the R.A., 1847; influenced by the Pre-Raphaelites; exh. at the R.A. and elsewhere from 1849. Landscape painter.

PD. 2–1951 ANSTEY'S COVE, DEVON (1854) PLATE 48

Canvas, $19\frac{7}{8} \times 26\frac{7}{8}$ in ($50{\cdot}5 \times 68{\cdot}3$ cm).[1] The cliffs are in tones of grey and orange-brown; the grass is in blue-greens and ochre-greens, with darker, similar colours in the bushes. The sea is deep blue and deep green; the sky is strong blue. Signed and dated lower right, 'Inchbold / 1854'.

Bought from the Fairhaven Fund, 1951. Coll. Sir Bruce Ingram (1877–1963); with P. & D. Colnaghi & Co. Ltd, London, from whom bought; exh. Hazlitt, 1974 (29).

Anstey's (or Anstis) Cove, a celebrated beauty spot, is on the east coast of Devon, just north of Torquay. It is remarkable for the variety and brilliance of the colour of its rocks. As Inchbold submitted the picture to the R.A. in April 1854 (when it was rejected), work on it must belong in part to 1853. It forms one of a group of extensive landscape subjects painted during the years 1853–6.[2]

REPRODUCED. Allen Staley, *The Pre-Raphaelite landscape* (1973), pl. 61; exhibition catalogue, Hazlitt, 1974, pl. 37.

NOTES. [1] Lined; dimensions of the painted surface. [2] Allen Staley, *The Pre-Raphaelite landscape* (1973), p. 115.

INNES, James Dickson

1887–1914. Born in Llanelly. Slade School, London, 1905–8; produced his best work from 1910. Landscape painter, who found his strongest inspiration in the mountains of his native Wales; worked also in France, Spain and Morocco.

2457 ARENIG FAWR, NORTH WALES

Wood, 12 × 16⅛ in (30·5 × 40·9 cm). Beyond a narrow, distant foreground, green and yellow in the centre, deep red and brown at the right, a broad-based mountain rises, forming three separate peaks, the slopes orange and yellow in the centre, green and mauve at either side, dark in tone at the right, light at the left. Above the mountain spreads a large anvil-shaped cloud, warm white above, grey and mauve below, against a strong blue sky.

Bequeathed by Edward Maurice Berkeley Ingram, C.M.G., O.B.E., 1941. Coll. Lord Ivor Spencer-Churchill by 1934, when he lent it to the XIX[A] Biennale Internazionale d'Arte, Venice (66);[1] bt by E. M. B. Ingram from the Redfern Gallery, London, 1936; exh. London, Redfern Gallery, 1939, 'Augustus John, J. D. Innes, Derwent Lees, paintings 1910–1914' (53); New York, World's Fair, 1939, 'Contemporary British art' (British Council) (44); exh. in North and South America (British Council) 1941, or earlier, to 1945;[2] received by the Fitzwilliam Museum, 1946; exh. Hazlitt, 1974 (30).

Cleaned, 1974. Though there seems every probability that the title of *Arenig Fawr* for this picture is correct, it cannot be regarded as certain. After being exhibited in 1934 without identification (see n. [1]), the picture in 1939 bore the title *Tan-y-Griseau* (*sic*), to which topographical considerations lend some support.[3] The Moelwyn Hills above Tan-y-Grisiau, as well as Arenig Fawr, not far away, both have a resemblance in shape to the mountain in the picture, their general formation being characteristic of this region of Merioneth. But the topography of Arenig and comparison with other paintings of it by Innes both point to a probable identification as this mountain. In particular, the distant ridge silhouetted at the left is a feature in the view of Arenig from the north-west, with which the other shapes of the mountain in the picture accord, and it is to be seen in paintings of Arenig by Innes, such as no. 4385 in the Tate Gallery, with which a passage of small dots on the lower slopes also corresponds. The picture has been dated *c.* 1911,[4] which places it among the earlier of the series of North Wales mountain paintings.

REPRODUCED. Catalogue of 'Contemporary British art', World's Fair, New York, 1939; L. Browse and J. Fothergill, *James Dickson Innes* (1946), pl. 16; exhibition catalogue, Hazlitt, 1974, pl. 38.

NOTES. [1] From a printed label at the back, with the title *The hilltop*. [2] Labels at the back and papers in the Fitzwilliam Museum. [3] Information kindly supplied by Mr R. L. Charles, Keeper of the Department of Art, National Museum of Wales, Cardiff, letter of 1 May 1970 (Fitzwilliam Museum) [4] L. Browse, in L. Browse and J. Fothergill, *James Dickson Innes* (1946), p. 66, no. 16. The ownership is there given in mistake as the Hon. Vincent Massey.

JACKSON, John

1778–1831. Born in Yorkshire. Apprenticed as a tailor; to London, 1804, when he first exhibited at the R.A.; entered the R.A. schools, 1805; visited the Netherlands, 1816, and Italy, 1818–19; R.A., 1817. Portrait painter.

649 THOMAS STOTHARD, R.A.

Canvas, $29\frac{1}{2} \times 24\frac{1}{2}$ in ($74{\cdot}3 \times 62{\cdot}2$ cm).[1] Half-length, somewhat to left, eyes raised; right hand placed across in front, holding spectacles. Bare-headed, iron-grey hair; clean-shaven. Wears a black jacket with a high collar, white neck-cloth. Dark brown background.

Given by Charles Fairfax Murray, 1908. (?) Exh. R.A., 1829 (143); coll. Elhanan Bicknell, of London; sale by his executors, Christie's, 25 April 1863 (47), bt Palmer; John Palmer sale, Christie's, 14 March 1864 (108), bt White; with Sedelmayer, Paris.[2]

Thomas Stothard (1755–1834), painter, prolific book-illustrator, and designer; R.A., 1794; friend of John Flaxman. Another portrait of Stothard by Jackson in the City Art Gallery, Manchester, in which he looks a decidedly older man, may be the one exhibited at the R.A. in 1829, when he was aged seventy-four, rather than the present one.

REPRODUCED. *Principal pictures* (1908 edn), p. 88, (1929 edn), p. 107.

NOTES. [1] Lined; dimensions of the painted surface. [2] Wax seal impression on the stretcher.

JERVAS, Charles

c. 1675–1739. Born in Ireland. Studied under Kneller in London; in Paris, 1699; in Rome by early 1703; back in London by early 1709; friend of Alexander Pope; principal painter to George I and George II. Portrait painter.

After Charles Jervas

650 MARTHA AND TERESA BLOUNT

Canvas, $43\frac{5}{8} \times 44\frac{3}{4}$ in (110·8 × 113·7 cm).[1] Two three-quarter-length standing figures; at the left Martha, facing front, her head turned towards Teresa at the right, who is facing half left, her eyes looking front. Martha is fair-haired and wears a crimson dress over a white chemise, with a dark blue, scarf-like drapery, held by the left hand, floating round behind her, her right arm raised. Teresa, with dark brown hair in which is a posy of flowers, wears a pale grey dress with a pink girdle and pink edging to the sleeves; in both hands, held out towards the left, she holds a wreath-like spray of foliage entwined with a dark green ribbon. Both have a low décolletage. Brown background, with a small tree at the left.

Given by Charles Fairfax Murray, 1908.

Martha Blount (1690–1762), and her less famous elder sister Teresa (1688–1759), were celebrated in the fashionable world of their time for their grace and beauty, and for their friendship with the poet Alexander Pope. This double portrait of them is one of four extant examples, of which the prime original appears to be the painting by Jervas belonging to J. J. Eyston at Mapledurham House, Oxfordshire,[2] formerly the seat of the Blount family, from whom it passed by inheritance to the Eystons. In this picture the ribbon entwined with the spray of foliage is inscribed 'Martha Teresa Blount, sic positae quoniam suaves 1716', quoting line 55 of Virgil's second eclogue. With the preceding line, it has been translated, 'and you will I pluck, O laurels, and thee, bordering myrtles, since so set you will mingle your fragrant sweets',[3] an elegant compliment to the two ladies. The small tree at the left, of which a twig twines round Martha's arm, is thus to be recognised as a laurel, and Teresa is seen to be holding a myrtle wreath, neither very identifiable in the painting. The two sisters lived at Mapledurham until the marriage of their brother in 1715, when they moved with their mother to another house, an event to which the painting of the double portrait in the following year to hang at Mapledurham is perhaps related. The four versions of the portrait fall into two groups, distinguished predominantly by differences in the figure of Teresa. In the Mapledurham original, the features are stronger and the expression of character more vigorous than in the present version and she has a relatively elaborate coiffure, features which are repeated in an example belonging to

John Browne-Swinburne at Capheaton, Northumberland, only slightly inferior in quality to the Mapledurham picture. A version in the Earl Waldegrave sale, Christie's, 10 February 1900 (37), of upright proportions, otherwise corresponds with the Fitzwilliam Museum picture in all but some very small details, and is of similar rather weak quality, perhaps by the same hand.[4] The Mapledurham original is also of upright proportions, but the Capheaton version is expanded at right and left into a horizontally proportioned picture. No doubt these variations in proportion are explicable by the positions which the different versions were painted to fill.

REPRODUCED. *Principal pictures* (1912 edn), p. 89, (1929 edn), p. 109.

NOTES. [1] Lined; dimensions of the painted surface. [2] Exh. London, South Kensington, 1867, 'National portraits' (152), lent M. H. Blount (of Mapledurham). See *The correspondence of Alexander Pope*, ed. George Sherburn, 5 vols. (1956), I, p. 332, for a letter from Jervas to Thomas Parnell, dated February 1716, evidently referring to this picture, to which, he says, 'I have just set the last hand'. [3] J. W. Mackail, *The eclogues and georgics of Virgil* (1889), p. 8. [4] A fifth example, untraced, corresponding with the Mapledurham original, is known from the frontispiece to vol. I of *The poetical works of Alexander Pope*, ed. Robert Carruthers, 2 vols. (1858), lettered 'From the picture in Stanton Harcourt'.

JOHN, Augustus Edwin

1878–1961. Born at Tenby, Wales. Slade School, London, 1894–8; exh. with the New English Art Club, and at London galleries, from 1898; worked with J. D. Innes (1887–1914); R.A., 1928; O.M., 1942. Painter of portraits, landscape, figures and flowers.

851 THE WOMAN OF OWER (1914) PLATE 56

Wood, 18 × 12 in (45·7 × 30·5 cm). The dress is white edged with blue, blue head-scarf, and yellow shawl; warm flesh-colour. The herbage around her is pale yellow, the wall behind is brown, the trees deep green, and the sky a strong blue. Signed and dated lower left, 'John 1914'.

Given by the Friends of the Fitzwilliam Museum, 1917. With Dowdeswell & Dowdeswells Ltd, London; their sale, Christie's, 7–9 February 1917 (459), bt for the Friends of the Fitzwilliam Museum.

The title of the picture in the Dowdeswell sale was *In the corn-field*; its present title was supplied by Augustus John in 1918,[1] 'Ower being the name of the place where it was painted'. This must be Ower in Hampshire, rather than Ower in Co. Galway, as it does not appear that John was in Ireland in 1914.[2]

REPRODUCED. Friends of the Fitzwilliam Museum, *Annual Report* for 1917.

NOTES. [1] Letter of 20 February 1918 (Fitzwilliam Museum). [2] Michael Holroyd, *Augustus John*, 2 vols. (1974), II, pp. 38–41; it was not until 1915 that he was in Galway again.

1018 WOMAN WITH A DAFFODIL (1910)

Wood, 13 × $9\frac{3}{8}$ in (33·3 × 23·8 cm). She stands, just less than whole-length, in a landscape, turned half to the right, head in profile to the right, holding across to the right in both hands a long-stalked daffodil. She wears a pink-mauve tunic, edged green, over a pink-mauve skirt, and a long buff and grey-green apron, edged with orange; buff head-scarf. The landscape is predominantly in light and dark greens, and grey-greens; in the background at the right is a low hill-top with trees. Blue-green sky. Inscribed in ink on the back of the panel, 'Augustus John/1910'.

Given by Sir H. F. Herbert Thompson, Bart, 1920.

The inscription on the back appears to be in John's own hand. The picture bears the subtitle 'Sketch at Aix'; this is Aix-en-Provence, which John visited in the summer of 1910.[1]

NOTE. [1] Michael Holroyd, *Augustus John*, 2 vols. (1974), I, p. 341; the daffodil remains an anomaly.

1071 GEORGE BERNARD SHAW (1915) PLATE 58

Canvas, $30\frac{1}{8}$ × $18\frac{1}{8}$ in (76·5 × 46·3 cm). Fresh flesh-colour, grey hair and white beard. He wears a light blue jacket, with a white shirt and a brown tie. Grey-green background. Signed upper right, 'John'.

Given by George Bernard Shaw, 1922. Painted for the sitter;[1] exh. London, R.A., 1922, Summer Exhibition (675); R.A., 1968/9, 'Royal Academy of Arts, bicentenary exhibition' (488); London, National Portrait Gallery, 1975, 'Augustus John'.

One of three portraits of Shaw painted on the same occasion at Lady Gregory's house, Coole Park, Co. Galway, Ireland.[2] This was in the Spring of 1915.[3] Of the two others, one, similar to the present portrait and considered by John the best of the three,[4] belongs to the National Trust at Shaw's Corner, Ayot St Lawrence, Hertfordshire; the other, portraying the head from the opposite side, and depicting Shaw 'with his eyes shut as if in deep thought',[5] belongs to Queen Elizabeth the Queen Mother. Shaw apparently paid for all three.[6] The Fitzwilliam Museum picture seems to have been originally started with the head rather higher up the canvas. George Bernard Shaw (1856–1950), writer of wide celebrity, best known for his numerous plays; in 1926 he was awarded the Nobel Prize for Literature.

REPRODUCED. *Royal Academy Illustrated* (1922), p. 7; *Principal pictures* (1929), p. 111; Anthony Bertram, *A century of British painting, 1851–1951* (1951), p. 172, pl. 44; John Rothenstein, *Augustus John* (1944), pl. 45; Arland Ussher, *Three great Irishmen*, New York (1953), p. 13; *Das Kunstwerk* (1953), VI, p. 26; John Rothenstein, *Augustus John* (1962) (no pl. ref.); Stanley Weintraub, *Private Shaw and public Shaw* (1963), p. xviii (cut down); David Hughes, *The seven ages of England* (1966), p. 190, no. 333; *Burlington Magazine* (1975), CXVII, 309.

NOTES. [1] Augustus John, *Chiaroscuro* (1952), pp. 95, 97, 100. [2] John, *op. cit.*, pp. 95, 100. [3] Michael Holroyd, *Augustus John*, 2 vols, (1974), II, pp. 46–8. [4] Holroyd, *op. cit.*, II, p. 48 n. [5] John, *op. cit.*, p. 97. [6] John, *op. cit.*, p. 97.

1116 THOMAS HARDY (1923) PLATE 58

Canvas, $24\frac{1}{8} \times 20\frac{1}{8}$ in ($61{\cdot}3 \times 51{\cdot}1$ cm). Brownish-pink flesh tones, grey hair, white moustache. Green-grey jacket and waistcoat, with a white shirt and black tie. The books in the background are mainly yellow, brown, blue and grey. Signed and dated upper right, 'John / 1923'.

Given by Thomas Henry Riches, 1923. Bt from the painter for the Fitzwilliam Museum shortly after it was painted;[1] exh. London, National Portrait Gallery, 1975, 'Augustus John'.

Thomas Hardy (1840–1928), novelist and poet; his first published work, 1871; awarded the Order of Merit, 1910. Painted in Hardy's study at Max Gate, Dorchester;[2] a drawing in black chalk for the head is also in the Fitzwilliam Museum (no. 1605). Hardy was well satisfied with the portrait,[3] and its acquisition by the Museum gave him great pleasure;[4] its purchase was due in the first place to T. E. Lawrence, who saw it at John's house.[5]

REPRODUCED. *The Graphic* (1924), CIX, 251; *Principal pictures* (1299), p. 110; Elizabeth Bowen, *English novelists* (1932), p. 41 (colour); David Hughes, *The seven ages of England* (1966), p. 185, fig. 324.

NOTES. [1] Fitzwilliam Museum Syndicate, 27 November 1923, minute 6. [2] Augustus John, *Chiaroscuro* (1952), p. 134; Michael Holroyd, *Augustus John*, 2 vols. (1974), II, p. 95. [3] Holroyd, *loc. cit.* [4] Letter from Mrs Thomas Hardy to S. C. Cockerell, Director of the Fitzwilliam Museum, 25 November 1923, printed in *Friends of a lifetime, letters to Sydney Carlyle Cockerell*, ed. Viola Meynell (1940), p. 310. [5] Letter from Augustus John, 21 October 1948 (Fitzwilliam Museum).

1641 SIR WILLIAM NICHOLSON (1909) PLATE 57

Canvas, $74\frac{7}{8} \times 56\frac{5}{8}$ in ($190{\cdot}2 \times 143{\cdot}8$ cm). He wears a black overcoat, grey trousers and yellow gloves; the chair is black. The curtain to the right is ochre, that to the left buff-yellow with a blue, pink and brown pattern; the carpet is red. The picture is in a gold frame, the colours of the composition blue, buff and orange-brown, with a mauve figure.

Given by Miss Sydney Renée Courtauld, 1933. Coll. Sir William Nicholson; exh. London, New English Art Club, 1909, '41st exhibition of modern pictures' (58); Pittsburgh, Pennsylvania, U.S.A., Carnegie Institute, 1910, 'Fourteenth international exhibition of paintings' (166); Rome, International Fine Arts Exhibition, British Section, 1911 (227); on loan to the Fitzwilliam Museum, 1919–33; purchased from Sir William Nicholson for the Fitzwilliam Museum, 1933; exh. London, National Portrait Gallery, 1975, 'Augustus John'.

Painted for William Nicholson, at Augustus John's suggestion, at 153 Church Street, Chelsea, where John took up residence late in 1908.[1] The portrait had been started by 8 January 1909,[2] and was finished in time to be included in the New English Art Club's summer exhibition that year. Analogies of conception and design may be observed with W. R. Sickert's portrait of P. Wilson Steer of 1890 (National Portrait Gallery, no. 3116), which remained in Steer's possession until bequeathed to the Gallery in 1942. William Newzam Prior Nicholson (1872–1949), kt 1936, was a painter of figure-subjects, portraits, still-life and landscape. For paintings by him, see pp. 183–6 below.

REPRODUCED. Albert Rutherston, *Augustus John* (1923), pl. 10; Anthony Bertram, *Augustus John*, New York (1923), pl. 10; John Rothenstein, *Augustus John* (1944 and subsequent edns), pl. 50; Carl Winter, *The Fitzwilliam Museum* (1958), pl. 107; John Rothenstein, *Augustus John* (1962) (no plate number).

NOTES. [1] Marguerite Steen, *William Nicholson* (1943), p. 115; letter from Augustus John, 30 July 1946 (Fitzwilliam Museum); Michael Holroyd, *Augustus John*, 2 vols. (1974), I, p. 293. [2] Holroyd, *op, cit.*, I, p. 294.

2456 DAVID AND DORELIA IN NORMANDY

Canvas on millboard, $14\frac{5}{8} \times 17\frac{7}{8}$ in ($37{\cdot}2 \times 45{\cdot}4$ cm). In a landscape, a small boy wearing a buff coat and green breeches, his left hand up to his head, stands to the right of a seated woman, turned towards the right and facing front. She wears a long-skirted mauve dress, a blue scarf over her right shoulder, and a blue turban. Green fields rise to a low ridge behind the figures; to the left is a beach, with a distant bay beyond. Strong blue sky. Signed lower left, 'John'.

Bequeathed by Edward Maurice Berkeley Ingram, C.M.G., O.B.E., 1941, received 1945. Exh. London, Redfern Gallery, 1939, 'Augustus John, J. D. Innes, Derwent Lees, paintings 1910–1914' (9), lent Ingram; New York, World's Fair, British Pavilion, 1939, 'Exhibition of contemporary British art' (49); exh. in Canada and America, with other Ingram pictures, apparently under the auspices of the British Council;[1] London, National Portrait Gallery, 1975, 'Augustus John'.

The figures in the picture are John's second wife, Dorelia, and his eldest child by his first wife, 'David' Nettleship John.[2] The place has been recognised as Dielette, not far from Cherbourg, where John and his wife and family spent most of the summer of 1908.[3]

REPRODUCED. Exhibition catalogue, *Augustus John, J. D. Innes, Derwent Lees, paintings 1910–1914* (1939), Redfern Gallery, London (colour); catalogue, *Exhibition of contemporary British art* (1939), New York, World's Fair, British Pavilion; catalogue, *Exhibition of the collection of paintings formed by the late Maurice Ingram* (1941), Redfern Gallery, London (colour); Rhys Davies, *The story of Wales* (1943), p. 47; *Burlington Magazine* (1975), CXVII, 309.

NOTES. [1] Included as no. 1 in the catalogue of the 'Exhibition of the collection of paintings formed by the late Maurice Ingram' held at the Redfern Gallery, London, in 1941, although, as the catalogue states, with ten other pictures (also included) 'away on exhibition in Canada and America', which seems to have extended to South American states. [2] Born on 6 January 1902, and christened Nettleship John, but always known as David. [3] Recognised by Edna Clarke Hall, who was also at Dielette in 1908 (information kindly supplied by Mr A. D. Fraser Jenkins, letter of 16 December 1975, Fitzwilliam Museum). Though this is presumably correct, the boy looks more than David's age of about six and a half. For John's stay at Dielette, see Michael Holroyd, *Augustus John*, 2 vols. (1974), I, p. 292.

PD. 22–1961 OLIVES IN SPAIN

Canvas, 13 × 16⅛ in (33·0 × 40·9 cm). To right and left in the foreground are low banks, painted in mauves and greys, leading diagonally towards the right to an olive orchard beyond, with grey-green foliage and brighter green grass, which reveals in the distance a meadow with trees against a mauve-coloured hill. Light buff sky. Signed lower right, 'John'.

Bequeathed by Louis Colville Gray Clarke, LL.D., 1960, received 1961. Exh. London, New Chenil Galleries, 1926 'Paintings and drawings by Augustus E. John' (16);[1] R.A., 1954, 'Works by Augustus John, O.M., R.A.' (394),[2] lent L. C. G. Clarke.

John paid only two visits to Spain, of which this painting must belong to the first, in May 1922, as the second took place during the winter of 1954/5.[3]

NOTES. [1] With the title, *Sketch in Spain*. [2] With the title, *Spanish landscape*. [3] Information kindly supplied by Mr Michael Holroyd (letter of 28 August 1970, Fitzwilliam Museum); see also his *Augustus John*, 2 vols. (1974), II, pp. 113, 197.

PD. 23–1961 STUDY IN PROVENCE

Canvas, 15 × 15⅜ in (38·1 × 39·1 cm). A woman at whole-length, turned front, stands beside a tree, her head turned to the left, her left hand on her hip; she wears a blue blouse, a red skirt and a pink tam-o-shanter; reddish brown flesh-colour. To the left rises the trunk of the tree, and behind the figure stretches a thick, bare branch, both plum red in colour. In the background is a distant slope, in greenish and bluish greys; pale greyish green sky above. Signed lower right, 'John'.

Bequeathed by Louis Colville Gray Clarke, LL.D., 1960, received 1961. Exh. London, New Chenil Galleries, 1926, 'Paintings and drawings by Augustus E. John' (10); R.A., 1954, 'Works by Augustus John, O.M., R.A.' (195), lent L. C. G. Clarke.

John paid his first visit to Provence in 1910, and returned not infrequently in subsequent years. It has been suggested on grounds of style that this picture, which was not among the Provençal studies exhibited in London at the Chenil Galleries after this first visit, may be of a period not long before the exhibition of 1926.[1]

NOTE. [1] By Mr A. D. Fraser Jenkins (letter of 13 January 1976, Fitzwilliam Museum).

PD. 24–1961 GIRL LEANING ON A STICK (1910)

Wood, 13 × 9¼ in (33·0 × 23·5 cm). She stands, just less than whole-length, turned to front, her head to the left, leaning with both hands on a long stick at the right; she wears a short-sleeved, long dress. The figure is drawn in pencil outline on the unprimed wood; the head, neck, forearms and grey head-scarf only in paint. The background is painted darker blue in the lower part and lighter blue in the upper. Inscribed in ink on the back of the panel, 'Augustus John/1910'.

Bequeathed by Louis Colville Gray Clarke, LL.D., 1960, received 1961. Exh. London, R.A., 1954, 'Works by Augustus John, O.M., R.A.' (176), lent L. C. G. Clarke; Sheffield, Graves Art Gallery, 1956, 'Augustus John, O.M., R.A.' (4).

The inscription on the back appears to be in John's own hand.[1]

NOTE. [1] The catalogues of both the R.A. and the Sheffield exhibitions describe the picture as 'Signed and dated on the back'.

PD. 25–1961 DORELIA BY THE CARAVAN

Wood, 14 × 10½ in (35·5 × 26·7 cm). She stands, at three-quarter-length, turned slightly to left, her head bent towards the left, leaning slightly against the caravan at right, her left hand placed upon it. She wears a light mauve tunic with an emerald green skirt, a red ribbon round her neck; her hair is dark blue. The caravan is in blues and greys. The sky, which fills almost the whole background, is of blue turning lighter towards the low horizon, with white clouds. Painted on a gilt ground. Signed top right, 'John'.

Bequeathed by Louis Colville Gray Clarke, LL.D., 1960, received 1961. (?) Exh. London, Alpine Club Gallery, 1917/18, 'Pictures and decorations by Augustus John' (42);[1] coll. Augustus John, 1923;[2] exh. London, New Chenil Galleries, 1926, 'Paintings and drawings by Augustus E. John' (44), bt Mrs Rumsey; New York, World's Fair, British Pavilion, 1939, 'Exhibition of contemporary British art' (47), lent L. C. G. Clarke; (?) Toledo Museum of Art, Ohio, U.S.A.[3]; London, R.A., 1954, 'Works by Augustus John, O.M., R.A.' (230); Sheffield, Graves Art Gallery, 1956, 'Augustus John, O.M., R.A.' (15).

The head in a head and shoulders study, of which only the head is completed, at Cardiff, National Museum of Wales, corresponds with the head in the present picture, and is stated to have been 'Painted in Chelsea, 1911'.[4]

REPRODUCED. Albert Rutherston, *Augustus John* (1923), pl. 7; A. B. (Anthony Bertram), *Augustus John* (1923), pl. 7.

NOTES. [1] With the title *Leaning against the caravan*, as in the New Chenil Galleries exhibition of 1926, the label of which is at the back of the painting. [2] Albert Rutherston, *Augustus John* (1923), pl. 7. [3] From a label at the back of the painting. [4] *Catalogue of the Gwendoline E. Davies Bequest* (1952), p. 16, no. 45, *Study of a woman's head*; rep. *Connoisseur* (1952), CXXIX, 25.

JOHN, Gwendolen Mary

1876–1939. Born at Haverfordwest, Pembrokeshire; elder sister of Augustus John. Slade School, London, 1895–8, where she was much influenced by her contemporary Ambrose McEvoy; studied under Whistler in Paris. Settled in France in 1903; close friend of Auguste Rodin. Painted chiefly portraits and single-figure studies of women and children.

PD. 24–1951 THE CONVALESCENT

Canvas, $16\frac{1}{8} \times 13$ in ($40{\cdot}9 \times 33{\cdot}0$ cm). A girl with dark brown hair, wearing a blue-grey dress, who looks down at a book held in her lap, is seated in an armchair turned half to the left, a circular table to the right of it. Chair and table are brownish ochre and grey in colour, a grey cushion is in the chair and a grey cloth on the table, upon it a pink cup and saucer and a brown coffee-pot. Light grey background with small touches of soft orange.

Given by the Very Rev. Eric Milner-White, C.B.E., D.S.O., Dean of York, 1951. Coll. Captain Peto; Eardley Knollys, who sold it to Roland, Browse & Delbanco, London, 1950; bt from them by the Very Rev. E. Milner-White, 1951.

Seven other versions of this subject are known, one of them, of unidentified ownership, from a photograph.[1] The six belong (1970) respectively to the Tate Gallery, London (no. 4861), to Manchester City Art Gallery, to Mrs Cazalet-Keir, to (the late) Dennis Cohen, to Mrs Hugo Pitman, and to Mrs F. D. Samuel. The practice of painting several repetitions of the same subject became a feature of Gwen John's later work, though it seems to have begun as early as about 1908.[2] Information concerning two of the known versions provides some evidence for dating the series of *The convalescent*. The Manchester version was bought in Paris in 1924, at an exhibition at the Salon des Tuileries, by Albert Rutherston, who stated that it had been painted at Meudon in the same year.[3] Also in 1924 Ethel Nettleship brought over from Meudon Mrs Samuel's version.[4]

NOTES. [1] In the Tate Gallery archives. [2] Mary Taubman, catalogue of the Arts Council exhibition, 'Gwen John', 1968, p. 17. [3] He gave it to Manchester in 1925. Information from Miss E. Johnson, Keeper of Paintings, Manchester City Art Gallery, 5 February 1970. [4] Tate Gallery Catalogues, *Modern British paintings, drawings and sculpture* (1964), I, p. 338.

JOHNSON, Cornelius

1593–1661. Born in London. Earliest known dated work 1617; court painter, 1632; influenced successively by Mytens, van Dyck and Dobson; in Holland from 1643; died in Utrecht. Portrait painter and miniaturist in oils.

PD. 60–1958 UNKNOWN LADY (1646) PLATE 3

Canvas, 33 × 27¾ in (83·9 × 70·5 cm).[1] Her dress is black, the linen white; dark brown hair with a small, dark cap. The jewel has dark stones set in gold; the fan is pink and grey. Signed and dated lower right, 'C Jonson van Ceulen 1646'.

Given by the Garrison Officer Cadet Battalion Association, as a memorial to No. 22 (Garrison) Officer Cadet Battalion, Cambridge 1916–19, 1958. With A. J. Sully, London, from whom bought by Leggatt Bros., London, 1926;[2] sold to the Hon. Mountstuart Elphinstone (1871–1957), 1926; inherited from him by John, 17th Lord Elphinstone, for whom sold by Leggatt Bros.

From the date of the painting, the lady is most probably Dutch; with the companion portrait of a man,[3] the pair were formerly described as members of the Six family. While in England Johnson signed his pictures 'Cornelius Johnson', but after moving to Holland he modified the form of his surname to 'Jonson van Ceulen'; sometimes wrongly called 'Janssens'.

NOTES. [1] Lined; dimensions of the painted surface. [2] Together with a companion portrait of a man, also on sale by Leggatt Bros. for Lord Elphinstone, see below. [3] See n. [2]; M. Crabbe sale, Sotheby's, 29 July 1970 (1).

JONES, Thomas

1742–1803. Born at Cefnllys, Radnorshire. At William Shipley's School, and the St Martin's Lane Academy, London; pupil of Richard Wilson, 1763–5. Member of the Incorporated Society of Artists of Great Britain, 1766; in Italy, 1776–83; retired to his estate at Pencerrig, Radnorshire, 1789. Landscape artist.

PD. 21–1954 SCENE NEAR NAPLES (1783)

Paper, 9½ × 13⅝ in (24·1 × 34·6 cm). On a low hill a grey, two-storied, rectangular building rises against the sky, trees behind a wall running from it towards the right. The slopes are covered with deep green verdure, except for the yellow of an outcrop of rock below the building. In the immediate foreground is the outline of a brown wall. Blue sky with grey clouds. Inscribed in pencil at the back, 'Naples Aprile 1783 TJ'.

Purchased 1954. Sold Christie's, 'The Property of a Lady whose husband was a descendant of Thomas Jones', 2 July 1954 (220), bt P. & D. Colnaghi & Co. Ltd., London from whom it was purchased; exh. Twickenham, Marble Hill House, and Cardiff, National Museum of Wales, 1970, 'Thomas Jones' (73); Hazlitt, 1974 (31).

Cleaned 1974. This study is among the latest made by Jones in Italy, which he left on 3 August 1783. In his *Memoirs*, the one reference to 'Excursions ...into the Country' during the month of April 1783 only mentions specifically a visit to the Convent of Camaldole, a seventeenth-century building with a church.[1] Equally out of the question as an identification of the subject of the present study is its description when purchased as *The monastery of San Martino*, above Naples. No identification was offered in the catalogue of the 1954 Christie sale, when it was simply called *A mansion on a hillside*. The practice of making studies in oil on primed paper goes back to an early stage of Jones's Italian sojourn, but its main use was during the three final years in Naples.

REPRODUCED. Exhibition catalogue, Hazlitt, 1974, pl. 14.

NOTE. [1] *Walpole Society* (1951), XXXII, 122.

DE KARLOWSKA, STANISLAWA

1876–1952. Born in Poland. Studied in Paris; married Robert Polhill Bevan, 1897; from 1900 lived in Hampstead, London; original member of the London Group, 1913.

PD. 17–1968 LOCK ON THE CANAL

Canvas, 22⅛ × 18 in (56·2 × 45·7 cm). The canal runs centrally through the composition from a background of tall industrial buildings. A double lock is in the foreground; behind it an iron footbridge spans the canal. The predominant colouring is blue and pink-mauve, stronger towards the foreground, with yellow-green water; adjacent to the buildings on the left is an orange-coloured feature; on those to the right is a yellow name sign. The sky is in cool and warm greys. Signed lower left, 'S. de Karlowska'.

Given by Mrs E. H. Baty and R. A. P. Bevan, C.B.E., the artist's children, 1968. Exh. London, New Burlington Galleries, 1928, 'London Group, retrospective exhibition, 1914–1928' (99); Bedford, Cecil Higgins Art Gallery, 1969, 'The Camden Town Group' (31).

Dated 1913 in the catalogue of the 'London Group, retrospective exhibition, 1914–1928', with the title *The canal at Camden Town*. The canal would thus be the Regent's Canal, which runs through this part of London.

KERR-LAWSON, James

1864–1939. Born in Scotland. Student in Rome and Paris; worked in Canada, Italy, Paris, Spain and North Africa. Painted portraits, genre, and wall-decorations.

2507 PAUL VERLAINE

Canvas, $16\frac{3}{4} \times 12\frac{3}{4}$ in ($42{\cdot}6 \times 32{\cdot}4$ cm). Nearly half-length, to left, looking front. Bare-headed, bald; flowing fair moustache, beard and whiskers; very bright blue eyes. Wears a loose, dull mauve coat, with white linen showing at the neck. Signed lower left, 'J. KERR-LAWSON'.

Bought from the Coppinger Prichard Fund, 1943. Coll. Caterina Kerr-Lawson, the artist's widow, from whom it was bought; exh. London, Beaux-Arts Gallery, 1942, Kerr-Lawson memorial exhibition; Edinburgh, Institut français d'Ecosse, Kerr-Lawson exhibition, 1952.

Paul Verlaine (1844–1896), *fin-de-siècle* poet, friend of Arthur Rimbaud. In Paris in 1894, Kerr-Lawson made a drawing of him from the life, from which this portrait was painted, also in Paris.[1]

REPRODUCED. Francis Carco, *Verlaine* (1939), p. 100, pl. XI; *Apollo* (1939), XXIX, 263.

NOTE. [1] *Apollo* (1939), XXIX, 262, from which it might be assumed that the painting itself was from life; but the lines of squaring-up for enlargement visible through the paint indicate that this was not so. The drawing is reproduced in the *Connoisseur* (1952), CXXIX, 115.

KINGSFORD, Florence Kate

1871–1949. Born in Canterbury. Student at the R.A. schools; pupil of Edward Johnston; best known as a calligrapher and illuminator; married S. C. Cockerell (later Sir Sydney), 1907.

PD. 143–1975 JOAN AND OLIVE KINGSFORD, AND MALCOLM BURGESS

Card, 7⅝ × 8½ in (19·3 × 21·6 cm). A square, white tent stands on a garden lawn, behind it a flower bed with red and yellow flowers in front of a grey-brown wooden fence. Beside the tent, three figures recline upon the grass, to the left a girl in a pale blue dress and red hat, next to her a woman in a pale blue dress with a white hat, and to the right a man in a white shirt and dark breeches and stockings. Grey-blue sky with white clouds.

Inscribed at the back with the artist's initials, 'FKK', 'Joan, Olive, Malcolm, BURGESS / or Olive, Connie, Malcolm / Birch Grove, Lee. Kent', and 'Mine / Joan'. Joan, one of Florence K. Kingsford's five sisters, married the donor of this painting.

PD. 144–1975 JOAN KINGSFORD

Canvas, 11⅞ × 8⅞ in (30·2 × 22·5 cm). A young girl, at whole-length, is seated on a folding, brown wooden chair, turned slightly to the right, her knees crossed, reading a book open upon them. She has light brown hair, and wears a black dress with a white pinafore, and black stockings. Behind her is the wall of a room, light brown below, buff above, on which hang above the girl's head a Japanese fan, greyish-buff, and a European fan, light greenish yellow with brown sticks.

Inscribed at the back with the artist's initials, 'FKK', and 'Joan'. See no. PD.143–1975 above.

Given by Wilfred R. Wood, 1975.

KNAPTON, George

1698–1778. Born in London. Pupil of Jonathan Richardson; in Italy, 1725–32; painter to the Society of Dilettanti, 1736–63; Surveyer of the King's pictures, 1765. Portrait painter in oils and pastel.

22 EDWARD MORRISON PLATE 6

Canvas, 29⅝ × 24¾ in (75·3 × 62·9 cm).[1] His hair is light brown; he wears an olive-green jacket and a scarlet waistcoat with brown lapels. The back of the chair in which he is seated is dark brown, the ledge on which he rests his arm is of a lighter brown. Brown background.

Bequeathed by the Rev. James William Arnold, D.D. (d. 1865), with a life-interest to his widow, Lady Mary Arnold; received 1873. Sale by Phillips (of London) at Ashby Lodge, Northamptonshire, 20–2 April 1854 (171), bt Rev. J. W. Arnold, D.D.[2]

The identification as Edward Morrison rests upon nothing firmer than family tradition,[3] but that is to a certain extent supported by circumstantial evidence. From the costume the portrait may be approximately dated to the third quarter of the eighteenth century. At the back of the picture is a written label, similar to those on the other three pictures in the Arnold bequest (see n. [2]), correctly attributing it to Knapton, but describing it as 'General Morrison (as a boy)'. By this is presumably meant General George Morrison (1704(?)–1799), who was connected with the Arnold family by the marriage of his eldest daughter to George Arnold of Ashby Lodge in 1788; but he could not be the youthful figure in the portrait. General Morrison's will shows that he had an apparently only son, who was his ultimate heir, named Edward, and indicates a friendship with Knapton by the bequest to his son of a collection of drawings left to him by the painter. The drawing which Edward Morrison holds seems to be a plan of fortifications, a possible reference to his father's military career as an engineer.

REPRODUCED. Earp, p. 108; *Principal pictures* (1912 edn), p. 90, (1929 edn), p. 113.

NOTE. [1] Lined; dimensions of the painted surface. [2] Ashby Lodge was the seat of the Arnold family, and descended to Georgeana Arnold, who married James Coape in 1840 and died in 1849; the catalogue of the sale of the pictures and library at Ashby lodge in 1854, does not specify the seller, but it was presumably James Coape. The bequest of Dr J. W. Arnold, the uncle of Georgeana, included two Arnold family portraits by Hogarth (see nos. 21 and 24, pp. 108 and 109 above) and a view of Ashby Lodge (see under N. T. Dall, no. 26, p. 62', also bought at the 1854 sale. [3] Information from Miss Bertha Coape-Arnold in 1953; her grandfather, the son of James Coape (see n. [2]), took the name of Coape-Arnold. The portrait was not identified in the 1854 sale, where it was wrongly catalogued as by Thomas Hudson; in the Arnold bequest, it was correctly given to Knapton, but described only as 'A member of the Arnold family'.

KNEWSTUB, Walter John

1833–1906. Born in Colchester. Student at the R.A. schools; pupil and assistant to D. G. Rossetti; worked for Ford Madox Brown in Manchester, 1887. Genre painter.

673* O IF I WERE GRANDMA

Paper mounted on wood, mixed technique, $20\frac{7}{8} \times 13\frac{7}{8}$ in ($52{\cdot}7 \times 35{\cdot}7$ cm). A little girl, nearly whole-length, standing, turned almost in profile to the left, the head in full profile, looks at herself in a mirror on a chest of drawers. She has red-gold hair; she wears a long white dress, with a patterned red shawl across her left shoulder, on which she places her left hand; right arm behind her back holding a gilt lorgnette. To the left is the end of a mahogany chest of drawers; to the right is a dark red garment thrown over a chair, with a table covered in dark green behind it, on which lies a cat. Behind the girl is a dark brown hanging; to the right of it a glimpse into another room. Signed with a monogram lower left.

Given by Charles Fairfax Murray, 1909. Exh. R.A., 1873 (827).

The figure of the girl is painted in water-colours; elsewhere, gum and probably other mediums appear to have been used. The girl is Knewstub's daughter, Alice Mary, afterwards the wife of Sir William Rothenstein. She appears again, at about the same age, in a painting with her mother.[1]

NOTE. [1] Rep. *Artwork* (1930), VI, 80.

LAMB, Henry

1885–1906. Born in Australia, brought up in Manchester. Initially a medical student; attended the art school of J.-E. Blanche, Paris; returned to London, 1911; R.A., 1949. Painted portraits, landscapes and subject pictures.

2748 LYTTON STRACHEY PLATE 61

Canvas, 20×16 in ($50{\cdot}8 \times 40{\cdot}7$ cm). His hair is dark brown, the moustache and beard deep auburn. His clothes are brown; the background is green.

Given by Justin Edward Vulliamy, 1945. Exh. Cambridge, 6 King's Parade, 1921, lent Henry Lamb;[1] bt from him by C. K. Ogden, organiser of the exhibition;[2] sold by him to Mrs E. O. Vulliamy;[3] gvien by her to her son, the donor.

Giles Lytton Strachey (1880–1932), biographer and literary critic, a prominent member of the 'Bloomsbury' circle. During the winter of

1913–14, Lamb was painting his large portrait of Strachey, now in the Tate Gallery, London (no. T118). This painting is one of a number of studies he then made, and corresponds exactly with the head and shoulders of the large portrait.

NOTES. [1] Letters of 11 August 1921 and 26 September 1948 from Henry Lamb (Fitzwilliam Museum). [2] *Ibid.*, n. [1]. [3] Information from Mrs Vulliamy, 1948.

PD. 233–1961 THE RIVER EBBLE, WILTSHIRE (1937)

Canvas-covered millboard, $19\frac{7}{8} \times 23\frac{3}{4}$ in (50·5 × 60·3 cm). In a flat meadow, surrounded by trees, a winding stream runs from the centre of the picture to the left foreground, where it is crossed by a stone footbridge. In the distance, a curve of downland, with a narrow band of cloudy sky, appear above the trees. The grass is in a light, bright green and light ochre, the water bright blue with reflections mainly of mauve, the trees predominantly bluish green with blue-mauve shadows. Signed and dated lower right, 'Lamb/37'.

Bought from the Fairhaven Fund, 1961. Exh. London, Leicester Galleries, 1961, 'A memorial exhibition of paintings and drawings by Henry Lamb, R.A.' (76), where it was bought.[1]

The Ebble runs into the River Avon near Salisbury, not far from Coombe Bissett, where Lamb lived from about 1930.

NOTE [1] All the works in this exhibition had come from the artist's widow, Lady Pansy Lamb (information from the Leicester Galleries, 1970).

LANCE, George

1802–1864. Born at Little Easton, Essex. Pupil in B. R. Haydon's studio, London, and at the R.A. schools. Exh. from 1824 (R.A., B.I., Society of British Artists). Painted still-life and some subject pictures.

490 FRUIT-PIECE PLATE 40

Canvas, 11 × 14 in (27·9 × 35·6 cm).[1] The basket is straw-colour. The peach is red and yellow, the currants red, the pear an ochrish green; the black grapes are a brownish red on the shadowed side; the leaves are olive green, brown in the shadow. The shelf is greyish brown; the background is warm brown.

Given by Mrs Richard Ellison, 1862. (?) Exh. London, B.I., 1836 (284).[2]

NOTES. [1] Backed onto a larger canvas attached to the stretcher, which measures 12 × 15 in (30·5 × 38·1 cm). [2] Title *Fruit*; the exhibition catalogue gives the outside dimensions of the frame as 20 × 23 in (50·8 × 58·4 cm), close to the size of the present frame, 19½ × 22¾ in (49·5 × 57·8 cm).

LAVERY, Sir John

1856–1941. Born in Belfast. Studied in Glasgow, London, and Paris (Académie Julian); influenced by J. Bastien-Lepage; exh. R.A. from 1886; kt, 1918; R.A., 1921. Painted portraits, landscape and genre.

1072 STUDIES IN THE HOUSE OF LORDS

Canvas, 14 × 10 in (35·6 × 25·4 cm). Numerous small sketches of heads against a black background, of which twenty-five are carried to the point of recognisability. Signed lower right, 'J. Lavery'.

Given by the Friends of the Fitzwilliam Museum, 1922. Exh. London, Grosvenor Galleries, 1922, 'Paintings and drawings by contemporary British artists' (43, 44 or 45);[1] bt from the artist.

Sketches made for Lavery's painting of Viscount Morley moving the address in the House of Lords on 14 December 1921 in reply to the speech from the Throne opening a special session of Parliament to consider proposals for the establishment of the Irish Free State. Prominent among the heads which have been identified are the Earl of Birkenhead, Lord Chancellor, lower right, above him Lord Carson, in the centre Viscount Chaplin, and above him to the right the Marquess of Londonderry; Viscount Morley's head is not included. The large completed picture,[2] which shows Lord Morley in the act of speaking, painted in 1922, is at Glasgow (Art Gallery and Museum, no. 1544).

REPRODUCED. Friends of the Fitzwilliam Museum, *Annual Report* for 1922.

NOTES. [1] In the exhibition catalogue, these three items are bracketed together as 'Three sketches for the picture of the House of Lords, 15th. Dec. 1921', but which of them is the Fitzwilliam Museum sketch is not known. The date should correctly be 14 December 1921. [2] Rep. *Royal Academy Illustrated* (1922), p. 55.

LAWRENCE, Sir Thomas

1769–1830. Born in Bristol. Almost entirely self-taught; moved to London, 1787; briefly attended the R.A. schools; Painter in Ordinary to George III, 1792; R.A., 1794; kt, 1815; at the close of the Napoleonic wars painted for the Prince Regent the portaits of the heads of the allied states and armies; P.R.A., 1820. Portrait painter.

27 SAMUEL WOODBURN PLATE 30

Wood, 43 × 32⅞ in (109·2 × 83·5 cm). Black hair; chestnut brown coat with a darker brown velvet collar, white choker; fawn trousers. Red-upholstered chair; red curtain in the background, with a brown mirror to left.

Given by Miss Woodburn, 1865. Coll. Samuel Woodburn; exh. London, B.I., 1830, Lawrence memorial exhibition (84), lent Samuel Woodburn.

Samuel Woodburn (1786–1853), became the pre-eminent London art dealer, and one of the finest connoisseurs, of his day; his interests lay in paintings, Old Master drawings, and prints. He is said to have been employed by the Founder of the Fitzwilliam Museum in the acquisition of his works of art,[1] and was largely instrumental in the formation of Lawrence's matchless collection of Old Master drawings. The portrait has been dated *c.* 1820;[2] but on grounds of style and of Woodburn's apparent age, it could equally be of a few years later, 1823–4, if a passage in Lawrence's correspondence with him is to be interpreted as reliable evidence for this approximate date.[3]

REPRODUCED. Earp, p. 110; *Principal pictures* (1912 edn), p. 92, (1929 edn), p. 117; R. S. Clouston, *Sir Thomas Lawrence* (n.d.), p. 34.

NOTES. [1] If so, it can only have been towards the end of Lord Fitzwilliam's life, as when he died in 1816, Woodburn was only thirty; perhaps it was mainly in connection with his fine collection of prints, of which Woodburn drew up the inventory for Lord Fitzwilliam's executors in March 1816. [2] Kenneth Garlick, *Sir Thomas Lawrence* (1954), p. 63. [3] A possible reference to the painting of the portrait occurs in a letter from Lawrence to Woodburn, then in Paris, dated 8 March 1823, in which he says, 'May I see you in my painting room, with looks uninjured by the Italian climate' (D. E. Williams, *The Life and correspondence of Sir Thomas Lawrence, Kt.*, 2 vols. (1831), II, p. 293); other letters show that Woodburn was in Rome late in 1822 and early in 1823 (Williams, *op. cit.*, pp. 281, 285).

LEAR, EDWARD

1812–1888. Born in Holloway, London. Received amateur instruction from his sister Ann, and while still a youth became a zoological draughtsman. About the age of twenty-five, turned to landscape; in Italy, 1837–41, where he began painting in oils; entered the R.A. schools, 1850; from 1853 spent his time mostly abroad; settled in San Remo, 1872. Topographical draughtsman and painter.

460* THE TEMPLE OF APOLLO AT BASSAE (1854–5) PLATE 42

Canvas, 57⅝ × 90⅜ in (146·4 × 229·5 cm). The temple is buff colour, in a terrain of ochrish green; the hills behind are blue. The foreground rocks are in tones of pinkish brown and grey in the lights, in tones of greenish grey in the shadows; the trunks of the trees are in tones of warm and cool brown, their foliage green or light brown. Signed and dated lower right, 'EL. [in a monogram] 1854–55'.

Given by the subscribers, 1860.[1] Exh. London, R.A., 1855 (319);[2] London, Arts Council, and Southampton, Art Gallery, 1958, 'Edward Lear' (3).[3]

Lear visited Bassae in the course of a tour of Greece made in the spring of 1849, during which he drew assiduously.[4] There can be no doubt that it was drawings then made which formed the basis of the present picture, when it was painted some years later; but this topographical material was supplemented by detailed studies from nature made in England. William Holman Hunt, whom Lear met in 1852, had suggested this method of procedure, considering Lear's drawings to be much too summary to permit of their use as the sole basis for paintings.[5] Work on the picture is first recorded in 1853, when Lear visited Leicestershire to paint rocks and oak trees for the foreground, an excursion which was repeated in 1854.[6] Early in 1855 he was again at work upon the picture in London,[7] and it was completed in time to be shown at the R.A. in the summer. No drawings precisely connected with the painting have so far come to light, though one from a slightly different view-point is known, which is of interest from being dated in Lear's hand 18 March 1849.[8] The temple is far from accurately depicted in the painting, the whole of the cella within the colonnade, still standing, being omitted. The Doric temple of Apollo Epicurius, at Bassae near Phigalea in Arcadia, was discovered in 1765. From the style of the frieze of the cella, now in the British Museum, it is dated to the last decades of the fifth century B.C.[9]

REPRODUCED. Earp, p. 110; *Later letters of Edward Lear*, ed. Lady Strachey (1911), p. 306; *Principal pictures* (1912 edn), p. 93, (1929 edn), p. 118; Angus Davidson, *Edward Lear* (1938 and 1968 edns), p. 80; Vivien Noakes, *Edward Lear* (1968), p. 174.

NOTES. [1] Lear was writing personally to his friends at the end of 1859 asking for subscriptions towards the purchase of the picture; see Vivien Noakes, *Edward Lear* (1968), p. 173. A list of the subscribers is printed in *Last letters of Edward Lear*, ed. Lady Strachey (1911), Appendix F, p. 380, where their purpose is expressed as a desire to see the picture in a university museum. Cf. also

Angus Davidson, *Edward Lear* (1938 and 1968 edns), p. 132. [2] The entry in the exhibition catalogue reads, 'The Temple of Bassae or Phigalea, in Arcadia: from the oak woods of Mount Cotylium. The hills of Sparta, Athome and Navarino in the distance'. [3] The exhibition was first shown in the Moot Hall at Aldeburgh, Suffolk, but excluding the present picture on account of its size. [4] Davidson, *op. cit.*, p. 66; Noakes, *op. cit.*, p. 99. [5] Davidson, *op. cit.*, pp. 78–80, 82, 86; Noakes, *op. cit.*, pp. 111ff. [6] Davidson, *op. cit.*, pp. 89, 91; Noakes, *op. cit.*, p. 119. [7] Noakes, *op. cit.*, p. 126. [8] In 1947 in the possession of Miss Elisabeth Kitson. [9] D. S. Robertson, *Greek and Roman architecture* (2nd edn, 1969), pp. 136–8.

LEES, Derwent

1885–1931. Australian by birth. Studied in Paris and at the Slade School, London; associate and follower of J. D. Innes, Augustus John and Ambrose McEvoy. Member of the New English Art Club, 1911–19. Landscape painter.

2450 LYNDRA IN WALES PLATE 60

Wood, $12\frac{7}{8} \times 16$ in ($32{\cdot}7 \times 40{\cdot}6$ cm). She wears a mauve jacket over a pink jersey, with a grey skirt and grey hat. The ground around her is pink, the further fields yellowish green divided by a band of blue-grey. The hills are in tones of grey, the most distant is mauve. The blue sky shades to pink behind her head; cream clouds. Signed lower left, 'Lees'.

Bequeathed by Edward Maurice Berkeley Ingram, C.M.G., O.B.E., 1941. Bt by Ingram from the Redfern Gallery, London, 1937; exh. London, Redfern Gallery, 1939, 'Augustus John, J. D. Innes, Derwent Lees, paintings 1910–1914' (33); National Gallery, 1940, 'British painting since Whistler' (104); Redfern Gallery, 1941, 'The collection of paintings formed by the late Maurice Ingram' (29).

The woman in the picture is Mrs Derwent Lees, engaged in darning a pair of Augustus John's socks;[1] she was married to Lees in 1913, having formerly been a model of John's. The dates when the three of them were together in Wales are uncertain, but one such occasion is mentioned in a letter from John to his wife Dorelia, undated, but probably written in 1912.[2] They were then near Tan-y-Grisiau, in Merioneth, North Wales. Otherwise, the date limits of 1910–1914 of the Redfern Gallery exhibition of 1939 provide the only available information for dating the picture.

NOTES. [1] Note inscribed by E. M. B. Ingram at the back of the picture, of information given by him by Mrs Derwent Lees in 1937. [2] Information kindly supplied by Mr Michael Holroyd, letter of 26 March 1970 (Fitzwilliam Museum).

LEGROS, Alphonse

1837–1911. Born at Dijon. Trained in Paris; came to England, 1863; as Slade Professor of Fine Art, University College, London, 1875–92, influential as a teacher of draughtsmanship.

94* THE REV. ROBERT BURN (1880)

Canvas, 25 × 18 in (63·5 × 45·7 cm). Head and sketched-in shoulders, nearly profile left. Bare-headed, greying, dark hair; greying, dark moustache, beard and whiskers. The background unpainted.

Given by the artist,[1] (?) 1880.

The Rev. Robert Burn (1824–1904), fellow of Trinity College, Cambridge, known for his work on the archaeology of Rome and its neighbourhood. The portrait was executed by Legros at the Fitzwilliam Museum in 1880, as a practical demonstration of painting, and completed in two hours; it was considered an excellent likeness. The demonstration took the place of a lecture by the Slade Professor of Fine Art, Sidney Colvin.[2]

NOTES. [1] From a label on the frame of the picture; not officially registered as an acquisition. [2] *Cambridge Review* (1880), I, 85.

LEIGHTON, Frederick, Lord

1830–1896. Born in Scarborough. Studied in Florence, Frankfurt and Paris; and again in Frankfurt, for three years, under J. E. Steinle; exh. R.A. from 1855; R.A., 1869; visited the East; P.R.A., 1878; kt, 1878; raised to the peerage, 1896. Painter of subject pictures, and sculptor.

1501 MISS LAING (1853) PLATE 48

Canvas, 41⅞ × 29¾ in (106·4 × 75·6 cm). Black hair, with a black veil and white, yellow and red flowers; her dress is light blue. The column is buff-coloured, the curtain orange-red, the balustrade on which she rests her hand is grey. The fountain is a warm grey, the hedge behind it deep green, the tree a lighter green with red and yellow fruit. Pale sky of white, cream and blue. Signed and dated lower left, 'FL' [in a monogram] 1853'.[1]

Given by Miss Carolin Nias, 1928. Coll. John Laing; Lady Nias; exh. London, R.A., 1897, 'Works of the late Lord Leighton of Stretton' (109), lent Lady Nias; her daughter, Miss Carolin Nias.

Caroline Isabella Laing, daughter of John Laing; she married Admiral Sir Joseph Nias, K.C.B. (1793–1879), in 1855. The portrait was commissioned by her father, an old friend of the Leighton family,[2] and was painted during a visit of the Laings to Rome in the spring of 1853.[3]

REPRODUCED. Leonée and Richard Ormond, *Lord Leighton* (1975), pl. 25.

NOTES. [1] Leonée and Richard Ormond, *Lord Leighton* (1975), p. 150, no. 17. [2] Information from Mr Richard Ormond, 1974. [3] Mrs Russell Barrington, *The life, letters and work of Frederick Leighton*, 2 vols. (1906), I, p. 122.

M. 84 CLYTIE

Canvas, $33\frac{1}{2} \times 54\frac{1}{4}$ in ($85{\cdot}1 \times 137{\cdot}8$ cm). In the middle distance a dark brown hill slopes up from the right to its summit towards the left, at its foot dark green trees. In the foreground at the right a terrace, on which stands a column surmounted by a figure, at its base a kneeling woman in flowing red drapery who stretches out her arms towards the hill. Blue sky filled with light and dark brown clouds.[1]

Bequeathed by Charles Brinsley Marlay, 1912. Exh. London, R.A., 1892 (489); Manchester, City Art Gallery, 1892, 'Tenth autumn exhibition' (486), lent Leighton; Leighton sale, Christie's, 11 July 1896 (114); exh. London, West Ham, 1897, 'Free picture exhibition', lent C. B. Marlay; R.A., 1897, 'Works by the late Lord Leighton of Stretton' (22); on loan to Leighton House, London, since before 1912.

Cleaned 1966. Leighton was already working on this picture, exhibited in 1892, in 1890.[2] A sketch for it was lot 102 in the Leighton sale of 1896,[3] where lot 85 was a study for the sky painted at Malimnora in Donegal. Clytie, deserted by her lover Apollo, pined away and was transformed into a heliotrope flower, which, turning its head always to follow the course of the sun, betokens her undying love for him (Ovid, *Metamorphoses*, IV). The catalogue of the Leighton exhibition at the R.A. in 1897 describes the picture as showing Clytie 'with arms outstretched towards the sun, which is setting behind a range of moorland hills'. In 1896 Leighton painted a second picture on the subject of Clytie, in which the motive of the woman kneeling beside the column is developed into a life-size figure-subject.

NOTES. [1] Leonée and Richard Ormond, *Lord Leighton* (1975), p. 171, no. 368. [2] In a letter of 20 January 1890 (John Rylands Library, Manchester) to M. H. Spielmann, he says 'If I can possibly get the landscape Clytie finished for the exhibition I shall do so'. Writing to Charles Pooley about sending the picture to the 1892 Manchester exhibition (letter of 7 August 1892, John Rylands

Library), he says 'I myself have a weakness for this picture, which I brewed for some 15 years'. For the information in this Note, and for other details, thanks are due to Mr Richard Ormond. [3] Ormond, *op. cit.*, p. 171, no. 369.

LELY, Sir Peter

1618–1680. Born probably in Westphalia. Pupil in Haarlem of F. P. de Grebber, 1637; came to England about 1641; became the foremost portrait painter in the country; kt, 1680.

2442 PORTRAIT OF A LADY PLATE 4

Canvas, $49\frac{5}{8} \times 40\frac{5}{8}$ in (126·1 × 101·6 cm).[1] Dark brown hair; dress of amber satin, with white sleeves, and a chestnut-brown cloak, the scarf of grey-brown. The landscape in deep greens and browns, with grey clouds in a pale blue sky.[2]

Given by the Friends of the Fitzwilliam Museum, 1941. (?) With Henry Graves & Co., London; coll. Charles Heath Warner, of London, sold Christie's, 28 November 1879 (143),[3] bt Chalkley; anon. sale, Sotheby's, 23 April 1941 (164), bt for the Friends of the Fitzwilliam Museum.

From style and costume the picture may be dated to about 1665. A drawing for the hands and forearms, in black and red chalk heightened with white, belongs (1961) to Robert Lehman, New York.

REPRODUCED. Friends of the Fitzwilliam Museum, *Annual Report* for 1941, p. 3; Alison Settle, *English fashion* (1948), p. 24 (colour); Carl Winter, *The Fitzwilliam Museum* (1958), pl. 71.

NOTES. [1] Lined; dimensions of the painted surface. [2] R. B. Beckett, *Lely* (1951), p. 49, no. 275. [3] Probably this lot, described as 'Portrait of a lady', rather than lot 144, the only other Lely in the sale, described as 'Lady Ann Franklin', bt Martin Colnaghi.

LEWIS, John Frederick

1805–1876. Born in London. Taught by his father, the engraver F. C. Lewis; assistant to Sir Thomas Lawrence; travelled much abroad from about 1827; in the Near East, 1839–51. In 1829 adopted water-colour as his medium; resumed painting in oils about 1855. R.A., 1865. Began as an animal painter, but early turned to figures and scenes of the picturesque.

468 A SYRIAN SHEIK, EGYPT (1856)

Wood, 17 × 12 in (43·1 × 30·4 cm). Three-quarter-length standing, turned half to right, looking left; black beard. Wears a red and yellow head-cloth, draped round the shoulders, and a long, cream-coloured coat over a striped white robe, which is held by a broad red belt, into which is inserted a sheathed dagger. With his right hand he holds a rifle by the barrel across his right shoulder. Background of level desert of sand and pebbles, with low rocks, faintly green, rising to the right. Turquoise blue sky. Signed and dated lower right, 'J. F. Lewis. 1856'.

Given by Mrs Richard Ellison, 1862. Exh. R.A., 1857 (39).[1]

After his return to England from the Near East in 1851, Lewis's paintings were exclusively oriental in subject, based upon studies made during his travels. A water-colour version of no. 468, $8\frac{1}{4} \times 5\frac{3}{4}$ in (21·0 × 14·6 cm) was lot 55 at Sotheby's Belgravia, 9 April 1974.

REPRODUCED. *The Art Journal*, N.S. (1858), IV, no. XXXII, 41 (at half-length).

NOTE. [1] *The Art Journal*, N.S. (1858), IV, no. XXXII, 42.

LIN, Richard

b. 1933. Living artist.

PD. 67–1974 FRYDAY

Canvas, 25 × 25 in (63·5 × 63·5 cm). A canvas-covered rectangle, painted white, stands in relief in a shallow box; horizontally across the rectangle run narrow, applied white strips, varying in width, one bordered with yellow, one with a red stripe, one ruled with pencil lines; the spaces between the strips vary slightly in the colour of white.

Bought from the Gulbenkian and University Purchase Funds, 1974. Exh. London, Marlborough Fine Art Ltd, 1974, Richard Lin exhibition; bt from Marlborough Fine Art.

Dated by Marlborough Fine Art to 1973.[1]

NOTE. [1] Label at the back of the picture.

LINNELL, John

1792–1882. Born in London. Pupil of John Varley; entered R.A. schools, 1805; influenced by William Mulready; friend of William Blake. Portrait and landscape painter.

PD. 7–1950 SUNSET OVER A MOORLAND LANDSCAPE

Wood, $8\frac{3}{8} \times 10\frac{1}{8}$ in (21·3 × 25·6 cm). A partly reaped cornfield in the foreground, in tones of brown and olive-green, with standing corn to the right, recedes towards a dip in some low, tree-covered hills, olive-green in colour, which extend from the right; blue hills in the distance. Clouds above to the left illuminated by the setting sun, with sunset reds and yellows over the distant hills; to the right a veiled grey-blue sky with cream and grey clouds.

Bought from the Fairhaven Fund, 1950. Coll. Mrs John Linnell (d. 1865); given by John Linnell to his daughter Mary, 1868;[1] her niece, Mrs T. H. Riches (born Linnell); her posthumous sale, Sotheby's, 18 October 1950 (148), bt Fine Art Society; bt from the Fine Art Society.

Similar in style and execution to paintings of the earlier 1850s, such as *The disobedient prophet* of 1851–4[2] (Harris Museum and Art Gallery, Preston).

NOTES. [1] From an inscribed label at the back. [2] Alfred T. Story, *Life of John Linnell* (1892), p. 272.

PD. 55–1958 THE RIVER KENNET, NEAR NEWBURY (1815) PLATE 37

Canvas on wood, $17\frac{3}{4} \times 25\frac{5}{8}$ in ($45{\cdot}1 \times 65{\cdot}2$ cm). The buildings, the bridge, the path and the distant field in tones of brown; the trees and herbage in tones of olive-green. The blue of the sky, and the cream and grey of the clouds, are reflected in the water. Damaged signature and date lower left, '...innell 18(?)5', the '5' somewhat conjectural.

Bought from the Fairhaven Fund, 1958. Exh. London, Society of Painters in Oil and Water-colours, 1816, '12th Exhibition' (13);[1] B.I., 1826 (138); sold to 'Mr Blackie', 1831;[2] (?) Ralph Thomas sale, Phillips, London, 2 May 1848 (81);[3] (?) exh. Derby, 1870, 'Works of art and industrial products' (33), lent A. W. Lyon;[4] (?) sold Christie's, Executors of Arthur W. Lyon, of Rocester, Staffordshire, 19 May 1883 (100),[5] bt Tooth; (?) J. W. Adamson sale, Christie's, 7 May 1887 (122);[6] coll. Colonel M. H. Grant by about 1933; exh. London, Arts Council, 1952–3, 'Early English landscapes from Colonel Grant's collection' (34); London, P. & D. Colnaghi & Co. Ltd, 1958, 'Paintings by Old Masters' (17), bt Fitzwilliam Museum; Colnaghi, 1973, 'John Linnell and his circle' (40).

Retouched 1868.[7] Except for the figures and the barge in the background, the painting corresponds with a water-colour belonging to Air Vice-Marshal F. M. H. Maynard, which is inscribed in Linnell's hand, 'River Kennett J Linnell 1815'. During the summer of that year he was at Newbury, which stands on the Kennet, painting portraits.[8] The picture can therefore be identified with the '"View on the River Kennet" (near Newbury), 1815', listed by Story,[9] thus establishing also the correct reading of the damaged date.[10] The inclusion of the barge identifies the scene as on the stretch of the Kennet between Newbury and Reading (where the river flows into the Thames), which had been made navigable in 1714.[11] This must be distinguished from the Kennet and Avon Canal, completed in 1810, which continued the navigable stretch of the river from Newbury to form a waterway connecting the Thames with the Severn.[12] When purchased, and previously when in Colonel Grant's collection, the picture bore the title *The Newbury canal*, no doubt referring to the Kennet and Avon Canal by another name.

REPRODUCED. H. M. Grant, *Old English landscape painters* (? 1933), 3 vols., II, pl. 191, (2nd edn. 1961), 8 vols., VIII, pl. 332, fig. 669; J. Simmons, *Transport* (1962), pl. 105; exhibition catalogue, *A decade of English naturalism 1810–20*, Norwich, Castle Museum, and London, Victoria and Albert Museum, 1969–70, p. 13; exhibition catalogue, *John Linnell and his circle*, London, P. & D. Colnaghi & Co., Ltd., 1973, pl. XVI; *Bulletin of the Ceveland Museum of Art* (March 1974), p. 105.

NOTES. [1] Title, *View on the River Kennett, near Newbury, Berks.* [2] Alfred T. Story, *Life of John Linnell* (1892), II, p. 261. [3] Title, *Kennet bridge.* The possible identification with this picture, and with that belonging to A. W. Lyon (see n. [4] and [5]), rests upon their titles, and upon a single Kennet painting only, the present one, being listed by Story (*op. cit.*, n. [1]). For the acquaintance and transactions between Thomas and Linnell see Story, *op, cit.*, pp. 13, 14. [4] Title, *The swing bridge*, see n. [5]. (5) Title, *The swing bridge on the Kennet, near Newbury, Berks.*, with the date 1816, when the present picture was first exhibited. [6] Title, *A canal scene, with farm buildings and figures at a lock.* [7] Story, *op. cit.*, II, p. 261. [8] Story, *op. cit.*, I, pp. 94, 97. [9] Story, *op. cit.*, II, p. 261. [10] Published as 1826 in M. H. Grant, *Old English landscape painters* (? 1933), 3 vols., II, pl. 191, (2nd edn, 1961), 8 vols., VIII, pl. 332, fig. 669. [11] Victoria County History, *Berkshire*, IV (1924), p. 145. [12] *Op. cit.* n. [11], and William Money, *A popular history of Newbury* (1905), p. 86.

PD. 963–1963 AUTUMN WOODS

Wood, 7¾ × 12 in (19·7 × 30·5 cm). A small clearing in a wood; in the foreground are dark brown trees to right and left, and a fallen tree in the centre with figures round it. Across the clearing, the light falls to the right on trees in autumn foliage, a fallen tree to their left; in the centre the clearing opens to distant trees. Deep blue sky with white clouds.

Bequeathed by Wilfrid Ariel Evill, 1963. Coll. Mrs Joseph, Birmingam, by 1905; exh. London, Leicester Galleries, 1952, 'New Year exhibition' (47), lent W. A. Evill; Brighton, Art Gallery and Museum, 1965, 'The Wilfrid Evill collection' (102).

A type of subject painted by Linnell throughout his life; in style and execution characteristic of his mature work.

LINNELL, William

1826–1906. Born at Hampstead, London; son of John Linnell. Exh. R.A. from 1851; in Italy, 1851–61, and 1863–5; lived near Redhill, Surrey. Landscape and rural genre.

PD. 47–1971 VIEW NEAR REDHILL

Oils on paper, $12\frac{1}{8} \times 18\frac{7}{8}$ in (30·8 × 47·8 cm). A tree-covered hill rises sharply towards the left from an undulating landscape, lightly sketched in. The trees are in tones of green over a brown under-painting, which covers the uncompleted foreground. The distant landscape is in grey-greens and blues; blue sky with blue-grey clouds. On the back is a faint pencil drawing of another hill.

Bought from the Fairhaven Fund, 1971. Coll. the Linnell family; R. Hughes-Hallet; exh. London, Alpine Club Gallery, 1971, 'One hundred English water-colours and drawings' (66); bt from R. Hughes-Hallet.

It has been suggested that this is Box Hill near Dorking, in Surrey, only a few miles away from where Linnell lived. The view of Box Hill in the background of John Brett's *The stonebreaker* (Liverpool, Walker Art Gallery), of 1857–8, shows a certain similarity, though the aspect is different.

LINTON, William

1791–1876. Born at Liverpool. Self-taught; exh. from 1817 (R.A. and B.I.); in Italy, 1828–9; visited Greece and Italy, 1840–1. Painted landscapes and scenes from Greek history.

493 MISTRA

Canvas, $45\frac{1}{4} \times 42\frac{1}{8}$ in (114·9 × 107·0 cm). In a rocky, mountainous landscape, with a dark, tree-fringed cleft in the foreground, into which tumbles a waterfall, the buildings of a small town stand on a precipitous bluff in the centre middle distance, a fortress crowning a high hill above it and slightly to the left; in the distance misty hills to right and left. The foreground rocks are brown and grey, the trees dark green; the buildings of the town are pinkish brown; the bluff and high hill are in tones of grey-green and yellow-grey, as are the distant hills. Hazy sky of cream and blue. Signed lower right, 'W LINTON'.

Given by Mrs Richard Ellison, 1862.

Mistra, in Greece, is in the Peloponnese slightly to the west of Sparta; the castle was a medieval stronghold built by Guillaume de Villehardouin. The view in this picture is taken from the north, and is very similar to plate XXIX in Linton's *Scenery of Greece and its islands*[1] (1856), though from a slightly different view-point. The plate is entitled *Mistra, the ruined Turkish town*; in the preface Linton refers to the engravings as taken from sketches made in Greece, which he visited during his 1840–1 tour.

NOTE. [1] The volume has a dedication as follows: 'To Richard Ellison, of Sudbrooke Holm, in the county of Lincoln, Esquire, &c &c &c, a distinguished promoter of the fine arts of his country, this work is dedicated with feelings of gratitude, respect and esteem'; Richard Ellison was the husband of the donor.

LONSDALE, JAMES

1777–1839. Born in Lancashire. Pupil of George Romney; studied at the R.A. schools; worked in London; one of the founders of the Society of British Artists. Portrait painter.

25 DR SAMUEL PARR

Canvas, 30⅛ × 25¼ in (76·5 × 64·2 cm). Half-length, seated, turned half to right, his left hand placed in his girdle. Bare-headed, thick white wig; clean-shaven, fresh complexion, bushy eyebrows. Wears black Prebendary's coat over black cassock. Behind him the back of his red-upholstered gilt armchair.

Bequeathed by the Rt Rev. Edward Maltby, D.D., Bishop of Durham,[1] 1859. Exh. R.A., 1823 (586); coll. Augustus Frederick, Duke of Sussex (1773–1843), sold Christie's, 24 June 1843 (129), bt Hill.

Samuel Parr (1747–1825), LL.D. Cambridge, 1781, became Prebendary of St Paul's Cathedral, 1783. Classical scholar, pedagogue and political writer, he was regarded in his own day as the Whig equivalent of Dr Johnson. The portrait was probably painted for the Duke of Sussex, with whom Parr was on terms of friendship,[2] since Lonsdale was his painter-in-ordinary, and Skelton's engraving, bearing the publication date 20 August 1823, is inscribed to the Duke as 'from an original painting in H.R.H. possession'.

ENGRAVED. Line-engraving by W. Skelton, 1823.

NOTES. [1] Dr Maltby was a pupil of Parr's at Norwich grammar school, and later helped to raise a subscription for his benefit. [2] W. Field, *Memoirs of the life, writings and opinions of the Rev. Samuel Parr, LL.D.*, 2 vols. (1828), II, p. 151.

DE LOUTHERBOURG, PHILIP JAMES

1740–1812. Born in Strasbourg. Pupil of his father, and, in Paris after 1755, of C. van Loo and F. Casanova; to London, 1771; designer of scenery at Drury Lane Theatre; R.A., 1781. Landscape, marine subjects, and battle pictures.

PD. 46–1958 THE RIVER WYE AT TINTERN ABBEY (1805) PLATE 24

Canvas, $42\frac{1}{2} \times 63\frac{3}{4}$ in ($108{\cdot}0 \times 161{\cdot}9$ cm).[1] The water is indigo-blue with brown reflections, the rocks at the right are in tones of brown, the hills above indigo-green. The trees in the centre are in tones of brown and deep green, those to the left are deep green; the gothic ruin is deep brown. The distant slopes of hills are in tones of sage-green. Pale blue sky with cream clouds. Signed along the base towards the right, 'P. I. de Loutherbourg R.A.', and dated on the boat to right, '1805'.

Bought from the Fairhaven Fund, 1958. (?) Exh. R.A., 1806 (100);[2] anon. sale, Sotheby's, 9 May 1956 (172),[3] bt Agnew; exh. London, Thos. Agnew & Sons Ltd, 1957, 'Old Masters' (17); bt from Agnew's; exh. Kenwood, Iveagh Bequest, 1973, 'Philippe Jacques de Loutherbourg, R.A.' (47).

A degree of damage everywhere, from lining and cleaning. Though the subject of this painting is an actual locality, the scenery has been aggrandised and romanticised by de Loutherbourg in the Salvator Rosa vein he adopted in his later paintings. The glimpse of the abbey ruins at the left, although architecturally crudely inaccurate, is recognisable as meant for Tintern from the plate of this subject in the artist's *The romantic and picturesque scenery of England and Wales*, published in 1805. Both must be taken from the same drawing.[4] From the orientation of the abbey and its situation on the right bank of the river, the building can be identified as the end of the north transept, though brought nearer the river than in actuality. A trace of de Loutherbourg's early enthusiasm for Dutch painters such as Jan Both may be detected in his treatment of the cattle and sheep.

REPRODUCED. *Illustrated London News* (1957), CCXXXI, 1045.

NOTES. [1] Lined; dimensions of the painted surface. [2] Title, *Morning with an old abbey*, which fits the lighting of the present picture from a source relatively low at the left, which is south-easterly in general direction. [3] Title, *Tintern Abbey on the Wye*. [4] The title-page of the book describes the plates as 'from drawings made expressly for this undertaking', the inaccuracy of the Tintern subject notwithstanding. The volume is without pagination or plate numbers.

McEVOY, Arthur Ambrose

1878–1927. Born at Crudwell, Wiltshire. Entered the Slade School of Fine Art, London, 1893; initially a painter of landscape and interiors; about 1915 became popular as a portrait painter; worked in London; member of the New English Art Club; A.R.A., 1924.

1144 PROFESSOR JAMES WARD (1913) PLATE 55

Canvas, 36⅛ × 28 in (91·7 × 71·1 cm). Grey hair; white beard, moustache and whiskers. Black academical gown of a Doctor of Science of Cambridge over dark clothes; white collar and pink tie. Signed and dated lower right, 'A McEvoy 1913'.

Given to the University of Cambridge by the subscribers, 1914. Exh. London, New English Art Club, 1913, Winter Exhibition (12); in the keeping of Mrs James Ward, 1914–25, when it was placed in the Fitzwilliam Museum; exh. London, R.A., 1928, 'Works of late members of the Royal Academy' (493).

James Ward (1843–1925), philosopher and psychologist; first Professor of Mental Philosophy and Logic, Cambridge University, 1897; F.B.A. Painted to mark his seventieth birthday, but not considered a good likeness.

REPRODUCED. Claude Johnson, *The works of Ambrose McEvoy* (1919), I, pl. 25; *Principal pictures* (1929), p. 127; J. W. Goodison, *Catalogue of Cambridge portraits* (1955), I, pl. XXXI.

MARLOW, William

1740–1813. Born in London. Studied in London under Samuel Scott and at the St Martin's Lane Academy; in France and Italy, 1765–8; worked in London and in many parts of England and Wales. Landscape painter in oils and water-colours.

PD. 1–1952 VIEW NEAR NAPLES PLATE 24

Canvas, 28¾ × 38¾ in (73·0 × 98·4 cm).[1] The shadowed foreground and the trees to the right in tones of brown and dark green; one of the two trees to the left deep green, the other yellow-green. The sunlit middle distance in sage-greens and sandy browns, with blue water, the trees of a yellower green, light brown or russet; the ground in shadow beyond in similar colours of a darker tone. The house is cream-coloured, the buildings to its left green, the tower and roofs pink and grey. The hills in the background are grey; the sky is light blue merging to warm cream towards the horizon at the right, with cream and grey clouds.

Bought from the Fairhaven Fund, 1952. Coll. Sir George A. H. Beaumont, Bart (1881–1933), Coleorton Hall, Leicestershire; sold by the Trustees, Sotheby's, 30 June 1948 (48), bt Angew; exh. London, Thos Agnew & Sons Ltd, 1949, 'Summer Exhibition' (39); bt from Agnew's.

When sold at Sotheby's in 1948, catalogued generically as 'Wilson', but purchased as by Marlow, which seems to be correct. On both occasions the picture was simply entitled *Italian landscape*, but in the distance towards the right the island of Ischia may probably be recognised rising from the sea. If this is correct, the background embraces the Bay of Salerno to the right, with the hills of the Sorrento Peninsula to the left. Marlow exhibited Italian views, including several described as near Naples, at the Society of Artists of Great Britain between 1767 and 1783, and at the R.A. between 1788 and 1795, the great majority of them after his return to England in 1768.

NOTE. [1] Lined; dimensions of the painted surface.

MARTIN, John

1789–1854. Born near Newcastle-upon-Tyne. Pupil of Boniface Musso in Newcastle, 1804; to London 1806, employed as a painter on china and glass; turned to pictorial art in oils, 1812; worked also in water-colours and as an engraver. Biblical and historical subjects in a grandiose style; landscape.

1502 TWILIGHT IN THE WOODLANDS (1850)

Paper over wood, 15 × 30⅛ in (38·1 × 76·3 cm). Below the dense foliage of a grove of trees, dark brown relieved in detail by some grey-green, is seen in the distance a craggy hill with a town below it, from which flows a river, under a sky of yellow and orange. A rocky foreground rises at the right to a low cliff, all in tones of brown and deep green, which is surmounted by trees; a cloudy, blue-grey sky above. Within the grove at the left stands a figure in a long grey coat, turned towards the distant view. Signed and dated lower right, 'J. Martin / 1850'.

Given by Lancelot Hugh Smith, 1928. (?) Exh. R.A., 1852 (215), *Scene in a forest – twilight*; Newcastle-upon-Tyne, Laing Art Gallery, 1951, 'Festival of Britain' (149); London, Whitechapel Art Gallery, 1953, 'John Martin' (33); Newcastle-upon-Tyne, Laing Art Gallery, 1970, 'John Martin' (30).

Cleaned and restored, 1970. Landscapes form less than a quarter of Martin's oil-paintings, which otherwise consist of subject pictures.

MASON, George Heming

1818–1872. Born at Stoke-on-Trent. Self-taught; in Rome, 1845–58; settled in London, 1864; A.R.A., 1869.

1019 LANDSCAPE

Paper on wood, $10\frac{1}{8} \times 13\frac{7}{8}$ in ($25{\cdot}7 \times 35{\cdot}3$ cm). A small lake, bordered here and there with reeds and backed by dense trees, is seen between the stems of trees in the foreground, where there are a few sparse shrubs. The water and the distant trees are in bluish greens, which mainly predominate in the foreground, with some fresher greens, browns, and a subdued yellow; the tree-trunks are grey-green. Cream sky merging into grey at the top.

Given by Sir (Henry Francis) Herbert Thompson, Bart, 1920.

The approximate date of the picture is probably indicated by a manuscript label at the back, giving the artist's address as 7 Theresa Terrace, Hammersmith, London, where he moved in 1869 and remained for the rest of his life.

MEYER, Henry

c. 1782–1847. Born in London. Pupil of the engraver F. Bartolozzi; exh. R.A. and Society of British Artists, of which he became president. Portrait painter and draughtsman, and engraver.

609 GEORGE DYER (1819)

Canvas, $35\frac{1}{2} \times 27\frac{3}{4}$ in ($90{\cdot}2 \times 70{\cdot}5$ cm).[1] Half-length seated, slightly to right, his right arm on the arm of the chair, his left hand placed on the back of his dog Daphne, lower right. Bare-headed, rough grey hair; clean-shaven. Black jacket and trousers, the jacket partly buttoned; a small magnifying glass hangs on a ribbon round his neck. The chair is red, with a red curtain draped behind it; to the right a book and papers on a table.

Bequeathed to the University of Cambridge by Miss Sarah Travers, and placed in the Fitzwilliam Museum, 1897. Exh. R.A., 1821 (150).[2]

George Dyer (1755–1841), author and schoolmaster, friend of Charles Lamb; in 1814 he published a *History of the University and Colleges of Cambridge*. The portrait was painted in 1819 at Meyer's request, Dyer stipulating that his dog Daphne should be included; it was regarded as a good likeness.[3] Dyer was an old friend of Miss Travers.

ENGRAVED. Stipple by H. Meyer, published 1822.

REPRODUCED. *Principal pictures* (1912 edn), p. 106, (1929 edn), p. 128.

NOTES. [1] Lined; dimensions of the painted surface. [2] Dyer was moved to publish some verses on the portrait in the *Gentleman's Magazine* for July 1821, p. 65. [3] J. I. Wilson, *History of Christ's Hospital* (1821), p. 222.

MILLAIS, Sir John Everett, Bart

1829–1896. Born at Southampton. Entered the R.A. schools, 1840; with D. G. Rossetti and W. Holman Hunt, formed the Pre-Raphaelite Brotherhood, 1848; R.A., 1863; gradually abandoned Pre-Raphaelite principles; highly successful as painter of sentimental genre and portraits. Cr. baronet, 1885; P.R.A., 1896.

499* THE BRIDESMAID (1851)

Wood, 11 × 8 in (27·9 × 20·3 cm). Half-length figure to front, the head held somewhat back, the eyes gazing intently forward; in front a narrow strip of table on which stand a plate with a carmine band round it, containing an orange and a small piece of plum cake, and at the left a silver sugar caster. Long, abundant golden-brown hair falls to cover both shoulders; light green dress with a white pattern, at her bosom a sprig of orange blossom fastened into a white bow. Her hands are held before her, the left one holding a small ring, through which she is about to pass a fragment of cake with the right hand. Dark blue background. Signed and dated upper left with a monogram of the letters 'JEM', and '1851'.

Given by Thomas Richards Harding, 1889. Coll. B. G. Windus by 1855;[1] his sales, Christie's, 19 July 1862 (46), bt in, and 14 February 1868 (314), bt Gambart; anon. sale (= J. M. Wright, of Liverpool), Christie's,

4 February 1888 (143), bt Sheppherd;[2] exh. Leeds, Municipal Art Gallery, 1888, 'Inaugural loan collection of paintings and other works of art' (264), lent T. W. Harding; London, Whitechapel Art Gallery, 1905, 'British art fifty years ago' (381); Manchester City Art Gallery, 1911, 'Works by Ford Madox Brown and the Pre-Raphaelites' (272); London, Tate Gallery, 1923, 'Paintings and drawings of the 1860 period' (79); Bournemouth, Russell-Cotes Art Gallery, 1951, 'Paintings and drawings by the Pre-Raphaelites and their followers' (34); London, R.A., and Liverpool, Walker Art Gallery, 1967, 'Millais' (33); Toronto, Art Gallery of Ontario, 1969, 'The sacred and profane in symbolist art' (29).

In a letter of 15 January 1851 to Mrs Combe, Millais described the subject as 'a bridesmaid who is passing the wedding cake through the ring nine times',[3] adding the explanation, in a letter of 21 February 1888 to T. W. Harding,[4] that 'it is said' she would thus see 'a vision of her beloved', which explains the intent gaze in the picture. The picture was at one time known as *All Hallow's E'en*[5] (31 October), notable for a number of superstitious practices for divining the connubial future.[6] The head is said to have been painted from Jane Elizabeth Senior (1828–1877), the wife of Nassau John Senior,[7] whom she married in 1848; but the sitter is also stated to have been a professional model, Miss McDowall.[8]

REPRODUCED. *Principal pictures* (1912 edn), p. 110, (1929 edn), p. 132; Robin Ironside and John Gere, *Pre-Raphaelite painters* (1948), pl. 51; exhibition catalogue, *The sacred and profane in symbolist art* (1969), Toronto, pl. 27.

NOTES. [1] W. M. Rossetti, *Preraphaelite diaries and letters* (1900), p. 170; in a letter of March 1852, Millais mentions Windus as having already several pictures of his, 'one large and some small', see J. G. Millais, *The life and letters of Sir John Everett Millais*, 2 vols. (1899), I, p. 161. [2] As T. R. Harding appears to have already owned the picture by 21 February 1888 (letter of 16 June 1889, Fitzwilliam Museum), it may well have been bought for him at the sale, perhaps through Thos Agnew & Sons Ltd, whose Manchester label is at the back of the picture. Millais, *op. cit.*, II, p. 468, gives, as a former owner besides T. R. Harding, 'Mr. Knight'; this could be an error for Wright, or a confusion with another painting by Millais entitled *The bridesmaid*, of 1879, listed on p. 478 as once belonging to J. W. Knight. A J. W. Knight sale at Christie's (anon.) of 11 February 1882, includes as lot 179 a painting by Millais with the title *The olden style*, unlikely to be the present picture under another name, and not listed by J. G. Millais. [3] Millais, *op. cit.*, I, p. 94. [4] See n. [5] and also M. H. Spielmann, *Millais and his works* (1898), p. 146. [5] Given this title in the Wright sale of 1888, but T. R. Harding (letter of 16 June 1889, Fitzwilliam Museum) states that Millais told him in a letter of 21 February 1888 that he called it *The brides-*

maid. Spielmann, *op. cit.*, p. 146, and Millais, *op. cit.*, II, p. 468, both refer to the alternative title. [6] R. T. Hampson, *Medii aevi kalendarium*, 2 vols. (1841), I, p. 363ff. [7] Spielmann, *op. cit.*, p. 146, Millais, *op. cit.*, I, p. 150. [8] Rossetti, *op. cit.*, 'The PRB Journal kept by W. M. Rossetti', p. 295, under 9 March 1851, referring to Millais having 'finished a small study from Miss McDowall', which 'resulted in the small oil picture The Bridesmaid'; but writing to Mrs Combe in January 1851 (see n. [3]) Millais speaks of having completed the picture.

1010 MRS COVENTRY PATMORE (1851) PLATE 47

Wood, $7\frac{3}{4} \times 8$ in ($19{\cdot}7 \times 20{\cdot}3$ cm). She has black hair, and wears a black dress with a white collar and carmine bow; the flowers are white and pink with green leaves. Dark blue background.

Given by the Friends of the Fitzwilliam Museum, 1920. Coll. Coventry (Kersey Dighton) Patmore (1823–1896); exh. London, R.A., 1852 (156); Grosvenor Gallery, 1886, 'Works of Sir John Millais, Bt, R.A.' (78A);[1] coll. Edward Andrews, brother of the subject of the portrait; on his wife's death in 1892, passed to Milnes Patmore, son of the subject of the portrait;[2] in 1899, coll. Coventry Patmore's third wife, Harriet (Robson);[3] bt by the Friends of the Fitzwilliam Museum from the Serendipity Shop, London, 1920; exh. London, Tate Gallery, 1923, 'Paintings and drawings of the 1860 period' (75); R.A., 1951–2, 'The first hundred years of the Royal Academy' (654); R.A., and Liverpool, Walker Art Gallery, 1967, 'Millais' (37).

Emily Augusta Andrews (1824–1862), the first wife of the poet Coventry Patmore, for whom the portrait was painted in 1851.[4] They married in 1847, and his poem *The angel in the house*, written during the first years of the marriage, was dedicated to her.

REPRODUCED. Basil Champneys, *Memoirs and correspondence of Coventry Patmore*, 2 vols. (1900), I, p. 116; Friends of the Fitzwilliam Museum, *Annual Report* for 1920; exhibition catalogue, R.A. and Walker Art Gallery, *Millais* (1967), pl. 11.

NOTES. [1] A circular, gilt wooden mount, concealing most of the flowers and the two corners of the chair back, which was removed in 1951, is mentioned in the catalogue. [2] Information from Mrs Barbara Rennie, great-grand-daughter of Edward Andrews (letter of 11 April 1973, Fitzwilliam Museum). [3] J. G. Millais, *The life and letters of Sir John Everett Millais*, 2 vols. (1899), II, p. 468. [4] Letter from Millais to Mrs Coventry Patmore, undated but written during the summer of 1851, when the portrait was not quite finished, and another dated 11 October 1851, to Coventry Patmore when it had been completed (originals in the Fitzwilliam Museum, printed in Basil Champneys, *Memoirs and correspondence of Coventry Patmore*, 2 vols. (1900), II, pp. 326–7).

MILLAR, James

c. 1735 (?)–1805. Worked in Birmingham; exh. at the Incorporated Society of Artists, London, 1771, and subsequently at the R.A. until 1790. Painter of history, portraits and still-life.

PD. 21–1951 YOUNG MAN IN RED (1769) PLATE 22

Canvas, 29¼ × 24¾ in (74·3 × 62·2 cm).[1] His clothes are light red, with white stockings and black shoes. The pedestal is light brown; the foliage dark olive-green; the ground brown in the foreground, green beyond; the house grey. Light blue sky with grey-blue and cream clouds. The relief on the pedestal shows the standing figures of Hercules and a woman, with part of a seated figure at the right, inscribed above, '...Alcid...';[2] inscribed above the relief, 'Millar XI', and 'Nov. 28 1769 Ꜻom. Ætatis suæ / 18'.

Bequeathed by Roger Francis Lambe, 1951.

Attempts to identify the house, which appears to go back to the early seventeenth century, in the hope of establishing the identity of the young man, have proved unsuccessful.[3]

NOTES. [1] Lined; dimensions of the painted surface. [2] Alcides is a name of Hercules; preceding 'Alcid...', above the head of the woman, are indications of some obliterated letters. [3] Thanks are due to Dr P. Cannon-Brookes for help in the search.

MOORE, Albert Joseph

1841–1893. Born in York. Early tuition from his father, William Moore; exh. R.A. from 1857; briefly at the R.A. schools, 1858; in Rome, 1862–3; influenced by Greek art. Figure painter.

2518 THE UMPIRE

Canvas, 17¾ × 7⅛ in (45·1 × 18·2 cm). Whole-length standing figure of a young woman to front, her head inclined to her left, fair hair; she rests on the left leg, the right knee bent, and holds a pink rod in her left hand; bare feet. Draped over a white dress, she wears a white robe passing over the left shoulder and under the right arm, which she holds behind her, and brought across over the left forearm; pink bead necklace. Behind her is a grey wall, with green foliage at the top. She stands on grass, which is edged along the front with a stone moulding, on which at the right is Moore's Greek anthemion signature.

Given by Louis Colville Gray Clarke, LL.D. (1881–1960), 1943. With the Nicholson Gallery, London.

This is closely related to the central figure in a group of three in *A river side*, exhibited at the R.A. in 1888, no. 139.[1] It could either precede this picture or follow it, as Moore sometimes combined studies of single figures to compose a group, or alternatively repeated separately a single figure from a group.[2] These paintings are often quite small in size, and show variations from the figures with which they correspond, as here. A small picture entitled *The footpath* relates to another of the figures in *A river side*,[3] which belongs to the period of Moore's best work.[4]

NOTES. [1] Whereabouts not known; the cartoon for it is reproduced in Alfred Lys Baldry, *Albert Moore, his life and works* (1894), p. 78. [2] Baldry, *op. cit.*, pp. 48ff., 53, 74. [3] Baldry, *op. cit.*, p. 63. [4] Baldry, *op. cit.*, p. 55.

MORE, JACOB

1740(?)–1773. Born in Edinburgh. Apprenticed in Edinburgh to John and Robert Norie, house decorators; in London by 1771; to Italy, 1773; worked in Rome. Landscape painter.

7 BONNINGTON LINN ON THE RIVER CLYDE — PLATE 24

Canvas, $27\frac{3}{4} \times 35\frac{1}{2}$ in ($70{\cdot}5 \times 90{\cdot}2$ cm).[1] The water is light blue-grey and brown, with cream-coloured foam; the rocks are in tones of brown; the trees are in subdued greens with golden brown lights, the foliage on the shadowed eminence a darker green; the distant trees are of a light grey-green. Pale blue sky with cream clouds.

Bequeathed by the Rev. Charles Lesingham Smith (b. 1806), 1878. Exh. London, Incorporated Society of Artists, 1771 (94).[2]

Bonnington Linn is the uppermost of the four celebrated falls, known collectively as the Falls of Clyde, which occur within a distance of three and three-quarter miles on the River Clyde near Lanark. The picture was bequeathed as by Richard Wilson, with the title *Falls of Clyde*. It was identified as the work of More in 1932,[3] and was re-entitled *Corehouse Linn*, alternatively known as Corra Linn,[4] the grandest of the falls, of which there is a painting by More at Edinburgh (National Gallery of Scotland, no. 1897). In the latter part of the eighteenth century the Falls were much admired as examples of the picturesque.

REPRODUCED. Earp, p. 214.

NOTES. [1] Lined; dimensions of the painted surface. [2] A presumed identification from the title in the catalogue of the exhibition, *A view of Bannington Linn* (*sic*), no other painting of this subject by More being known. [3] By Sir Alec Martin; catalogued by Earp, p. 217, as 'Attributed to Wilson'. [4] Thus also David Irwin, 'Jacob More, neo-classical landscape painter', *Burlington Magazine* (1972), CXIV, 776–7. But more recent investigation at the National Gallery of Scotland has now established the correct identification; thanks are due to Dr Lindsay Errington for kindly supplying this information.

MORLAND, George

1763–1804. Born in London. Apprenticed to his father, the painter Henry Robert Morland; possibly a student at the R.A. schools; exhibited from 1773 (R.A., Society of Artists, Free Society of Artists). His earlier artificial, often sentimentalised, subject-pictures were succeeded in the 1790s by rustic genre, for which he is now principally known.

6 ENCAMPMENT OF GIPSIES

Canvas, 25¼ × 30¼ in (64·1 × 76·5 cm). Towards the left, in a woodland glade with a large, leaning tree in the centre, is a party of gipsies, who turn towards a sportsman leaning over a fence to right of the tree in conversation with them. Directly in front of the tree is a group of a seated woman in a light brown cloak and red head-scarf, holding a baby in blue with a white bonnet, a young child to the left of her, and a small boy in grey clothes standing at the right, watching a white and brown dog drinking from a pool. In the foreground to the left of this group is a standing woman in a red cloak with her back turned, and another woman kneeling behind her, in a grey bodice, blue skirt and white mob-cap, who washes some linen; beside them a pan and a bucket. Further to the left, in shadow, is a seated man in grey. A second brown and white dog stands in front of the sportsman, who is in light blue with a black hat. Behind him rises a sandy cliff covered with scrubby growth. Olive-green and brown foliage and herbage, brown ground. Signed on a bank at the right, 'G Morland'.

Given by Mrs Richard Ellison, 1862. Exh. London, 1862, 'International exhibition' (113), lent Mrs Ellison.[1]

This, of a late type among Morland's paintings, may be assigned to his last decade. A version with minor differences, of the same dimensions, signed and dated 1794, with the Leger Galleries, London, in 1952, appears from a reproduction to be probably a copy, with a false signature.[2]

NOTES. [1] With the title *Gipsies.* [2] Advice and information from Mr David Winter in the cataloguing of this and the following paintings by Morland are gratefully acknowledged.

13 CALF AND SHEEP

Canvas, 12 × 15¼ in (30·5 × 38·7 cm). In the left foreground a man in a cream coat, blue breeches and light brown boots, lies asleep, his sleeping dog, pale brown, beside him. Behind him, turned in profile to the right, is a group of a brown and white calf at the left, a greenish grey sheep standing to nibble some ivy on the trunk of a dead tree, grey-green and orange brown, at the right, and a recumbent sheep, reddish brown, in front of them. Behind the calf is a low, sandy bank on which grows a hedge. Sky with dark grey clouds to the left, lightening towards the right, with a patch of blue. Signed on the tree-trunk, 'G. Morland'.

Bequeathed by Daniel Mesman, 1834. Exh. Reading, Museum and Art Gallery, and Southampton, Art Gallery, 1975, 'George Morland' (3).

Cleaned 1904.

REPRODUCED. Earp, p. 138; *Principal pictures* (1912 edn), p. 113, (1929 edn), p. 136.

14 DONKEY AND PIGS (1789)

Canvas, 12 × 15 in (30·5 × 38·1 cm).[1] A donkey, warm grey with a yellow muzzle, stands in the centre turned to the left, in front of it a recumbent pig in tones of cream, brown and pink, with three piglets beside it and two more to the right, dark grey, brown, cream or grey in colour. To the left is a pig-sty with the trunk of a large tree beyond, in tones of grey-green and yellow; at the door of the sty, the head of a second pig. Behind the donkey is a grey fence, and at the right a tub with a besom beside it, some planks covering the tub, yellow-grey in colour. The ground is yellow and yellow-grey. Above and to the right is a grey and cream sky, with a patch of blue. Signed and dated lower left, 'G Morland 1789'.

Bequeathed by Daniel Mesman, 1834. On loan to the City of Cambridge, 1972–5; exh. Reading, Museum and Art Gallery, and Southampton, Art Gallery, 1975, 'George Morland' (2).

Cleaned 1904.

REPRODUCED. *Principal pictures* (1912 edn), p. 114, (1929 edn), p. 137.

NOTE. [1] Lined; dimensions of the painted surface.

19 LANDSCAPE WITH FIGURES

Canvas, $11\frac{3}{4} \times 14\frac{1}{2}$ in ($29{\cdot}8 \times 36{\cdot}8$ cm).[1] At the top of a gentle slope running up from the foreground stands an old tree, with a thatched building to the left and the trees of a small wood behind. Broken ground recedes to the left, with a pool in the foreground, in front of which lies a tree trunk. At the right are sandy banks crowned with trees, beside which a track runs up. Along it two groups of figures advance from the foreground, a man, accompanied by a woman with two small children, and beyond them a man and woman walking beside a laden animal, on which sits a baby, a child and a dog to the right. Trees and herbage in tones of olive-green, grey-green and yellow-green; ground in tones of orange-yellow; the tree-trunk grey-green and pink-buff; some touches of red in the figures. Blue sky with cream, pink and grey clouds. Signature lower left, 'George Morland'.

Bequeathed by Daniel Mesman, 1834.

Cleaned 1904. A work of about 1790–3; the signature is false.[2]

NOTES. [1] Lined; dimensions of the painted surface. [2] David Winter, letter of 23 October 1973 (Fitzwilliam Museum).

20 COAST SCENE

Canvas, $10 \times 11\frac{7}{8}$ in ($25{\cdot}4 \times 30{\cdot}2$ cm).[1] A line of low, chalky cliffs, their grassy tops olive-green, extends into the distance from the right, where there is the sandy beach of a cove, on which two standing men face a third who is half kneeling, their clothes in tones of brown, grey, blue and pink; beside them a basket with a fish in it. To left the green-grey sea stretches to the horizon, dashing against the further cliffs, to the left of which is a distant sailing vessel; near the beach the water swirls in foam around some dark, green-brown rocks to the left. Dark, stormy sky with grey clouds, a break to left of centre with cream clouds and some blue sky. Signed and dated lower right, 'G. Morland 1798'.

Given by Mrs Richard Ellison, 1862.

A weak, late example of Morland's work, the signature and date of doubtful authenticity.[2] A larger version ($23\frac{1}{2} \times 29$ in ($59{\cdot}7 \times 73{\cdot}7$ cm), sight), with different and elaborated action in the foreground, is at Mottistone Manor, Isle of Wight (National Trust). It is entitled Compton Bay, which is on the Mottistone estate, and this may well be correct, though Morland's coast scenes in the Isle of Wight tend to be very similar in scenic character.

NOTES. [1] Lined; dimensions of the painted surface. [2] It is unusual for Morland's pictures to be signed after 1793 (David Winter, letter of 23 October 1973, Fitzwilliam Museum).

1604 WATERING HORSES

Canvas, $33\frac{5}{8} \times 46\frac{1}{4}$ in ($85{\cdot}4 \times 117{\cdot}5$ cm). In the foreground to the left are a brown and a white horse drinking, a dog beside the white one, on which a man in a red coat is mounted; behind rises the stump of a tree, and in the background is a group of three buildings inside a wall, in tones of greenish grey with passages of dull pink; birds in flight above. To the right stands an ancient, hollow tree, grey-green and buff, a felled tree lying at its base, behind it the foliage of other trees. Open ground in the centre is covered with shrubby growth and herbage of light green. Stormy effect, with a dark sky of warm grey clouds, a break of cream and blue above the houses. Signed lower right on the felled tree, 'G. Morland / pix^{t}'.

Bequeathed by Joseph Roe, 1931. Exh. London, Dowdeswell Galleries, 1894.[1]

Another version of the composition, of the same size, signed and dated 1791, is in the Hermitage Museum, Leningrad, no. 5834. In it, the two trees right and left are omitted, and the group of three buildings is replaced by a single one. The Fitzwilliam Museum picture may be regarded as a later re-working by Morland.[2]

NOTES. [1] See *The World* for 21 February 1894; it seems likely that the exhibition noticed was one of Dowdeswell's series of 'Early English masters', and that the picture belonged to them, but no copy of a catalogue has been traced. [2] Information from David Winter (letter of 23 October 1973, Fitzwilliam Museum).

1786 MORNING, OR THE BENEVOLENT SPORTSMAN (1792) PLATE 28

Canvas, 40×54 in ($101{\cdot}6 \times 137{\cdot}2$ cm).[1] The sportsman, on a white horse, wears a buff jacket, white breeches and a black hat; the man behind him is in darker buff; the nearer dog is white and brown, the other two in tones of grey and light brown; the donkey is in tones of grey. The standing gipsy wears dark grey breeches, his legs are light brown; the seated woman has a pink jacket, white skirt and cap; the man, a dark grey jacket and light grey shirt; the child's garment is in tones of pale brown, the flesh a darker brown; their dog is brown and white; the tent is in tones of varied greys, the straw inside cream-coloured. The herbage and foliage are in tones of varied greens and browns; the sky in tones of warm and cool greys. Signed and dated to left, above the tent, 'G. Morland Pin^{xt} 1792'.

Bequeathed by Arthur William Young, 1936. Coll. Lieut.-Gen. the Hon. Sir Charles Stuart (1753–1801), for whom it was painted;[2] exh. R.A., 1792 (23); Robert Wedd[3] sale, Christie's, 22 May 1807 (57), bt Linnell; (?) coll. J. Fairlie;[4] J. E. Fordham, of Melbourn Bury, Royston; exh. London, 1862, 'International exhibition' (103);[5] London, Thos. Agnew & Sons Ltd, 1905, 'Eleventh annual exhibition' (19); coll. Sir Joseph Beecham, Bart; exh. London, 1908, 'Franco-British exhibition' (48); Rome, 1911, 'International fine arts exhibition' (65); Beecham sale, Christie's, 3 May 1917 (46), bt Robson;[6] exh. Reading, Museum and Art Gallery, and Southampton, Art Gallery, 1975, 'George Morland' (18).

Cleaned 1956. Painted as a companion to *Gipsies kindling a fire* of 1789, also commissioned by Lt-Gen. Stuart.[7] When lined in 1956, a former lining was removed, together with additions to the original canvas enlarging it at the top by 3½ in (8·9 cm), at the left-hand side by ¾ in (1·9 cm), and at the right-hand side by 3 in (7·6 cm). These additions were estimated to be upwards of a hundred years old.[8] An identical version of the present picture, signed with initials, from Sudeley Castle, sold by Mrs J. H. Dent-Brocklehurst at Sotheby's, 17 March 1971, lot 103, appears from comparison with a photograph to be a good copy, confirmed by the close correspondence of its dimensions, 42½ × 56¼ in (107·9 × 142·8 cm), as given in the sale catalogue, with those of the Fitzwilliam Museum picture as enlarged. In the collection of Mr and Mrs Paul Mellon, U.S.A., there is a small oil sketch (entitled *The Indian girl*), which corresponds with the seated gipsy child, though different in dress, signed by Morland and dated 1793,[9] a date which suggests that both figures were done from the same drawing.

REPRODUCED. Walter Gilbey, *George Morland* (1907), p. 112 (colour); *Connoisseur* (1913), XXXV, 69; catalogue of the Beecham sale, Christie's, 3 May 1917 (46).

ENGRAVED. Mezzotint by Joseph Grozer, 1795; stipple, with some variations, by W. Nicolls.

NOTES. [1] Lined; dimensions of the painted surface. [2] George C. Williamson, *George Morland* (1904), p. 52. [3] Morland's solicitor. [4] A *Benevolent squire* by Morland was exhibited at the Society of British Artists, Suffolk Street, London, in 1832, no. 55, lent by J. Fairlie. [5] With the title *Gipsies.* [6] Evidently for A. W. Young, as the price at the sale is the same as he is recorded to have paid for it. [7] Williamson, *op. cit.*, pp. 41, 52. [8] Information from H. A. Buttery, who carried out the restoration (letter of 12 October 1956, Fitzwilliam Museum). [9] Information from David Winter (letter of 23 October 1973, Fitzwilliam Museum).

After G. Morland

1603 THE FARMYARD

Canvas, $35\frac{7}{8} \times 47\frac{3}{4}$ in (91·2 × 121·3 cm).[1] A yard covered with straw lies in the angle between a thatched building at the right and a small, lower extension to left of it; the walls, and the woodwork of two doors in the extension and a boarded window at the right, are in tones of grey-green, the thatch similarly coloured with slight yellow passages. Beside a low lean-to at the right a kneeling man empties food from a bucket into a trough, at which two pigs are feeding, a third approaching from the left; behind the man stands a woman in a mob-cap, holding a vegetable in her apron; the man wears a light buff coat with a pink waistcoat, the woman a grey dress with yellow fichu, and a pink skirt; the pigs are coloured cream, grey and pink. To left a brown horse stands in front of a white one, both facing right, behind them lies a dark grey horse, turned to the left. Signed and dated on the trough lower right, 'G. Morland 1797'.

Bequeathed by Joseph Roe, 1931. Coll. J. W. Garrad.

Copy of a larger original dated 1792, formerly belonging to W. Lockett Agnew.[2] Perhaps the date accompanying the spurious signature indicates the date of the copy. Another version was with Trotti, Paris, in 1972.

NOTES. [1] Lined; dimensions of the painted surface. [2] His sale, Christie's, 15 June 1923 (39), rep., $57\frac{1}{2} \times 79\frac{1}{2}$ in (146·1 × 201·9 cm).

MOSER, MARY

1744–1819. Born in London. Daughter of George Michael Moser, enamellist; foundation member of the R.A., 1748; exh. from 1760 (R.A. and Society of Artists); upon marrying, 1793, became Mrs Lloyd. Painted flowers and subject pictures.

PD. 38–1966 VASE OF FLOWERS

Canvas, $28\frac{3}{8} \times 21\frac{1}{8}$ in ($72{\cdot}1 \times 53{\cdot}6$ cm).[1] In a yellow-brown urn-shaped vase standing on a light brown stone ledge, is a tall group of flowers; at the top are tulips and a purple iris, mixed flowers below include roses, sweet peas, auriculas and morning glory. Lying on the ledge around the base of the vase are four bunches of grapes and three yellow apples, on one of which perches a chaffinch. At either side of the flowers flutter two butterflies.[2]

Given by Major the Hon. Henry Rogers Broughton (2nd Lord Fairhaven), 1966.

REPRODUCED. *Country Life* (1974), CLV, 1185 (colour).

NOTES. [1] Lined; dimensions of the painted surface. [2] Maurice H. Grant, *Flower paintings through four centuries. A descriptive catalogue of the collection formed by Major the Honourable Henry Rogers Broughton* (1952), p. 92.

MÜLLER, William James

1812–1845. Born in Bristol. Pupil there of J. B. Pyne about 1827; influenced by J. S. Cotman; tours to Italy, Greece and Egypt between 1834 and 1839, when he moved from Bristol to London; visits to Wales, 1841–2, to Lycia, 1843–4; exh. from 1833 (R.A., B.I. and Society of British Artists, Suffolk Street). Painter of landscapes and picturesque figure subjects.

1103 MILLPOND WITH CHILDREN FISHING (1843)

Canvas, $36\frac{1}{4} \times 28\frac{1}{8}$ in ($92{\cdot}1 \times 71{\cdot}4$ cm). A pool, mainly in tones of grey, cream and brown, fills the foreground, with two children in the centre, a kneeling boy in dark grey fishing, with a little girl, wearing a pink skirt and blue bodice with white sleeves, standing beside him. Behind them, extending to the right, is a bank with a sluice-gate in it, and further back the gable-end of a cottage in tones of varied creams and greys, the red roof of a lean-to at the left. A tree rises beside the cottage to the left, and further left is a group of taller trees. Flat, open ground at the left, cream and brownish green, extends to cream and grey village buildings with red roofs, and a church, among trees. Foliage and herbage in brownish greens. Sky of broken cream and grey clouds against blue. Signed and dated lower right, 'W. J. Müller, 1843'.

Bequeathed by Samuel Sandars (1837–1894), with a life-interest to his widow, received 1923.

Pastoral landscapes of Müller's latter years, such as this, can probably be referred to the neighbourhood either of London or of Bristol. The scenery of the lower Thames and of nearby Gillingham on the Medway, were favourite subjects at this time.[1]

NOTE. [1] See N. Neal Solly, *Memoir of the life of William James Müller* (1875), p. 118.

PD. 1–1974 RIVER LANDSCAPE WITH AN ANGLER (1842)

Millboard on wood, $11\frac{7}{8} \times 17\frac{7}{8}$ in ($30{\cdot}2 \times 45{\cdot}5$ cm). A river runs diagonally across the canvas from the left to the lower right corner, where it cascades among some rocks, on one of which towards the left is a man fishing; trees rise along the further bank. The water is dark green, with white foam, the rocks are in tones of brown and dark green; the lower left corner, uncompleted, is light brown; the trees are dark green to the right, a lighter green to the left. Above is a pale grey sky with white clouds. Signed and dated lower left, 'W. Muller 1842'.

Given by the Friends of the Fitzwilliam Museum, 1974. With the Hazlitt Gallery, London; coll. the Hon. M. A. Tennyson; his sale, Christie's, 22 October 1971 (105), bt Field; with Thos Agnew & Sons Ltd, London; bt from Agnew's, 1974; exh. Hazlitt, 1974 (35).

In the early autumn of 1842, Müller was painting in north Wales, staying first at the village of Roe near Conway, until he moved to Bettws-y-Coed, where he worked more particularly in the valley of the River Lledr,[1] noted for its fishing.

REPRODUCED. Exhibition catalogue, Hazlitt, 1974, pl. 15.

NOTE. [1] N. Neal Solly, *Memoirs of the life of William James Müller* (1875), pp. 148ff.

MULREADY, William

1786–1863. Of Irish extraction, brought up in London. Student at the R.A. schools, 1800; pupil and then instructor in John Varley's school, London; R.A., 1816. Painter of landscape and of genre, for which he is principally known.

952 THE FARRIER'S SHOP PLATE 35

Canvas, $16\frac{1}{8} \times 20\frac{1}{2}$ in ($40{\cdot}9 \times 52{\cdot}1$ cm).[1] The farrier's shop has reddish pink walls; the roof is brown at the right and chocolate-coloured at the left; the horse is white. The foliage of the trees is green, grey-green and brown;

the ground is pale buff in the lights and warm grey in the darks, with grass of a clear, light green. The house at the left has white walls and a red roof. The woman is in black and white with a red cloak, the man in tones of buff, the group at the grindstone in brown, white and black. Clouds of strong blue-grey below, with lighter greys above and patches of clear blue.

Bequeathed by Joseph Prior (1834–1918), received 1919. Coll. Mrs B. Gibbons, of Hanover Terrace, London; her sale, Christie's, 5 May 1883 (27), bt Angew; Thomas Woolner, R.A., who lent it to the Grosvenor Gallery, London, Winter Exhibition, 1888, 'Century of British art from 1737 to 1837' (114);[2] exh. Paris, Petit Palais, 1972, 'La peinture romantique anglaise et les Préraphaelites' (199); London, P. & D. Colnaghi & Co. Ltd, 1973, 'Drawings, watercolours and paintings by John Linnell and his circle' (123); Hazlitt, 1974 (36).

The painting of landscape, which at first principally occupied Mulready's earlier years, was gradually superseded from about 1808 by genre.[3] The Dutch influence, which is evident from the beginning in these genre paintings, only becomes apparent in his landscapes in 1811, in the first of two Kensington subjects, *The Mall*, which was followed in 1812 by *Near the Mall*[4] (both Victoria and Albert Museum, Sheepshanks Collection). In these pictures, which were commissioned together, he turns abruptly away from the picturesque paintings, such as *An old gable* (formerly coll. Col. M. H. Grant), which he was still exhibiting in 1811.[5] The Fitzwilliam Museum landscape marks a further development, in which Mulready has discarded his Dutch exemplars in favour of a naturalism which reveals the influence of Constable's paintings of the later 1820s.

REPRODUCED. Catalogue, *A loan exhibition of drawings, watercolours and paintings by John Linnell and his circle*, P. & D. Colnaghi & Co. Ltd. (1973), pl. XLIV; exhibition catalogue, Hazlitt, 1974, pl. 17; *Burlington Magazine* (1974), CXV, 351, fig. 87.

NOTES. [1] Lined; dimensions of the original canvas, which has unpainted margins of ⅜ in (0·9 cm) along the top, and ½ in (1·3 cm) at the right and along the base. [2] Entitled in the Gibbons sale *The smithy*, in the Grosvenor Gallery exhibition *The farrier's shop*; Frederick G. Stephens, *William Mulready, R.A.* (1890), p. 80, note, no. 3, gives it the title *Landscape, the forge*, and says it 'is sometimes called *The blacksmith's shop*'. [3] Stephens, *op. cit.*, p. 75. [4] Stephens, *op. cit.*, p. 61; they were rejected both by the patron who had commissioned them and for exhibition at the R.A. (p. 64). [5] Stephens, *op. cit.*, p. 62.

MURRAY, Charles Fairfax

1849–1919. Pupil of D. G. Rossetti; worked for Morris & Co.; exh. R.A., and elsewhere in London; spent much of his life in Italy. Well-known connoisseur; collector and dealer. Painted mainly domestic subjects.

2293 THE FLAMING HEART

Wood, 13 × 11 in (33·0 × 27·9 cm). Half-length figure of a young woman, turned half right, facing front, the head slightly inclined to her right, both hands touching a small medallion at the base of her throat. Bare-headed; thick, waving fair hair, parted in the middle, falls over her shoulders; pale complexion, with green-blue eyes. She wears a loose robe with wide sleeves, yellow in colour with passages of white, red and green, and a triple necklace of blue, green and white beads. On the medallion is an emblem of a golden torch from which issue three red flames, the latter indicated by the first finger of the left hand. Behind the head is a dark background of a conflagration within town walls, in front of which are ships with red sails. Signature and date lower left, 'DGR', in a monogram, '1863'.[1]

Bequeathed by Charles Haslewood Shannon, R.A., 1937 Anon. sale (= H. J. Brown), Christie's, 3 March 1924 (34); late W. Lawson Peacock sale, Christie's, 6 February 1925 (117), bt Stone; coll. Charles Ricketts, R.A., and C. H. Shannon, R.A., by 1926;[2] on loan to the Fitzwilliam Museum from C. H. Shannon, 1933–7.

This is a copy by Fairfax Murray of D. G. Rossetti's painting of 1863, *Helen of Troy*, now at Hamburg (Kunsthalle, no. 2469).[3] At the back of this original Rossetti has transcribed a passage from the *Agamemnon* of Aeschylus, translating the Greek, 'destroyer of ships, destroyer of men, destroyer of cities'. The figure was painted from a model named Annie Miller.[4] The title borne by this copy appears to have no connection with Rossetti, and the origin of the false signature and date, reproduced carefully from the original, remains equally unexplained.

REPRODUCED. *Museum und Kunst, Beiträge für Alfred Hentzen* (1970), pl. 81.

NOTES. [1] Virginia Surtees, *The paintings and drawings of Dante Gabriel Rossetti* 2 vols. (1971), I, p. 92, no. 163 (R.1). [2] The date is on a frame-maker's label at the back of the picture, with Ricketts's name as the owner. [3] Surtees, *loc. cit.* no. 163, rep. II, pl. 232. [4] *Old Water-Colour Society's Club* (1941), XIX, 'Extracts from G. P. Boyce's diaries, 1851–1875', p. 44, 13 March 1863.

NASH, Paul

1889–1946. Born in London. Chelsea Polytechnic, London, 1906–7; Slade School of Art, London, 1910–11; member of the London Group, 1914; of the New English Art Club, 1919; appointed Official War Artist, 1917, and again 1940; exhibited with the Surrealists, 1936 and 1938. Landscape painter, book-illustrator, designer.

PD. 6–1955 NOVEMBER MOON (1942) PLATE 62

Canvas, 30 × 20 in (76·2 × 50·8 cm). The sky is blue-grey to the left and pink to the right, with a greenish grey moon; the foreground is an ochrish grey, the fungus to the left is mushroom pink, the one to the right brown. The trees repeat these colours in varying tones; the tall group have white stems. Signed lower right with the initials 'PN' in a monogram.

Given by the Contemporary Art Society, 1955. Coll. Ivor Novello, who bought it from Arthur Tooth & Sons Ltd, London, February 1943; exh. Leeds, Temple Newsam House, 1943, 'Paul Nash, Barbara Hepworth' (30); London, Tate Gallery (Arts Council), 1948, 'Paul Nash, a memorial exhibition' (55); Canada, British Council, 1949–50, 'Paul Nash' (19), lent Ivor Novello (d. 1951); coll. Sir Edward Howard Marsh, K.C.V.O., C.B., C.M.G., who bequeathed it to the Contemporary Art Society, 1953; exh. London, Arts Council, 1953, 'Paintings and drawings from the Sir Edward Marsh collection' (17): Leicester Galleries, 1953, 'The collection of the late Sir Edward Marsh' (73); Guildhall Art Gallery (Art Exhibitions Bureau), 1954, 'Trends in British Art, 1900–1954' (19); Finsbury Town Hall, 1955, lent Contemporary Art Society; Tate Gallery, 1960, 'Contemporary Art Society, 50th anniversary exhibition' (46); Tate Gallery, 1975, 'Paul Nash' (196).

This is one of a group of pictures painted by Nash with the garden of Hilda Harrisson's house, Sandlands, on Boar's Hill, Oxford, as their basic theme. It is a group which contains some of the best of his late work. His attention was first caught by this garden in November 1942,[1] the date of the present painting,[2] and the series continued into 1944. Nash described these landscapes as transcendental, and the fungi, on the one hand, the sun and the moon on the other, assume a special significance in this connection,[3] the fungi symbolising death, the sun life, and the moon fertility, to put it very briefly.[4] The presence of the moon and the fungi together in the present picture is exceptional in the Boar's Hill series, in which otherwise the two sets of symbols occur separately.[5] Fungi alone are found in *Land-*

scape of the brown fungus and *Landscape of the red fungus*, of 1943, and sun and moon in numerous paintings, one of the best known (in three versions) being *Landscape of the vernal equinox*, of 1943–44,[6] in which both occur together. Closely similar to the present picture, but without either moon or fungus, is *Michaelmas landscape*, of 1943.[7]

REPRODUCED. Exhibition catalogue, *Paul Nash, a memorial exhibition* (1948), Tate Gallery (Arts Council), pl. XIII; exhibition catalogue, *Paintings and drawings from the Sir Edward Marsh collection* (1953), Arts Council, pl. IV; Contemporary Art Society, Annual Report for 1952–3; Anthony Bertram, *Paul Nash, the portrait of an artist* (1955), frontispiece (colour); John Rothenstein, *Paul Nash* (1957), cover (colour); John Woodward, *A picture history of British painting* (1962), p. 149 (colour).

NOTES. [1] Anthony Bertram, *Paul Nash, the portrait of an artist* (1955), pp. 259, 286; Margot Eates, *Paul Nash* (1973), pp. 85–6, 133. [2] Bertram, *op. cit.*, p. 323; John Rothenstein, *Paul Nash* ('The masters' series, no. 85) (1967), p. 8. [3] Bertram, *op. cit.*, p. 287. [4] Bertram, *op. cit.*, pp. 288–90. [5] Bertram, *op. cit.*, pp. 287–9. [6] Bertram, *op. cit.*, pp. 287–93, and Index of pictures. [7] *Paul Nash, paintings, drawings and illustrations*, ed. Margot Eates (1948), p. 79, pl. 116.

NASMYTH, ALEXANDER

1758–1840. Born at Edinburgh, where he was a student at the Trustees' Academy under A. Runciman; assistant to Allan Ramsay, 1775–8; portrait painter in Edinburgh; in Italy, 1782–4; in Edinburgh from 1786; turned to landscape painting; hon. academician, R.S.A., 1832. Painted portraits and landscape.

PD. 2–1974 LOCH DOON, AYRSHIRE PLATE 27

Canvas, $17\frac{7}{8} \times 24$ in ($45{\cdot}2 \times 61{\cdot}0$ cm).[1] The foreground is in tones of brown and green; similar colours in the middle distance to the left, to the right tones of grey-green; the distant hills in opalescent tones of mauve and buff; the water is blue and cream. Cream and orange clouds in a blue sky.

Bought from the Fairhaven Fund, 1974. Coll. James Harrison; his sale, Christie's, 6 April 1973 (129), bt Perman; bt from Thos Agnew & Sons Ltd, London, 1974; exh. Hazlitt, 1974 (38).

Nasmyth exhibited landscape paintings from 1807, the great majority of them of Scottish subjects.

REPRODUCED. Sale catalogue, Christie's, 6 April 1973, lot 129; exhibition catalogue, Hazlitt, 1974, pl. 16.

NOTE. [1] Lined; dimensions of the painted surface.

NASMYTH, Patrick

1787–1831. Born in Edinburgh. Pupil of his father, Alexander Nasmyth; moved to London, 1807; exhibited from 1809 (R.A., B.I. and Society of British Artists, Suffolk Street); influenced by the Dutch. Landscape painter.

1787 VIEW NEAR NORWOOD

Wood, $11\frac{3}{8} \times 15\frac{1}{4}$ in ($28{\cdot}8 \times 38{\cdot}7$ cm). A pool extends across the foreground, narrowing towards the right; from its indented, sandy margin the ground slopes up diagonally to a wood in the centre and at the right, where a sportsman with a gun and two black dogs advances along a path towards it, a tall tree to the left of him. Beyond the pool a line of trees runs across to the left from the wood, beyond it higher ground with a red-roofed house at the left. Blue sky with grey and cream clouds. The foliage and herbage are grey-green or brown-green, the tree-trunks grey and brown; the water is in tones of grey and grey-green, tinged with brown.

Bequeathed by Arthur William Young, 1936. Coll. David Jardine, of Liverpool; his posthumous sale, Christie's, 16 March 1917 (120), bt Robson;[1] exh. London, Guildhall Art Gallery, 1971, 'London and the great painters' (13); Hazlitt, 1974 (39).

Cleaned 1974. Norwood subjects were exhibited by Nasmyth in 1821 (R.A., no. 404) and 1822 (B.I., no. 221).

REPRODUCED. Exhibition catalogue, Hazlitt, 1974, pl. 16.

NOTE. [1] Evidently for A. W. Young, as the price at the sale is the same as he is recorded to have paid for it. A label of Thos Agnew & Sons Ltd at the back suggests that at some time it passed through their hands.

PD. 8–1956 VIEW IN LEIGH WOODS (1830) PLATE 37

Canvas, $28\frac{1}{8} \times 40\frac{1}{8}$ in ($71{\cdot}4 \times 101{\cdot}9$ cm).[1] The foliage is olive-green and brown, the tree-trunks are mainly grey and grey-green, with some light brown; the herbage is olive-green and brown towards the left, yellow-green towards the right; the water reflects the colours of the foliage, with a sky reflection in varied greys. The distant fields are light brown, with grey hills beyond. Sky of grey and warm cream clouds against grey-blue. Signed on the large stone lower left, 'Pat^{k} Nasmyth', and dated to right of it, '1830'.

Bought from the Fairhaven Fund, 1956. Coll. John, 2nd Lord Northwick (1770–1859), for whom it was painted;[2] his posthumous sale, Thirlstane

House, Cheltenham, by Phillips, 26 July 1859 (351), bt Grundy; Thomas Walker sale, Christie's, 16 June 1888 (142), bt Agnew; Charles P. Matthews sale, Christie's, 20 June 1891 (72), bt Vokins; R. Kirkman Hodgson sale, Christie's, 23 February 1907 (47), bt Williams; J. Vavasseur deceased sale, Christie's, 23 April 1910 (32), bt Agnew; B. Lewis sale, Christie's, 3 March 1930 (138), bt Tooth; with Arthur Tooth & Sons Ltd, London, in 1933; with Leggatt Bros., London; Eric Richter sale, New York, Parke-Bernet Galleries, 2–3 November 1950 (307); van Doorn Estate sale, New York, Parke-Bernet Galleries, 29 February 1956 (65), bt Julius Baer; bt from Leggatt Bros,. London.[3]

Cleaned 1956. This is Leigh Woods, Bristol, across the Avon Gorge from Clifton Downs.

REPRODUCED. Sale catalogues: B. Lewis, 1930; Eric Richter, 1950; van Doorn Estate, 1956.

NOTES. [1] Lined; dimensions of the painted surface. [2] So stated in the 1859 Northwick sale catalogue. [3] Obtained by them in the United States.

NEWTON, Herbert Herman

1881–1959. Born in London. After a career in business, began painting in 1921; studied drawing under Leon Underwood; influenced by the Impressionists; exhibited with the New English Art Club, the London Group, and at the R.A. Landscape painter.

1522 THE VALLEY OF THE PALUD, TOWARDS SUNSET (1928)

Canvas, 20 × 30 in (50·8 × 76·2 cm). A tree-covered line of hill in sunlight, pale grey-green and orange-buff, closes the distance, a dark shadow, deep green, running along its base. At the right, in front of it, a green, shrub-covered slope in shadow runs down into the valley, which fills the centre, its uneven floor covered in plant growth and shrubs, mainly in tones of orange, green and red-brown. Signed and dated lower left, 'H. H. Newton 1928'.

Given by the artist, 1929. Exh. New York, C. W. Kraushaar Art Galleries, 1928; London, Goupil Gallery, 1929, 'Herbert H. Newton, oil paintings' (24); placed on loan to the City of Cambridge, 1972.

The valley of the Palud is on the island of Port Cros, one of the four Iles d'Hyères, near Toulon. Newton painted another version of the subject, *Early morning*, and projected two more, *Gathering storm* and *Moonlight*.[1]

REPRODUCED. C. St C. Graham, *H. H. Newton* (British artists of to-day series, VII) (1929), pl. 2; Herbert B. Grimsditch, *The paintings of H. H. Newton* (1952), pl. 20.

NOTE. [1] H. H. Newton, *An artist's experience* (1953), pp. 37, 39.

NICHOLSON, Sir William Newzam Prior

1872–1949. Born at Newark-on-Trent. Student at Herkomer's school, London, and at the Académie Julian, Paris; influenced by Whistler; kt, 1936. Painter mainly of portraits, landscape and still-life.

892 THE GIRL WITH A TATTERED GLOVE (1909) PLATE 54

Canvas, 35⅜ × 28 in (89·8 × 71·1 cm). Her hat is black, her jacket an ochrish dark grey; the surface upon which she rests her arms is a dull, dark mauve, the scarf is blue, the gloves are dark grey. Green-grey background. Signed and dated lower left, 'Nicholson 1909'.

Given by Mr and Mrs Edward Owen Vulliamy, 1917. Exh. London, Goupil Gallery, 1911, 'Oil paintings by William Nicholson' (31),[1] bt by Mr and Mrs Vulliamy; Huddersfield Public Library and Art Gallery, 1946, 'Two hundred years of British painting' (304).

Cleaned and restored, 1961. The sitter was Mrs Lottie Stafford, a popular London model of her day.[2] The picture was painted in a studio at The Pheasantry in King's Road, Chelsea, London.[3]

REPRODUCED. *Principal pictures* (1929), p. 141; S. Kennedy North, *Contemporary British artists – William Nicholson* (1923), pl. 21; Frank Rutter, *Modern masterpieces*, part 5 (1935), p. 76 (colour); Robert Nichols, *William Nicholson* (1948), pl. 12.

NOTES. [1] With the title *The girl with the tattered gloves.* [2] Marguerite Steen, *William Nicholson* (1943), p. 114. [3] Steen, *loc. cit.*

907 FIELD MARSHAL J. C. SMUTS (1923)

Canvas, 23⅝ × 21⅝ in (60·0 × 54·9 cm). Nearly half-length, turned half left; bare-headed, grey, receding hair; grey chin beard and moustache; warm complexion. Wears dark suit, with white shirt and grey tie.

Given by Almeric, Lord Queenborough, 1924. Exh. London, Goldsmiths' Hall, 1953, 'Treasures of Cambridge' (38).

In 1917 Nicholson painted a portrait of Smuts in khaki uniform (Johannesburg Art Gallery, South Africa), of which he made a replica for presentation by Lord Queenborough to the Fitzwilliam Museum. This being unsuccessful, fresh sittings were obtained in 1923 for the present portrait, though Nicholson again was critical of the result.[1] The Rt Hon. Jan Christiaan Smuts (1870–1950), South African statesman and military leader of international repute. Among many other distinctions, he became a Privy Councillor in 1917, and Chancellor of the University of Cambridge in 1948.

REPRODUCED. J. W. Goodison, *Cambridge portraits* (1955), I, pl. XXXII.

NOTE. [1] He thought it gave Smuts 'no dignity', and made him 'look ordinary and unsuccessful' (letter of 20 March 1924, Fitzwilliam Museum). The portrait was painted over the earlier one, but reduced in size.

1125 THE GATE OF HONOUR UNDER SNOW (1924)

Canvas, $24\frac{1}{8} \times 20\frac{1}{4}$ in ($61{\cdot}2 \times 51{\cdot}4$ cm). The tall gateway, a classical design in solid masonry, rises in the centre, with a stretch of wall at either side, laden with snow; behind the wall at right and left are portions of high buildings. In the open space of the foreground a flagged path runs through deep snow to the gateway, chains slung between low posts at either side. The architecture is in tones of ochrish grey-brown; the snow is pale greyish or mauvish; cream-coloured sky. Signed and dated lower left 'N 1924'.

Given by the artist, 1924. Exh. Nottingham, Museum and Art Gallery, 1933, 'William Nicholson, retrospective exhibition' (130).

The Gate of Honour is the third of three gateways at Gonville and Caius College, Cambridge, symbolising the career of a student, the others being named Humility (the first one) and Virtue. It was built about 1575, but when Nicholson painted it had lost some of its original features, since restored. The view-point is inside the College, with the end of the Senate House seen above the wall at the left, and part of the Old Schools at the right.

1138 A. C. BENSON (1924) PLATE 54

Wood, $22\frac{3}{8} \times 26\frac{1}{4}$ in ($56{\cdot}9 \times 66{\cdot}7$ cm). Warm complexion; grey hair and moustache. He wears a black suit and academical gown. The chair is red. The screen in the background is deep green.

Given by Arthur Christopher Benson, C.V.O., LL.D., 1924. Painted as a gift to Dr Benson from Madame de Nottbeck;[1] exh. Fitzwilliam Museum, 1924, shortly prior to being given.

Nicholson began a first portrait of Benson, never finished, in 1917.[2] The present one was painted in May 1924, and successfully completed in three days after four previous attempts; Benson did not care for it as a likeness.[3] Arthur Christopher Benson (1862–1925) was a man of letters and Master of Magdalene College, Cambridge.

REPRODUCED. *Principal pictures* (1929), p. 142; Robert Nichols, *William Nicholson* (1948), pl. 30; J. W. Goodison, *Cambridge portraits* (1955), I, pl. XXXII.

NOTES. [1] Letter from Benson, 3 November 1924 (Fitzwilliam Museum). [2] *The diary of Arthur Christopher Benson*, ed. Percy Lubbock, n.d. (1926), p. 292. [3] Lubbock, *op. cit.*, p. 306.

1498 ARMISTICE NIGHT

Canvas, 21¼ × 23¼ in (54·0 × 59·1 cm). View down a street with tall buildings on either side. A large piece of artillery, seen from the side, is in the centre, with another, partly visible, beyond, and the barrel of a third at the right. Figures swarm over them, and a crowd fills the street, two wounded soldiers in hospital blue in the foreground. Flags hang from buildings at the right, and the street is lit by fireworks. Predominantly painted in tones of ochrish grey, with touches of red and blue.[1]

Given by Mrs Frederick Leverton Harris, 1928. Exh. London, International Society of Sculptors, Painters and Gravers, 1919, '26th exhibition' (19).[2]

Painted at 11 Apple Tree Yard in London, just off Piccadilly, where Nicholson had moved into a studio not long before the end of the 1914–18 war, which was concluded by an armistice on 11 November.

REPRODUCED. Lillian Browse, *William Nicholson* (1956), pl. 17.

NOTES. [1] Inscribed on the back of the canvas with a brush in black paint, 'Nov. 11th/1918', and 'Nicholson'. [2] With the title *November 11, 1918*.

1524 STILL-LIFE, FRUIT ON A DISH

Wood, 21⅜ × 23⅜ in (54·3 × 59·4 cm). The oval dish lies diagonally across the canvas on the corner of a table, which has a cloth patterned in white and puce with a few passages of grey-green. The dish is white with a faint blue pattern. On it are a green and yellow corn-cob, five small yellow (?) plums, a (?) pear in light greens, and an apple, partly pale green. A plain background above the table is in tones of dark green with passages of dull red and mauve. Signed lower left 'N'.

Given by the Friends of the Fitzwilliam Museum, 1929. Bt from the artist; exh. Nottingham Museum and Art Gallery, 1933, 'William Nicholson, retrospective exhibition' (157).

REPRODUCED. Friends of the Fitzwilliam Museum, *Annual Report* for 1929.

PD. 10–1967 MATADERO, SEGOVIA (1935)

Wood, $14\frac{7}{8} \times 18$ in ($37{\cdot}7 \times 45{\cdot}7$ cm). Filling the centre is a rocky, grassy bluff, the rock grey and cream, surmounted by the square end of a building with buff walls and red roof, which runs along a ridge into the background. Behind, a town stretches to left and to right, where a tall, square tower rises. The town is in pale tones of pink, buff and grey; light blue sky. Signed lower left, 'N', and 'Nicholson' (incised into the paint). On the back is a rough sketch in pencil of another subject.

Given by Emanuel Vincent Harris, O.B.E., R.A., in memory of his wife Edith, 1967. Exh. London, Leicester Galleries, 1936, 'Paintings by William Nicholson' (27), bt Harcourt Johnstone; his sale, Sotheby's, 12 June 1940 (164), bt E. V. Harris; exh. London, National Gallery, 1942, 'Nicholson and Yeats' (62).

The town is Segovia, with the square tower of its cathedral. The picture dates from 1935.[1] On this visit to Segovia, which ended in May,[2] the Matadero (slaughter house) particularly caught Nicholson's attention as a subject.[3] A second, larger version of the present painting is recorded,[4] and 'another view' of the same building is also known.[5]

REPRODUCED. Robert Nichols, *William Nicholson* (1948), pl. 27 (colour).

NOTES. [1] Robert Nichols (Nicholson's son-in-law), *William Nicholson* (1948), pl. 27, and Lillian Browse, *William Nicholson* (1956), p. 104, no. 449. [2] Marguerite Steen, *William Nicholson* (1943), pp. 167–77, though the year is not given. [3] Steen, *op. cit.*, p. 169. [4] In the catalogue of the 1936 exhibition at the Leicester Galleries, the present painting is described as 'small version'; no. 22 in the exhibition is catalogued *tout court* as *Matadero*. The Fitzwilliam Museum picture alone is listed by Browse, *op. cit.*, p. 104, no. 449; Steen, *op. cit.*, p. 169, only refers to a single painting of the subject, which she describes as completed, after some delay, in England. [5] Browse, *op. cit.*, p. 104, no. 450, coll. Guy Dixon.

NORTHCOTE, JAMES

1746–1831. Born in Plymouth. Came to London 1771, and worked as an assistant in the studio of Sir Joshua Reynolds until 1776; in Italy, 1777–80; R.A., 1787. Portrait and history painter.

23 JOSEPH NOLLEKENS

Canvas, $23\frac{5}{8} \times 19\frac{1}{8}$ in (60·0 × 48·6 cm).[1] Bust to front, the head slightly right. Bare-headed, grey hair; clean-shaven. Wears a brown jacket open over a yellow waistcoat, with a white tie and jabot frill. Dark brown background.

Given by the Rev. Richard Edward Kerrich, 1861. Exh. London, South Kensington, 1867, 'National portraits' (627).

Joseph Nollekens (1737–1823), sculptor, pupil of Peter Scheemakers; celebrated for his portrait busts; R.A., 1772. The portrait shows him as an old man, but the features are unmistakably the same as those in the engraving by W. Bond after a drawing of him when younger by John Jackson, which forms the frontispiece to J. T. Smith's *Nollekens and his times* (1828). The attribution to Northcote was tentative at the time of the gift in 1861, but comparison with his portraits of elderly men of about the same date, such as *The falconer* of 1796 (Master of Kinnaird, Rossie Priory), confirms it through similarities in the rather tense presentation, the lighting, the modelling and the treatment of the eyes.[2] Nollekens's statue of William Pitt was commissioned by the subscribers in 1812 for presentation to Cambridge University, where it stands in the Senate House.

REPRODUCED. Earp, p. 146; *Principal pictures* (1912 edn), p. 119, (1929 edn), p. 143.

NOTES. [1] Lined; dimensions of the painted surface. [2] Not listed in Stephen Gwynn, *Memorials of an eighteenth century painter* (1898).

ORPEN, Sir William Newenham Montague

1878–1931. Born in Ireland. Trained in Dublin, and at the Slade School of Fine Art, London; member of the New English Art Club, 1900; official war artist, 1917–19; K.B.E., 1918; R.A., 1919. Portrait and subject painter.

1143 THE RT HON. SIR CLIFFORD ALLBUTT

Canvas, $50 \times 40\frac{1}{4}$ in (127·0 × 102·2 cm). To knees, seated, turned half right, looking front, the right hand gripping the end of the chair arm, the left hand on his left leg. Bare-headed, receding white hair; white chin-beard and heavy, pointed moustache. Wears black jacket and waistcoat, with dark grey trousers; stiff white cuffs and stand-up collar, with a bright blue tie. Brown curtain draped behind the figure. Signed lower left, 'ORPEN'.

Bequeathed by the Rt Hon. Sir (Thomas) Clifford Allbutt, K.C.B., M.D., F.R.S., 1925. Given to him by the subscribers, 1920; placed on loan in the Fitzwilliam Museum, 1922; deposited on indefinite loan at Addenbrooke's Hospital, Cambridge, 1961.

Thomas Clifford Allbutt (1836–1925), physician, the inventor of the clinical thermometer, was F.R.S. and became Regius Professor of Physic at Cambridge in 1892; K.C.B., 1907; P.C., 1920. The portrait was subscribed for by the medical profession, and was given to Allbutt when President of the British Medical Association at its meeting in Cambridge in 1920.[1] He did not consider it a satisfactory likeness.

REPRODUCED. *Principal pictures* (1929), p. 144.

NOTE. [1] Sir H. D. Rolleston, Bart, *The Cambridge medical school* (1932), p. 188.

1486 SELF-PORTRAIT

Wood, $31\frac{1}{8} \times 25\frac{1}{2}$ in ($79{\cdot}1 \times 64{\cdot}8$ cm). A head and shoulders reflection in a mirror, to right of centre, is repeated in a perspective of secondary mirror reflections, somewhat to left of centre. He is turned in profile to left, the head half left, holding a large palette and brushes in the right hand. Bare-headed, dark hair, clean-shaven, warm complexion; the shoulders sketched in in black, the space below thinly rubbed in in green. The palette and brushes sketchily indicated; blobs of white, red, yellow and blue paint on the palette. To right the upright bar of a window-frame, warm grey, with the scalloped edge of a curtain, outlined in black, to right of it, and the black railing of a balcony; in the distance a view across Paris to the church of the Sacré-Coeur in Montmartre. Blue sky with cream and pink-grey clouds.[1]

Given by the artist, 1928.

Very similar in his general appearance and apparent age to Orpen's self-portrait, *The man with the paintbrush*, of 1925 in the Uffizi Gallery, Florence. Perhaps painted when he was in Paris in 1924.[2] Orpen made occasional use of his reflection in a mirror in other self-portraits. See p. 43, no. 923.

NOTES. [1] Listed in P. G. Konody, *Sir William Orpen, artist and man* (1932), pp. 281, 282, with the title *Paris.* [2] Detailed information on Orpen's movements is scarce, but another self-portrait is entitled *Orpsie boy, you're not so young as you were, my lad, Paris, 1924* (Konody, *op. cit.*, p. 239).

OULESS, Walter William

1848–1933. Born in Jersey. Trained at the R.A. schools; exh. R.A. from 1869, initially with subject paintings; R.A., 1881. Painter of subject pictures and portraits.

495 PROFESSOR SIR GEORGE MURRAY HUMPHREY (1886)

Canvas, $25\frac{3}{4} \times 21\frac{1}{2}$ in ($65{\cdot}4 \times 54{\cdot}6$ cm).[1] Nearly half-length, turned almost half right, head slightly right. Bare-headed, thick, dark hair; dark moustache, whiskers and bushy beard. Wears double-breasted black jacket with black academical gown and scarlet hood of a Cambridge Doctor of Medicine. Chestnut brown background. Signed and dated lower left, 'W.W.O. 1886'.

Given to the University by the subscribers, and placed in the Fitzwilliam Museum, 1887. Exh. London, R.A., 1886 (1073).

George Murray Humphrey (1820–1896), surgeon; F.R.S., 1859, Professor of Human Anatomy, Cambridge University, 1866–83, when he became Professor of Surgery; kt, 1891. Through his influence the Cambridge Medical School was raised to a high level of excellence. The portrait was subscribed for by former pupils.[2]

ENGRAVED. Mezzotint, anonymous, published 1887.

NOTES. [1] Dimensions of the painted surface, which does not extend quite to the edges of the canvas. [2] Cambridge University Library, Cambridge Papers no. BP 653.

PATCH, Thomas

1725–1782. Born in Exeter. In Rome by 1747; pupil there of C. J. Vernet, 1750–3; moved to Florence, 1755, where he remained; visited Venice, 1760. Landscape painter and caricaturist.

87 INTERIOR OF AN ITALIAN COFFEE-HOUSE

Canvas, $15\frac{1}{4} \times 19\frac{7}{8}$ in ($38{\cdot}7 \times 50{\cdot}5$ cm).[1] Standing along a buff wall behind a black brazier, at the left, are three men all wearing light brown coats or cloaks and black tricorne hats, the centre one smoking a pipe; to the right of the brazier sits a woman in a striped pink dress with a light green cap, her back turned, with a hunch-backed dwarf, dressed like the other men, to her right facing her. At the right the wall breaks back above a step, on which stands a priest in black, regarding the group round the brazier through a quizzing-glass; in front of the step and to the right stands a man in similar dress to the others, turned towards the priest. Brown floor partly covered with darker brown tiles.

Bequeathed by Daniel Mesman, 1834. Exh. Exeter, Royal Albert Memorial Museum and Art Gallery, 1932, 'Works by early Devon painters' (240).

Considered as dating from an early period of Patch's stay in Rome from 1747 to 1755.[2]

REPRODUCED. Earp, p. 150.

NOTES. [1] Lined; dimensions of the painted surface. [2] F. J. B. Watson, 'Thomas Patch', *Walpole Society* (1940), XXVIII, 37.

PEPLOE, Samuel John

1871–1935. Born in Edinburgh. Studied there and in Paris; exh. R.S.A. from 1901; lived in Paris, 1910–13; R.S.A., 1927. Painter of landscape, still-life and figure-subjects.

700 STILL-LIFE PLATE 56

Wood, $9\frac{5}{8} \times 13\frac{3}{4}$ in ($24{\cdot}4 \times 34{\cdot}9$ cm). The melon is yellow on the outside, in tones of very pale grey-green and pink inside; the plums are brown-black and grey-blue; the pears in tones of ochre, pink and green. The knife and fork have pale grey handles and darker grey blade and prongs; the linen of the same pale grey. Deep grey background. Signed lower left, 'peploe'.

Given by Mr and Mrs Edward Owen Vulliamy, 1910. With the Goupil Gallery, London, where it was bought by the donors in 1910.

A painting of the years preceding Peploe's departure for Paris in 1910. The flowing technique, the rich quality of the paint, and the restrained colour indicate a date of about 1906–7.

PETTIE, John

1839–1893. Born in Edinburgh, where he was trained. First exhibited, 1858; to London, 1862; R.A., 1873. Painted subject pictures, genre and portraits.

2132 MRS BOSSOM, THE ARTIST'S MOTHER (1870)

Canvas, $13\frac{1}{2} \times 11\frac{1}{2}$ in ($34{\cdot}3 \times 29{\cdot}2$ cm). Bust, somewhat to left. An old lady, with grey hair; on her head, a small black cap or ornament, in which are red flowers, black ribbons hanging from it at either side in front of her shoulders. Grey dress, with black buttons down the front, an oval brooch at the neck. Brown background. Signed and dated lower left, 'J. Pettie 1870'.

Bequeathed by Charles Haslewood Shannon, R.A., 1937. Coll. Charles Ricketts, R.A., and C. H. Shannon, R.A.; on loan to the Fitzwilliam Museum from C. H. Shannon, 1933–7.

Inscribed at the back, 'Portrait of Mrs. Bossom, J. Pettie's mother'.

PHILLIP, John

1817–1867. Born in Aberdeen. Pupil of T. M. Joy in London; student at the R.A. schools, 1837; in Aberdeen, 1840–6, when he returned to London, and there remained. Visited Spain, 1851, 1856–7 and 1860; R.A., 1859. Painter of portraits and genre, principally of Spanish subjects.

1021 SPANISH CARNIVAL

Millboard, 23⅞ × 20 in (60·7 × 50·8 cm). In the centre is the half-length figure of a woman, turned in profile to right, the head half right; she has dark hair with a red rose in it, and wears a yellow and green dress with a black scarf round the shoulders; the left arm is raised to her head. To left, behind and turned towards her, stands a man in black wearing a cocked hat, with a mandolin under his right arm; he holds up near his face a mask half yellow and half black. Light cream-grey background.

Given by Sir (Henry Francis) Herbert Thompson, Bart, 1920. Coll. Sir Henry Thompson, Bart (1820–1904), his father, to whom it was given by the artist's executors, 1867.[1]

A sketchily painted picture, which is described by Sir Henry Thompson as an unfinished work begun in Seville, given to him by Phillip's executors in lieu of his portrait which the artist did not live to paint.[2] A finished version of the subject, with some variations, slightly larger in size (29 × 22 in, 73·7 × 55·9 cm) and on canvas, is in the Graves Art Gallery, Sheffield (no. 1547), entitled *Carnival time, Seville* and dated 1860.

NOTES. [1] See n. [2]. [2] Note by Sir Henry Thompson at the back of the picture. Conflicting with this is the information from Sir Herbert Thompson (letter of 11 January 1921, Fitzwilliam Museum) that in an old note made by his father it is recorded that the picture was painted at Cadiz.

PHILLIPS, Thomas

1770–1845. Born at Dudley, Warwickshire. Came to London, 1790; entered the R.A. schools; assistant to Benjamin West; exh. R.A. from 1792; R.A., 1808; Professor of Painting, R.A., 1824. Initially a history painter, but turned early to portraiture.

10 HUGH PERCY, 3RD DUKE OF NORTHUMBERLAND (1803)

Canvas, 30 × 25 in (76·2 × 63·5 cm). Nearly half-length, turned front, facing half right; within a painted oval. Bare-headed, light brown hair; clean-shaven, fair complexion. Wears dark coat, buttoned, with white choker. Behind the figure, a red curtain draped across towards the left, landscape view to right. Inscribed on the back of the (original) canvas, 'Earl Percy./Phillips pinxt/1803'.

Given by George Crauford Heath, 1850. Coll. Dr George Heath, his father (1745–1822).

Hugh Percy, 3rd Duke of Northumberland (of the third creation) (1785–1847); styled Earl Percy until he succeeded his father in 1817; K.G., 1819; ambassador extraordinary at the coronation of Charles x of France, 1825; Chancellor of the University of Cambridge, 1840–7. In the copy of Phillips's note-book recording his paintings (National Portrait Gallery), under 23 April 1803, is the entry, 'Lord Percy 3 time for Dr. Heath No. 181', preceded, under the date of 7 April 1803, by 'Lord Percy 2nd time for Dr. Goodall, No. 180'. The entry for no. 180 refers to the portrait now at Eton College,[1] where it was customary for a boy on leaving, if so requested, to present his portrait to the head master. Earl Percy left Eton in 1802, at the end of the headmastership of Dr Heath, who was succeeded by Dr Goodall. It thus appears that when the official leaving portrait was painted a year later for presentation to Dr Goodall, a second portrait was commissioned as a gift to the headmaster under whom Earl Percy had spent his schooldays from 1795 to 1802. The two portraits, which are of the same size, are similar in scheme, but in the Eton portrait the figure is turned towards the right, and the two heads, though very close in pose, are different enough to indicate separate sittings. The first of the series of three portraits occurs in the note-book under 30 March 1800, no. 118, described as a whole-length, 'exhibited', no doubt the portrait shown at the R.A. in 1800, no. 274, to be identified with the whole-length of him as a youth, in uniform, at Alnwick Castle.

ENGRAVED. Mezzotint by S. W. Reynolds, published 1805.[2]

REPRODUCED. J. W. Goodison, *Catalogue of Cambridge portraits* (1955), I, pl. XIX.

NOTES. [1] Rep. Lionel Cust, *Eton College portraits* (1910), pl. XXXI. [2] Alfred Whitman, *Samuel William Reynolds* (1903), p. 75, no. 235; dedicated to the Duke of Northumberland.

PHILPOT, Glyn Warren

1884–1937. Born in London. Trained at the Lambeth School of Art, London, and in Paris under J. P. Laurens; exh. R.A. and New English Art Club; R.A., 1923. Painter of portraits and subject pictures.

1121 SIEGFRIED SASSOON (1917) PLATE 61

Canvas, 24 × 20 in (61·0 × 50·8 cm). Dark brown hair; black jacket and grey shirt. Dark grey background. Signed and dated lower left, 'Glyn Philpot 1917'.

Given by Siegfried Sassoon, C.B.E., M.C., 1924. On loan to the Fitzwilliam Museum from the donor, 1918–24; exh. London, Royal Water Colour Society's Galleries, 1965, 'Fifty years ago' (41); Cambridge, University Library, 1968, Siegfried Sassoon exhibition.

Siegfried Sassoon (1886–1967), poet and prose writer; M.C., 1916; C.B.E., 1951. The idea of the portrait, which was painted in London during the summer of 1917, seems to have originated with Robert Ross. Sassoon regarded it as a romantic, though externalised, image of him, and as 'an ideal "posterity portrait" ' for a writer.[1] The pose recalls that of Philpot's *A young Breton*, exhibited at the R.A. in 1917, the year of this portrait (London, Tate Gallery, no. 3218).

NOTE. [1] Siegfried Sassoon, *Siegfried's journey, 1916–1920* (1945), pp. 49–51 (rep. frontispiece).

2472 LA ZARZAROSA (1910–11)

Canvas, 102¼ × 72¼ in (259·7 × 183·5 cm). A young woman in yellow, turned towards the left, sits on a couch leaning back against its raised end at the right, an ochre-coloured scarf across her lap; an embroidered yellow shawl covers the seat of the couch; its end is draped in black, with a grey cushion upon it on which she rests her left arm. She has black hair with pink flowers in it; beside her on the couch are some grapes and a black Spanish hat. A young man in black, wearing a similar hat, leans on the raised end of the couch with his right arm, his left hand on his hip. Behind him and a little to the left, stands an older woman, in a black and grey dress, with pink flowers in her black hair. The background is deep brown, with lighter brown curtains at either side. Signed and dated lower right, 'G. W. Philpot 1910–11'.

Bequeathed by Mrs Emile Mond, in memory of her sons Captain Francis Mond and Alfred William Mond,[1] 1942. Exh. London, Tate Gallery, 1938, 'Paintings and sculpture by the late Glyn Philpot, R.A.' (14), lent Mrs Emile Mond.

'Zarzarosa' is the Spanish for a dog-rose. Philpot twice visited Spain, in 1906 and 1910.

REPRODUCED. A. C. Sewter, *Glyn Philpot* (1951), pl. 1 (colour).

NOTE. [1] Francis Mond was a member of King's College, Cambridge, and his younger brother, Alfred William Mond, of Peterhouse; Francis Mond was killed on military service during the 1914–18 war, and his brother died in 1928.

POND, Arthur

1705(?)–1758. Student at the St Martin's Lane Academy, London, 1720; follower of J. Vanderbank; visited Italy, returning 1727; Fellow of the Royal Society, 1752; well known as a connoisseur. Portrait painter in oils and pastel; engraver.

1752 RICHARD SNOW (1738)

Canvas, $29\frac{5}{8} \times 24\frac{3}{4}$ in ($75{\cdot}2 \times 62{\cdot}9$ cm).[1] Half-length, slightly to left. Bareheaded, white wig to shoulders; clean-shaven; fresh complexion with dark blue eyes. Wears dark brown coat, buttoned at the waist, over dark brown waistcoat; white cravat with fringed ends. Deep brown-grey background, the corners of a lighter brown forming an oval. Signed and dated lower right, 'Pond. pinxit. 1738', and inscribed lower left, 'Rich: Snow. Esq. Æt. 85'.

Given by the Friends of the Fitzwilliam Museum, 1935. Coll. Dorothea Snow, Lady Harrison; descended to the daughters of Archdeacon Harrison, Brixham; their (anon.) sale, Christie's, 14 December 1934 (42),[2] bt Spink; bt from Spink & Son, London, 1935.

Richard Snow, born about 1653, barrister-at-law, was of Clipsham, Rutland; he was the father of Lady Harrison.[3] Pond, not much esteemed by George Vertue in 1727 as a painter in oils, is commended by him in 1743 both for his oil paintings and his pastels.[4]

REPRODUCED. Friends of the Fitzwilliam Museum, *Annual Report* for 1935.

NOTES. [1] Lined; dimensions of the painted surface. [2] Wilfred J. Cripps, *Pedigree of the family of Harrison* (1881), p. 17 (information from Professor Sir Ellis Waterhouse) and C. H. Collins Baker, *British painting* (1933), p. 90; three other paintings by Pond were in the same sale, lots 41 and 43. [3] Label at the back of the picture, and Cripps, *loc. cit.* [4] *Walpole Society* (1934), XXII, Vertue III, pp. 33, 117, 118.

Attributed to Arthur Pond

8 THOMAS GRAY PLATE 6

Canvas, $49\frac{3}{4} \times 39\frac{7}{8}$ in ($126{\cdot}3 \times 101{\cdot}3$ cm).[1] His hair is light brown; the brocaded coat is light blue, lined with shot pink and grey, over a pink and grey shot waistcoat, with a white shirt, black velvet breeches, white stockings and red slippers. The table cover is deep green; the silver standish pale grey; the brown books have red labels, two of them are lettered 'LOCK', a third 'TEMPLE'.

Given by Henry Hazard, 1858. Coll. Thomas Gray; bequeathed, 1771, to his cousin Mary Antrobus, who married Thomas Robinson of Cambridge, 1786; passed to her younger sister, Dorothy Comyns (or Comings) of Cambridge (d. 1807); bequeathed to her son, Richard Comyns (or Comings), of Cambridge (d. 1838); bequeathed to his brother-in-law, Henry Hazard, of Cambridge;[2] exh. London, Goldsmiths' Hall, 1959, 'Treasures of Cambridge' (31); placed on loan to Pembroke College, Cambridge, 1970.

Thomas Gray (1716–1771), poet and scholar, Regius Professor of History and Modern Languages, Cambridge, 1758; resided in Cambridge, initially at Peterhouse, and from 1756 at Pembroke College. The portrait shows him as a boy, but there is no contemporary evidence as to his age, to which the earliest known reference is the statement on J. Hopwood's engraving of 1814 (see below) that he was in his fifteenth year, presumably the family tradition. This gives a date for the painting of, probably, 1731, as Thomas Gray's birth in 1716 took place on 26 December. Presumably also due to family tradition is the attribution of the portrait in the engraving to Jonathan Richardson the elder,[3] but this is out of the question on grounds of style and quality. This may well be the 'picture of him by Pond, taken when he was very young, but badly executed' referred to by Jacob Bryant in a letter of 1798.[4] Other portraits by Pond show a similar restlessness of gesture in the pose and prominence given to the hands, similar treatment of the features, and a similar tendency to an undue emphasis on the dress ornaments; compare particularly two large groups of the children of Captain F. Delaval at Doddington Hall, Lincolnshire.

ENGRAVED. Stipple by J. Hopwood, published 1814, figure to the shins only; lettered 'THOMAS GRAY, ann. aet. xv. From an original painting by Richardson in the possession of Robinson Esqr of Cambridge'.

REPRODUCED. *Principal pictures* (1912 edn), p. 137, (1929 edn), p. 163; *The correspondence of Gray, Walpole, West and Ashton*, ed. Paget Toynbee, 2 vols. (1915), frontispiece to vol. II; Lord David Cecil, *Two quiet lives* (1948), p. 82; R. W. Ketton-Cremer, *Thomas Gray* (1955), p. 8.

NOTES. [1] Lined; dimensions of the painted surface. [2] Provenance given in a contemporary note to the entry registering the picture in the Fitzwilliam Museum *Acquisition book*, 1817–1907, p. 25, with additional details taken from *The correspondence of Thomas Gray*, ed. Paget Toynbee and Leonard Whibley, 3 vols. (1935), pp. 1309–10; the latter gives the name of Dorothy Comyns's son as Richard, with the date of his death, which has been adopted in preference to 'the late W. Comyns' in the Fitzwilliam Museum *Acquisition book*. An unresolved anomaly is the statement in the inscription on the engraving by J. Hopwood (see below), published in 1814, that the original was 'in the possession of Robinson Esqr of Cambridge', by which must be meant Thomas Robinson, the husband of Mary Antrobus, from whom the portrait is stated to have passed to her sister Dorothy Comyns, who died in 1807, bequeathing it to her son. [3] Assumed to be what is meant by the 'Richardson' of the engraving. [4] *Gentleman's Magazine* (1846), I, 140–3, see R. W. Ketton-Cremer, *Times Literary Supplement*, 28 October 1949, p. 697.

PORTER, Frederick James

1883–1944. Born at Auckland, New Zealand. Student at the Académie Julian, Paris; worked mostly in France and England; member of the London Group and the London Artists' Association. Painted landscape and still-life.

2402 TULIPS

Millboard, $25\frac{3}{4} \times 18\frac{5}{8}$ in ($65{\cdot}4 \times 47{\cdot}3$ cm). In a blue bowl with a yellow band round it, standing on a table covered with a cloth patterned in grey, cream and chocolate, are nine mauve tulips. Behind, to the right, is a vertical strip broadly brushed in in deep blue-green, to the left an area broadly brushed in in yellow-green, with a passage of buff-colour between it and the edge of the table.

Bequeathed by Frank Hindley Smith, 1939. Exh. London, London Artists' Association, 1933, 'Summer show' (30).

Frank Hindley Smith was one of the guarantors of the London Artists' Association.

RAEBURN, Sir Henry

1756–1823. Born in Edinburgh. Largely self-taught; began as a miniaturist; in Italy, 1784–6, when he returned to Edinburgh; exh. R.A. from 1792; R.A., 1815; kt, 1822; His Majesty's Limner for Scotland, 1823. Portrait painter.

220 WILLIAM GLENDONWYN PLATE 26

Canvas, $49\frac{1}{8} \times 40$ in ($124{\cdot}8 \times 101{\cdot}6$ cm).[1] He wears a yellowish brown coat over a white waistcoat, which is grey and light brown in the shadows; ruddy complexion. The landscape is of a similar brown to the coat, the trees and sky of a red-brown.

Purchased 1892. Anon. sale (= H. O. Collins), Christie's, 22 February 1890 (78), bt Lesser;[2] with William Holder, London, from whom it was bought.

William Glendonwyn, of Glendonwyn and Sarton; he was married in Edinburgh in 1781, when he is recorded as of College Kirk parish.[3] His name is an archaic form of Glendinning, not uncommon as a Scots surname, and is derived from a property in Westerkirk parish, Dumfriesshire, where it no longer survives.[4] The portrait may be approximately dated 1795–1800. It displays similarities of style, and has similarities of costume, with a number of portraits painted ten years or so after Raeburn's return from Italy in 1786, such as the *Sir John Sinclair* and the *Mrs Campbell of Ballimore*, about 1795, the *Captain David Burrell*, 1798, and the *Macdonald children of Clanranald*, of about 1800.[5]

REPRODUCED. Earp, p. 160; *Principal pictures* (1912 edn), p. 132, (1929 edn), p. 158; C. Winter, *The Fitzwilliam Museum* (1958), p. 383, pl. 96.

NOTES. [1] Lined; dimensions of the painted surface. [2] Sold together with lot 79, also by Raeburn, of Glendonwyn's wife and child. [3] *Scottish Record Society*, 1922, p. 286. His eldest daughter and heiress, Mary, married Sir James Gordon, Bart, in 1801, and died in 1845 (*Gentleman's Magazine* (1845), July, 101). [4] Thanks are due for the biographical information to Professor Bruce Dickins. [5] See James L. Caw, *Scottish painting past and present* (1908), p. 73.

REINAGLE, Philip

1749–1833. Admitted to the R.A. schools, 1796; assistant to Allan Ramsay; studied and copied the Dutch seventeenth-century landscapists; R.A., 1812. Painted portraits, animals, and from 1794 chiefly landscape.

PD. 892–1973 LILIUM SUPERBUM

Canvas, $17\frac{3}{4} \times 13\frac{5}{8}$ in ($45{\cdot}0 \times 34{\cdot}7$ cm).[1] The head of a lily in full bloom, the recurved flowers of yellow flushed with carmine, with black spots, reverse of the petals carmine. Below it, a dark, rock-strewn foreground, brown and green; to left and behind, a dark green cliff; to right, more distant, the slope of a hill, ochre and blue-grey in colour. Dark blue-grey sky with dark grey clouds.

Bequeathed by Henry (Broughton), 2nd Lord Fairhaven, 1973. Coll. Robert John Thornton, M.D. (1768(?)–1837); sale of the Linnaean Gallery, Christie's, 2 July 1813 (32); exh. Cambridge, Fitzwilliam Museum, 1974, 'Botanical drawings from the Broughton Collection' (3).

Painted for Robert John Thornton's 'The Temple of Flora', the third section of his *New illustration of the sexual system of Linnaeus* (1799–1807), for which it was engraved by Richard Earlom (see below). This engraving was the first to appear of the twenty-eight plates of 'The Temple of Flora', which were issued in successive parts. *Lilium superbum* (the superb lily) was introduced from eastern North America in 1738.

ENGRAVED. Mezzotint by Richard Earlom, 1799 (see above).

REPRODUCED. Wilfrid Blunt, *The art of botanical illustration* (1950), pl. 35 (colour).

NOTE. [1] Lined; dimensions of the painted surface.

PD. 65–1974 CUPID INSPIRING THE PLANTS WITH LOVE PLATE 25

Linen, $17 \times 13\frac{5}{8}$ in ($43{\cdot}2 \times 34{\cdot}6$ cm). Cupid is pink, with light brown hair and white wings, his quiver is gold, held by a light blue ribbon. The foliage and herbage are in muted greens, except for the tall banana-trees at the right, which are light green; the flowers of the strelitzia at the right are orange-red. The ground is in muted browns; the water is blue-grey; the mountains are soft light blue with pink lights; the sky is blue with grey and cream clouds.

Bequeathed by Henry (Broughton), 2nd Lord Fairhaven, 1973, received 1974. Exh. London, R.A., 1799 (111); coll. Robert John Thornton, M.D.

(1768(?)–1837); sale of the Linnaean Gallery, Christie's, 2 July 1813 (44), bt Richardson.

Painted for Robert John Thornton's *New illustration of the sexual system of Linnaeus* (1799–1807),[1] for which it was engraved by Thomas Burke (see below), the engraving, with other matter, preceding the twenty-eight plates of 'The Temple of Flora' (see no. PD.892–1973, above).

ENGRAVED. Mezzotint by Thomas Burke, 1805 (see above).

NOTE. [1] Described in the catalogue of the R.A. exhibition of 1799 as 'for Dr Thornton's Botanical work', which had been advertised in 1797.

Attributed to P. Reinagle

453 LANDSCAPE WITH FIGURES

Paper on wood, $5\frac{1}{8} \times 9\frac{1}{8}$ in ($13{\cdot}0 \times 23{\cdot}2$ cm). Behind a small group of trees in the foreground stands to the left a low house with a roof of red tiles, beside the trees the figure of a seated man; to right is a dead tree with timber and a ladder propped against it, a signpost at its base; the ground is brown, the herbage deep green with yellowish lights, the foliage yellowish grey-green with similar lights. A landscape recedes in the centre, greenish yellow with grey-green hedges, with a group of three figures; in the distance a line of grey-blue hills. Sky of cream and grey clouds, light blue in the centre.

Bequeathed by Daniel Mesman, 1834.

Bequeathed as by Philip Reinagle, but it is unlike his extant landscapes, which are in a tradition deriving from Richard Wilson and George Lambert. From his study of Dutch seventeenth-century landscape, he could possibly, however, be the author of such a picture as this, giving the impression, as it does, of being a pastiche based on the Dutch seventeenth-century painters. It is worthy of note that the attribution to Reinagle is contemporaneous with him.

REINAGLE, Ramsay Richard

1775–1862. Born in London. Pupil of his father, Philip Reinagle; studied in Italy and Holland; exh. R.A. from 1788; R.A., 1823. Painter of portraits, landscape and animals.

448 LANDSCAPE NEAR TIVOLI, WITH PART OF THE CLAUDIAN AQUEDUCT

Canvas, 20½ × 28⅞ in (52·1 × 73·3 cm). Beyond a pool in the foreground, with a herd of goats to the right, four arches of the ruined aqueduct extend across from the right, where some trees rise in front of them; at the left and further away, are more of the ruins partly concealed by trees, and between the two is a view of open country receding to distant hills. The ruins, lit from the further side, are pink grey, the illuminated return walls terracotta pink; the foreground is in tones of pinkish brown, greyer in the shadows, with reflections in the water of blue and terracotta colour; the foliage is a yellowish green, deep grey-green in the darks; the landscape repeats the foreground colours in tones of reduced intensity, with blue-grey distant hills. The sky is light grey-blue with a few light, warm grey clouds.

Founder's Bequest, 1816. Exh. London, R.A., 1808 (299);[1] B.I., 1811 (133).[2]

The scene is to the south-east of Tivoli, in the Valle d'Empiglione, near where this stream joins the River Anio.

NOTES. [1] Entitled, *Part of the Claudian aqueduct near Tivoli – evening.* [2] Entitled, *Part of the remains of the Claudian Aqueduct beyond Tivoli on the Road to Horace's Villa*, though the poet never possessed a villa at Tivoli.

REYNOLDS, ALAN

b. 1926. Living artist.

PD. 48–1958 DUSK – THE OUTBUILDINGS (1957)

Hardboard, 17⅞ × 24 in (43·5 × 60·9 cm). Beyond a pale, open foreground, white over grey-green, a range of barns and sheds stretches across the picture, in tones of dark grey-greens and brown-greys, with some brown in the roofs; rising in the background are the tops of two oast-houses and the branches of some trees. Signed and dated lower right, 'Reynolds 57'.

Given by the Friends of the Fitzwilliam Museum, 1958. Exh. London, Leicester Galleries, 1958, 'Paintings and watercolours 1956–58 by Alan Reynolds' (46), where it was bought for the Friends of the Fitzwilliam Museum; placed on loan to the City of Cambridge, 1972.

REYNOLDS, Sir Joshua

1723–1792. Born at Plympton, Devon. Apprenticed to Thomas Hudson in London, 1740–3; in Devon and London until he left for Italy, 1749; back in England, 1752; settled in London, 1753; first President of the R.A., 1768; Principal Painter to the King, 1784. Painted portraits and fancy subjects.

653 LORD ROCKINGHAM AND EDMUND BURKE PLATE 14

Canvas, 57¼ × 62⅝ in (145·4 × 159·1 cm).[1] The unfinished figure of Rockingham at the right is carried further than Burke's; the faces of both are laid in in light grey, Rockingham's with some warm tones added; his dress is dull reddish grey, the Garter ribbon slightly blue; the wig and body of Burke in warm cream. The chair is dull crimson, with brown wood, the carpet on the table has dull reds, blues and greys; the papers are white. The column at the right is light grey, with a pale crimson curtain, the other column is dark grey. The unfinished landscape is in tones of blue with a blue, grey and cream sky.

Given by Charles Fairfax Murray, 1908. Coll. Mary Palmer, Marchioness of Thomond (d. 1820);[2] her sale, Christie's, 26 May 1821 (14), bt Coles; coll. Thomas Phillips, R.A., sold Christie's 9 May 1846 (12), bt Sir Francis Grant, P.R.A.; his sale, Christie's, 28 March 1879 (84), bt Sir Frederick Leighton, P.R.A.; exh. London, Grosvenor Gallery, 1883–4, 'Works of Sir Joshua Reynolds, P.R.A.' (197); Leighton sale, Christie's, 13 July 1896 (335), bt Fairfax Murray.

Unfinished. Cleaned 1961. Charles Watson-Wentworth, 2nd Marquess of Rockingham, K.G. (1730–1782), Whig statesman, became premier in a brief administration lasting from July 1765 to July 1766; upon its formation, Edmund Burke (1729–1797), statesman and orator, was appointed his private secretary. This double portrait no doubt commemorates these events; it was probably inspired by van Dyck's group of the Earl of Strafford and his secretary, Sir Philip Mainwaring, then in the possession of the Marquess of Rockingham. Three sittings each by Rockingham and Burke between January and December 1766 presumably relate to this painting, for which no entries are identifiable in Reynolds's ledgers.[3] The figures remain very incomplete after so few sittings, but the accessories have been fully realised by an assistant.[4]

REPRODUCED. *Principal pictures* (1912 edn), p. 136, (1929 edn), p. 162; Sir Philip Magnus, *Edmund Burke* (1931), p. 28; *BurlingtonMagazine* (1966), CVIII, 122.

NOTES. [1] Lined; dimensions of the painted surface. [2] Mary Palmer, Reynolds's niece, inherited virtually all his property; later in the year of his death she married the Marquess of Thomond. This double portrait does not appear in the sale of Reynolds's 'Portraits, Fancy Pictures, Studies and Sketches' held by his executors in 1769. [3] A. Graves and W. V. Cronin, *A history of the works of Sir Joshua Reynolds, P.R.A.* (1899), I, p. 131 and II, pp. 838–9; E. K. Waterhouse, *Reynolds* (1941), p. 58, dates it 1766–8, thus including one sitting by Burke in 1767 and two by Rockingham in 1768, though it seems more probable that these relate to other portraits. [4] In Derek R. Hudson, *Sir Joshua Reynolds* (1958), Appendix B, 'Reynolds's painting techniques', H. A. Buttery refers on p. 249 to the methods exemplified in this unfinished picture.

1179 HENRY VANSITTART

Canvas, oval, 29 × 23¾ in (73·7 × 60·3 cm).[1] Nearly half-length, turned slightly right, facing slightly left. Bare-headed, his own powdered hair, curled at the sides; clean-shaven. Wears a sky-blue coat and waistcoat, the coat unbuttoned; lace jabot. Dark, warm grey background.

Bought from the Spencer George Perceval Fund, 1926. Coll. Colonel Robert Arnold Vansittart, of North Cray Place, Kent; sold by him about 1913; purchased from Thos Agnew & Sons Ltd, London, who obtained it from another dealer.[2]

The paint of the head flattened by ironing and considerably damaged by over-cleaning, some re-touching. Henry Vansittart (1732–1770) entered the service of the East India Company in 1745; in England, 1751 – late 1753/4; Governor of Bengal, 1760–4, when he returned to England; M.P. for Reading, 1768; left for India, 1769. Sittings recorded in Reynolds's sitter-books show the painting of two portraits of Henry Vansittart; one series of nine sittings took place between September 1767 and May 1768, a second series of ten in June and July 1769. He was then in his later middle thirties, which accords with his appearance in each of two portraits, in one wearing a blue coat and scarlet waistcoat (formerly at Kirkleatham Hall, Yorkshire, sold Sotheby's, 23 March 1949 (38), bt Agnew),[3] in the other wearing scarlet uniform (in 1928 coll. D. H. Farr, Philadelphia, U.S.A.).[4] By comparison with these, his appearance in the Fitzwilliam Museum portrait is almost boyish. In view of this evidence and the dates of Vansittart's movements, it can only be concluded that the portrait was painted during his visit to England from 1751 to late 1753 or 1754, when he was twenty-one or twenty-two, for which no sitter-books are known. Reynolds settled in London early in 1753, which narrows still further the date assignable to the painting.[5] Though the damage to the face makes a precise estimation of style impossible, the painting does not seem stylistically inconsistent with such a portrait of this period as the *Ann Eliot, Mrs Hugh Bonfoy* (Earl of St Germans, Port Eliot). A repetition of the portrait, oval within a rectangle,[6] belonged to Lord Vansittart (d. 1957) at Denham Place, Buckinghamshire. Payments for Vansittart portraits in Reynolds's ledgers run from 12 December 1767 to 12 July 1769, and though difficult to analyse they evidently cover the two portraits of Henry Vansittart discussed above, besides some portraits of his children for which sittings are recorded.

REPRODUCED. *Principal pictures* (1929), p. 161.

NOTES. [1] Lined; dimensions of the painted surface. [2] The other dealer is the source of the information that the portrait belonged to Colonel R. A. Vansittart, but it is to some extent borne out by the fact of the design of the frame being identical with that of the later portrait by Reynolds of Henry Vansittart in scarlet uniform (see below), also an oval, which Graves and Cronin record as in his possession; information of the sale of about 1913 kindly communicated by the late Lord Vansittart (letter of 14 March 1947, Fitzwilliam Museum). [3] A. Graves and W. V. Cronin, *A history of the works of Sir Joshua Reynolds, P.R.A.*, 4 vols. (1899–1901), III, p. 1001. [4] Graves and Cronin, *loc. cit.* [5] Graves and Cronin, *op. cit.*, III, p. 1000, give the stylistically impossible date of 'about 1745'. [6] Engraved in mezzotint by S. W. Reynolds, published 1822 (Alfred Whitman, *Samuel William Reynolds* (1903), p. 156, no. 39).

1775 MRS ANGELO

Canvas, $21\frac{7}{8} \times 17\frac{7}{8}$ in ($55{\cdot}6 \times 45{\cdot}4$ cm).[1] Bust, to front, the head slightly inclined to her right. Darkish hair dressed close to the head, braided with pearls, a pink bow on top; a string of pearls, caught in a double loop in front and tied with a pink bow, encircles the neck; pearl ear-drops. She wears a grey-pink dress over a white bodice, with low décolletage, leaving her left shoulder bare, the dress sketchily brushed-in. Blue-green background.

Bought from the Spencer George Perceval Fund, 1936. Coll. Angelo family, Edinburgh; bt from them by David Thomson for James Smith of Jordanhill, Renfrewshire (d. 1867), 1811; his son, Archibald Smith of Jordanhill (1813–1872); Mrs Archibald Smith; exh. London, R.A., 1892, Winter Exhibition (33);[2] her son, the Rt Hon. James Parker Smith, P.C. (1854–1929); sold by his trustees to Mrs G. E. Wade, 1930;[3] John McDowell; his sale, Sotheby's, 25 March 1936 (106), bt H. A. Buttery; bt from Buttery.

Marie Françoise Dubourg (d. 1809), wife of John Angelo (or Ainslie), known also as Angelo Tremamondo (d. 1805), riding-master and Master of the Royal Academy of Exercises in Edinburgh, whose elder brother was the celebrated London riding- and fencing-master, Domenick Angelo.[4] Each brother had his wife's portrait painted by Reynolds, Mrs Domenick Angelo's being now in the Metropolitan Museum, New York (no. R33-9). Corresponding with the two portraits are two distinct series of sittings in Reynolds's sitter-books, the first consisting of eight between 8 January and 12 March 1759, with two more in September, and the second of another eight between 5 January and 6 March 1760, with one more in May. In every instance, the sitter's name is given simply as 'Mrs Angelo', and nothing is to be derived from Reynolds's ledgers to indicate which series of sittings was for which lady.[5] But as John Angelo's marriage only took place late in 1758 or in 1759,[6] it seems more likely that the first series of sittings was for Domenick Angelo's wife, whom he had married in 1755, than for John Angelo's, to whom the 1760 series may therefore be attributed.

REPRODUCED. *The Ancestor* (1904), VIII, 52; *Burlington Magazine* (1948), XC, 320.

NOTES. [1] Lined; dimensions of the painted surface. [2] Described as an oval, the portrait being then in an oval mount. [3] The history of the picture down to this point kindly communicated by Mr A. Parker Smith, 1947. [4] Biographical information derived from 'The Angelo family' by the Rev. Charles Swynnerton, *The Ancestor* (1904), VIII, 1–72; the date of Mrs Angelo's death comes from *The Scots Magazine* (1809), p. 959. [5] See J. W. Goodison, 'Portraits of "Mrs. Angelo" by Sir Joshua Reynolds', *Burlington Magazine* (1948), XC, 320–2. [6] In London, where he remained until moving to Edinburgh in 1763.

PD. 10–1955 THE BRADDYLL FAMILY PLATE 15

Canvas, $93\frac{3}{4} \times 58$ in ($238{\cdot}1 \times 147{\cdot}3$ cm).[1] He wears a red coat, his wife a white dress with a black scarf, the boy a blue coat with buff waistcoat and breeches; the dog is white and brown. The seat, urn and pedestal, and tree-trunk are brownish ochre, the foliage red-brown, the clouds pinkish grey.

Given by the National Art-Collections Fund, from the Ernest Edward Cook collection, 1955. Coll. Lt-Col. Thomas Richmond-Gale-Braddyll (1776–1862);[2] his sale, Christie's, 23 May 1846 (44), bt Bishop; W. J. Isbell, of Stonehouse; T. Pooly Smyth, of Plymouth, by 1857;[3] exh. Manchester, 1857, 'Art treasures' (52); Pooly Smyth sale, Christie's, 13 June 1859 (213), bt in; Rev. W. C. Randolph; exh. London, R.A., 1890, 'Old masters' (124); Lionel, 2nd Lord Rothschild (d. 1937), Tring Park, by 1899;[4] his nephew, Nathaniel, 3rd Lord Rothschild; given by him to the Lord Baldwin Fund for Refugees, sale at Christie's, 25 May 1939 (256), bt Gooden & Fox; bt from Gooden & Fox, London, by E. E. Cook, 1939, who bequeathed his collection to the National Art-Collections Fund, 1955.

The group consists of Wilson Gale-Braddyll (1756–1818), of Conishead Priory, Lancashire, his wife, Jane Gale, whom he married in 1776, and their son Thomas, born 1776, who became Richmond-Gale-Braddyll, lieutenant-colonel in the Coldstream Guards. The sittings are recorded in Reynolds's sitter-book for 1789, eight for Mrs Braddyll and five each for the father and the son, between 23 March and 30 May. But none of the entries of payments for Braddyll portraits in Reynolds's ledgers, can be related to this group. The figure of the son Thomas has a considerable similarity of conception to an earlier, whole-length portrait of him by Reynolds, exhibited in 1784.[5] The group is among the last pictures painted by Reynolds, who abandoned painting in July 1789 upon suffering a defect in his eyesight.

REPRODUCED. A. Graves and W. V. Cronin, *A history of the works of Sir Joshua Reynolds, P.R.A.*, 4 vols. (1899–1901), I, p. 112 (large paper edition); Newnes Art Library, *Reynolds* (n.d.), pl. 48; *Country Life* (1955), CXVII, 1502; *Illustrated London News* (1955), p. 871; Carl Winter, *The Fitzwilliam Museum* (1958), p. 379, pl. 95.

NOTES. [1] Lined; dimensions of the painted surface. [2] Presumably inherited from his father, Wilson Gale-Braddyll, see below. [3] For the ownership of W. J. Isbell and T. Pooly Smyth, see William Cotton, *A catalogue of the portraits painted by Sir Joshua Reynolds, Knt., P.R.A.* (1857), p. 11. [4] A. Graves and W, V. Cronin, *A history of the works of Sir Joshua Reynolds, P.R.A.*, 4 vols. (1899–1901), I, pp. 111–12. [5] Graves and Cronin, *op. cit.*, I, p. 111; rep. Newnes Art Library, *Reynolds*, pl. 46.

RICHARDSON, Jonathan the elder

1665–1745. Pupil of John Riley in London about 1688–91; influenced by Kneller; in active practice before 1700; influential writer on the arts. Portrait painter.

16 ALEXANDER POPE (1742) PLATE 6

Canvas, $13\frac{3}{8} \times 11\frac{1}{4}$ in ($33{\cdot}9 \times 28{\cdot}6$ cm).[1] Dark brown hair; crimson gown with brown fur; brown background. Signed, in a monogram, and dated, lower right, 'JR 1742'.

Bequeathed by Daniel Mesman, 1834.[2] Exh. London, South Kensington Museum, 1867, 'Exhibition of national portraits' (136); National Portrait Gallery, 1961, 'Portraits of Pope'.

Cleaned 1904. Alexander Pope (1688–1744), celebrated Augustan poet. One of a number of portraits of Pope painted by Jonathan Richardson, and perhaps the last; it is the only one bearing a signature and date.[3] Another version by Richardson, with slight differences and somewhat smaller, but of equal quality, belongs to Colin Broun Lindsay at Colstoun, East Lothian. At the back of it is the inscription, said to have been copied from an old label, now lost, 'This picture Mr Pope sate to my father for at my request for me 1742'. It may be identified with lot 46 in the posthumous sale of Jonathan Richardson the younger, London, Langford's, 18 February 1772, 'Mr Pope, from the life'.[4] A rather poor derivative[5] belonged in 1966 to Professor Maynard Mack. A painting by Richardson belonging to Anthony Storer (1746–1799), known from an engraving of 1793 by R. Clamp,[6] has a great similarity to the two portraits discussed above, but both in the pose and the details of the costume diverges decidedly from them.

REPRODUCED. Earp, p. 166; *Principal pictures* (1912 edn), p. 138, (1929 edn), p. 164; C. R. L. Fletcher and Emery Walker, *Historical portraits* (1919), III, p. 40; W. K. Wimsatt, *The portraits of Alexander Pope* (1965), p. 221.

NOTES. [1] Lined; dimensions of the painted surface. [2] Described, together with several other paintings in the Mesman bequest, as 'From the collection of Lord Mitford' (John Massey, *A catalogue of the paintings, drawings, etc., bequeathed to the University of Cambridge by the late Daniel Mesman, Esq.* (1846), no. 45), but no peerage of Mitford appears to have ever existed. [3] W. K. Wimsatt, *The portraits of Alexander Pope* (1965), p. 220, no. 55.2. [4] Wimsatt, *op. cit.*, p. 220, no. 55.1. [5] Wimsatt, *op, cit.*, p. 357, no. 41. [6] Plate to S. and E. Harding's *Shakespeare illustrated* (1793).

Follower of Richardson

456 HENRY, LORD HERBERT, LATER 10TH EARL OF PEMBROKE (1748)

Canvas, 33 × 27⅛ in (83·8 × 68·9 cm). Half-length to front, the left hand held across the body; bare-headed. Wears a 'van Dyck' costume of a blue slashed doublet, with white, lace-edged collar and cuffs; a deep pink drapery is taken over his left shoulder to reappear behind his right arm. Brown background.

Founder's Bequest, 1816.

Henry, Lord Herbert (1734–1794), succeeded his father as 10th Earl of Pembroke in 1750. An expert in horsemanship, he reformed the standard of riding in the British army, in which he rose to the rank of general in 1782, when he was appointed Governor of Portsmouth. His mother was the daughter of the 5th Viscount Fitzwilliam, and thus the aunt of the Founder of the Fitzwilliam Museum, in whose handwriting an inscription at the back of the picture identifies the portrait and dates it 1748, when Lord Herbert was fourteen.[1] Formerly mistakenly identified as a portrait of the 9th Earl of Pembroke, and ascribed to George Knapton,[2] which is out of the question, but there is a certain affinity with the work of Richardson's pupil Thomas Hudson.

NOTES. [1] 'Ld Herbert, son to the Earl of Pembroke, 1748'. [2] Ascribed to Knapton since William Seguier's 'Inventory of the pictures, portraits and drawings...' in the Founder's Bequest, dated March 1816 (Fitzwilliam Museum).

RICHMOND, George

1809–1896. Born at Brompton, Middlesex. Pupil of his father, Thomas Richmond; entered R.A. schools, 1824; friend of William Blake; in Italy, 1837–9; R.A., 1866. Portrait draughtsman and painter; subject painter.

1204 MRS WILLIAM FOTHERGILL ROBINSON (1870) PLATE 42

Wood, 37 × 27¾ in (94·0 × 70·5 cm). Her cap is white, her hair grey; fresh complexion. Black velvet dress. The table cover is red; the cushion on which she rests her book is red patterned in blue and grey. Brown wall behind her. The landscape is brown with a blue distance; blue sky with cream and grey clouds.

Given by the Rev. W. Fothergill Robinson, 1927.

Mrs William Fothergill Robinson was the grandmother of the donor, whose father, William Fothergill Robinson (1833–1895), married George Richmond's daughter Julia,[1] and no doubt commissioned the portrait.[2] In a chronological list of Richmond's paintings, extracted from his diaries, which belongs to the Richmond family, an entry for the portrait occurs under 1870.[3] A miniature reduction of it, the head said to be by Richmond, has also descended in the family.

NOTES. [1] A. M. W. Stirling, *The Richmond papers* (1926), p. 71. [2] The donor, in a letter of 28 November 1927 (Fitzwilliam Museum), remarks that his father, who was of Trinity College, Cambridge, 'adored his mother', and the choice of a painter was obvious; as the eldest son, Richmond Fothergill Robinson, died in 1915, the portrait presumably came to the donor through him. [3] With a payment of 200 guineas. In 1959 the list was in the possession of Mr G. Richmond, of Ashford, Kent (Fitzwilliam Museum records).

PD. 179–1975 SELF-PORTRAIT (1840)

Canvas, 16⅛ × 16 in (40·9 × 40·6 cm). Bust, turned right, facing half right, the eyes shaded with his right hand. Bare-headed, brown hair; clean-shaven; somewhat dark complexion. Wears a black jacket, with a red tie. Brown background, dark at left, lighter at right. Inscribed on the canvas at the back, 'Geo. Richmond, Sketch of Himself made on his return from Italy in 1840', and 'Wax used in this'.

Allocated by the Standing Commission on Museums and Galleries, under the terms of settlement of the death duties on the estate of the late Kerrison Preston (1884–1974), 1975. Coll. Mrs John Richmond, daughter-in-law of George Richmond, R.A.; bought from her by Kerrison Preston; exh. London, Arts Council, 1962, 'British self-portraits, *c.* 1580 – *c.* 1860' (79); sale by the executors of Kerrison Preston, Sotheby's, 20 March 1974 (30), withdrawn.

As the inscription at the back of the canvas testifies, this was painted by Richmond in 1840, upon returning from his second visit to Italy. Two earlier self-portraits precede it, a miniature of 1830 (coll. the Richmond family), and a drawing of about the same date (coll. Sir Geoffrey Keynes, F.R.C.S.).[1]

REPRODUCED. Sale catalogue, Sotheby's, 20 March 1974 (30).

NOTE. [1] Richard Ormond, *Early Victorian portraits*, National Portrait Gallery Catalogue, 2 vols. (1973), I, p. 395, nos. 1, 2 and 3.

ROGERS, CLAUDE MAURICE

b. 1907. Living artist.

PD. 4–1960 CLOVER FIELD, SOMERTON, SUFFOLK (1959)

Canvas, 30 × 40⅛ in (76·2 × 101·9 cm). Beyond a bright green field in the foreground, is a line of hedge in a slight dip, with some trees at the left, in darker greens with some passages of brown; beyond the hedge open fields slope gently upwards, a large mauve area in the centre surrounded by light yellow, to the sky-line, which is broken by dark green trees and a group of dark farm buildings. Signed and dated lower left, 'C. Rogers 59'.

Bought from the D. M. McQuaid Fund, 1960. Exh. London, Leicester Galleries, 1960, 'Anne Dunn, Earl Haig, Claude Rogers' (cat. p. 11, no. 8), where it was bought; placed on loan to the City of Cambridge, 1972; exh. London, Whitechapel Art Gallery, 1973, 'Claude Rogers'.

Cleaned 1972.

REPRODUCED. *The Listener*, 17 March 1960, p. 506; exhibition catalogue, *Claude Rogers* (1973), Whitechapel Art Gallery, no. 52.

PD. 90–1974 ATHENS

Millboard, $9\frac{7}{8} \times 8\frac{1}{8}$ in ($25{\cdot}1 \times 20{\cdot}6$ cm). In the right foreground is the corner of a white house, with a yellow roof and a window with grey panes; to the left of it are the pink roofs of other houses among green trees. In the distance are hills, grey-blue, grey-green and bright blue, with lower green hills in front of them, from which stretches up to the houses an uncompleted area of green and bright blue with the white of the unpainted, primed canvas. Along the top is a narrow strip of grey-blue sky.

Given by Keith Stuart Baynes, 1974. Given to him by the artist, 1970.[1]

NOTE. [1] Inscription by the donor at the back of the picture.

ROMNEY, George

1743–1802. Born at Dalton-in-Furness, Lancashire. Apprenticed to the portrait painter Christopher Steel, 1755–7; established in Kendal; moved to London, 1762; visited Paris, 1764; in Rome and elsewhere in Italy, 1773–5; worked in London. Chiefly a portrait painter.

654 (?) WILLIAM THOMAS MEYER

Canvas, $21\frac{1}{4} \times 16$ in ($54{\cdot}0 \times 40{\cdot}6$ cm).[1] Bust to front, the head half right. Bare-headed, light-coloured hair to shoulders; clean-shaven. Wears a dull crimson coat, buttoned up, with a white neck-cloth. Dark brown background.

Given by Charles Fairfax Murray, 1908. Coll. William Long (1747–1818); by inheritance to his great-nephew, Walter J. Long, by 1858;[2] his sale, Christie's, 28 June 1890 (118), bt Agnew; exh. London, R.A., 1892, 'Old Masters' (25), lent William Agnew (1825–1910).

When belonging to Walter J. Long, and subsequently, described as a portrait of the poet William Hayley (1745–1820);[3] but, although its original owner, William Long, was Hayley's doctor, comparison with authentic portraits of Hayley by Romney show this to be incorrect. There is, however, a strong facial resemblance with the portrait in profile of William Thomas Meyer in Romney's group of Hayley, his son Thomas, Meyer and Romney himself, at the Abbot Hall Gallery, Kendal, painted in 1796.[4] William Thomas Meyer, baptised 1779, was the son of the portrait miniaturist Jeremiah Meyer, and a close friend of Hayley's son Thomas; he took his degree of Bachelor of Arts at Cambridge in 1801, and seems to have been destined for the church.[5] In the group he was aged eighteen, and the young man in the present portrait appears to be of much the same age. The portrait is in the nature of a study. A copy belongs to the Hon. Sir Patrick Browne, Thriplow Bury, Cambridgeshire.

REPRODUCED. *Principal pictures* (1912 edn), p. 140, (1929 edn), p. 166; *Connoisseur* (1915), XLIII, 76; Reginald Grundy, *English art in the XVIII century* (1928), pl. XXV.

NOTES. [1] Lined; dimensions of the painted surface. [2] Sir Herbert Maxwell, Bart, *George Romney* (1902), p. 181, no. 203. [3] In Humphrey Ward and W. Roberts, *Romney*, 2 vols. (1904), II, p. 74, no. 2 of the portraits of Hayley, it is related to a sitting of 1777, but this was for a three-quarters size portrait, i.e. 30 × 25 in (76·2 × 63·5 cm). [4] Ward and Roberts, *op. cit.*, p. 75, rep. Lord Ronald Sutherland Gower, *George Romney* (1904) (plates not numbered). [5] William Hayley, *Memorials of the life and writings of William Hayley*, 2 vols. (1823), II, p. 466; he was admitted at Trinity College, Cambridge, in March 1796, and in the portrait wears academical gown and cap.

ROSSETTI, DANTE GABRIEL

1828–1882. Painter and poet; properly Gabriel Charles Dante Rossetti. Born in London. After some early instruction at Sass's Drawing Academy, attended the R.A. schools, 1845–7; worked under Ford Madox Brown; co-founder of the Pre-Raphaelite Brotherhood with J. E. Millais and W. Holman Hunt, 1848; patronised by Ruskin. Painter in oils and water-colour, and draughtsman; subject pictures.

685 JOAN OF ARC (1882)

Wood, 20¾ × 18 in (52·7 × 45·7 cm).[1] Half-length figure, turned almost in profile to the left, the head held back with the eyes gazing upwards, a sword held by the hilt in both hands above her right shoulder.

Bare-headed, auburn hair; over armour wears an embroidered, deep gold-coloured mantle; in the background a design of brownish conventionalised fleurs-de-lis against indigo blue. Inscribed upper left, 'Jehane la Pucelle'. Signed and dated top right, 'DGR' [in a monogram] '1882'.[2]

Given by Charles Fairfax Murray, 1909. Painted for L. R. Valpy,[3] but included in the posthumous Rossetti sale, Christie's, 12 May 1883 (107), bt in; coll. L. R. Valpy; exh. London, Burlington Fine Arts Club, 1883, 'Pictures, drawings, designs and studies by the late Dante Gabriel Rossetti' (93); L. R. Valpy sale, Christie's, 26 May 1888 (100), bt F. S. Ellis; with Thos Agnew & Sons Ltd, in 1899.[4]

This design is a simplified variant of a painting of 1863, in which Joan of Arc faces to the right and kisses a sword before an altar at the foot of a crucifix.[5] It is a replica of a water-colour of 1864 now in the Tate Gallery, London (no. 5235), of which there is another, reduced replica in water-colour, also of 1864.[6] This is the last painting upon which Rossetti worked, being finished within a few days of his death at Birchington-on-Sea on 9 April 1882.[7] The subject relates to Joan of Arc's discovery under the altar of a church, to which she had been directed by her 'voices', of an ancient sword, which she carried to the relief of Orleans in 1429.

REPRODUCED. *Principal pictures* (1912), p. 143.

NOTES. [1] Dimensions of the painted surface; the panel measures 21⅜ × 18⅞ in (54·3 × 47·9 cm). [2] Virginia Surtees, *Dante Gabriel Rossetti*, 2 vols. (1971), I, p. 92, no. 162(R.3). [3] One of the pictures painted for Valpy in exchange for the large *Dante's dream* which he bought from Rossetti in 1873 and returned to him for re-sale in 1878, see H. C. Marillier, *Dante Gabriel Rossetti* (1899), p. 184, n. 1. [4] Marillier, *op. cit.*, p. 256, no. 304; Agnew's label is at the back of the picture. [5] Surtees, *op. cit.*, I, p. 91, no. 162. [6] Surtees, *op. cit.*, I, p. 91, nos. 162 (R.1), (R.2); see also nos. 162A, 162B. [7] W. M. Rossetti, 'Notes on Rossetti and his works', *The Art Journal* (1884), p. 208; Marillier, *op. cit.*, pp. 174, 184 (n. 1), 199.

728 GIRL AT A LATTICE (1862) PLATE 47

Canvas, 12 × 10⅝ in (30·5 × 27·0 cm).[1] Dark complexion, warmly coloured in the cheeks, similar flesh-colour in the hands, dark brown hair; dress patterned in mauve on white; coral necklace. The window-sill is brown and grey; white jug and dish with a blue design, the wallflowers red and deep yellow. The lead of the lattice is deep greenish grey; the curtain is a greenish white, very thinly painted. Signed and dated lower left, 'DGR', in a monogram, '1862'.[2]

Given by Charles Fairfax Murray, 1911. Coll. G. P. Boyce, who bought it from Rossetti in 1862;[3] exh. London, Burlington Fine Arts Club, 1883, 'Pictures, drawings, designs and studies by the late Dante Gabriel Rossetti' (50); late G. P. Boyce sale, Christie's, 1 July 1897 (212), bt C. Fairfax Murray; exh. London, Tate Gallery, 1923, 'Paintings and drawings of the 1860 period' (27); Brussels, 1929, 'Exhibition of retrospective British art' (54); Newcastle-on-Tyne, Laing Art Gallery, 1971, 'Dante Gabriel Rossetti' (49); London, R.A., 1973, 'Dante Gabriel Rossetti' (303).

Painted from a maidservant at Ford Madox Brown's house at Hampstead.[4] The picture is among the first works produced by Rossetti after the death in February 1862 of his wife Elizabeth Siddal,[5] whose features it strongly recalls.[6]

REPRODUCED. *Masterpieces of Rossetti* (1912), front cover and p. 23; *Principal pictures* (1912 edn), p. 148, (1929 edn), p. 173; Virginia Surtees, *The paintings and drawings of Dante Gabriel Rossetti*, 2 vols. (1971), II, pl. 220.

NOTES. [1] Painted on a square canvas, with a blank strip along either side. [2] Virginia Surtees, *The paintings and drawings of Dante Gabriel Rossetti*, 2 vols. (1971), I, p. 88, no. 152. [3] *Old Water-Colour Society's Club* (1941), XIX, 'Extracts from G. P. Boyce's diaries, 1851–1875', p. 41, 7 May 1862. [4] See n. [3]. [5] H. C. Marillier, *Dante Gabriel Rossetti* (1899), pp. 124, 244, no. 131. [6] Cf., for example, *Regina cordium* of 1860, Johannesburg Art Gallery, South Africa, rep. Surtees, *op. cit.*, II, pl. 187.

SANDYS, Anthony Frederick Augustus

1829–1904. Born in Norwich. Student at the School of Design, Norwich, about 1845; to London, 1850 or 1851; exh. R.A. from 1851; friend of D. G. Rossetti. Painter of portraits and subject pictures, best known as a draughtsman.

724 EMMA SANDYS

Canvas on wood, oval, $9\frac{3}{8} \times 7\frac{3}{8}$ in ($23{\cdot}8 \times 18{\cdot}7$ cm). Head and shoulders, front, the head turned half right. Bare-headed, auburn hair; grey-pink flesh colour; low cut yellow and green dress; grey-green background. The hair and dress unfinished.[1]

Given by Charles Fairfax Murray, 1911. Exh. Brighton, Museum and Art Gallery, 1974, 'Frederick Sandys' (79).

Emma Sandys (1843–1877), the sister of Frederick Sandys, also an artist, exhibited portraits at the R.A. between 1868 and 1874. She is seen here as a young girl, aged about ten or twelve.

REPRODUCED. Exhibition catalogue, *Frederick Sandys*, Brighton Museum and Art Gallery (1974), pl. 50.

NOTE. [1] Inscribed at the back, 'Emma Sandys by her brother F. A. Sandys', and, on a label, 'Emma Sandys by F. A. Sandys'.

881 MRS SANDYS

Canvas, $18\frac{1}{4} \times 14\frac{1}{8}$ in ($46{\cdot}3 \times 35{\cdot}8$ cm).[1] Head, turned and looking half left, in the centre of the canvas, the rest of which, thinly rubbed in in light brown, is blank. Black hair; greyish-pink flesh colour.

Given by Charles Fairfax Murray, 1917.

Given as a portrait of the artist's mother, Mary Anne Negus. It appears to be contemporary with no. 887 below, of the later 1840s, when Sandys would have been about eighteen.

NOTE. [1] Lined; dimensions of the painted surface.

886 PORTRAIT OF A YOUNG MAN

Wood, $8\frac{1}{4} \times 6\frac{1}{2}$ in ($20{\cdot}9 \times 16{\cdot}5$ cm). Head and shoulders, turned half left, the hands held together before him. Bare-headed, dark auburn hair; clean-shaven; wears brown dress. Dark green background. The dress and hands unfinished.

Given by Charles Fairfax Murray, 1917. Exh. Brighton, Museum and Art Gallery, 1974, 'Frederick Sandys' (10).

Cleaned 1974. Copy after a painting by Rogier van der Weyden (Netherlandish, *c.* 1399–1464) at Upton House, Oxfordshire, no. 171[1] (National Trust, Bearstead Collection). It has been dated 'Probably before 1850'.[2]

REPRODUCED. Exhibition catalogue, *Frederick Sandys*, Brighton Museum and Art Gallery (1974), pl. 2.

NOTES. [1] See M. J. Friedländer, *Early Netherlandish painting* (1972), II, p. 69, no. 45, rep. pl. 65. [2] By Mrs Betty O'Looney, exhibition catalogue, *Frederick Sandys*, Brighton Museum and Art Gallery (1974), p. 21, no. 10.

887 MRS SANDYS

Wood, $16\frac{1}{8} \times 12$ in ($40{\cdot}9 \times 30{\cdot}5$ cm). Three-quarter-length standing, turned and facing almost in profile to the right, looking front, the arms folded. Bare-headed, black hair. Black dress with a narrow white collar, a red ribbon round her neck; a red shawl with white stripes passes over her left shoulder and behind her back to cross in front. Behind the figure to the left is a wall, surmounted by a column with a draped red curtain; to the right sky and landscape.

Given by Charles Fairfax Murray, 1917. Exh. Brighton, Museum and Art Gallery, 1974, 'Frederick Sandys' (75).

Cleaned and restored, 1974. Given as a portrait of the artist's mother, Mary Anne Negus, see no. 881 above. From the costume and the style of hairdressing, it may be dated to the later 1840s. A drawing by Sandys, which could almost be a study for it, is at Birmingham (City Art Gallery and Museum, no. 812'06), accompanied by one of his father (no. 813'06), both, like the painting, from the Fairfax Murray collection.

REPRODUCED. Exhibition catalogue, *Frederick Sandys*, Brighton Museum and Art Gallery (1974), pl. 47.

SARGENT, JOHN SINGER

1856–1925. Born in Florence of American parents. Student at the Ecole des Beaux-Arts, and pupil of Carolus Duran, Paris, 1874; moved from Paris to London, 1885; mural paintings at Boston, U.S.A., commissioned 1890; R.A., 1897; travelled extensively. Influenced by the Impressionists, and studied Velasquez and Hals. Predominantly a painter of portraits and landscape.

753 STUDY OF A SICILIAN PEASANT (1907) PLATE 49

Canvas, 23⅝ × 18⅛ in (60·0 × 46·0 cm). Ochre-brown complexion with pink ears; black hair and moustache; dark ochre jacket and white shirt; grey-ochre background. Signed lower left 'John S. Sargent', and dated lower right, '1907'.[1]

Given by the artist, 1914. Exh. London, R.A., 1926, 'Works by the late John S. Sargent, R.A.' (351).

Described by the artist as 'rather a study than a picture'.[2]

REPRODUCED. *Principal pictures* (1929), p. 189.

NOTES. [1] Evan Charteris, *John Sargent* (1927), listed p. 288. [2] Letter of 7 February 1914 (Fitzwilliam Museum); the Museum's records state that the picture was 'Painted in Sicily by the donor' (Syndicate Book, 20 February 1914, minute 6).

1067 OLIVES IN CORFU PLATE 49

Canvas, 22¼ × 28¼ in (56·5 × 71·7 cm). The foliage is brownish green, the tree-trunks mainly in tones of brown, the ground is green. The two shrubs to left are a strong green, with pink flowers, the fence light buff; white goats; light blue and cream sky. Signed lower left, 'John S. Sargent', and dated lower right, 'Corfu 1912'.[1]

Given by the Friends of the Fitzwilliam Museum, 1922. Bt from the artist, 1922; exh. London, R.A., 1926, 'Works by the late John S. Sargent, R.A.' (5); Birmingham, City Museum and Art Gallery, 1964, 'Works by John Singer Sargent, R.A.' (46).

The date of 1912 placed by Sargent upon this picture must be regarded as an error; in 1912 he was in Spain, and the picture, with its typical choice of an olive-grove as a subject,[2] dates from his visit to Corfu in 1909.[3] It is known that Sargent often signed and dated his pictures some time after they were painted, and his recollection of the date was not always reliable.[4] It may well be that he signed and dated this picture when it was bought from him in 1922.

REPRODUCED. Friends of the Fitzwilliam Museum, *Annual Report* for 1922; *Principal pictures* (1929), p. 190.

NOTES. [1] Evan Charteris, *John Sargent* (1927), p. 289; C. M. Mount, *John Singer Sargent* (1957), p. 359 (KO913). [2] Richard Ormond, *John Singer Sargent* (1970), p. 76. [3] Charteris, *loc. cit.*, Mount, *loc. cit.* [4] Charteris, *op. cit.*, p. 39; Mount, *op. cit.*, p. 335.

1169 SANTA MARIA DELLA SALUTE, VENICE

Canvas, $25\frac{1}{4} \times 36\frac{3}{8}$ in ($64{\cdot}2 \times 92{\cdot}4$ cm). Above steps leading up from eye-level rise two projecting features of the architecture of the church; that at the left, at an angle, is enriched with pilasters below a cornice and with niches which hold sculpture, a semi-circular window above; that at the right has two detached columns on high plinths, a statue in a niche between them. The stonework is in tones of slightly ochre or slightly grey cream, with grey-green shadows. At the extreme right is part of the shadowed entrance doorway, deep blue-green in colour.[1]

Given by Harold, 1st Viscount Rothermere, 1926. Sale by J. S. Sargent's executors, Christie's, 24 July 1925 (102), bt Martin; exh. London, R.A., 1926, 'Works by the late John S. Sargent, R.A.' (22), lent Viscount Rothermere; Wildenstein & Co. Ltd, 1972, 'Venice rediscovered' (39).

Entitled in the 1925 Sargent sale, *Entrance to Santa Maria della Salute, Venice*, though the entrance doorway itself is barely indicated at the right. Two other paintings of part of the church from the same low view-point are: Johannesburg Art Gallery, South Africa, and anonymous sale, Christie's, 13 November 1964 (50). None of the three is dated, but the Johannesburg picture was exhibited at the New English Art Club, London, in 1910. Together with the Fitzwilliam Museum picture it has been dated to 1904,[2] but the latter has also been assigned to 1908.[3]

REPRODUCED. Christie sale catalogue, 24 July 1925.

NOTES. [1] Evan Charteris, *John Sargent* (1927), listed p. 289; C. M. Mount, *John Singer Sargent* (1957), listed p. 358 (KO43). [2] Mount, *loc. cit.* [3] Charteris, *loc. cit.*

1506 NEAR THE MOUNT OF OLIVES, JERUSALEM

Canvas, $26\frac{1}{8} \times 38\frac{1}{2}$ in (66·3 × 97·8 cm). A stretch of open ground, falling to a slight depression in the centre, and in places broken by rocks, recedes and rises from the foreground to a line of low buildings at the right along the sky-line; from them low hills in the distance run to the left. In the lights the foreground is in tones of pale blue-grey and ochre, in the lighter shadows blue-grey or grey-green, and brown in the deeper shadows. Similar colours are in the buildings, with some deep green foliage. The hills to the left are orange-brown. Light blue-grey sky.[1]

Given by Miss Sargent and Mrs Ormond, sisters of the artist, 1929. Exh. London, National Gallery, Millbank [Tate Gallery], 1926, *List of loans at the opening of the Sargent Gallery*, p. 9, lent Miss Emily Sargent; R.A., 1926, 'Works by the late John S. Sargent, R.A.' (272).

Sargent paid his second visit to Palestine in the autumn of 1905, returning in January 1906. Each date has been assigned to the picture.[2]

NOTES. [1] Evan Charteris, *John Sargent* (1927), listed p. 287; C. M. Mount, *John Singer Sargent* (1957), listed p. 358 (KO515). [2] Charteris, *loc. cit.*, 1906; Mount, *loc. cit.*, 1905.

PD. 34–1949 PORTRAIT OF DOROTHY BARNARD (1889)

Canvas, $27\frac{3}{4} \times 15\frac{1}{2}$ in (70·5 × 39·4 cm). Half-length standing, in profile to the right, leaning with her hands behind her against the end of a pale grey wall at the left. Bare-headed, auburn hair to shoulders; cream-coloured complexion with pink cheeks. Over a white blouse, wears a yellow jacket with an orange pattern. Dark brown background.[1]

Bequeathed by Miss Dorothy Barnard, 1949. Coll. Mrs Frederick Barnard, her mother; the Misses Barnard; exh. London, National Gallery,

Millbank [Tate Gallery], 1926, *List of loans at the opening exhibition of the Sargent Gallery*, p. 3; R.A., 1926, 'Works by the late John S. Sargent, R.A.' (595); National Gallery, 1941, 'A Whistler and early 20th. century oils' (21); Birmingham, City Museum and Art Gallery, 1964, 'Works by John Singer Sargent, R.A.' (19).

Unfinished. Miss Dorothy Barnard (1878–1949) was the daughter of the artist Frederick Barnard; she and her sister Polly posed for the two little girls in Sargent's *Carnation, lily, lily, rose* (Tate Gallery, London, no. 1615), painted in 1885/6. Painted at Fladbury, Worcestershire, where Sargent had taken a house, in 1889.[2]

NOTES. [1] Evan Charteris, *John Sargent* (1927), listed p. 261; C. M. Mount, *John Singer Sargent* (1957), listed p. 340 (891). [2] Charteris, *loc. cit.*; Mount, *loc. cit.*; David McKibbin, *Sargent's Boston* (1956), listed p. 83, but wrongly dated to 1887.

SCULLY, Sean

b. 1945. Living artist.

PD. 105–1975 PAINTING 20/7/74, NO. 3/3

Acrylic on canvas, 48 × 48 in (121·9 × 121·9 cm). The square of the canvas is divided into twelve rectangles by narrow vertical and horizontal bands, three vertical and two horizontal. The rectangles are sage-green; the vertical bands are light blue with some pink along the edges, the much narrower horizontal bands pink with some dark blue along the edges.

Bought from the Gulbenkian and University Purchase Funds, 1975. Exh. London, Rowan Gallery Ltd, 1975, 'Sean Scully, recent paintings'; bt from the Rowan Gallery.

SEYMOUR, James

1702–1752. Born in London. Student at the St Martin's Lane Academy, London, 1720; influenced by John Wootton; worked at Newmarket and elsewhere. Among the earliest of British sporting painters. Painter and draughtsman of horses.

450 HORSE AND GROOM

Canvas, $11\frac{7}{8}$ × 14 in (30·2 × 35·6 cm). A grey horse stands in profile towards the left, with a young groom mounted on his back looking towards the front. The groom, who is clean-shaven, wears a black cap, buff jacket, yellow breeches and black riding-boots, and holds the reins in his left hand and a switch in his right; red saddle-cloth. Behind are grey-green trees, and to the left are a brown gate and a stile, a landscape with a windmill beyond. The ground is grey-green and brown; grey sky.

Bequeathed by Daniel Mesman, 1834.

This belongs to what seems to be Seymour's mature style of painting, when he was no longer imitating Wootton. It is comparable with two more elaborate pictures, *Sir William Jolliffe preparing for the chase* (Lord Hylton, Ammerdown, Somerset), and *Sir Richard Leighton, Bart, Sir J. Kynaston, Bart, and John Corbet Esq., of Sundorne Castle, with their hunters and hounds* (sale of H. D. Corbet, of Sundorne Castle, Sotheby's, 21 May 1935 (155), rep.). Lord Hylton's pictures by Seymour were painted for Sir William Jolliffe (1665–1750), and one, *A huntsman*, is dated 1745;[1] John Corbet inherited Sundorne Castle in 1741. Little is known of the details of Seymour's career, but from these considerations a speculative dating in the 1740s may perhaps be advanced for the Fitzwilliam Museum painting.

NOTE. [1] See C. H., 'Horses by James Seymour at Ammerdown', *Country Life* (1929), LXV, 126–9, illustrated.

SHANNON, Charles Haslewood

1863–1937. Born at Quarrington, Lincolnshire. Student at the Lambeth School of Art, London, 1882; exh. at the Grosvenor Gallery, and later at the R.A., with the New English Art Club, and elsewhere; R.A., 1920. Painted figure subjects and portraits; wood-engraver and lithographer.

2294 SELF-PORTRAIT (1917)

Canvas, 27 × 26¾ in (68·6 × 68·0 cm). Half-length, turned in profile to the right, facing half right, leaning forward across a table towards a canvas at the right on which he is painting, his left hand resting on the table holds a drawing. Bare-headed, grey hair; clean-shaven; a paint-brush held in the mouth. Wears black clothes, with a white collar and blue bow-tie. To the right a blue cloth, on which are two paint-brushes, lies on the table beside a brown and buff jar. Dark brown background. Signed and dated lower right, 'CHARLES SHANNON / 1917'.

Bequeathed by Charles Haslewood Shannon, R.A., 1937.[1] Exh. London, R.A., 1918 (98); Bradford, Corporation Art Gallery, 1919, 'Twenty-sixth spring exhibition' (57); Liverpool, Walker Art Gallery, 1922, 'Jubilee autumn exhibition' (422); London, Barbizon Gallery, 1928, 'Paintings and drawings by Charles Shannon, R.A.' (4); London, R.A., 1956–7, 'British portraits' (489).

The composition is repeated, with minor modifications, in a lithograph by Shannon of 1918.

REPRODUCED. *Charles Shannon, A.R.A.*, Masters of Modern Art Series (n.d.), p. 1 (colour); *Studio* (1918), LXXIV, 14.

NOTE. [1] Bequeathed with the Ricketts and Shannon Collection.

SHAYER, WILLIAM, THE ELDER

1788–1879. Born in Southampton. Self-taught; influenced by the landscape and marine painter John Wilson; member of the Society of British Artists. Landscape and marine genre painter.

1104 THE PRAWN FISHERS PLATE 39

Canvas, 24 × 29⅞ in (60·9 × 75·9 cm).[1] On a beach in the foreground is a group, towards the right, of a youth seated between two baskets talking to a standing fisher-girl to left of him, a small child beside her. The beach is ochre; the youth wears dark grey trousers, a yellow waistcoat over a white shirt and a pink cap; the girl wears a grey bodice with white sleeves, a yellow scarf and a pink skirt. Behind the youth stands a donkey, to the right is a timber stump, and to the left of the girl is a seated black and white dog. Low grey cliffs run from the right behind the group, with high, rocky cliffs in the distance of a paler grey. Running out towards the left in the middle distance is a jetty, dark grey-brown in colour, with boats beside it and grey-blue sea with the white sails of some ships beyond. Cream and pale grey cloudy sky. Signed lower right, 'Wm Shayer'.

Bequeathed by Samuel Sandars (1837–1894), with a life-interest to his widow, received 1923. Exh. London, B.I. 1835 (496);[2] Society of British Artists, Suffolk Street, 1843 (181), 1855 (238), 1857 (215).[3]

Not later than 1835. Very similar in motive, style and composition, but in reverse, is a *Welsh fisher folk*, signed and dated 1851 (Leger Galleries Ltd, London, 1959).

NOTES. [1] Lined; dimensions of the painted surface. [2] The dimensions of the frame given in the catalogue correspond closely with those of the present frame, which has every appearance of being the original. [3] The title in each case is the same, *The prawn fishers*, as in the B.I. exhibition of 1835. If the evidence of titles is to be trusted, it appears from the catalogues of the Society of British Artists, which include many pictures by Shayer, that he not infrequently exhibited the same painting on more than one occasion.

SICKERT, Walter Richard

1860–1942. Born in Munich; came to England, 1868. Briefly at the Slade School of Art, London, 1881; in Whistler's studio; influenced by Degas; frequently in France, often residing in or near Dieppe; several visits to Venice, 1895–1904; returned to London, 1905; Dieppe, 1919–22; mainly in London until settling in Bath, 1938. R.A., 1934; resigned, 1935. Painter of urban scenes, figure compositions and portraits.

2410 THE TRAPEZE (1920) — PLATE 51

Canvas, $25\frac{1}{2} \times 31\frac{7}{8}$ in ($64{\cdot}7 \times 81{\cdot}0$ cm). The canvas of the tent is khaki-coloured, with greener shadows; the tent-poles are buff. The figure is in blue; the platform is deep pink, its supports are green. Signed and dated lower left, 'Sickert 1920', signed lower right, 'Sickert'.[1]

Bequeathed by Frank Hindley Smith, 1939. Exh. Norwich, 1925, 'Centenary of the Norwich Museum' (51), lent Hindley Smith; London, Thos Agnew & Sons Ltd, 1933, 'Retrospective exhibition of pictures by W. R. Sickert, A.R.A.' (10);[2] London, Tate Gallery, 1960, 'Sickert, paintings and drawings' (153).

From the date of 1920, it is probable that the scene is taken from a circus at Dieppe, where Sickert is known to have made studies in a circus during his 1919–22 visit.[3] In 1920 he was living at Envermeu, about ten miles distant. The composition is distinctly reminiscent of the painting by Degas of 1879, *Mademoiselle Lala at the Cirque Fernando, Paris* (National Gallery, no. 4121). Another version, with slight variations and sketchier in treatment, belongs to Mr and Mrs Paul Mellon, U.S.A. The trapeze artist is named as Mademoiselle Leagh.[4]

REPRODUCED. Lillian Browse, *Sickert* (1943), pl. 53; Anthony Bertram, *Sickert* (1955), pl. 37; Wendy Baron, *Sickert* (1973), pl. 276.

NOTES. [1] Wendy Baron, *Sickert* (1973), pp. 160, 378, no. 396. [2] With title *The trapeze, Dieppe*. [3] Gabriel White, *Notes and sketches by Sickert*, Arts Council exhibition catalogue (1949), p. 17, no. 42; Lillian Browse, *Sickert* (1943), p. 58, and listed in her *Sickert* (1960), p. 92. [4] The Mellon version was exhibited at the winter exhibition of the London Group, 1923 (57), as *Mlle. Leagh*.

2411 WOMAN WITH RINGLETS

Canvas, 14 × 12 in (35·6 × 30·5 cm). The head and naked shoulders of a woman, her head in profile to the right, with hair falling in ringlets at the sides and back. Behind to the right, part of the end of a black iron bedstead. Flesh tones pale pink in the lights, ochre or brown in the shadows; hair orange-brown in the lights, dark brown in the shadows. Background ochrish brown. Signed lower right, 'Sickert'.[1]

Bequeathed by Frank Hindley Smith, 1939.

This has been dated *c.* 1911.[2] The model appears to be the same as in no. 2727, *Oeillade*, p. 225 below, of almost the same dimensions, and assigned to the same date.[3]

NOTES. [1] Wendy Baron, *Sickert* (1973), pp. 117, 359, no. 317. [2] Lillian Browse, *Sickert* (1960), p. 92, no. 4; Baron, *op. cit.*, p. 359, no. 317. [3] Browse, *loc. cit.*, no. 5; Baron, *op, cit.*, p. 358, no. 316.

2458 THE OLD BEDFORD (1894–5)

Canvas, 21⅝ × 15 in (54·9 × 38·1 cm). View in a theatre of the end of a balcony, with a large wall mirror to the left, seen from below, the spectators in the balcony and parts of the architecture illuminated by light from the stage. The predominant colours are the orange-browns (in the lights), the darker browns (in the shadows), and the grey-greens, of the architecture; with passages of grey and lighter blue-grey, warm yellow highlights on the gilt decoration, the light brown tones of the people's faces and the dark greys of their clothes. Signed lower right: 'Sickert'.[1]

Bequeathed by Edward Maurice Berkeley Ingram, C.M.G., O.B.E., (b.1890), 1941. With the Leicester Galleries, London, 1930; exh. Venice, Biennale XIV, 1936, catalogue (3rd edn), p. 367, no. 13; London, National Gallery, 1940, 'British painting since Whistler' (186), lent Ingram;[2] National Gallery, 1941, 'Sickert' (18); Redfern Gallery, 1941, 'Collection of paintings formed by the late Maurice Ingram' (12); Leeds, Temple Newsam House, 1942, 'The life work of Walter Richard Sickert' (121); London, Guildhall Art Gallery, 1971, 'London and the greater painters' (34).

The 'Old Bedford' theatre was a music-hall in Camden Town, London, built in 1861 and destroyed by fire in 1899, when it was rebuilt on the same site. Both 'Old Bedford' and 'New Bedford' subjects occur in Sickert's work, mainly during the earlier years of his career. The present

Old Bedford subject is known in a number of versions, which all vary in some degree one from another. Documentation is slight; an etching of the composition is dated 1894,[3] and a painting at Liverpool (Walker Art Gallery, no. 47–139) was exhibited in London at the New English Art Club in November 1895.[4] Taking progressive changes in the group of figures as a guide to relative dating, the etching is seen to be the earliest known worked-out example of the composition, and the Fitzwilliam Museum picture to precede the one at Liverpool. Directly linking the two paintings is a careful charcoal drawing of the whole composition,[5] corresponding closely with the Fitzwilliam Museum painting and of the same dimensions, in which some alterations in the figures are tried out leading towards the grouping in the Liverpool picture. The present painting may thus be dated 1894–5.[6] Connected with this transition are two drawings of the whole composition, respectively in the British Museum (Department of Prints and Drawings, no. 1914–10–5–2),[7] and at Cape Town (South African National Gallery, no. 628), both squared for enlargement. Apparently intermediate between the etching and the Fitzwilliam Museum picture, and therefore possibly Sickert's preliminary oil sketch for it, is a small painting on wood ($9\frac{3}{4} \times 6\frac{1}{2}$ in, $24{\cdot}7 \times 16{\cdot}5$ cm),[8] formerly in the collection of Edward Le Bas.[9] Versions subsequent to the Liverpool painting are at Ottawa (National Gallery of Canada, Massey Collection), assigned to about 1898,[10] and a much later, sketchily painted example, of about 1915–20, belonging to Mr and Mrs Peter Hughes.[11] Finally come two paintings in which the composition has been modified by extension to the right, with an enlarged group of figures, and by reduction at the left; one belonging to William Shand-Kydd[12], the other in a private collection, London, both assigned in date to about 1898.[13] A small painting entitled *The Bedford* was in an anonymous sale at Christie's, 13 July 1925 (132).

There are a number of early drawings for the composition, some of them evidently sketched in the theatre during performances, as was Sickert's wont. Three drawings of the whole subject were respectively with the Mercury Gallery, London, in 1970, belonging to R. A. MacAlpine, and in a private collection in England, in 1973. A detailed study of the curving front of the balcony and the similar feature below the mirror, formerly belonged to C. Maresco Pearce. A sketch of the mirror with the reflection of a single man in it, as in the 1894 etching, is at Liverpool (Walker Art Gallery, no. 5311). Sketches of the head of the boy leaning his chin on his hand, first used in the Fitzwilliam Museum painting, occur among other figure sketches in two sheets of drawings, respectively in the British Museum (Department of Prints and Drawings, no. 1938-5-14-17) and at Islington, London (Public Libraries). A drawing of the whole composition in chalk, water colour and gouache, in an English private collection, shows a late stage in working out the composition.[14]

Though the subject is usually known as *The Old Bedford*, alternative titles which occasionally occur are *The boy I love is up in the gallery*, and *Cupid in the gallery*.

REPRODUCED. *Studio* (1930), C, 318 (colour); Lillian Browse, *Sickert* (1943), pl. 5; Anthony Bertram, *Sickert* (1955), pl. 4; *Shell-B.P. News* (1958), May, cover (colour); *Capolavori nei secoli*, Milan (1964/5).

NOTES [1] Wendy Baron, *Sickert* (1973), pp. 40–4, 311, no. 73, Version 2. [2] In substitution for no. 186 in the printed catalogue, *Interior of St Mark's* by Sickert. [3] Rep. in *The Idler* for March 1895, p. 169, with the title *The music hall* opposite, and below the reproduction, in quotation marks, 'The boy I love is up in the gallery'. [4] 'Fifteenth exhibition of modern pictures', no. 73, entitled *The boy I love is up in the gallery*; see Ronald Pickvance, 'The magic of the halls and Sickert', *Apollo* (1962), LXXVI, 107ff.: rep. Lillian Browse, *Sickert* (1960), pl. 15; Baron *op. cit.*, pp. 40, 310, no. 73, rep. pl. 45. [5] Formerly belonging to Mrs George Swinton, now in an English private collection, rep. *Image* 7 (1952), p. 19, John Rothenstein, *Sickert* (1961) (plates not numbered), erroneously described as belonging to the Arts Council of Great Britain, and Baron, *op. cit.*, pl. 44. [6] A date as early as *c.* 1890 has been proposed, e.g. Lillian Browse, *Sickert* (1943), p. 35, and *Sickert* (1960), p. 91, no. 1. [7] Virtually identical with Sickert's etching, *The Old Bedford*, published by Carfax & Co., London (in 1915, see Robert Emmons, *The life and opinions of Walter Richard Sickert* (1941), p. 184). [8] For Sickert's use of preparatory oil sketches on wood, see Browse, *op. cit.* (1960), p. 48. [9] Baron, *op. cit.*, p. 311, no. 73, Version 1. [10] Browse, *op. cit.* (1960), p. 87, no. 2; Baron, *op. cit.*, p. 312, no. 78. [11] Browse, *op. cit.* (1960), p. 65, no. 15; Baron, *op. cit.*, p. 312, no. 78. [12] Browse, *loc. cit.*, n. 11; Baron, *op. cit.*, p. 311, no. 75, rep. pl. 46. [13] Browse, *loc. cit.*, n. 11; Baron, *op. cit.*, p. 311, no. 76, rep. pl. 47. [14] For notes on these ten drawings, see Baron, *op. cit.*, p. 310, under no. 73.

2515 SIR HUGH WALPOLE (1928)

Canvas, $16\frac{7}{8} \times 16\frac{1}{2}$ in ($42{\cdot}9 \times 41{\cdot}9$ cm). Head, facing and looking nearly quarter left; bare-headed, receding fair hair, clean-shaven; horn-rimmed spectacles. To either side of his blue shirt collar, is a patch of the terracotta red of his jacket. Behind, two small boys (at the right) and a small girl (at the left) are playing at the edge of some water, which stretches away to trees in the background. Signed and dated lower right, 'Sickert 1928'.[1]

Bequeathed by Sir Hugh Walpole, C.B.E., 1941, received 1943. With the Savile Gallery Ltd, London; bt from them by Sir Hugh Walpole, 1929;[2] exh. London Group, 1929, '26th Exhibition' (19); Arts Council, 1970, 'Decade 1920–30' (1).

The portrait was begun at the end of October 1928, at 1 Highbury Place, London, and finished before the end of the year. From Sir Hugh Walpole's account of the sittings, the portrait appears to have been painted direct, without preliminary drawings or other studies, though whether or not Sickert made use of photographs is not clear.[3] Of Sickert's two portraits of Walpole, only this was painted from life; the other, different in design and larger, is in the Glasgow Art Gallery (no. 2607).[4] Sir Hugh Seymour Walpole, C.B.E. (1884–1941), novelist; kt, 1937.

REPRODUCED. Rupert Hart-Davis, *Hugh Walpole* (1952), p. 300.

NOTES. [1] Wendy Baron, *Sickert* (1973), pp. 174–5, 381, no. 406. [2] Letter from the Savile Gallery Ltd, 20 October 1948 (Fitzwilliam Museum). [3] Rupert Hart-Davis, *Hugh Walpole* (1952), pp. 298–9. It was at 1 Highbury Place, a studio which Sickert took in 1927, that he is supposed to have begun painting from photographs (Lillian Browse, *Sickert* (1960), p. 41); but the practice dates from much earlier, cf. Baron, *op. cit.*, pp. 168–9. [4] Hart-Davis, *op. cit.*, p. 299, n. 1; Baron, *op. cit.*, p. 381, no. 406, rep. pl. 282.

2726 THE GARDEN OF LOVE

Canvas, $32\frac{1}{4} \times 24\frac{1}{4}$ in ($81{\cdot}9 \times 61{\cdot}6$ cm). Seen from above at an oblique angle through the open lower half of a sash window, is a garden, with the wall of a high building beyond it. A lawn with an urn in the centre is bordered to right and left by a path, and along the end runs a series of light arches, with a woman beside a centrally placed piece of sculpture, reaching up towards the plants which climb over them. Above the arches is a line of dark brown trellis, and to the left the foliage of a tree. The lawn is light green, and the foliage dark green, except for some yellow-green along the arches. Above this view is part of the upper sash of the window, covered with a curtain striped and patterned in deep red, green and buff. Signed lower right, 'Sickert'.[1]

Given by Howard Bliss, 1945. Anon. sale, Christie's, 4 March 1932 (67), bt Lessore; exh. London, Beaux-Arts Gallery,[2] April–May 1932, 'Paintings by Richard Sickert, A.R.A.' (34), lent Howard Bliss; Liverpool,

Walker Art Gallery, 1933, 'Fifty-ninth autumn exhibition' (99); Leeds, Temple Newsam House, 1942, 'Exhibition of the life work of Walter Richard Sickert' (186); Bedford, Cecil Higgins Art Gallery, 1969, 'The Camden Town group' (48).

A drawing of this subject, virtually identical with the painting , also in the Fitzwilliam Museum (no. 2775), is inscribed in Sickert's hand, 'Lainey's garden' and 'Londra benedetta II'. 'Lainey' was Sickert's third wife, the painter Thérèse Lessore, whom he married in 1926, and the garden can be identified as that of their house in Quadrant Road, Islington, where they settled in 1927. The urn and the piece of sculpture (a cast of Michelangelo's *Madonna and Child* at Bruges) were subsequently in their garden at Barnsbury Park, where they moved in 1931. The figure is no doubt Mrs Sickert, who was an enthusiastic gardener.[3] The drawing is not squared for enlargement, suggesting that drawing and painting come independently from a common source.[4] Both may be dated *c.* 1927–31.[5]

REPRODUCED. Wendy Baron, *Sickert* (1973), pl. 267.

NOTES. [1] Wendy Baron, *Sickert* (1973), pp. 164, 374–5, no. 383. [2] Then run by Jules Lessore. [3] This circumstantial information about the Sickerts and their garden has been kindly communicated by Mrs Helen Lessore, who knew the house at Barnsbury Park (letter of 19 September 1973, Fitzwilliam Museum). [4] Baron, *op. cit.*, pp. 374–5, no. 383. [5] Lillian Browse, *Sickert* (1960), p. 92, nos. 8 and 13, dates them *c.* 1928; Baron, *op. cit.*, p. 374, no. 383, dates *c.* 1924–7; Mrs Lessore, *c.* 1927.

2727 OEILLADE

Canvas, 15 × 12 in (38·1 × 30·5 cm). A woman reclines across a bed, turned away from the spectator, whom she regards over her left shoulder. Part of the end of a black iron bedstead at the left. She has a ruddy complexion and lightish brown hair, and wears a cream-brown dress. Grey-blue bed clothes; background greenish grey with dull red markings. Signed lower left, 'Sickert'.[1]

Given by Howard Bliss, 1945. Exh. London, Carfax Gallery, 1912, 'Paintings and drawings by Walter Sickert' (18); Brighton, Public Art Galleries, 1913–14, 'Work of English post-impressionists, cubists, and others' (58).

This has been dated on stylistic grounds *c.* 1911.[2] The model appears to be the same as in no. 2411, *Woman with ringlets*, p. 221 above, of almost the same dimensions and assigned to the same date.[3]

NOTES. [1] Wendy Baron, *Sickert* (1973), pp. 117, 118, 129, 358, no. 316. [2] Lillian Browse, *Sickert* (1960), p. 92, no. 5; Baron, *loc. cit.* [3] Browse, *loc. cit.*, no. 4; Baron, *op. cit.*, p. 359, no. 317.

PD. 25–1953 RUSHFORD MILL (1915–16)

Canvas, 25⅛ × 30⅛ in (63·8 × 76·5 cm). On the further bank of a stream crossed by stepping stones, beyond a foreground of grass with bushes at the right, the large mill building stands at the left. Behind it and in the centre rise some tall trees, with a few house roofs seen at the right against a hill-side. The herbage and foliage range in colour from yellow-green to blue-green; the water is mainly brown with blue reflections. The mill building, which has a grey roof, and some of the ground nearby, are in buffs and browns. Grey-blue sky with pale buff clouds. Signed lower right, 'Sickert'.[1]

Bought from the Fairhaven Fund, 1953. Exh. Carfax & Co. Ltd., London, 1916, 'Paintings by Walter Sickert' (5);[2] coll. Thomas Geoffrey Blackwell (1884–1943); sold for him by Arthur Tooth & Sons Ltd, London, to Horace Noble, 1943; anon. sale, Christie's, 25 July 1952 (46), bt Roland, Browse & Delbanco, London; bt from Arthur Tooth & Sons Ltd.

Rushford Mill on the river Teign in Devon, which still stood, with its stepping stones, in 1971 scarcely changed from the painting, is within less than a mile of the village of Chagford, where Sickert spent the summer of 1915.[3] Many drawings and small oil studies on panel date from this visit.[4] Among the few which were later used to paint full-scale pictures in the studio, is a panel painting for this picture of Rushford Mill, belonging to Dr S. Charles Lewson.[5] Two drawings of the composition, one an elaborated tracing of the other, both bearing a few colour notes and squared for enlargement, are in the Walker Art Gallery, Liverpool.[6] As it was November before the painting was exhibited in 1916, it may be approximately dated 1915–16.

REPRODUCED. Fitzwilliam Museum, *Annual Report* for 1953, pl. III; Wendy Baron, *Sickert* (1973), pl. 258.

NOTES. [1] Wendy Baron, *Sickert* (1973), pp. 152, 371, no. 378. [2] With the title *Rushford Mill*, though the picture was later known as *The mill pool.* [3] Robert Emmons, *The life and opinions of Walter Richard Sickert* (1941), p. 183. [4] Baron, *op. cit.*, p. 152. [5] Baron, *op. cit.*, p. 371, no. 368. [6] Original, no. 5528, tracing, no. 5420; both were bought in 1948, with other drawings by Sickert, from his studio. On the traced drawing, an inscription in an unknown hand mistakenly identifies the subject as at Auberville, which is close to the village of Envermeu, near Dieppe, where Sickert was living in 1919–20.

PD. 2–1955 MRS SWINTON PLATE 51

Canvas, 30×25 in (76·2×63·5 cm). She wears a red dress, and has dark hair; the flesh tones are greenish and ochrish in colour. The sea is green with grey-blue shadows; mauve-blue sky.[1]

Bequeathed by James William Freshfield, 1955. Probably exh. Paris, Bernheim Jeune & Cie, January 1907, 'Exposition Sickert' (36);[2] with William Marchant & Co., London; their sale, Christie's, 28 and 31 January 1927 (145), bt Cremetti; (?) with the Savile Gallery, London; coll. the Hon. Mrs Maurice Glyn; exh. London, Thos Agnew & Sons Ltd, 1933, 'Retrospective exhibition of pictures by W. R. Sickert, A.R.A.' (49);[3] sold by Agnew's for Mrs Glyn to J. W. Freshfield, 1936; on loan to the Fitzwilliam Museum, 1938–46.

Mrs Elsie Swinton (1874–1966), wife of Captain George Sitwell Swinton, was a singer and a close friend of Sickert, who 'painted a number of portraits' of her.[4] Two others are known, *The lady in the gondola*, belonging to Martin Halperin, and a smaller version of it at Oxford (Ashmolean Museum, no. 407) dated 1905.[5] A drawing of her, from the Emmons collection, was in 1947 with the Ferrers Gallery, London. Mrs Swinton, in 1956, recalled this portrait as having been painted in Sickert's studio at 8 Fitzroy Street, London, about 1908,[6] but this seems too late. In technique there are similarities with the portrait of 1905, and closer similarities with paintings of 1906, such as *The Belgian cocotte*, belonging to the Arts Council of Great Britain, and *Le lit de cuivre*, in the possession of Nigel Haigh.[7] Considering also the strong probability that the portrait was exhibited in Paris in January 1907, a date of 1905–6 is indicated. The portrait is based on a photograph,[8] but only the pose and lighting are common to both, the costume and the background[9] being inventions.

REPRODUCED. *Burlington Magazine* (1971), CXIII, 550; Wendy Baron, *Sickert* (1973), pl. 157.

NOTES. [1] Wendy Baron, *Sickert* (1973), pp. 53, 88, 339, no. 223, with date *c.* 1906. [2] Robert Emmons, *The life and opinions of Walter Richard Sickert* (1941), p. 137, states that Sickert sent over to Paris some of the portraits he painted of Mrs Swinton. The present one was evidently among them, as it has on the back of the canvas the impression of a *douane* rubber stamp. In the Bernheim Jeune exhibition catalogue, no. 36 is entitled simply *Etude pour portrait*, with no dimensions for positive identification; but a link is provided by the curious Franco-English title of the Fitzwilliam Museum picture when in the Marchant sale of 1927, *Etude pour portrait: lady in a red dress.* [3] As depicting Mrs Swinton, who was a friend of Mrs Glyn. [4] Emmons, *loc. cit.* [5] Baron, *op. cit.*, p. 337, no. 203. [6] Letter from her son, Brigadier A. H. C. Swinton, 13 March 1956 (Fitzwilliam Museum). [7] Baron, *op. cit.*, p. 339, no. 220, p. 337, no. 209. [8] A print belongs to Mrs Swinton's daughter, Lady William Percy, who has kindly allowed use to be made of it; see *Burlington Magazine* (1971), CXIII, 551–2, rep. p. 550. [9] Not in any way Venetian, as tends to be assumed, presumably by analogy with the 1905 portrait with its background of the church of Sta Maria della Salute.

PD. 17–1959 THE LION OF ST MARK PLATE 50

Canvas, $35\frac{1}{2} \times 35\frac{3}{8}$ in. (90·2 × 89·8 cm).[1] The pattern on the upper part of the walls is dull pink on buff, both darker on the shadowed side; the stonework is buff-ochre, on the shadowed side ochre-brown and blue-grey. The dome is ochre-brown, on a drum of Venetian red; the stonework below is in ochre-browns and blue-greys. The column is in warmer browns and buffs, the lion grey. Blue water and sky. Signed lower right, 'Sickert'.[2]

Bequeathed by Guy John Fenton Knowles, 1959. Coll. André Gide (1869–1951); bought from his family by the Leicester Galleries, London; exh. Leicester Galleries, 1952, 'New Year exhibition' (57), bt G. J. F. Knowles; London, Tate Gallery, 1960, 'Sickert paintings and drawings' (70).

The Doge's Palace, Venice. The painting is connected with Sickert's first visit to Venice in 1895–6, when it is known that he painted at least one version of this subject.[3] This may be the picture belonging to Mrs Peter Hastings,[4] which was exhibited at the New English Art Club in 1896[5] ('Sixteenth exhibition of modern pictures' (96)), and is considerably smaller than the present one (23 × 23 in, 58·4 × 58·4 cm), in which also the composition extends somewhat further on all four sides. The present picture is possibly among the paintings of Venetian subjects done in the studio by Sickert after his return to London in 1896,[6] but in the absence of precise information a dating of *c.* 1895–6 is to be preferred.[7] A small painting with this title, measuring $7\frac{1}{2} \times 6\frac{1}{4}$ in (19·6 × 15·9 cm), was in an anonymous sale at Christie's, 4 March 1932, lot 76. Paintings entitled *The lion of St Mark*, which cannot now be identified, as the exhibition catalogues give no dimensions, were in Bernheim Jeune's Sickert exhibition in Paris, 1904, no. 1,[8] and at the Leicester Galleries, London, 1948, 'Paintings...in the collection of Sir Louis Fergusson, K.C.V.O.', no. 49,[9] sold by the Leicester

Galleries in the same year. An etching of the subject by Sickert, published by Carfax & Co., 1915,[10] seems to be based upon Mrs Hastings's version.

REPRODUCED. Lillian Browse, *Sickert* (1960), pl. 29; *Architectural Review* (1960), CXXVII, 224, fig. 9; John Rothenstein, *Sickert* (1961) (plates not numbered); Wendy Baron, *Sickert* (1973), pl. 56.

NOTES. [1] Lined; dimensions of the painted surface. [2] Wendy Baron, *Sickert* (1973), pp. 47, 49–51, 313, no. 86. [3] Lillian Browse, *Sickert* (1960), p. 26. [4] Formerly belonging to Captain Sir Malcolm Bullock, Bart, from whom inherited 1966; Baron, *op. cit.*, pp. 313–14, no. 86. [5] Information from a label at the back of the picture, kindly communicated by Mrs Hastings (letter of 11 October 1970, Fitzwilliam Museum). In 1929 it was with the Leicester Galleries, London (reproduced *Burlington Magazine* (1929), LV, December, 'Notable works of art now on the market', pl. 15); it was bought by Sir Malcolm Bullock in 1947 from Thos Agnew & Sons Ltd, London, no. 42 in their 'Exhibition of paintings and drawings by W. R. Sickert from the collection of Robert Emmons'. [6] Baron, *op. cit.*, p. 46. [7] Baron, *op. cit.*, p. 313, no. 86; it has been dated 1896, Browse, *op. cit.*, pp. 69, 91, and catalogue of the Tate Gallery Sickert exhibition, 1960, no. 70, and 1900, Leicester Galleries, catalogue of their 'New Year exhibition', 1952, no. 57. [8] Perhaps the present picture, see Baron, *op. cit.*, pp. 313–14, no. 86. [9] The catalogue states that it was exhibited in 1929 in their 'Sickert retrospective exhibition', but the only painting in this catalogue with which it could be identified is no. 92, with the title *San Marco*. Perhaps this is a confusion with Mrs Hastings's picture, see n. [5] above. [10] Robert Emmons, *The life and opinions of Walter Richard Sickert* (1941), p. 184.

PD. 28–1970 CHURCH OF ST JACQUES, DIEPPE

Wood, $6\frac{9}{16} \times 4\frac{11}{16}$ in (16·7 × 12·0 cm). The west front of the church is seen down a street, with the fronts of buildings in steep perspective at either side. To the left of the church, across an open space, stands a light-coloured, three-storey building (Hôtel du Commerce). The darker parts are in tones of pink-grey, with accents of very dark grey, the lighter parts in tones of ochre-yellow; the church doors are dull Venetian red. Pink-grey sky. Signed lower right, 'Sickert'.[1]

Bequeathed by the Very Rev. Eric Milner-White, C.B.E., D.S.O., Dean of York, 1963, received 1970. With Arthur Tooth & Sons Ltd, London; exh. Tooth's, 1950, 'Paris–Londres' (14),[2] bt by the Very Rev. E. Milner-White.

When Sickert took up his residence in Dieppe in 1898, the church of St Jacques became one of his most frequent subjects. This view of the west front, in particular, is known in many versions, both paintings and drawings, each with its individual variations,[3] but not all include in the composition the open space to the left of the church, as in the present example. This, which is one of several small paintings on wood, could well be a study for the large painting on canvas at Manchester (Whitworth Art Gallery, no. 0.1.1970).[4] The paintings and drawings forming this long series are assigned to *c.* 1899–1900.[5]

NOTES. [1] Wendy Baron, *Sickert* (1973), pp. 58–9, 321–2, no. 118, panel version 4. [2] The catalogue of the exhibition describes it as 'A collection of pictures recently purchased in France'. [3] Baron, *op. cit.*, p. 321, no. 118. [4] Rep. Baron, *op. cit.*, pl. 85; for Sickert's use of small preliminary studies on wood, see Lillian Browse, *Sickert* (1960), p. 48. [5] Baron, *op. cit.*, pp. 321–2, nos. 118–120.

PD. 91–1974 GIRL AT A LOOKING-GLASS, LITTLE RACHEL

Canvas, $20\frac{1}{8} \times 16\frac{1}{8}$ in (51·1 × 41·0 cm). A girl standing in front of a dressing-table, seen from the back and turned half towards the right, looks at her reflection in an oval looking-glass; behind the dressing-table is a window with glazing-bars, and in the distance to the right a church. The girl's red hair is brown at the back in shadow; her dress is in tones of dark grey and grey-green, slightly toned white trimming runs down her right arm; in her reflection the face is in tones of grey-brown, the hair in tones of dark brown, the dress in tones of blue-grey. The dressing-table is dark brown with passages of blue and grey; the woodwork of the looking-glass is deep grey and brown with light grey-blue along the top of the frame. The glazing-bars of the window are greenish grey; the church is mauve-grey with orange accents, below it a passage of grey-white changing lower down to dull yellow. The sky is light grey. Signed lower left, 'Sickert'.[1]

Given by Keith Stuart Baynes, 1974. Given to him by the artist, 1925;[2] coll. L. G. Hoare (d. 1959); exh. New York, Thos Agnew & Sons Ltd, 1929, 'Contemporary British artists' (7);[3] coll. K. S. Baynes; exh. London, Thos Agnew & Sons Ltd, 1960, 'Sickert' (59); Columbus, Ohio, U.S.A., Columbus Gallery of Fine Art, 1971, 'British art, 1890–1928' (101).

One of a series of paintings and drawings of 'Little Rachel' done by Sickert in Mornington Crescent, London, in 1907; he described her as 'a little Jewish girl of 13 or so with red hair', and she is identified as Miss

Siderman, who died in 1963 aged seventy.[4] Two drawings for the painting are known, a complete composition study in a private collection in London, and another belonging to the University of Reading. The picture formerly bore the title *Chez Verney*, under which it appeared at Agnew's exhibition in 1960, presumably through some confusion with no. PD. 92–1974 (see below).

REPRODUCED. Exhibition catalogue, *British art, 1890–1928*, Columbus Gallery of Fine Art, U.S.A. (1971), fig. 67.

NOTES. [1] Wendy Baron, *Sickert* (1973), pp. 102, 347 (no. 263 (1)). [2] On the occasion of K. S. Baynes buying from Sickert for L. G. Hoare *Chez Vernet* below, no. PD. 92–1974, which see, n. (2). [3] With the title *The mirror*. [4] Baron, *loc. cit.*; a different account is given in the catalogue of the exhibition at the Columbus Gallery of Fine Art in 1971, by Denys Sutton, where it is stated that K. S. Baynes saw it being painted at 8 Fitzroy Street, London, about 1910, but this is not confirmed by Mr Baynes, whose recollection of seeing the picture goes no further back than 1919 (letter of 23 January 1976, Fitzwilliam Museum).

PD. 92–1974 CHEZ VERNET (1925)

Canvas, $24\frac{1}{8} \times 19\frac{7}{8}$ in ($61{\cdot}3 \times 50{\cdot}5$ cm). A group of two men and a woman sit to the left at a rectangular table in the foreground, looking to the right; the nearer man is in grey, the woman beyond him has a dark grey hat and bluish white dress, the further man has clothes and a cap of ochre-brown; the faces are buff, orange, blue and cream in colour; the table top is in tones of grey and mauve-grey; at the right is part of the back of a bentwood chair. Receding at the right is a wall with two openings in it, the sides of the openings light yellow, the wall green; figures at the openings are in greys, yellows, browns and blues; a coat hanging at the right is grey. A wall at the back, crossed by a yellow-brown shadow, is orange-coloured above it and ochre below; a strip of ceiling above is ochre. Through a rectangular doorway at the back, in tones of grey and yellow, is seen a blue-green plant against a yellow-green wall, with the figure of a standing woman in grey. Signed and dated lower left, 'Sickert '25'.[1]

Given by Keith Stuart Baynes, 1974. Coll. L. G. Hoare (d. 1959), bt from the artist 1925;[2] exh. London, Thos Agnew & Sons Ltd, 1933, 'Retrospective exhibition of pictures by W. R. Sickert, A.R.A.' (5); Liverpool, Walker Art Gallery, 1935, 'Sixty-first Autumn Exhibition' (81).

Vernet's was a café-concert in Dieppe, the subject, in varying aspects, of many drawings and paintings by Sickert.[3] One of the paintings, different in subject from the present picture, is dated 1920,[4] the year in which Sickert moved to Dieppe after the death of his first wife. He left Dieppe for London in 1922, where he was still living in 1925, the date of this painting. Two other versions of it are known, one now or formerly belonging to Mrs Lewis Cohen, the other in a private collection in London, for which there are some drawings.[5] The title of the present picture was formerly mis-spelt *Chez Verney*, as at Agnew's in 1933, under which form it was at one time, by some confusion, attached to no. PD. 91–1974 above, also from the collection of L. G. Hoare.

NOTES. [1] Wendy Baron, *Sickert* (1973), p. 378 (no. 397(2)). [2] The purchase was made on L. G. Hoare's behalf by K. S. Baynes (his letter of 23 January 1976, Fitzwilliam Museum); the date of 1925 is given in Baron, *loc. cit.*, n. 1. [3] Baron, *op. cit.*, pp. 161, 378 (no. 397). [4] Baron, *op. cit.*, p. 378 (no. 397), fig. 276. [5] Baron, *op. cit.*, p. 378 (no. 397 (1)).

SIMS, Charles

1873–1928. Born in London. Studied at the National Art Training Schools, South Kensington (later the Royal College of Art), 1890; in Paris, Académie Julian, 1891–2; R.A. schools, London, 1893–5; exh. R.A. from 1896; R.A., 1915. Painted landscapes, portraits and allegorical subjects.

1505 STUDY OF A DEAD RAIL

Canvas on millboard, 12 × 16 in (30·5 × 40·6 cm). The bird lies on its side across the centre of the canvas, the head at the right, the breast towards the spectator. The feathers are grey, lighter on the lower part of the body, darker on the breast, head, neck and wings; greenish yellow legs and feet. The (?) rushes on which it lies are in tones of pinkish, greyish and greenish ochre. Dark grey background, a lighter grey-green towards the left.

Given by the Friends of the Fitzwilliam Museum, 1928. With Barbizon House, London, from whom it was bought.

REPRODUCED. Friends of the Fitzwilliam Museum, *Annual Report* for 1928.

2547 THE LITTLE FAUN — PLATE 55

Canvas, $20\frac{1}{8} \times 24\frac{1}{8}$ in (51·1 × 61·3 cm). The table-cloth is white; the nearer woman wears white with a red sash, the further woman is in pink; the boy's shorts are white, his jersey white and black; the faun has brown legs and a light pinkish body. The trunk and branches of the tree are in tones of grey-green and brown-green, the blossom is white; the faun parents are in tones of deep brown. Light blue-grey sky. Signed lower right, 'Sims'.

Given by Mrs Sigismund Goetze, 1943. Exh. London, (Royal) Institute of Oil Painters, 1906, '24th Exhibition' (51), bt L. F. Floersheim; anon. sale, Christie's, 31 July 1931 (48), bt Goetze; coll. Sigismund C. H. Goetze (1866–1939); exh. London, R.A., 1933, 'Commemorative exhibition of works by late members' (450).

Study for the larger version (40 × 50 in, 101·6 × 127·0 cm) in the Cornwall County Museum and Art Gallery, Truro (A. A. de Pass Collection no. 223),[1] painted in 1907.[2] Presumably to be dated 1905–6. A water-colour version in reverse belonged in 1929 to George Clough.[3]

NOTES. [1] So described in the catalogue of the 1933 R.A. exhibition. [2] Charles Sims, *Picture making, technique and inspiration*, with a memoir by Alan Sims (1943), rep. pl. 24 and so dated on the caption. [3] Rep. *Old Water-Colour Society's Club* (1929), vol. for 1928–9, pl. XXXIII.

SMIBERT, John

1688–1751. Born in Edinburgh. Student at the St Martin's Lane Academy, London; in Italy, 1719–22; to America, 1728; to Boston, Mass., U.S.A., by 1729, where he remained. Portrait painter.

Attributed to John Smibert

642 UNKNOWN MAN

Canvas, $29\frac{7}{8} \times 24\frac{7}{8}$ in (75·9 × 63·2 cm).[1] Half-length slightly left, head turned somewhat to the right; wears a crimson, soft cap; clean-shaven. Crimson jacket open over an open white shirt. Dark brown background.

Given by Charles Fairfax Murray, 1908. Coll. C. F. Huth; his sale, Christie's, 19 March 1904 (35).

In the Huth sale, and when given, described as of the poet James Thomson (1700–1748), by William Aikman, and so catalogued. But comparison with authentic portraits of Thomson does not support this identification, and despite some points of likeness with the work of Aikman, the picture appears to be by a less vigorous hand with different habits of drawing. The style has a considerable similarity to the work of Smibert, which it resembles in lighting, modelling and treatment, and in the expression, particularly of the eyes, but the impastoed use of the paint is less characteristic. A date in the first half of the eighteenth century is broadly indicated by the costume.

REPRODUCED. *Principal pictures* (1912 edn), p. 1, (1929 edn), p. 1; C. R. L. Fletcher and Emery Walker, *Historical portraits* (1919), III, p. 84.

NOTE. [1] Lined; dimensions of the painted surface.

SMITH, Sir Matthew Arnold Bracy

1879–1959. Born at Halifax, Yorkshire. Slade School of Art, London, 1905–7; in Brittany; briefly at Matisse's school, Paris, 1911; worked much in France; studied the Old Masters, particularly Ingres; influenced by the Post-Impressionists and the *fauves*. Painter of the figure, landscape and still-life. C.B.E., 1949; kt, 1954.

2453 LANDSCAPE AT AIX-EN-PROVENCE PLATE 60

Canvas, 18⅛ × 21⅝ in (46·3 × 54·9 cm). The hill-side, orange-red with blue-green trees, is green towards the top with a darker green tree, and at the base is yellow. The belt of trees beyond is dark green, the distant line of hills olive-green and red-brown. The sky is mainly blue, cream and green, with some passages of red. Signed lower left, in a monogram, 'MS'.

Bequeathed by Edward Maurice Berkeley Ingram, C.M.G., O.B.E., 1941. Sold for the artist by Arthur Tooth & Sons Ltd, London, to G. Shakespeare, 1936, and for him to E. M. B. Ingram, 1938; exh. London, National Gallery, 1940, 'British painting since Whistler' (180); Redfern Gallery, 1941, 'Collection of paintings formed by the late Maurice Ingram' (36); R.A., 1960, 'Memorial exhibition of works by Sir Matthew Smith, C.B.E.' (170).

During the 1930's, which Matthew Smith spent in France, the chief development in his painting lay in the direction of landscape. The present picture belongs to the period, 1934–40, when he was established in Aix-en-Provence; it has been dated *c.* 1936,[1] with other landscapes of the same locality.[2]

NOTES. [1] Catalogue of the R.A. memorial exhibition, 1960, p. 22, no. 170. [2] E.g., Birmingham Museum and Art Gallery, no. P. 14/46.

PD. 51–1971 STILL-LIFE WITH POMEGRANATES AND PEARS

Canvas, 15 × 18⅛ in (38·1 × 46·3 cm). A red and yellow earthenware bowl, seen rather from above, standing on the grey and green top of a table, is filled with whole and split pomegranates, in varying tones of red, on top of them three large green pears; two large yellow pears lie on the table at the left. Background of ochre-yellow, turning to brown-red at the right.

Bequeathed by Claude William Guillebaud, C.B.E. (d. 1971), with a life-interest to his widow, who relinquished it 1971. Bt from the artist by Alex Reid & Lefevre Ltd, London; sold to C. W. Guillebaud, 1942.

A label of Reid & Lefevre at the back gives a date for the painting of 1935.

SOEST, Gerard

c. 1605(?)–1681. Of German or Dutch origin. Perhaps in England by 1644; worked in London. Portrait painter.

2356 UNKNOWN MAN PLATE 4

Canvas, 29⅝ × 24⅝ in (75·3 × 62·6 cm).[1] He has white hair and moustache; fresh complexion. The clothes are black, with white linen. Brown background. Signed lower left, 'Soest Pinxit'.

Given by Claude Dickason Rotch, 1939. Sale of the late Richard Manley Foster, of Liverpool, Christie's, 17 June 1927 (42), bt Pawsey & Payne, London; anon. sale, Christie's, 20 December 1929 (149), bt Rodd.[2]

This portrait takes its place among Soest's later works, which are thought to have been comparatively few.[3] It may be dated *c.* 1670–5, or possibly a little later. A portrait of Admiral Jeremiah Smith,[4] who died in 1675, is practically a repetition save for the head; and a portrait of William Chiffinch by Soest's pupil John Riley (Dulwich Gallery. no. 568), of *c.* 1670–80, is virtually another repetition of the same portrait-formula.

NOTES. [1] Lined; dimensions of the painted surface. [2] As *Portrait of a gentleman* in the Foster sale of 1927, but in the anonymous sale of 1929 as *Mr Manley of Overleigh*, an identification evidently derived from a manuscript label at the back of the picture reading 'from Overleigh, Mr. Manley'; this inscription remains unelucidated. [3] C. H. Collins Baker, *Lely and the Stuart portrait painters* (1912), 2 vols., I, p. 205. [4] Lord Queenborough sale, Christie's, 28 April 1950 (72), bt Colnaghi.

van SOMER, Paul

1576–1621. Born at Antwerp. Worked in the Netherlands; in London by December 1616; employed as a court painter from at least 1617. Portrait and history painter.

442 CATHERINE, LADY ABERGAVENNY PLATE 3

Canvas, $30\frac{1}{2} \times 25\frac{1}{8}$ in ($77{\cdot}5 \times 63{\cdot}8$ cm).[1] The black dress is embroidered in gold and grey; brown hair; the locket is dark grey, the jewels black. Red background. The inscription reads 'Catherine Vaux wife to Henry Baron Abergavenny'.

Founder's Bequest, 1816.

Catherine Vaux, second wife of Henry Nevill, 9th Baron Abergavenny (or Bergavenny), married before 1616, died 1649. The portrait presumably came into the Fitzwilliam family through Lady Abergavenny's great-grand-daughter, Frances Shelley, wife of the 5th Viscount Fitzwilliam and heir-general of her grandfather, the 11th Baron Abergavenny. Unattributed in the Founder's Bequest, it may confidently be ascribed to van Somer from the similarity of style with the head of his portrait of Queen Anne of Denmark, dated 1617, at Windsor Castle,[2] and the costume confirms this as the approximate date of the painting. A whole-length version of the portrait, including the figure of a child, belonged in 1951 to the Hon. S. Stonor at Stonor Park,[3] and as the Fitzwilliam Museum painting has evidently been cut down,[4] it too may originally have been a whole-length.

REPRODUCED. Earp, p. 230.

NOTES. [1] Lined; the dimensions are those of the canvas to the edge of the stretcher, beyond which are turned-over portions painted with a continuation of the design. [2] Oliver Millar, *The Tudor, Stuart and early Georgian pictures in the collection of Her Majesty the Queen* (1963), p. 81, no. 105, rep. pl. 42. [3] Thomas Stonor married Elizabeth Nevill, daughter of Catherine Vaux, Lady Abergavenny. [4] Indicated by the scale of the figure in relation to the present size of the canvas, and by its truncated appearance; see also n. [1].

2484 ELIZABETH, COUNTESS OF KENT

Canvas, $49\frac{1}{4} \times 40\frac{1}{4}$ in ($125{\cdot}1 \times 102{\cdot}2$ cm).[1] Three-quarter-length standing, to right, looking front, the left hand placed on a red-covered table right, a fan held in the right hand at her side. She wears a black dress with a deep décolletage edged with lace, round which runs a black necklace; from a double thread round her neck hangs an oval jewelled pendant; on a black band round her right wrist is secured a ring. Deep white cuffs, edged with lace; a three-layered white hanging ruff edged with lace;

black feathers in her light-coloured hair at the back of the head; pearl ear-drops. Behind the figure a fringed, draped red curtain.

Given by Claude Dickason Rotch, 1942. Coll. Penruddocke family, of Compton Chamberlayne, Wiltshire; Captain G. W. Penruddocke sale, Robinson, Fisher & Harding, Willis's Rooms, London, 13 November 1930 (5),[2] bt Major Craig; coll. Major Sir Algernon Tudor-Craig, K.B.E.; anon. sale, Christie's, 28 February 1936 (121), bt Deane.

In the Penruddocke sale of 1930, and subsequently, as a portrait of Dame Joan Penruddocke, wife of Sir John Penruddocke (d. 1648), by Marcus Gheeraerts. But it is, in fact, a slightly larger version on canvas of the portrait on wood (45 × 32½ in, 114·3 × 82·6 cm) of Elizabeth, Countess of Kent (1581–1651), daughter of the 7th Earl of Shrewsbury, in the Tate Gallery, London (no. T 398), documented as by van Somer.[3] The latter must be regarded as the prime original from the fact of its inclusion in the royal collection at the time of Charles I,[4] but the Fitzwilliam Museum repetition is also acceptable as from the hand of van Somer. The portrait may be dated from costume *c.* 1615–20. The oval pendant is probably a piece of jewellery much favoured at this period, a locket containing a portrait miniature, which in this case could well have been a portrait of Anne of Denmark, consort of James I. The jewels on the pendant compose a monogram of the letters AR, resembling in form these letters, standing for Anna Regina, in a more elaborate monogram which includes Queen Anne's personal ciphers, upon a locket in the Fitzwilliam Museum enclosing a miniature of the Queen.[5] As the Countess of Kent was in attendance upon Queen Anne, it seems likely that the pendant may be another such locket, a gift to the Countess from the Queen. In the Tate Gallery painting, the stone in the ring fastened round the right wrist appears to bear a monogram of the letters ER, perhaps standing for the initials of the Countess of Kent before her husband, Lord (Grey de) Ruthyn, became Earl of Kent in 1623. No monogram is discernible on the ring in the present version.

NOTES. [1] Lined; dimensions of the painted surface. [2] 'Family portraits of the Penruddocke family...removed from Compton Park, Salisbury'. [3] See *The Tate Gallery Report, 1960–61* (1961), pp. 30–2, for a fully raisonné catalogue entry. [4] *Loc. cit.*, n. 3. [5] Illustrated in Joan Evans, *A history of jewellery, 1100–1870* (1953), pl. 103a, b.

SPENCER, Gilbert

b. 1893. Living artist.

PD. 48–1956 DORSET DOWNS

Canvas, $16\frac{1}{8} \times 22$ in ($40{\cdot}9 \times 55{\cdot}8$ cm). A green meadow, with a cornfield to the left and rising ground to the right, slopes down to a fold in the downs. On the rising ground beyond are fields of green, yellow or brown. Scattered trees and hedges are of a darker green. A cloudy, cream-coloured sky.

Given by Mrs Florence Image (sister of the artist), 1956. (?) Exh. London, Goupil Gallery, 1923, 'Gilbert Spencer, English landscapes and figure pieces' (29).[1]

Stated by the donor to have been painted in 1919, upon Spencer's demobilisation from the army.[2]

NOTES. [1] The title of this picture in the exhibition was 'Dorset downs'; this was his first one-man exhibition. [2] Letter of 14 June 1956 (Fitzwilliam Museum).

SPENCER, Sir Stanley

1891–1959. Born at Cookham, Berkshire. Slade School of Art, London, 1908–12; saw service in Macedonia during the war of 1914–18; wall-paintings for the Sandham Memorial Chapel, Burghclere, 1926–32; R.A., 1950; C.B.E., 1950; kt, 1959. Lived mainly at Cookham. Painter of figure subjects, landscape and some portraits.

1481 SARAJEVO, BOSNIA (1922)

Canvas, 24×22 in ($60{\cdot}9 \times 55{\cdot}9$ cm). A straight stretch of river between stone-faced embankments runs into the depth of the composition, terminating with a bridge, where there are tall buildings at either side. Trees line the embankments, with two tall cypresses beyond the bridge. The distance is closed with steep, rounded hills. The water is in blues and mauves, the illuminated embankment at the right is pale greenish grey, the shadowed one at the left is mauve. The buildings at the left are pale buff and orange, those at the right are mauve-grey. The hills are in tones of reddish brown, with a narrow band of bright blue sky above.

Given by Mrs Frederick Leverton Harris, 1928.

In the summer of 1922, Spencer went to Yugoslavia with his friends the Carlines on a painting expedition. The party, which included his future wife Hilda Carline, returned to England in the autumn.[1] During this visit he is said to have painted ten landscapes,[2] of which this must be one. In its atmospheric use of colour and free handling of the paint, the picture is stylistically in marked contrast with Spencer's later work.

NOTES. [1] Maurice Collis, *Stanley Spencer* (1962), pp. 74–5. [2] Collis, *op. cit.*, p. 74.

1553 COTTAGES AT BURGHCLERE PLATE 63

Canvas, 24½ × 63 in (62·2 × 160·0 cm).[1] The houses are russet-coloured, with white palings and gates. The foliage and herbage are in quiet tones of varying greens. The sky is cream with grey clouds.

Given by the Friends of the Fitzwilliam Museum, 1930. Exh. London, Goupil Gallery, 1930, 'Goupil Gallery Salon' (56), bt for the Friends of the Fitzwilliam Museum; Tate Gallery, and Birmingham, City Museum and Art Gallery, 1955, 'Stanley Spencer, a retrospective exhibition' (27); Cookham, Stanley Spencer Gallery, April–November 1969.

Burghclere is a small village in Hampshire, south of Newbury. Spencer moved there in May 1927, to begin work on the paintings commissioned by J. L. Behrend for the Sandham Memorial Chapel,[2] thus giving a date for the present painting between 1927 and 1930.[3]

REPRODUCED. Friends of the Fitzwilliam Museum, *Annual Report* for 1930; *Fine Art, special Spring number of The Studio* (1931), p. 92; Frank Rutter, *Modern masterpieces* (1935), part I, p. 11 (colour); Mary Chamot, *Modern painting in England* (1937), p. 76, pl. VII (colour).

NOTES. [1] Dimensions of the painted surface; the stretcher is slightly larger. [2] Maurice Collis, *Stanley Spencer* (1962), p. 90. [3] The catalogue of the Tate Gallery exhibition in 1955, p. 18, no. 27, gives as the date '*c.* 1930'.

2452 LANDSCAPE IN NORTH WALES (1938) PLATE 63

Canvas, 22 × 27⅞ in (55·9 × 70·8 cm). The slate of the fence and the tree-trunk at the right are grey; foliage and herbage are in muted tones of varying greens; the patch of cultivated ground is pinkish brown. The hut is in stripes of light and dark bright pink, which is repeated in the spray of blossom at the left. The rocks of the distant hills are mainly mauve, the fields on them in patches of varying greens; some of the distant fields in the valley are mauve or brown. Grey and cream sky.

Bequeathed by Edward Maurice Berkeley Ingram, C.M.G., O.B.E., 1941.[1] Exh. London, National Gallery, 1940, 'British painting since

Whistler' (131); Redfern Gallery, 1941 'Collection of paintings formed by the late Maurice Ingram' (40).

This belongs to Spencer's visit to North Wales in 1938,[2] when he was in the Snowdon district during part of September and October.[3]

NOTES. [1] On the back is the label of Arthur Tooth & Sons Ltd, London, who became Spencer's agents in 1932. [2] Maurice Collis, *Stanley Spencer* (1962), p. 245. [3] Collis, *op. cit.*, p. 148.

2506 SELF-PORTRAIT (1939)

Canvas, $15\frac{5}{8} \times 21\frac{3}{4}$ in ($39{\cdot}7 \times 55{\cdot}2$ cm). Head and shoulders, turned half right, holding up a paint-brush at the right in his left hand; in front of the figure is part of a brown rectangular palette with patches of paint on it, held in his right hand. Dark brown hair covering the forehead, clean-shaven; large, round spectacles. He wears a brown jacket, with a white shirt and blue tie. Flesh tints are predominantly in green-greys, with pinks and mauves. Behind the figure, at both sides of the head, are folds of cloth, light blue-grey, with an even expanse of light buff above.

Given by the Friends of the Fitzwilliam Museum, 1942. Exh. London, Leicester Galleries, 1942, 'Stanley Spencer' (16), bt for the Friends of the Fitzwilliam Museum; Cookham, Stanley Spencer Gallery, April–October 1965.

In the catalogue of the Leicester Galleries exhibition of 1942, the portrait is dated 1939, no doubt correctly as the exhibition was 'arranged in conjunction with Arthur Tooth & Sons Ltd',[1] who had been Spencer's agents since 1932. As he is shown painting with his left hand, and was not left-handed,[2] the portrait is seen to be a single-mirror image in reverse.

REPRODUCED. Frontispiece to the catalogue of the exhibition at the Leicester Galleries, London, 1942, 'Stanley Spencer'.

NOTES. [1] Title-page of the Leicester Galleries exhibition, 1942, 'Stanley Spencer'. [2] Letter from his brother Gilbert Spencer, June 1971 (Fitzwilliam Museum).

PD. 966–1963 SELF-PORTRAIT WITH PATRICIA PREECE

Canvas, 24×36 in ($61{\cdot}0 \times 91{\cdot}2$ cm). She lies on her right side naked on a bed, facing the spectator, her head at the left, the knees drawn up; his head and naked shoulders, seen from the back, are in front of her, the head turned to the left; he has black hair and wears spectacles, she has fair hair.

In the background is the angle of a room, with a wallpaper of pink and yellow flowers on a buff ground, the head of a bedstead to the left. The flesh-tones of the woman are mauvish pink and yellowish; his are greenish with pinker passages, he has a warm complexion.

Bequeathed by Wilfrid Ariel Evill, 1963.[1] Exh. Cambridge, Fitzwilliam Museum, 1949–50, lent W. A. Evill; Brighton, Art Gallery, 1965, 'The Wilfrid Evill collection' (206).

Patricia Preece became Spencer's second wife in May 1937, a few days after his divorce from Hilda Carline.[2] They had been lovers for two years,[3] and at least as early as 1936 he had been painting intimate nudes of her.[4] This picture has been dated to 1937,[5] and if so it is likely to have been painted before the wedding on 29 May, as the marriage was ruined within a few days by Spencer's adultery with Hilda[6] to gratify his fantasy of having now two wives.[7] The picture appears to illustrate Spencer's practice of painting nudes at very close range, because, as he explained, he liked to feel he was crawling over the forms like an ant.[8]

REPRODUCED. Elizabeth Rothenstein, *Stanley Spencer* (1945), p. 11 (detail of Spencer's head); *Burlington Magazine* (1965), CVII, 595; Louise Collis, *A private view of Stanley Spencer* (1972), p. 40.

NOTES. [1] W. A. Evill was Spencer's solicitor, and possessed a number of his figure-paintings; see Maurice Collis, *Stanley Spencer* (1962), p. 118. Cf. also, nos. PD. 967–1963 and PD. 968–1963, below and p. 242. [2] Collis, *op. cit.*, p. 129. [3] Collis, *op. cit.*, p. 131. [4] Collis, *op. cit.*, p. 123, see also Louise Collis, *A private view of Stanley Spencer* (1972), pp. 62, 106. [5] M. Collis, *op. cit.*, p. 245. [6] M. Collis, *op. cit.*, pp. 131–3. [7] M. Collis, *op. cit.*, pp. 124ff. [8] M. Collis, *op. cit.*, p. 125.

PD. 967–1963 LOVE AMONG THE NATIONS

Canvas, $37\frac{5}{8} \times 110\frac{1}{4}$ in (95·6 × 280·0 cm). A crowd of people of varying colour and nationality, some clad, some not, engaged in embracing one another, stretches across the canvas. At the left is the stone wall of a building in perspective; in the right background is an open room full of people. The costumes and skin colours are in muted tones, in which browns, buffs and greys predominate, with a little red. Squared for transfer.

Bequeathed by Wilfrid Ariel Evill, 1963.[1] Coll. J. L. Behrend; exh. London, Arthur Tooth & Sons Ltd, 1936, 'Recent paintings by Stanley Spencer' (21); Leeds, Temple Newsam House, 1947, 'Paintings and drawings by Stanley Spencer' (30); sold to W. A. Evill, *c.* 1948;[2] exh. London,

Tate Gallery (Contemporary Art Society), 1952, 'Seventeen collectors' (229); Tate Gallery, 1955, 'Stanley Spencer' (34); Brighton, Art Gallery, 1965, 'The Wilfrid Evill collection' (205).

This picture and one entitled *The dustman* (or *Lovers*), herald a series of erotic paintings begun in 1937, in which Spencer sought to convey his belief in the mystical illumination to be gained from the act of sex. In all his figure-paintings he had aimed at presenting a kind of golden age, which was now to be more surely attainable.[3] This is the theme of the present painting, originally entitled *Humanity*,[4] in which love-making harmoniously unites different peoples and races. The seated man at the right is identified as Spencer and the standing woman further to the right as his first wife Hilda.[5] It was painted for J. L. Behrend, and has been dated both 1935[6] and 1935–6.[7] A 'complete study for the composition' was in 1955 in Spencer's possession,[8] presumably one of the drawings in pencil which were always the initial and principal stage in his figure-paintings.[9]

REPRODUCED. *Burlington Magazine* (1965), CVII, 595; Louise Collis, *A private view of Stanley Spencer* (1972), p. 89 (detail).

NOTES. [1] See n. [1] to no. PD. 966–1963, p. 240 above. [2] Catalogue of the exhibition 'Stanley Spencer', Tate Gallery, 1955, p. 20, no. 34. [3] Maurice Collis, *Stanley Spencer* (1962), pp. 137–9. [4] In the exhibition at Tooth's in 1936. [5] Louise Collis, *A private view of Stanley Spencer* (1972), caption to plate p. 89. [6] *Loc. cit.*, n. 2. [7] M. Collis, *op. cit.*, p. 244. [8] *Loc. cit.*, n. 2. The catalogue entry states that *Love among the nations* developed out of Spencer's visit to Yugoslavia in 1922 (see no. 1481, p. 238 above), but the connection, if any, must be slight. [9] M. Collis, *op. cit.*, pp. 137, 227.

PD. 968–1963 LOVE ON THE MOOR

Canvas, $31\frac{1}{8} \times 122\frac{1}{8}$ in ($79{\cdot}1 \times 310{\cdot}2$ cm). On a wide, open space of grass, bounded at the back by a high, curving, red brick wall, with a house at the left and a stream at the right, is a large crowd of animated people standing in several groups. To left of the centre is a statue on a pedestal of of the naked Venus with a crouching man embracing her legs. Painted in muted tones of the local colouring.

Bequeathed by Wilfrid Ariel Evill, 1963.[1] Exh. Brighton, Art Gallery, 1965, 'The Wilfrid Evill collection' (204).

The theme of the painting is the apotheosis of Spencer's first wife, Hilda Carline, whom he married in 1925 and divorced in 1937, as the goddess of love.[2] He took up the subject again in a huge painting, never completed, which was to have formed part of a projected Apotheosis series devoted to the glorification of the three women to whom he owed his enlightenment as to the sacred and mystical nature of sexual love.[3] The other two were his second wife, Patricia Preece (see no. PD. 966–1963, p. 240 above), and a lady who remains anonymous.[4] But the closest bond was with Hilda, represented in the statue of Venus, with Spencer as the crouching man in the posture of adoring abasement which was psychologically characteristic of his erotic relationships.[5] The painting of the picture was spread over the years 1949–54.[6] Though Hilda had died in 1950, his feeling for her, which soon revived after their divorce, was such as to remain unaffected by this event.[7] In some of the two hundred or so figures, the erotic significance of the picture is self-evident; but it is also expressed in the preoccupation of many of them with articles of women's clothing, for which Spencer had a strong fetishism. The frequent introduction of figures both of Hilda and of his second wife,[8] indicates a pervasive, if enigmatic, autobiographical element, as might be expected. The 'moor' is Cookham Moor,[9] a common in the beloved Berkshire village where Spencer was born and spent the greater part of his life.

REPRODUCED. Maurice Collis, *Stanley Spencer* (1962), p. 176 (centre detail); *Burlington Magazine* (1965), CVII, 595; Louis Collis, *A private view of Stanley Spencer* (1972), p. 137 (detail to right).

NOTES. [1] See n. [1] to no. PD. 966–1963, p. 240 above. [2] Maurice Collis, *Stanley Spencer* (1962), pp. 213–14, and Louise Collis, *A private view of Stanley Spencer* (1972), pp. 107, 158–9. [3] M. Collis, *op. cit.*, pp. 220–4. [4] M. Collis, *op. cit.*, pp. 192–3. [5] M. Collis, *op. cit.*, pp. 144–5. [6] M. Collis, *op. cit.*, pp. 213, 247. [7] M. Collis, *op. cit.*, pp. 167, 213–14. [8] Information from Lady Spencer (Patricia Preece), kindly communicated by Miss Louise Collis (letter of 22 June 1971, Fitzwilliam Museum). [9] M. Collis, *op. cit.*, pp. 213–14.

STANFIELD, CLARKSON[1]

1793–1867. Born in Sunderland. Apprenticed as a boy to a heraldic painter in Edinburgh. At sea from 1808 to about 1818; began as a theatrical scene painter; travelled in Italy, Holland and France; R.A., 1835; worked in London. Best known as a marine painter.

501 COAST SCENE NEAR GENOA (1846)

Canvas, $28\frac{1}{8} \times 44\frac{1}{4}$ in ($71{\cdot}4 \times 112{\cdot}4$ cm). At the left, the blue, rough water of a bay recedes to the light brown cliffs of a rocky coast, with distant snow-clad heights above; on the beach rises a detached mass of rock crowned with buildings. At the right, precipitous rock cliffs descend to the sea, where a huge single rock stands at the water's edge; from behind it a track leads down to the foreground, where two men are pulling ashore a broken ship's mast; on the summit of the further cliffs stand the buildings of a domed church. Sunlit scene, with warm cream clouds in a blue sky, the grey mass of an advancing storm at the left. Signed and dated lower right, 'C Stanfield/1846', the 'C' and 'S' in a monogram.

Given by Mrs Richard Ellison, 1862.

REPRODUCED. Earp, p. 188.

NOTE. [1] Sometimes erroneously called William Clarkson Stanfield.

STANNARD, JOSEPH

1797–1830. Born in Norwich, where he was a pupil of Robert Ladbroke. In Holland, 1821–2; briefly in London, 1823–4; worked in Norwich. Landscape and marine painter.

PD. 69–1948 BOATS ON THE YARE NEAR BRAMERTON, NORFOLK (1828) PLATE 38

Wood, $18\frac{1}{8} \times 25\frac{1}{2}$ in ($46{\cdot}0 \times 64{\cdot}8$ cm). The large sail is tan-brown, with a grey one next to it; the sails of the smaller boat are cream and tan-brown; the hulls of both vessels are dark brown; the sail at the left is grey. In the background, the trees are of a subdued green and brown, which, in a lighter key, are the colours of the fields; the houses are cream-coloured. The water is pale blue and grey; the sky light blue with cream and grey clouds. Signed and dated lower left, 'J .Stannard 1828'.[1]

Bought from the Fairhaven Fund, 1948. Coll. Donald D. Day, Norwich; exh. Norwich, Castle Museum, 1927, 'Norwich school of painting' (103); Castle Museum, 1934, 'Paintings and drawings by members of the Stannard family' (73); bt from Mr Day by W. Boswell & Son, Norwich, who sold it to H. G. Wilton, East Carleton, Norfolk; exh. Norwich, St Ethelbert's House, 1939, 'Centenary of the house of Boswell' (Room 3, no. 16);[2] bt from Mr Wilton by W. Boswell & Son, who sold it to P. M. Turner, London, from whom it was bought; exh. London, Hazlitt, 1974 (54).

Cleaned 1974.

REPRODUCED. Norwich, Castle Museum, catalogue of the exhibition 'Paintings and drawings by members of the Stannard family', 1934; *Illustrated London News* (1949), CCXIV, 282; exhibition catalogue, Hazlitt, 1974, pl. 19.

NOTES. [1] Listed in Harold A. E. Day, *Life and work of Joseph Stannard* (n.d.), p. 36, no. 31. The last figure of the date is not very clear, but appears to be an '8'. [2] With the title *Whitlingham*, though previously exhibited as a scene at Bramerton, which from the topography appears undoubtedly to be correct.

STARK, JAMES

1794–1859. Born in Norwich. Pupil there of John Crome 1811–14, when he moved to London; influenced by William Collins; admitted R.A. schools, 1817; in Norwich, 1819–30, when he returned to London; Windsor, 1839–49; London again for the rest of his life. Landscape painter.

PD. 6–1954 NEAR NORWICH PLATE 38

Wood, $22\frac{1}{2} \times 30\frac{3}{8}$ in ($57{\cdot}2 \times 77{\cdot}2$ cm). The lighter trees at the left have pale brown foliage and pale brown and green stems; the rest of the trees are in tones of deep, subdued green, which is also the colour of the herbage in shadow at the right, where the water is blue and cream. The road and most of the background seen through the trees are light brown; the cattle are brown and white, and black and white. The line of the distant hill is light blue. Grey and cream clouds in a blue sky, which is suffused with a warm tone towards the sky-line.

Bought from the Fairhaven Fund, 1954. Coll Samuel Montagu, 1st Lord Swaythling (1832–1911); exh. London, 1908, 'Franco-British Exhibition' (44), lent Lord Swaythling; sold by his grandson, the 3rd Lord Swaythling, Christie's, 12 July 1946 (36), bt R. J. Burrell; exh. London, Leggatt Bros., 1949; bt from Mrs R. J. Burrell; exh. Norwich, Castle Museum, 1959, 'James Stark, centenary exhibition' (36).

Cleaned 1954. A characteristic type of subject occurring in Stark's work in numerous examples. This particular composition, recalling motives found in Hobbema's landscapes, is known in three other versions, two in the Castle Museum at Norwich, *The forest gate* (no. 10.4.99) and *Wood scene* (no. 60.939), and a third at one time with Leggatt Bros., London, each of the four displaying its own variations. They may be broadly dated to the period of Stark's residence in Norwich from 1819 to 1830.[1]

REPRODUCED. Sale catalogue, Christie's, 12 July 1946, lot 36.

NOTE. [1] W. F. Dickes, *The Norwich school of painting* (1905), p. 467, includes *The forest gate* at Norwich in a list of paintings given this general date (p. 461). Upon his return to Norwich in 1819, Stark was in poor health and for a time did no painting (Dickes, *op. cit.*, p. 452).

STEER, Philip Wilson

1860–1942. Born in Birkenhead. Student in Paris at the Académie Julian and the Ecole des Beaux-Arts, 1882–4; initially influenced by Whistler and the Impressionists; foundation member of the New English Art Club, 1886; O.M., 1931. Painted landscape, with some figure studies and portraits.

1008 SELF-PORTRAIT (1920)

Canvas, 29 × 23¼ in (73·7 × 59·0 cm). Half-length to front, the right forearm resting on a table on which lie a palette and paint-brushes, the fingers of the right hand held by the left. Bare-headed, light hair; light moustache. Wears grey jacket and waistcoat, blue and white striped shirt, with a stiff white collar and blue bow tie. Dark grey-blue background. Signed and dated lower left, 'Philip Wilson Steer 1920'.[1]

Given by the artist, 1920. Exh. London, New English Art Club, 1920, 'Sixty-second Exhibition' (48); Arts Council of Great Britain (travelling exhibition), 1962, 'British self-portraits from Sickert to the present day' (46).

Painted for presentation to the Fitzwilliam Museum (see p. 43, no. 923). A self-portrait at the age of eighteen belongs to W. R. Hornby Steer, together with a study for the self-portrait of 1906 in the Uffizi Gallery, Florence, a related sketch for which is in the possession of Mrs M. Braine.

REPRODUCED. James Laver, *Portraits in oil and vinegar* (1925), p. 77; Frank Rutter, *Modern masterpieces* (1936), p. 46.

NOTE. [1] Bruce Laughton, *Philip Wilson Steer* (1961), p. 153, no. 556.

1513 SUMMER EVENING (1912)

Canvas, 24⅛ × 36¼ in (61·3 × 92·1 cm). Across a stretch of bright blue water lies a small group of buildings on a low shore dominated by a long red structure with two tall chimneys, a dark jetty to the right. Several small ships with brownish sails lie at the end of the jetty, and some small boats dot the water. To left and right are distant stretches of low, flat, green landscape, and in the foreground is a sandy shore with three figures at the left. Above, a large expanse of sky is filled with broken, creamy clouds half veiling some patches of blue. Signed and dated lower right, 'P. W. Steer 1912'.[1]

Bequeathed by Henry Blackwall Harris, 1929. Exh. London, Goupil Gallery, 1912, 'Goupil Gallery Salon' (45); (?) Goupil Gallery, 1924,

'Recent and earlier works by P. Wilson Steer' (50);[2] Tate Gallery, 1929, 'Loan exhibition of works by P. Wilson Steer' (119), lent Henry B. Harris; Gloucester, City Museum, College of Art Centenary, 1959, 'Paintings, drawings and water-colours by P. Wilson Steer' (36).

When exhibited at the Tate Gallery in 1929, the picture bore the title *Porchester: summer evening*, but at the Goupil Gallery in 1912 it was called simply *Summer evening*. Though Steer's annual painting expedition in 1912 took him to Porchester (or Portchester),[3] a village in Hampshire on Portsmouth harbour, the buildings across the water cannot be those of Porchester itself, which possesses a prominently situated castle distinguished by a round tower, and the scene is presumably located in the vicinity. A slightly larger version of the subject, also dated 1912, from the same viewpoint but with changes of detail and a different sky, formerly in the E. J. Hesslein collection, belongs (1971) to Viscount Mackintosh;[4] this version also bore the unspecific title *With the tide*, but has been reproduced as *Near Porchester*.[5]

NOTES. [1] Bruce Laughton, *Philip Wilson Steer* (1971), p. 150, no. 474. [2] With the title *Summer evening*, as in the 1912 Goupil Gallery exhibition, but D. S. MacColl, *Life, work and setting of Philip Wilson Steer* (1945), p. 214, makes no reference to the exhibition of 1924. [3] MacColl, *op. cit.*, pp. 91–2, 186. [4] Laughton, *op. cit.*, p. 150, no. 471. [5] By D. S. MacColl, *Artwork* (1929), vol. 5, p. 26.

2415 SURF

Wood, 6¼ × 29⅛ in (15·9 × 74·0 cm). An expanse of grey, rolling sea extends across the picture, with waves breaking on the shore in a line of foam in the foreground. The distant horizon is broken towards the right by a small steamer, and at the left by the sails of three boats. Grey-blue sky. Rich, fluid impasto. Signed lower left, 'P. W. Steer'.[1]

Bequeathed by Frank Hindley Smith, 1939. Exh. London, Royal Society of British Artists, Winter Exhibition, 1887–8 (364);[2] Arts Council of Great Britain (London and elsewhere), 1960–1, 'P. Wilson Steer, 1860–1942' (7).

An early painting, associated with two other small sea paintings on wood, *Grey sea* (coll. A. D. Peters) and *The open sea* (coll. Conrad Ormond), both dated 1886. Stylistically there is reason to consider the present painting the earliest of the three, and there are arguments for a date of 1885.[3] A small sketch for the composition is in an early sketch-book in the Victoria and Albert Museum, no. E287 – 1942.

REPRODUCED. Robin Ironside, *Wilson Steer* (1943), p. 15; *Apollo* (1966), LXXXIII, 49; Bruce Laughton, *Philip Wilson Steer* (1971), pl. 9.

NOTES. [1] Bruce Laughton, *Philip Wilson Steer* (1971), p. 127, no. 16. [2] With the title *Surf*, which appears on a manuscript label at the back of the picture giving Steer's address as 6 Trafalgar Studios, Chelsea, where he was from 1885 to 1888, thus identifying the present picture as the one exhibited in 1887–8, see Laughton, *op. cit.*, p. 10, n. 15. [3] Laughton, *op. cit.*, pp. 10, 127, no. 16, with a date of '*c.* 1885'; in *Apollo* (1966), LXXXIII, 49, 'Some early panel sketches by Wilson Steer', he favours a date of 'about 1886'. D. S. MacColl, *Life, work and setting of Philip Wilson Steer* (1945), lists it on p. 190 under 1887; his statements that it was in anonymous sales at Christie's in 1910, bt Sampson, in 1918, bt Mrs Weldon, and in 1919, bt Bates, have not proved verifiable.

2416 THE THAMES FROM RICHMOND HILL (1893)

Wood, $8\frac{1}{4} \times 10\frac{3}{8}$ in (21·0 × 26·4 cm). Under a deep expanse of sky, filled with broken cream and grey clouds against blue, a bend of the river, with blue water, occupies the centre of the landscape. Along the outer edge of the bend, at the left, runs flat, open ground, mainly in ochres and greens, backed by a mass of dark trees, in greens and greys; across the river, a similar mass of trees fills the curve at the right. Isolated trees run across a flat, open foreground.[1]

Bequeathed by Frank Hindley Smith, 1939.[2] Exh. London, Hazlitt, 1974 (55).

This dates from 1893, when Steer spent the summer at Richmond, Surrey.[3] It is one of a group of small panel paintings of this period, all executed in a similar free, sketching technique, owing something to Whistler and quite distinct from Steer's contemporaneous essays in Impressionism. Distinct also from these paintings is the adoption of a traditional type of landscape design.

REPRODUCED. Exhibition catalogue, Hazlitt, 1974, pl. 39.

NOTES. [1] Bruce Laughton, *Philip Wilson Steer* (1971), pp. 30, 84, 134 (no. 136). [2] D. S. MacColl, *Life, work and setting of Philip Wilson Steer* (1945), p. 194, listed as *View from Richmond Hill*, with a reference to the Goupil Gallery, London, 1919, presumably a trade reference as the picture is not to be found in the exhibition catalogues of that year. [3] Laughton, *loc. cit.*, and MacColl, *op. cit.*, pp. 47, 86, listed p. 194, of this year.

2449 RICHMOND, YORKSHIRE (1905)

Canvas, $16 \times 21\frac{5}{8}$ in (40·6 × 54·9 cm). Towards the left in the middle distance, the castle stands on an eminence with the town of Richmond on lower ground towards the right, all in shadow in greys and grey-browns. An open sunlit foreground in tones of ochre with dark patches of grey-blue and grey-brown shadow, runs down towards the curve of the river, with blue and grey water, below the town; a ridge in shadow crowned with trees rises at the left from the open ground, mainly in green-greys and yellow-greys. Cloudy sky, mainly in tones of cream, with some grey clouds above the castle. Signed and dated lower right, 'P. W. Steer 1905'.[1]

Bequeathed by Edward Maurice Berkeley Ingram, C.M.G., O.B.E., 1941. Exh. Venice, 1936, Biennale XX, catalogue p. 367, no. 10; London, National Gallery, 1940, 'British painting since Whistler' (58), lent E. M. B. Ingram; Redfern Gallery, 1941, 'Exhibition of the collection of paintings formed by the late Maurice Ingram' (15); Gloucester, City Museum, College of Art Centenary, 1959, 'Paintings, drawings and water-colours by P. Wilson Steer' (24).

Steer's last visit to Richmond, Yorkshire, was in 1903.[2] Besides the pictures in oils which he painted on this visit, he made some careful topographical washed drawings, which later were used as a basis for oil-paintings.[3] It is from one of these drawings[4] that the present freely-handled painting of 1905 is taken.

NOTES. [1] Bruce Laughton, *Philip Wilson Steer* (1971), p. 143, no. 324. [2] D. S. MacColl, *Life, work and setting of Philip Wilson Steer* (1945), pp. 78, 186; Laughton, *op. cit.*, p. 126. [3] Laughton, *op. cit.*, p. 92. [4] J. R. Gabbitas sale, Sotheby's, 26 June 1940 (79), dated 1903.

2455 MONTREUIL FROM THE RAMPARTS (1907)

Canvas, $19\frac{3}{4} \times 24$ in ($50{\cdot}2 \times 60{\cdot}9$ cm). Framed between trees at left and right, is a view of part of a town with a large building rising among the houses at the right; the predominating colours are greyish pinks, ochrish greens, and cream, with some passages of orange. The trees, sketchily painted, are in pale tones of green. The sky is light, yellowish grey. Signed and dated lower left, 'P. W. Steer 1907'.[1]

Bequeathed by Edward Maurice Berkeley Ingram, C.M.G., O.B.E., 1941, received 1946. Coll. Montague Shearman, London; exh. London, Redfern Gallery, 1940, 'The Montague Shearman collection of French and English paintings' (1); exh. in Canada (British Council), 1941 or earlier to 1945.[2]

Montreuil (or Montreuil-sur-Mer, though over nine miles from the coast), still largely enclosed within its ancient ramparts planted with trees, is a small town in the Pas-de-Calais. Steer was first there in 1889, and his second visit in 1907 marks his last painting expedition abroad.[3] The same view of the town, but taken from rather further back, forms the subject of two other paintings by Steer respectively in the Tate Gallery, London (no. 6184) and in the Ashmolean Museum, Oxford (no. 421).

REPRODUCED. Redfern Gallery exhibition catalogue, 1940, *The Montague Shearman collection of French and English paintings*, p. 11; *Connoisseur* (1940), cv, p. 224.

NOTES. [1] Bruce Laughton, *Philip Wilson Steer* (1971), pp. 97–8, listed p. 146, no. 402. [2] Included as no. 8 in the catalogue of the 'Exhibition of the collection of paintings formed by the late Maurice Ingram' held at the Redfern Gallery, London, in 1941, although, as the catalogue states, away on exhibition. Listed in D. S. MacColl, *Life, work and setting of Philip Wilson Steer* (1945), p. 209, with a reference to the London firm of dealers, Barbizon House, which it has not proved possible to verify. [3] MacColl, *op. cit.*, pp. 85–7, 186; Laughton, *op. cit.*, pp. 125–6.

PD. 18–1951 WALBERSWICK, CHILDREN PADDLING (1894) PLATE 52

Canvas, $25\frac{1}{4} \times 36\frac{3}{8}$ in ($64{\cdot}2 \times 92{\cdot}4$ cm). The water is light, bright blue, the beach orange-yellow and blue-grey. The seated figure is in white, blue on the shadowed side; the bending girl wears blue-grey with a red skirt and cream-coloured hat; the girl behind her to the right is in blue-green with a cream-coloured hat; her companion is in pink, with a blue skirt and white knickers. The jetty and the boat alongside it are blue; the small boat at the right is green, blue and white, with a pink sail. Light blue and cream sky. Signed and dated lower left, 'Steer '94'.[1]

Given by Lady Daniel, in memory of her husband, Sir Augustus Moore Daniel (1866–1950), 1951. Exh. London, Goupil Gallery, 1894, 'A collection of paintings by P. Wilson Steer' (11); New English Art Club, 1925, 'Retrospective exhibition, 1886–1924' (125), lent A. M. Daniel; Tate Gallery, 1929, 'Loan exhibition of works by P. Wilson Steer' (12); French Gallery (Wallis & Son), 1931, 'An anthology of English painting' (52); Leicester Galleries, 1951, 'The collection of the late Sir Augustus Daniel' (93); London and elsewhere, Arts Council of Great Britain, 1960–1, 'P. Wilson Steer' (22); London, Arts Council of Great Britain, 1967, 'Decade 1890–1900' (42).

This belongs to an early phase of Steer's landscape painting, when his work began to take a new direction, first in evidence in 1888, under the influence of Impressionism.[2] The condition of the paint indicates a considerable process of re-working. Though Steer's date on the painting is 1894, as a Walberswick subject[3] its genesis must go back some years earlier, as he was last there in 1891.[4] The shingle beach on the left is reminiscent in its treatment and colour of two Walberswick paintings exhibited in December 1889, *Figures on the beach, Walberswick* (Tate Gallery, no. 5766) and *Knucklebones* (Ipswich Museums and Art Galleries).[5] As this area is free of re-working, save for a small passage in the distance, this seems undoubtedly to give an approximate date for the inception of the picture.[6] Elsewhere, areas of re-working occur sporadically throughout the painting. They include the figures of the three children and the expanse of sky, which bear comparison in their treatment with two paintings of 1890, the children in *The ermine sea*, dated 1890 (formerly coll. Sir Augustus M. Daniel), and the sky in *Poole harbour* (Leeds City Art Gallery), datable by Steer's visit in that year to nearby Swanage.[7] The curious blobs of paint in the water to indicate flashing reflections, recur in *A sunlit sea* (coll. Mrs Hugo Pitman), also assigned to about 1890.[8] Evidently some of the revision thus took place at an early stage, but it can only be concluded that the process was not completed until 1894, when Steer dated the picture as finished.[9]

REPRODUCED. *Studio* (1930), C, 255 (colour); Robin Ironside, *Wilson Steer* (1943), pl. 13; D. S. MacColl, *Life, work and setting of Philip Wilson Steer* (1945), p. 45, pl. 19(b); Arts Council of Great Britain, catalogues of the exhibitions, 'P. Wilson Steer', 1960, pl. III, and 'Decade 1890–1900', 1967, p. 14; Jeremy Maas, *Victorian painters* (1969), p. 251; Bruce Laughton, *Philip Wilson Steer* (1971), pl. 79 (colour).

NOTES. [1] Bruce Laughton, *Philip Wilson Steer* (1971), p. 131, no. 69. [2] Laughton, *op. cit.*, pp. 14, 17. [3] When originally exhibited in 1894, and subsequently, entitled simply *Children paddling*. D. S. MacColl, *Life, work and setting of Philip Wilson Steer* (1945), p. 195, lists the picture with this title, identifying the place as Swanage, which Steer only visited once, in 1890. Laughton, *op. cit.*, p. 27, n. 29, corrects this on the evidence of old photographs of Walberswick. [4] Laughton, *op. cit.*, pp. 27–8. [5] Laughton, *op. cit.*, pp. 27, 129 (no. 46), 130 (no. 54), which seems certainly to have been the picture exhibited in 1889, rather than no. 55, which is signed and dated 1891. [6] Laughton, *op. cit.*, p. 27, concludes that it was begun 'about 1889/90'. [7] Laughton, *op. cit.*, pp. 27, 130 (no. 65), 131 (no. 73). [8] Laughton, *op. cit.*, pp. 25, 27, 131 (no. 75). [9] Laughton, *op. cit.*, p. 125, describes this as 'post-dating...for exhibition'.

PD. 183–1975 CHILDREN PLAYING, LUDLOW WALKS (1899)

Canvas, 22⅝ × 36½ in (57·5 × 92·7 cm). On the brow of a hill in the foreground, which turns towards the distance at the right, in tones of yellow-brown, are three girls in white, one of them, towards the left, running with a white and brown dog. Below the hill an extensive landscape, full of trees, recedes to low, distant hills, in its nearer stretch the arches of a cream-coloured bridge in the centre, with red roofs to left and right of it among trees in varying shades of green; on the hill as it recedes at the right are trees in brighter greens, with deep shadows in greens and browns. The landscape, level towards the left and rising at the right, merges in the distance with the hazy cream-colour of the hills and the sky, which breaks above into blue with some clouds. Signed and dated lower right, 'P Wilson Steer 99'.[1]

Bequeathed by Mrs G. John Scaramanga, 1975. Exh. London, New English Art Club, 1899 (65); Glasgow, 1901, 'International exhibition' (373), lent by the artist; coll. Geoffrey Thomas Blackwell (1884–1943); with Arthur Tooth & Sons Ltd, 1934; coll. G. John Scaramanga; bequeathed to his widow, 1972.

The upper part of the sky re-worked. This is connected with Steer's first visits to Ludlow in 1898 and 1899; for stylistic reasons the picture is considered to have been almost certainly painted in the studio, based upon drawings made during these visits.[2] Two other versions of the composition, related to Steer's visit to Ludlow in 1906, which are similar to one another, display variations from the earlier painting.

REPRODUCED. Bruce Laughton, *Philip Wilson Steer* (1971), pl. 180.

NOTES. [1] Bruce Laughton, *Philip Wilson Steer* (1971), p. 139 (no. 232). [2] Laughton, *op. cit.*, pp. 88 and 95, n. 27, referring to drawings in Steer's sketch-book at the Victoria and Albert Museum, London, no. E289–1942 (Laughton, *op. cit.*, p. 124, no. 27).

PD. 184–1975 THE BLUE DRESS (1892) PLATE 53

Canvas, 35⅞ × 28 in (91·2 × 71·2 cm). The dress and bonnet are dark blue; her hair is auburn; the chair is dark brown. The walls, curtains and window-frame are each in a different shade of broken, green-tinted ochre; the shadow on the wall is broken brownish grey-green. Signed and dated upper left, 'P W Steer' 92.[1]

Bequeathed by Mrs G. John Scaramanga, 1975. Exh. London, New English Art Club, 1892 (60); coll. F. H. Hoare; exh. London, Goupil Gallery, 1894, 'Paintings by P. Wilson Steer' (3); with Lockett Thomson, Barbizon House, London, 1937; coll. G. John Scaramanga; exh. London (Tate Gallery) and elsewhere, Arts Council, 1960–1, 'P. Wilson Steer' (18); bequeathed by G. John Scaramanga to his widow, 1972.

The sitter was a well-known model named Rose Pettigrew, much employed by Steer.[2] Though dated 1892, the picture appears to have been started in 1891.[3] In place of the present title, it was first exhibited with the legend, 'Molle meum levibus cor est violabile telis / Et semper causa est cur ego semper amem' (My soft heart is always liable to injury by light weapons/And the perpetual reason is that I am always in love).

REPRODUCED. *Barbizon House Record, 1937*, no. 2; exhibition catalogue, *P. Wilson Steer*, Arts Council (1960), pl. 1; Bruce Laughton, *Philip Wilson Steer* (1971), frontispiece (detail), pl. 89.

NOTES. [1] Bruce Laughton, *Philip Wilson Steer* (1971), pp. 42–3, 132 (no. 98). [2] She was afterwards Mrs H. Waldo Warner, see Laughton, *op. cit.*, pp. 113ff. [3] D. S. MacColl, *Life, work and setting of Philip Wilson Steer* (1945), p. 192, where it is included under 1891 in the 'Catalogue of oil paintings' by Alfred Yockney, for which see also p. 6.

PD. 185–1975 HYDRANGEAS (1901)

Canvas, $33\frac{5}{8} \times 44\frac{1}{4}$ in (85·4 × 112·4 cm.) On a sofa which fills the width of the composition and reaches to the top of it, a woman with a spreading skirt is seated at the right turned towards the left, dangling a string of pearls from her outstretched right hand to play with a black cat on the sofa at the left. The cover of the sofa is pale green, with a red and sage-green decorative motif; the woman wears a light blue dress with a green and mauve pattern, and a white jacket edged with lace; she has light brown hair. A plant of white hydrangeas stands in the lower left corner, and at the top, at either side above the curved back of the sofa, are other white flowers with dark green foliage, with the glimpse of a wall at the left in tones of grey. Signed and dated lower left, 'P. Wilson Steer 1901'.[1]

Bequeathed by Mrs G. John Scaramanga, 1975. Exh. London, New English Art Club, 1901 (66); coll. Sir Cyril Kendall Butler, K.B.E.; exh. London, Tate Gallery, 1929, 'Loan exhibition of works by P. Wilson Steer' (9); with Lockett Thomson, Barbizon House, London, exh. 1937, 'Paintings by P. Wilson Steer, O.M.' (4); coll. G. John Scaramanga; exh. Paris,

New English Art Club, 1938 (103); London (Tate Gallery) and elsewhere, Arts Council, 1960–1, 'P. Wilson Steer' (44); bequeathed by G. John Scaramanga to his widow, 1972.

The model in this painting was probably Miss Ethel Warwick, as may be deduced from a portrait of her in the National Gallery of South Africa, Cape Town, also of 1901, in which she is apparently wearing the same lace-edged jacket. Related drawings are in the Victoria and Albert Museum, Steer sketch-books, nos. E279–1942 and E289–1942.[2]

REPRODUCED. Exhibition catalogue, *Paintings by P. Wilson Steer, O.M.*, Barbizon House, London (1937); *Connoisseur* (1937), XCIX, 293; *Barbizon House Record, 1937*, no. 8; Robin Ironside, *Wilson Steer* (1943), pl. 35; Bruce Laughton, *Philip Wilson Steer* (1971), pl. 133.

NOTES. [1] Bruce Laughton, *Philip Wilson Steer* (1971), pp. 75, 140 (no. 269). [2] Laughton, *op. cit.*, p. 140 (no. 269).

STEVENS, Alfred

1817–1875. Born at Blandford, Dorset. In Italy, 1833–42; studied at the Florentine Academy; visited Venice and Rome, where he was assistant to B. Thorwaldsen; teacher at the Government School of Design, London, 1845–7; worked as a sculptor and painter, designed many schemes of architectural decoration, and designed for manufactures in metal and ceramics.

2204 THE ASCENSION OF CHRIST

Wood, 36 × 16⅞ in (91·4 × 42·8 cm). At the base to the left is a group of four figures of Apostles, two of them looking upwards, and to the right is part of another figure in an otherwise blank area, all are more or less incomplete; above, on a bank of cloud crossing the picture, an angel with outstretched arms steps forward and down towards the Apostles; at the top to the right are two figures of angels, one, seen from behind, in flight, to left of them a fragment of the figure of Christ bordering a blank area to the left. The blank areas are of white gesso; the clothing of the figures is dull pink or white, with brown shadows.

Bequeathed by Charles Haslewood Shannon, R.A., 1937. Coll. Mrs Gamble;[1] exh. London, Tate Gallery, 1911–12, 'Loan collection of works by Alfred Stevens' (39); coll. Charles Ricketts, R.A., and C. H. Shannon, R.A.; on loan to the Fitzwilliam Museum, 1933–7.

Unfinished and somewhat defaced; in the group to the left at the base, one figure has been erased and drawn in in outline; the head of the incomplete figure at the right is erased; at the top the figure of Christ, of which a fragment remains to the left of the angels, has been erased; the outline drawing of the figures is visible in many places. A drawing in black chalk for this composition in the Victoria and Albert Museum (no. E.2499–1911), which only extends upwards to include the angel on the band of cloud, is incomplete in much the same respects as is the painting; the two figures of angels at the top are depicted in the lower right corner, but with no indication of the erased Christ figure. At the Royal Institute of British Architects are seven drawings for portions of the composition,[2] including a study for the figure of Christ; none are more than sketches, some very slight. They and the present painting are assigned to *c.* 1845–6.[3] The subject also occurs in a series of Bible illustrations begun about 1858; the most complete drawings for it are in the Fitzwilliam Museum (nos. 2223, 2224), showing certain similarities with the painting. When Stevens was in Italy he made a copy of Titian's *Assumption of the Virgin* in Sta Maria dei Frari in Venice, and, as has been suggested,[4] it seems likely that the present composition was inspired by that of the Frari picture. The ascension of Christ into heaven is mentioned in the gospel of St Mark, XVI. 19, in St Luke's gospel, XXIV. 51, and in the Acts of the Apostles, I. 9–11.

REPRODUCED. Susan Beattie, *Alfred Stevens, 1817–75*, exhibition catalogue, Victoria and Albert Museum (1975), p. 22, no. 11.

NOTES. [1] Probably the widow of James Gamble, a pupil of Stevens, who died in 1910; she contributed a number of other loans to the Stevens exhibition of 1911–12 at the Tate Gallery. [2] Susan Beattie, *Catalogue of the drawings collection of the Royal Institute of British Architects. Alfred Stevens* (1975), p. 18, no. 9, 1–7. [3] *Ibid.* [4] *Ibid.*

2228 LEONARD W. COLLMANN PLATE 44

Canvas, $18\frac{1}{8} \times 13\frac{7}{8}$ in (46·0 × 35·3 cm).[1] Brown hair; black clothes and tie. Dark brown background to left, grey-brown to right.

Bequeathed by Charles Haslewood Shannon, R.A., 1937. Coll. Mrs Gamble;[2] exh. London, Tate Gallery, 1911–12, 'Loan collection of works by Alfred Stevens' (23); coll. Charles Ricketts, R.A., and C. H. Shannon, R.A.; on loan to the Fitzwilliam Museum, 1933–7; exh. London, R.A., 1956–7, 'British portraits' (427).

Leonard Collmann, who was born about 1816 and died before 1891, was an architect and decorator, and a personal friend of Stevens, whom he assisted over some of the business matters concerning the monument to the Duke of Wellington in St Paul's Cathedral. The portrait is in the nature of a study, and could possibly have been preliminary to the larger, full-face portrait in the Fogg Art Museum, Harvard University, U.S.A., painted, together with a portrait of Collmann's wife, in 1854.[3]

REPRODUCED. Illustrations to the R.A. exhibition, 'British portraits', 1956–7, p. 55.

NOTES. [1] Lined; dimensions of the painted surface. [2] See no. 2204 above, n. [1]. [3] Hugh Stannus, *Alfred Stevens* (1891), para. 130; the portrait of Mrs Collmann is in the Tate Gallery, no. 1775.

STRANG, William

1859–1921. Born at Dumbarton. Student at the Slade School of Art, London, 1875, under Alphonse Legros, by whom he was strongly influenced; best known as a draughtsman and etcher; R.A., 1921.

981 SELF-PORTRAIT (1919)

Canvas, 25 × 19⅞ in (63·5 × 50·5 cm). Nearly half-length, turned half right, his right hand placed on his chest. Bare-headed, greying dark hair and moustache, pink complexion; gold-rimmed spectacles. Wears green-grey waistcoat over a white shirt; white-spotted blue knotted tie. Dark grey background. Signed and dated lower right, 'W. STRANG/1919'.

Given by the artist, 1919.

Many self-portraits of Strang are known, some in oils, some drawn or etched. Another oil-painting of 1919, larger than the present portrait, is in the Tate Gallery (no. 3629). See p. 43, no. 923.

STUART, Gilbert

1755–1828. Born in Rhode Island, U.S.A. Pupil in America of Cosmo Alexander; accompanied him upon his return to Scotland, 1772; in America, 1773/4–75, when he returned to England; assistant to Benjamin West, 1777–82; in Dublin, 1787–92/3, when he returned finally to America.

785 UNKNOWN MAN

Canvas, 23¾ × 19¾ in (60·3 × 50·3 cm).[1] Bust to left; bare-headed, dark brown hair; clean-shaven. Wears a purplish brown coat open over a waistcoat of the same colour. Grey-green background. Within a painted oval.

Given by Mrs George Frederic Watts, 1916. Coll. G. F. Watts, O.M., R.A., by 1893.[2]

Much damaged by flattening and abrasion of the paint. Despite its condition, which seriously limits a clear estimation of style and original quality, an attribution to Gilbert Stuart can be made with reasonable confidence.[3] From the costume, the portrait may be dated about 1775–80, and much similarity is to be found with portraits by Stuart of approximately this date. The head is strongly lit, and appears broadly modelled in his manner, with a richness of impasto similar to his handling; and characteristic of his general style of portraiture are the presentation and the proportion of the figure within the oval, a form of bust portrait to which Stuart was addicted. The portrait is of a young man, and a close comparison is afforded by Stuart's painting of his friend Dr Benjamin Waterhouse (b. 1754) of about 1776[4] (Redwood Library and Athenaeum, Newport, Rhode Island), soon after the painter's arrival in London.

NOTES. [1] Lined; dimensions of the painted surface. [2] From a label at the back of the picture. [3] Originally suggested by H. A. Buttery (1933) and Harry B. Wehle (1940); when given the portrait was attributed to Francis Cotes. [4] Lawrence Park, *Gilbert Stuart*, 4 vols. (1926), II, pp. 790–1, rep. IV, pl. 884.

Copy after Gilbert Stuart

1142 GEORGE WASHINGTON

Canvas, $28\frac{5}{8} \times 24$ in ($72{\cdot}7 \times 60{\cdot}9$ cm).[1] Nearly half-length, turned half left. Bare-headed, powdered hair curled at the sides; clean-shaven; high colour on the cheek-bones. Wears black coat and waistcoat, white neck-cloth and lace jabot. Behind the figure a dull, deep crimson curtain, revealing a glimpse of blue sky with grey clouds lower left.

Given by Mrs T. T. Greg, 1925.[2]

Restored 1936. George Washington (1732–1799), Commander-in-chief in the American War of Independence, first President of the United States. Gilbert Stuart painted Washington from the life three times, once in 1795 and twice in 1796.[3] It is to the last of these three portraits that the present copy goes back, a head on an uncompleted canvas belonging to the Boston Athenaeum Society, deposited since 1876 with the Boston Museum of Fine Arts.[4] It is upon this 'Athenaeum Head' that Stuart based the numerous portraits of Washington which he painted for the rest of his career, and the type has long been accepted as the standard Washington portrait.[5] Stuart's portraits of him have been liberally copied. The present example, manifestly an old copy, bears much resemblance to a Stuart original belonging (in 1931) to Herbert L. Pratt in New York, in which the head is of a modified form of the Athenaeum Head known as the 'Monro-Lenox' type, found principally in standing whole-length portraits.[6] It is probable that portraits with this type of head were painted before 1801.[7] The small area of sky beyond the curtain in the lower left corner in the Pratt portrait, repeated on a larger scale in this copy, provides a link with the whole-lengths, in which the figure is posed against a column with a draped curtain which has sky to the left of it.

REPRODUCED. *Principal pictures* (1929), p. 204.

NOTES. [1] Lined; dimensions of the painted surface. [2] An old label at the back reads, '11 by Stewart. General Washington by the same painter who painted the original. One of 6 brought to this country on speculation'. Not listed among copies after Gilbert Stuart in John Hill Morgan and Mantle Fielding, *The life portraits of Washington and their replicas*, Philadelphia (1931), pp. 339ff.; but among the portraits listed as attributed to Stuart, no. XXXVIII, pp. 328–9, with an inconclusive history, is similar in its description to the present copy and of the same sight dimensions. [3] *Ibid.*, p. 223. [4] *Ibid.*, pp. 223–4, 273, no. 34, rep. p. 272. [5] *Ibid.*, pp. 231–2, 229. [6] *Ibid.*, p. 284, no. 51, rep. p. 224; another portrait, not reproduced, which seems from the description to be very similar to no. 51, is no. 42, p. 279. [7] *Ibid.*, p. 245.

STUBBS, George

1724–1806. Born in Liverpool. Briefly pupil of Hamlet Winstanley, but essentially self-taught; worked in the north of England; in Rome, 1754; began to study the anatomy of the horse about 1758; to London about 1759; A.R.A., 1780; elected R.A., 1781, rescinded 1783. Painter of horses and other animals, portraits, scenes of country life, and subject pictures.

PD. 45–1971 ISABELLA SALTONSTALL AS UNA IN SPENSER'S 'FAERIE QUEENE' (1782) PLATE 16

Ceramic plaque, oval, $18\frac{7}{8} \times 25\frac{1}{8}$ in (47·9 × 63·8 cm).[1] She wears a white dress and veil; the donkey is white, the drapery covering it (Una's 'black stole') dark grey; tawny-coloured lion. The rocks to the right are warm grey, the ground in front of them brown. The prominent tree to the left has a stem in tones of yellowish grey, and foliage of a subdued grey-green, which is the colour of the herbage on the ground. In the glade beyond, the light passages are grey-green, used in a warmer tone in the darker parts. Signed and dated on the rocks to the right, 'Geo: Stubbs pinxit/1782'. Written on the back in brown ink, is the following inscription: 'Isabella Saltonstall Aged sixteen. / In the character of Una, Spenser's Faery Queen – / From her fayre eyes he took commandment / and ever by her looks conceived her intent.'[2]

Bought from the Paintings and Duplicates, the Perceval, and the Cunliffe Funds, 1971. Exh. R.A., 1782 (70); (?) coll. Miss Isabella Saltonstall (d. 1829);[3] Sir Walter Gilbey, Bart (1831–1914);[4] his executors' sale, Christie's, 11 June 1915 (409), bt S. Gilbey; Leslie T. Good (d. 1965); exh. London, Whitechapel Art Gallery, 1957, 'George Stubbs' (13); Harold Good (brother of L. T. Good), from whom bought; exh. London, Tate Gallery, 1974, 'Stubbs & Wedgwood' (25).

Cleaned 1971. Stubbs had begun experimenting with painting in enamels by 1769,[5] at first upon copper; but wishing to make larger paintings than this material permitted, he turned to the use of a ceramic ground for his purpose. The plaques he required were made by Josiah Wedgwood, who produced the first suitable examples between the end of 1778 and the end of 1779. Stubbs was using them until at least 1795, the year of the latest known dated plaque; he is said to have evolved a range of nineteen pigments which would withstand the necessary second firing of the plaque, but the details of his method are unknown.[6] The subject of the present picture is taken from Book I of Edmund Spenser's *Faerie Queene*, 'The Legende of the Knight of the Red Crosse or of Holinesse'. The knight errant is the champion of Una, personifying Truth,[7] who accompanies him mounted upon a 'lowly Asse more white than snow', her attire covered by 'a black stole...as one that inly mourned' (Canto I, verse 4). He is deceived into deserting her, and in the course of Una's search for him a lion is tamed through pity for her and becomes her guardian, as described in verses 1–10 of Canto III, concluding with the lines inscribed upon the back of the plaque, 'From her faire eyes he tooke commaundment,/And euer by her lookes conceiued her intent'. Isabella Saltonstall, daughter of Robert Saltonstall, was born about 1766 (i.e. aged 16 in 1782), and died unmarried in 1829 at Hatchford, near Cobham, in Surrey.[8] When signing his will in 1806, Stubbs added her name as co-executrix to that of Mary Spencer,[9] his lifelong companion, which appears to have led to her identification as the unnamed lady, mentioned twice in Joseph

Farington's diary for 1807, to whom Stubbs was in debt for a considerable amount of money at the time of his death.[10] She had a large collection of his works.[11]

REPRODUCED. Basil Taylor, *Stubbs* (1971), pl. 97; *Gazette des Beaux-Arts* (1972), LXXII, 'Chronique des arts, Supplément', p. 136, fig. 497; Fitzwilliam Museum, *Annual Report* for 1971, pl. VIII; exhibition catalogue, *Stubbs & Wedgwood*, Tate Gallery (1974), p. 83 (colour).

NOTES. [1] The ceramic material of the plaque is cane-coloured. [2] Written in a careful but not a formal hand, which does not appear to be that of Stubbs, cf. a letter of 1787 rep. in Walter Shaw Sparrow, *George Stubbs and Ben Marshall* (1929), p. 40. [3] A probable inference since she is the subject and possessed many works by Stubbs (see n. [11]), and it does not appear among his paintings in the posthumous sale held by his executrix (Coxe, 26–7 May 1807); on the other hand it is not included in the list of her collection as given in *The Sporting Magazine* for November 1809 (reprinted in Sir Walter Gilbey, Bart, *Life of George Stubbs, R.A.* (1898), p. 230). [4] Presumably acquired after 1898, as Gilbey, *op. cit.*, pp. 144–67, does not enumerate it among his collection of works by Stubbs. [5] Basil Taylor, *Stubbs* (1971), p. 15. [6] Basil Taylor, 'Josiah Wedgwood and George Stubbs', *Proceedings of the Wedgwood Society* (1961), no. 4, pp. 210–12, 224. [7] *Spenser's poetical works*, ed. J. C. Smith and E. de Selincourt (1965 edn), p. xliv. [8] Information kindly supplied by Basil Taylor (letter of 17 January 1972, Fitzwilliam Museum). The little girl in Stubbs's portrait group of *The Saltonstall family* of 1769 (private collection; formerly coll. James A. E. de Rothschild) appears too old to be another portrait of Isabella. [9] Gilbey, *op. cit.*, pp. 232–4. [10] Basil Taylor, *Stubbs* (1971), pl. 97, p. 212; *The Farington diary* (1924), IV, pp. 143, 146 (3 June and 6 June 1807). [11] Gilbey, *op. cit.*, p. 230.

SUTHERLAND, GRAHAM

b. 1903. Living artist.

PD. 969–1963 THE DEPOSITION (1946) PLATE 64

Millboard, $59\frac{7}{8} \times 48$ in (152·0 × 121·9 cm). The flesh colour of Christ, the Virgin Mary and St John is greenish grey, of Mary Magdalen pink. She and the Virgin Mary wear blue robes, St John a brown robe. The blood which runs down from the feet of Christ is crimson. The upper part of the background is green-grey, the lower part bright green; the upper rectangle at the right is orange-red, the two triangles below it are orange-brown, as is the larger rectangle; the circular form is green-grey and black. The ground is orange-brown. Signed and dated lower right, 'Sutherland 23.11.46'.

Bequeathed by Wilfrid Ariel Evill, 1963. Exh. Cambridge, Fitzwilliam Museum, 1949–50, lent W. A. Evill; London, Tate Gallery, 1952, 'Seventeen collectors' (233); Venice, XXVI Biennale, British Pavilion, 1952; Paris, Musée National d'Art Moderne, 1952, 'Exposition Graham Sutherland' (16); Amsterdam, Stedelijk Museum, 1953, 'Sutherland' (16); Zürich, Kunsthaus, 1953, 'Graham Sutherland' (16); Brazil, São Paulo, Museum of Modern Art, 1955, 'Sutherland' (2); Brighton, Art Gallery, 1965, 'The Wilfrid Evill Collection' (251); Turin, Galleria Civica d'Arte Moderna, 1965, 'Sutherland' (50); Basel, Kunsthalle, 1966, 'Sutherland' (40); Arts Council, Whitechapel and elsewhere, 1972 'Decade 1940s' (113).

Sutherland's religious paintings originated with the commissioning of a *Crucifixion* for St Matthew's Church, Northampton, in 1944,[1] which was eventually painted in the course of 1946.[2] While working on it, other pictures of related New Testament subjects were painted, among them this *Deposition*, precisely dated 23 November 1946.[3] It belongs to a period of transition from 1944 to 1948 between Sutherland's earlier style and that of his maturity.[4] In considering Sutherland's religious paintings, account is to be taken of his Christian faith as a Roman Catholic, to which church he became a convert in 1926.

REPRODUCED. Paris, Musée National d'Art Moderne, catalogue of the 'Exposition Graham Sutherland', 1952, colour (no pagination); Douglas Cooper, *The work of Graham Sutherland* (1961), pl. 73; Fitzwilliam Museum, *Annual Report* for 1963, pl. XX; Turin, Galleria Civica d'Arte Moderna, catalogue of the 'Sutherland' exhibition, 1965, p. 131; *Burlington Magazine* (1965), CVII, 596.

NOTES. [1] Douglas Cooper, *The work of Graham Sutherland* (1961), pp. 29, 66; the subject initially proposed was an *Agony in the garden*. [2] Cooper, *op. cit.*, pp. 32, 34, 66. [3] Cooper, *op. cit.*, pp. 35, 75 (no. 73). [4] Cooper, *op. cit.*, pp. 38, 66.

TOVEY, Samuel Griffiths

1808–1873. Exh. Bristol Society of Artists, from 1832; established in Bristol by at least 1841; exh. R.A., B.I., and Society of Artists, Suffolk Street, 1847–8 (from a London address), 1850–65, from a Bristol address. Painted portraits, and architectural and topographical scenes both at home abroad.

3987 WILLIAM BEARD

Canvas, $51\frac{1}{4} \times 40\frac{7}{8}$ in ($130{\cdot}2 \times 103{\cdot}9$ cm). To below knees, seated in a high-backed, carved wooden chair, his left arm resting on a wooden table right, the hand placed upon some bones, his right hand resting on his knee holding the skeleton of a large paw. Bare-headed, grey hair, clean-shaven; wears a light-coloured overall over black clothes, with a white neck-cloth. Beside his arm on the table lie some long bones, and a paper inscribed 'Mr William Beard / Bone Cottage / Banwell', and 'Member of the Philosophical Societies of P.... and Colchester'. In the dark background a large, carved wooden cabinet stands behind the figure.

Bequeathed by Spencer George Perceval, 1922.

William Beard (1772–1868), of Banwell in Somerset, where he discovered a deposit of the bones of animals now extinct in this country. His collection, which was augmented by the addition of bones from neighbouring finds at Hutton, Bleadon and Sandford, is now in the Somerset County Museum at Taunton Castle. A portrait of him in lithography, which is based on this painting, occurs opposite p. 154 of John Rutter's *Delineations of the north-western division of the county of Somerset* (1829), where it is described as 'an excellent likeness'. Rutter mentions on p. 154 that Beard kept his collection of bones in 'a curious old carved oak cabinet', no doubt to be recognised in the cabinet in the painting.[1] The lithograph is lettered 'Aetatis LVII', giving a date for the painting of 1828–9, when Tovey was aged nineteen or twenty.[2]

NOTES. [1] The paw which Beard is holding is perhaps the 'claw of the bear... beautifully perfect' mentioned by Rutter (*op. cit.*, pp. 155–6) as successfully reconstructed by him. [2] The attribution to Tovey is derived from an inscription painted on the back of the canvas, 'S. G. Tovey / No 1'.

TOWNE, Francis

1739/40–1816. Birthplace unknown. Possibly pupil at Shipley's School, London; exh. from 1762; worked much at Exeter; in Rome, 1780–1. Landscape painter in oils and water-colours.

1616 HILLY LANDSCAPE (1780)

Canvas, $15\frac{1}{4} \times 20\frac{1}{8}$ in ($38{\cdot}7 \times 51{\cdot}1$ cm).[1] From an elevated foreground, with trees at the right, and at the left trees and boulders with a hillside beyond, the view extends over a flat valley to a distant range of rounded hills; crossing the centre is a road, on which a wagon, followed by a horseman, descends to the right. In the middle distance hills slope down from the right into the valley, where some houses are seen among trees. The ground is in tones of brown and grey-blue; the foliage of the trees at the right is of a subdued sallow green or dark brown-green, that of the trees at the left is tan brown. Pale blue sky with cream and light brown clouds. Signed and dated lower left, 'F. Towne / Pinx^{t} 1780'.

Given by Captain Stanley William Sykes, O.B.E., M.C., 1932. Exh. Exeter, Royal Albert Memorial Museum and Art Gallery, 1932, 'Works by early Devon painters' (10), lent S. W. Sykes.

When exhibited at Exeter in 1932, entitled *Landscape at Morrill*, perhaps from an inscription on the back of the original canvas, now concealed; but if so it must be a mis-reading, as 'Morrill' is not identifiable as a place name. Towne exhibited two paintings only in 1780, both entitled simply *View in Devonshire* (R.A., nos. 21 and 24), in which county, or elsewhere in the neighbourhood of Exeter, the scene could well be located, as his departure for Rome in 1780 did not take place until early September.[2] Alternatively the painting could be taken from one of the drawings made on his Welsh tour in 1777, as was his practice,[3] some of which, in the neighbourhood of Dolgelly, show a landscape of very similar character.[4]

NOTES. [1] Lined; dimensions of the painted surface. [2] A. P. Oppé, 'Francis Towne, landscape painter', *Walpole Society* (1920), VIII, 97, Adrian Bury, *Francis Towne* (1962), p. 73. [3] Oppé, *op. cit.*, pp. 105–6. [4] E.g., *Dolgelly*, rep. Bury, *op. cit.*, p. 71.

TUCKER, Rev. James Justus

1795/6–1842. Born at Hull. Bachelor of Arts, Cambridge, and ordained priest, 1821; chaplain on the Bengal Establishment, India; exh. Society of British Artists, Suffolk Street, 1835–41. Painted subject pictures and portraits.

3988 THE ANGEL PROCLAIMING THE END OF TIME

Canvas, $34\frac{1}{8} \times 27\frac{1}{2}$ in ($86{\cdot}4 \times 69{\cdot}9$ cm). The winged angel, turned towards the front, strides across the foreground, pointing upwards with his right arm and holding a small scroll in his left hand; he is draped in a pink robe and has golden hair, his wings are green-grey; behind his head is a semi-circular glory of prismatic colours. In the foreground to the right are brown rocks, to the left clouds through which lightning strikes, and a torrent of green water. Behind the figure are green-grey cloud masses. Signed lower right, 'J. J. Tucker'.

Bequeathed by the Rev. James Justus Tucker, 1842. Exh. Society of British Artists, Suffolk Street, 1841 (448).

The subject is taken from the Book of Revelation of St John the Divine, x. 5, 6.[1] A label at the back of the picture identifies the subject, and a second one is inscribed, 'J. J. Tucker, B.A./Simla'.

NOTE. [1] Quoted in the exhibition catalogue of the Society of British Artists, 1841.

TURNER, Joseph Mallord William

1775–1851. Born in London. Pupil of Thomas Malton; entered the R.A. schools, 1789; exh. R.A. from 1790; worked in Dr Monro's 'academy'; influenced by Richard Wilson and Claude Lorrain; R.A., 1802; travelled extensively in the British Isles and abroad. Painted landscape and marine subjects in both oils and water-colours.

M.Add. 17 WELSH MOUNTAIN LANDSCAPE PLATE 31

Canvas, $25\frac{1}{4} \times 38\frac{7}{8}$ in ($64{\cdot}1 \times 98{\cdot}8$ cm).[1] The foreground in deep tones of green and reddish brown, with lighter brown passages; the lower portions of the mountain mass to the left in lighter grey-greens, browns and brownish creams, the higher part in similar colours to the foreground, lighter in tone. The further hills in light grey-greens and browns, paler towards the summit, the shadowed portion towards the left in darker and greyer greens. The clear part of the sky light grey-blue, the mists among the hills cream and grey, the cloud mass in tones of grey and cream.[2]

Bought from the Marlay Fund, 1925. (?) Coll. Sir John Swinburne, Bart (d. 1860);[3] coll. H. A. J. Munro, of Novar (*c.* 1797–1864), by 1857;[4] Munro sale, Christie's, 11 May 1867 (180), bt White; bt from White by Thos Agnew & Sons Ltd, 1869; sold to K. D. Hodgson, 1870; bt from him by Agnew's, 1893, and sold the same year to James Orrock;[5] exh. London, R.A., 1894, 'Old Masters and deceased masters of the British school' (10); Orrock sale, Christie's, 27 April 1895 (308), bt in; bt from him by Agnew's, 1901, and sold the same year to Humphrey Roberts; Roberts sale, Christie's, 21 May 1908 (102), bt Agnew's; sold to Messrs W. B. Paterson, London, 1908; bt through Paterson's from an anonymous owner.

Much damaged by rubbing and over-cleaning, and much repainted, especially in the clouds, there seems to be more than one system of craquelure. The picture formerly bore the title of *The Trossachs*, which appears to derive from the Munro sale of 1867, where it was entitled *Loch Katrine, or The Trossachs*. Previously, during Munro's lifetime, it seems to have been known simply as *Landscape*.[6] In William Frost's 1865 catalogue of the Munro collection,[7] the picture is mistakenly called *Loch Katrine*,[8] and this title was adopted, presumably from Frost,[9] in the 1867 sale catalogue, with the addition, for reasons unknown, of the alternative title of *The Trossachs*, by which the picture has since been known.[10] On Turner's first visit to Scotland in 1801, his route ran at a distance from the region of The Trossachs and Loch Katrine,[11] which he did not reach until his 1831 visit.[12] This is much too late a date for the present picture, which belongs with the paintings of a strongly romantic character which he produced over a few years from 1797, largely based upon the style of Richard Wilson.[13] Among his exhibited pictures, *Morning amongst the Coniston fells*, R.A. 1798 (Tate Gallery, no. 461), *Kilgarren Castle*, R.A. 1799 (National Trust, Wordsworth House, Cockermouth), and *Dolbadern Castle*, R.A. 1800 (R.A.), together with *Mountain scene* (Tate Gallery, no. 465), unexhibited but assigned to 1798–1800,[14] may be cited for purposes of comparison.[15] As in this picture, these subjects of wild scenery are romantically treated with a sombre, dark foreground against a pale-coloured distance, wreathed in mists, with rolling clouds above. The comparison is particularly close with the *Mountain scene*,[16] where the treatment, the handling of the paint, the colour, and even the foreground design, complete with a seated figure, are remarkably similar. In the sketch-books of Turner's 1798 North Wales tour there are many drawings and water-colours depicting mountain scenery of similar character to the hills in this painting. Some of the water-colours are also close to it pictorially, and a few of them could well be of the same district, if not actually of the same range from differing view-points. Such are nos. 95 and 99 in the 'Hereford Court' sketch-book, *Dinas Bran* and *Lake with mountains*, and no. 49a, *Mountain scene*, in the 'Academical' sketch-book.[17] None of the oil-paintings exhibited during Turner's lifetime can be identified with the present one,[18] but the available evidence points to its identification as a North Wales subject, painted about 1799–1800.[19]

REPRODUCED. Constable, pl. XXXI.

NOTES. [1] Lined; dimensions of the painted surface. [2] Sir Walter Armstrong, *Turner* (1902), p. 233. [3] William Frost, A.R.A., *A complete catalogue of the paintings, water-colour drawings, drawings and prints, in the collection of the late Hugh Andrew Johnstone Munro Esq., of Novar, at the time of his death deposited in his house No. 6 Hamilton Place, London; with some additional paintings at Novar* (1865), p.94, no. 705, as *Loch Katrine*, stating mistakenly that it was included in the Swinburne sale, which was held at Christie's on 15 June 1861. At this sale there were no Turners among the Swinburne pictures, but in a property sold anonymously, and unidentifiable, lot 96 was by Turner entitled *Loch Katrine*, bought in for 750 guineas, the sum quoted by Frost as the price fetched by the supposed Swinburne picture. But mistaken though he was, the possibility cannot be ignored that Frost may have had some independent reason to believe that the Munro picture came from the Swinburne collection. [4] *The Art Journal* (1857), p. 135. [5] A torn manuscript label at the back, with the remains of Orrock's signature, 'J.O....', states impossibly in view of its early date that the picture was painted for Munro. [6] Thus described in an account of the Munro collection at Hamilton Place, London, in *The Art Journal* (1857), p. 135; the other Turners are all given specific titles. [7] *Loc. cit.*, n. [3]. [8] See n. [3]. Frost was perhaps misled by a reference in the 1861 sale catalogue to *The Art Journal* for 1857 (see n. [6]), and from the inclusion of this reference it is possible that the anonymously sold property did in fact belong to Munro, who, on at least one other occasion (Christie's, 26 March 1860) sold pictures in this way. But if so the picture seems to have been wrongly identified, as *The Art Journal*'s description is of 'an early picture', and in the sale catalogue it is referred to as of Turner's 'middle period'. No *Loch Katrine* is enumerated in *The Art Journal.* [9] Together with his descriptive phrase 'in the style of Gaspar Poussin'. [10] An oil-painting with this title is mentioned by Ruskin, as in the possession of a London dealer named Grundy, in the 1851 edition of vol. I of *Modern painters* (*The works of John Ruskin*, ed. E. T. Cook and Alexander Wedderburn (1903), III, p. 245); but the reference occurs as a footnote to a paragraph in which he is discussing Turner's paintings of about 1810–12, much too late a date for the Munro picture. The guess might be hazarded that lot 96 in the 1861 sale (see n. [3]) was, or was thought to be, the Grundy picture and that the previous confusion (see n. [8]) was worse confounded by the addition to Frost's title for the Munro picture, itself derived from lot 96, of the Grundy title. The Trossachs is a mountain defile running at one end from Loch Katrine. [11] A. J. Finberg, *The life of J. M. W. Turner, R.A.* (2nd edn. 1961), pp. 73–4. [12] Finberg, *op. cit.*, p. 332. [13] A. J. Finberg, *Turner's sketches and drawings* (1910), pp. 32–4, 35–6, 37, 41. [14] National Gallery, Millbank, *Catalogue, Turner collection* (1920), p. 3. [15] To these oil-paintings may be added two water-colours in the British Museum, Department of Prints and Drawings, *A view in North Wales* and *Lake Llanberis with Dolbadern Castle*, both Turner Bequest, numbered respectively LX (a)–A and LXX–X; see Andrew Wilton, *Turner in the British Museum*, exhibition catalogue (1975), p. 35, nos. 19 and 20 (rep.), as *c.* 1799. [16] Rep. John Rothenstein and Martin Butlin, *Turner* (1964), pl. 8, as *Mountain scene, Wales.* [17] British Museum, Department of Prints and Drawings, Turner Bequest, nos. XXXVIII and XLIII; no. 95 in the 'Hereford Court' sketch-book is rep. Rothenstein and Butlin, *op. cit.*, pl. 3b, with the title *Welsh valley*. [18] John Gage, 'Turner and Stourhead', *The Art Quarterly* (1974), XXXVII, 86–7, n. 51, suggests that the Fitzwilliam Museum picture may be the *Ben Lomond mountains, Scotland*, exhibited by Turner at the R.A. in 1802, no. 862; but there is uncertainty as to whether this was an oil or a water-colour, though in any case presumably small; see C. F. Bell, *A list of the works contributed to public exhibitions by J. M. W. Turner, R.A.* (1901), p. 44, no. 63, and A. J. Finberg, *The life of J. M. W. Turner, R.A.* (2nd edn, 1961), pp. 80, 465 (n. 81). [19] Thanks are due to Mr Evelyn Joll for items of information contributed to this catalogue entry.

VAUGHAN, Keith

b. 1912. Living artist.

PD. 15–1960 STANDING FIGURE (1960)

Canvas, 30 × 25 in (76·2 × 63·5 cm). Naked male figure, almost to the ankles, turned front, resting on the left leg. The torso, without arms, is light brown, with a dark brown, rectangular central dot, and a medium brown rectangle upper left; above is a dark green rectangle tilted to the left. The right leg is brown, terminating in passages of white, yellow and light blue; the left leg is brown at the top, changing to light blue above the knee, below it is dark blue bordered with brown. The background is in dark blues. Signed and dated in black paint on the back of the canvas, 'Keith Vaughan 1960'.

Bought from the D. M. McQuaid Fund, 1960. With the Matthiesen Gallery, London, from whom it was bought; exh. London, Whitechapel Art Gallery, 1962, 'Keith Vaughan retrospective exhibition' (258).

Abstract treatment in a flat, linear pattern.

VINCENT, George

1796–(?)1831. Born in Norwich. Pupil there of John Crome; to London, 1816; worked in the School of Painting of the B.I., 1817–18; made a tour in the north, 1819; last exhibited, 1831. Landscape painter.

PD. 50–1949 VIEW IN THE HIGHLANDS (1827)

Canvas, 40 × 50¾ in (101·6 × 127·9 cm).[1] Below a mountain peak in the centre, in tones of grey, steep broken ground in greens and browns descends abruptly to a lake; from it low cliffs rise in the foreground at either side, that at the right rocky and in shadow, deep brown in colour, that at the left covered with trees, with foliage in tones of golden brown. Light blue sky with cream and grey clouds. Signed and dated on the stern of a rowing boat in the centre foreground, 'GV [in a monogram] 1827'.

Bought from the Fairhaven Fund, 1949. Acquired in 1949 by Leggatt Bros., London, from whom it was bought.[2]

Vincent visited Scotland in 1819;[3] he exhibited his first painting of a Scottish subject in 1820, and others followed at intervals until 1830,[4] but there appears to be no record of a repetition of the visit.[5] The present painting may therefore be based upon sketches or drawings of 1819, but so far none have come to light.

NOTES. [1] Lined; dimensions of the painted surface. [2] A picture exhibited in London at the B.I., 1830, no. 349, has this title, but is unlikely to be the present painting as the outside dimensions of the frame as given in the catalogue, 42 × 50 in (106·7 × 127·0 cm), are for a smaller picture. [3] W. F. Dickes, *The Norwich school of painting* (1905), p. 498, H. A. E. Day, *East Anglian painters* (1968), II, p. 106. [4] Dickes, *op. cit.*, pp. 509–10. [5] Day, *op. cit.*, speculates that visits after 1819 may be deduced from the later dates on certain paintings of Scottish subjects.

PD. 4–1954 LOCH ETIVE, ARGYLLSHIRE (1821)

Canvas, 21¼ × 30 in (54·0 × 72·2 cm).[1] In the foreground a stream is bounded at the left by a rocky cliff, from which issues a small waterfall, and at the right by lower, sloping ground partly covered by trees; in the centre the view opens to the loch, with hills rising in the distance; a brown and white cow stands in the stream, with an angler beyond. Signed and dated on a rock lower right, 'GV [in a monogram] 1821'.

Bought from the Fairhaven Fund, 1954. Coll. Sir Jabez Edward Johnson-Ferguson, Bart (1849–1929); his executors' sale, Christie's, 30 May 1930 (72),[2] bt Storey; bt from Leggatt Bros., London.

See no. PD. 50–1949 above. It may be presumed that this also is based on sketches or drawings of 1819, but none are so far known.

NOTES. [1] Lined; dimensions of the painted surface. [2] In Christie's catalogue the date is incorrectly read as 1824.

WALKER, DAME ETHEL

1861–1951. Born in Edinburgh. Westminster School of Art, London, 1892; Slade School of Art, London, 1892–4, and again 1912–13, 1916–19, 1921–2. Member of the New English Art Club, 1900; influenced by Puvis de Chavannes, the Impressionists and Gauguin. Lived and worked mainly in London and at Robin Hood's Bay, Yorkshire; A.R.A., 1940; D.B.E., 1943. Painted portraits, seascapes, flower-pieces and decorative compositions.

2317 GIRL'S HEAD

Canvas, 13⅞ × 11 in (35·2 × 27·9 cm). Head and shoulders, turned slightly to the right, facing front. Bare-headed, red hair falling in plaits; blue jacket over a white blouse; chalky flesh-tones. Background mainly in tones of white, light blue, grey and yellow; a white, patterned curtain to the left. Signed lower left, 'Ethel Walker'.

Bequeathed by Miss Edith Bateson, 1938.

This picture, directly painted in clear tones of pure colour, and somewhat flat in design, is of the later phase of Ethel Walker's work, in the style she developed under the influence of the Impressionists during the first decade of the 1900s.[1] It appears to belong in date to the late 1920s or early 1930s. The portrait of a child, *Christopher Robin* (Sotheby's, 9 July 1969, lot 19), signed and dated 1923, bears comparison in technique but seems less developed; close in style is a portrait of *Jean Werner Laurie* (Tate Gallery, no. 4669) probably of 1927–8, and also similar is a portrait of *Flora, daughter of J. Havard Thomas*, bought by the City Art Gallery, Manchester, in 1933, which has been dated on grounds of costume to the second half of the 1920s.[2] Later, to judge from the portrait of *Vanessa* of 1937 (Tate Gallery, no. 5038), the dense, solid paint gives way to a lighter impasto and to more muted colour. Together with paintings of the sea, portraits of girls were the favourite subjects of Ethel Walker's later work, known in many examples.[3]

NOTES. [1] John Rothenstein, *Modern English painters* (1962), I, p. 93. [2] Letter of 10 December 1971 (Fitzwilliam Museum) from the Manchester City Art Gallery. [3] Rothenstein, *loc. cit.*

WALTON, Edward Arthur

1860–1922. Born at Glanderston, Renfrewshire. Studied mainly at the Glasgow School of Art and the Düsseldorf Academy; influenced by Velasquez and Whistler; R.S.A., 1905; died in Edinburgh. Painter of landscape and portraits.

1119 SELF-PORTRAIT

Canvas, 26⅜ × 20¼ in (67·0 × 51·5 cm). Half-length, turned almost in profile right, head half right, a palette held in the left hand, a brush in the right, with which he is painting on a pale, blank canvas. Bare-headed, dark hair, clean-shaven; wears a grey jacket. Background scumbled over in dark grey, some passages of dark green to left. Signed lower right, 'E. A. Walton'.[1]

Given by Mrs Edward Arthur Walton, in accordance with the wishes of her husband, 1923.

The portrait, which, except for the head, is somewhat sketchy in treatment, was painted for presentation to the Fitzwilliam Museum (see p. 43, no. 923). The signature was added after the artist's death on the instructions of his executors, the small 'o' under the W of Walton being placed there to distinguish it from a true signature.[2]

NOTES. [1] Under the 'W' of Walton is a small 'o'. [2] Information from the son of the artist, December 1958 (Fitzwilliam Museum records).

WALTON, Elijah

1832–1880. Born near Birmingham. Entered the R.A. schools at the age of eighteen; exh. R.A. from 1851; from 1860 travelled extensively in the British Isles, Norway, Switzerland, Greece, Egypt, Syria, etc. Landscape painter.

456* THE TOMBS OF THE SULTANS NEAR CAIRO (1865)

Canvas, 54 × 72⅛ in (137·2 × 183·2 cm). An open expanse of rocky ground in tones of grey and blue-grey extends from the foreground towards low, dark blue hills in the middle distance, a figure mounted on a camel crossing the foreground towards the right, a small cavalcade of others behind him; a single domed building rises from the foothills to right of centre, with groups of others with minarets extending to the left. Above is a sunset sky with clouds in tones of brilliant orange, yellow and red, with blue above. Signed and dated lower right, 'Elijah Walton 1865'.

Given by the artist, 1866. Exh. R.A., 1865 (346).

WARD, James

1769–1859. Born in London. Trained as an engraver under J. R. Smith and William Ward; began exhibiting oil-paintings, 1792; R.A., 1811. Painter of genre, animals, landscape and portraits.[1]

60 FIGHT BETWEEN A LION AND A TIGER (1797) PLATE 29

Canvas, 40 × 53⅝ in (101·6 × 136·2 cm). The animals are painted in their natural local colours; the rocks in tones of brown, with the sparse herbage in tones of brown-green. Indigo-blue sky with grey clouds. Signed and dated lower left, 'James Ward / Pinx^{t} 1797'.

Given by Mrs Richard Ellison, 1862. Exh. London, R.A., 1798 (209).

When Ward, originally trained as an engraver, began the practice of oil-painting about the late 1780s, his pictures were based in both subject and style upon the sentimental genre of his brother-in-law, George Morland. But as early as 1793, when he exhibited a *Tiger snarling over his prey* (R.A., no. 587), he displayed a vein of realism and dramatic intensity which was to play an important part in his subsequent development. A note to H. R. Cook's engraving of the present picture[2] comments, 'The Tiger is here supposed to have caught the small antelope deer, and at that moment he is sprung upon by the lion. In the encounter between them, the deer is struggling to escape'.

ENGRAVED. Mezzotint by James Ward, R.A., published 1799;[3] line-engraving by H. R. Cook, published 1807.

NOTES. [1] Thanks are due to Mr E. J. Nygren for his help in the cataloguing of this and the three following paintings by James Ward. [2] *The Sporting Magazine* (1807), XXIX, 215. [3] Julia Frankau, *William Ward, A.R.A., James Ward, R.A., their lives and works* (1904), p. 104, no. 51; the background is somewhat modified, and the antelope is omitted.

2261 TWO CHILD STUDIES

Paper,[1] 24¼ × 20¼ in (61·6 × 51·4 cm). The head and naked shoulders of a young child lying asleep in bed, facing towards the left, are seen at the right, a white pillow behind the head, a green and brown cover on the bed. Towards the left, a naked little boy, seen to the knees, is seated on the bed, turned to the front, looking downwards and to the right, both arms extended to the left. Both children have fair hair and very pink cheeks. The background is scumbled in brown, bronze green and grey.

Bequeathed by Charles Haslewood Shannon, R.A., 1937. (?) Exh. London, 6 Newman Street, 1822, 'Pictures painted by James Ward Esq., R.A.' (27);[2] coll. Charles de Sousy Ricketts, R.A. (1866–1931), and Charles Haslewood Shannon, R.A. (1863–1937); on loan to the Fitzwilliam Museum, 1933–7.

The two figures are evidently studies of the same child. Though less infantile than the standing little boy in Ward's R.A. diploma picture, *A bacchanalian*, dated 1811, there is a distinct resemblance between them, and the Fitzwilliam Museum picture is also comparable in technique, although sketchier in treatment. On this basis, the painting may be dated *c.* 1812. It is tempting to speculate that the model is Ward's son, Somerville Man, who died in 1821, aged eleven, or nearly.[3] Ward frequently painted on paper at about this period.[4]

NOTES. [1] Mounted on a canvas, which has been lined. [2] The catalogue entry for no. 27 runs 'Infantine Animation and Repose – Study from Nature'. [3] C. Reginald Grundy, *James Ward, R.A.* (1909), pp. xl, xliv, and Julia Frankau, *William Ward, A.R.A., James Ward, R.A., their lives and works* (1904), p. 68. [4] Information from Mr E. J. Nygren.

2577 PIGS

Canvas, 15 × 23¼ in (38·1 × 59·1 cm).[1] A cream-coloured sow lies with her head to the right across the left centre foreground, a litter of seven piglets in front of her; the straw on which she lies is light brown, ground to the right is dark brown. Behind her and to the left is an open timber structure, dark brown, with a half-grown pig standing to the right of it, silhouetted against an indigo-blue sky with a mass of cream-coloured clouds.

Given by Sir Frank Brangwyn, R.A., 1943.

Pigs recur periodically as a subject in Ward's work during the earlier years of his career as a painter. *Feeding pigs* was exhibited as early as 1793 (R.A., no. 145), and paintings entitled simply *Pigs*, were shown (R.A. or B.I.) in 1807, 1808, 1809 and finally in 1813. The motive of the present painting is found again in a painting in the Victoria and Albert Museum (no. 217), dated 1813, but without the litter of piglets, and in an undated drawing, complete with piglets, in the City Museum and Art Gallery, Birmingham (no. 1010'27).[2] A suckling sow is introduced into a painting of *The farm-yard*, dated 1810, in the collection of Mr and Mrs Paul Mellon, U.S.A. (no. 464), which is known also in a larger version, dated 1811, belonging to G. M. Daintry. The young pig in the background of the Fitzwilliam Museum picture, which is found also in the painting of 1813 and in the drawing at Birmingham, corresponds in form, with its rounded rump and angular snout, with a *Chinese sow* in the Victoria and Albert Museum (no. 218).

NOTES. [1] Lined; dimensions of the painted surface. [2] An undated soft-ground etching corresponding in reverse with this drawing by Ward is thought probably to be of about 1794 (information from Mr E. J. Nygren).

3939 SLEEPING LIONESS

Canvas, 22⅛ × 25⅞ in (56·2 × 65·7 cm).[1] Lying on rocky ground, the lioness is seen in a foreshortened view with her head towards the spectator. To the right of a rock rising behind her is a distant landscape. Golden brown monochrome, with some dark green for a little sparse foliage.

Source of acquisition unknown.

A very similar, but not identical, reclining lioness occurs in an oil sketch of *Daniel in the lions' den* at the Tate Gallery, no. 4985,[2] of which a finished study belonged in 1960 to Basil Taylor;[3] paintings with this title were exhibited by Ward in London at 6 Newman Street in 1841[4] and at the R.A. in 1852 (no. 303). An earlier version of no. 3939, which must have served as the study for the Fitzwilliam Museum picture, is in a private collection in England.[5]

NOTES. [1] Lined; dimensions of the painted surface. [2] A small pencil study for the composition is also at the Tate Gallery, no. 4986. [3] Catalogue of the Arts Council exhibition, 'James Ward', 1960, p. 33, no. 54. [4] *Description of Ward's gallery of paintings, models and engravings*, no. 108. [5] Information from Mr E. J. Nygren, who dates the Fitzwilliam Museum painting on grounds of style about 1840–50.

WATTS, George Frederic

1817–1904. Born in London. Pupil of the sculptor William Behnes, and enrolled, 1835, in the R.A. schools, but mainly self-taught. In Italy, 1843–7; much influenced by Venetian painting. A.R.A. and R.A., 1867; O.M., 1902. Painted principally portraits and allegorical subjects.

503 WILLIAM CAVENDISH, 7TH DUKE OF DEVONSHIRE (1883)

PLATE 44

Canvas, 50 × 40 in (127·0 × 101·6 cm). His hair is white, side-whiskers grey; warm complexion. Over black clothes he wears the black and gold gown of Chancellor of the University of Cambridge, with the blue ribbon of the Order of the Garter. Venetian red background. Signed and dated lower left, 'G F Watts / 1883'.

Given to the University by a body of subscribers, and accepted to be placed in the Fitzwilliam Museum, 1883.[1] Commissioned by the subscribers; exh. Fitzwilliam Museum, October 1883.

William Cavendish, 7th duke of Devonshire (1808–1891) became in 1861 Chancellor of the University of Cambridge, to which in 1870 he gave, with all its equipment, the Cavendish Laboratory of Experimental Physics, for which he is commemorated among the benefactors of the University. The subscribers to the portrait were members of the University,[2] for whom Watts painted from the same series of sittings a second portrait for presentation to the Duke, now at Chatsworth, which is closely similar though not a replica.[3] A copy by Cecil Schott, a pupil of Watts, 1892, is in the Oxford and Cambridge University Club, London; other copies are in the Cavendish Laboratory, Cambridge, and at Eastbourne College, founded by the Duke in 1867.

REPRODUCED. *Principal pictures* (1912 edn), p. 208, (1929 edn), p. 237.[4]

NOTES. [1] *Cambridge University Reporter* (1883–4), p. 312, Grace 1, 13 December 1883. [2] *Ibid.*, 1881–2, pp. 282–92. [3] Although the Duke wrote accepting the portrait in December 1883 (*Cambridge University Reporter* (1883–4), p. 294), it is signed and dated 'G. F. Watts 1885'. [4] In each case erroneously captioned 'Spencer Compton, 9th Duke of Devonshire'.

784 CHAOS

Canvas, $7\frac{5}{8} \times 29\frac{1}{4}$ in (19·3 × 74·3 cm).[1] At the left, among broken rocks, are a number of naked, agonised figures, behind them a conflagration against which rises a single figure with arms outstretched. The figures and rocks are brown, the conflagration orange-brown and grey. At the right reposes on rocky ground a group of gigantic reclining figures, golden brown in colour; below them a chain of lively small figures. In the centre foreground a single large naked figure rises from rolling blue water. In the background deep blue sky at the right lightens to yellow and white in the centre, distant crags below.

Given by the Friends of the Fitzwilliam Museum, 1916. Acquired from the Watts Collection[2] through the artist's widow, Mrs M. S. Watts.

As early as 1848, Watts had in mind a scheme for a cycle of wall-paintings on the epic subject of the history of mankind, a series which he was later to call 'The House of Life'. His description at this time of one of the first designs in the series corresponds with the right-hand portion of the composition of *Chaos*.[3] Paintings of this design, known as *The Titans*, are to be found in several examples. The largest of them, described as 'the first completed version'[4] and dated to 1873–5,[5] is in the Watts Gallery at Compton, Surrey; two others, of smaller size, belong to Mr Ronald Chapman, and another was in the Charles Handley-Read collection.[6] The Fitzwilliam Museum painting is the earliest sketch for the complete composition of *Chaos*.[7] On a large scale it is known in two versions, one in London, Tate Gallery no. 1647, assigned in date to 1882,[8] the other in the Watts Gallery at Compton, left unfinished by Watts in the same year.[9] Another small version ($12\frac{7}{8} \times 31\frac{1}{8}$ in, 32·7 × 79·1 cm) is at Liverpool, Walker Art Gallery no. 2097, sold by the artist in 1898.[10] These later versions only differ from the Fitzwilliam Museum sketch in minor respects. A number of drawings for the *Chaos* composition belong to Mr R. Brinsley Ford, and a discarded figure for it in fresco is at Leighton House, London. In 1896 Watts wrote of 'the long unfinished design *Chaos*', that 'The intention of this picture is to convey in the language of symbol an idea of the passing of our planet from chaos to order...from the earliest periods on the left of the picture to where the reposeful giants on the right are suggestive of a state of stability and order', the small figures below them 'representing the cycles of time'[11]. As a title for the composition Watts came to prefer *Cosmos*, or *Chaos passing into Cosmos*, to the original *Chaos*.[12]

REPRODUCED. Friends of the Fitzwilliam Museum, *Annual Report* for 1916.

NOTES. [1] Lined; dimensions of the painted surface. [2] Paintings by Watts retained in his own possession. [3] M. S. Watts, *George Frederic Watts*, 3 vols. (1912), I, pp. 101–5. [4] Watts, *op. cit.*, I, p. 301. [5] Manuscript catalogue of Watts's works, compiled by his widow, Mrs M. S. Watts, at the Watts Gallery, Compton, Surrey. [6] Given by Watts to Alexander Fisher in 1907, one of 'Some three or four sketches...made on canvas of part of' the version of *Chaos* which is now no. 2097, Walker Art Gallery, Liverpool (*see* n. [5]). [7] *See* n. [5], where it is stated that the painting 'stood unframed upon the dresser of Mr. Watts's studio until his death'. [8] *See* n. [5], though dated by the Tate Gallery *c.* 1849–75. [9] *See* n. [5]. [10] To James Smith (Walker Art Gallery archives). [11] New Gallery, London, exhibition catalogue, *The works of G. F. Watts, R.A.* (1896), pp. 5, and 64, no. 148. [12] *See* n. [5], and see also Watts, *op. cit.* n. [3], I, p. 102, n. 1.

1761 THREE HEADS

Canvas, $11\frac{1}{8} \times 21$ in ($28{\cdot}2 \times 53{\cdot}3$ cm). The head of a young woman in the centre, inclined towards the right and tilted back, the lips parted and the eyes looking up, with fair hair, is flanked at the left by a similar head facing in profile to the right. The head of a child, at the right, leans close to the head of the central figure, to which the eyes look up. Sketchy background suggestive of light clouds against a blue sky.

Bequeathed by the Rt Hon. Professor Sir (Thomas) Clifford Allbutt, K.C.B., M.D., F.R.S. (1836–1925), received 1935. (?) Watts Collection.[1]

A sketched group of indeterminate date, not so far recognised as a preliminary study for a larger painting. The two older heads appear to be of the same person.

NOTE. [1] Paintings by Watts retained in his own possession. The frame is of Watts's standard pattern, and has the label of his framer, E. J. Uppard, at the back stamped with the date 3 January 1906, suggesting that the picture was probably in the Watts Collection, and left it only after being framed in 1906. Sir Clifford Allbutt, a distinguished physician (see p. 187, no. 1143), was a close friend of Watts and his wife, and it is tempting to suppose that he may have acquired this picture after Watts's death in 1904 from the Watts Collection.

WEBBER, John

1750(?)–1793. Born in London. Studied in Berne and Paris; student at the R.A. schools, 1775; draughtsman with Captain Cook's last voyage, 1776–80; R.A., 1791. Mainly a landscape painter.

454 A NATIVE OF OTAHEITE

Canvas, $18\frac{1}{8} \times 14\frac{1}{4}$ in ($46{\cdot}3 \times 36{\cdot}2$ cm).[1] Head and shoulders to left. Bareheaded, bushy, black hair; clean-shaven; dark complexion. Wears a light-coloured garment round the shoulders. Brown background.

Bequeathed by Daniel Mesman, 1834.

From the liveliness of expression, and the directness of the manner of painting, the head gives the impression of being a study from life, a conclusion reinforced by the sketchy treatment of the garment round the shoulders. In the Mesman collection given to William Hodges, with this title,[2] but later catalogued as by John Weber.[3] It is by the same hand as the large three-quarter length portrait of a girl, Poedooa, at Greenwich (National Maritime Museum, on loan from the Admirality since 1936), given to Webber, of which another version, with his signature, was in an anonymous sale at Sotheby's on 12 December 1956, lot 57, identified with the painting exhibited at the R.A. in 1785, no. 392. In the R.A. catalogue, Poedooa is described as the daughter of the chief of one of the Society Islands in the South Pacific, which include Otaheite, or Tahiti, lending support to the correctness of the title of the Fitzwilliam Museum picture. Webber was in this area with Cook's expedition in 1777, which may thus be accepted as the date of the present study. Another version of the painting of Poedooa is in the National Library of Australia, Canberra.

NOTES. [1] Lined; dimensions of the painted surface. [2] Manuscript 'Catalogue of the Pictures and Drawings etc. Bequeathed to the University of Cambridge by the late Daniel Mesman Esqr.', Fitzwilliam Museum, evidently made when the collection was sent to Cambridge. [3] John Massey, *Catalogue of the paintings, drawings, etc., bequeathed to the University of Cambridge by the late Daniel Mesman in the year 1834* (1846), p. 5, no. 76. In Earp, p. 95, the picture is mistakenly catalogued as by the portrait painter C. H. Hodges (1764–1837).

WEST, Benjamin

1738–1820. Born in Pennsylvania, U.S.A. Self-taught; practised as a portrait painter in Philadelphia and New York; in Italy, 1760–3, when he settled in London; foundation member of the R.A., 1768; P.R.A., 1792; much patronised by George III. History and portrait painter.

655 THE CONTINENCE OF SCIPIO PLATE 21

Wood, $39\frac{1}{2} \times 52\frac{1}{2}$ in (100·3 × 133·3 cm). Scipio, seated at the left, with a deep red cloak, extends his left hand towards the captive girl, in a pale pink mantle over a white dress, kneeling in the centre, who holds the right hand of her betrothed standing beside her, wearing olive-green. Behind the girl kneels an old woman in a blue-green mantle covering her head; further right are three men, two of them partly naked, carrying metal vessels. Behind the group stand two Roman soldiers in shadow. In the background several buildings rise against a sky of light blue and cream, tinged in places with pink. The rest of the colouring is brown, relieved by a few touches of deep red and blue-green in the three figures of men at the right.

Given by Charles Fairfax Murray, 1908. Exh. Incorporated Society of Artists, 1766 (179);[1] coll. John Knight, of Portland Place, London; his sale, Phillips, 23–4 March 1819 (37), bt Sir T. Hesketh.[2]

West first exhibited at the Incorporated Society of Artists in 1764, the year after he came to London, and again in 1765, so there is reason to suppose that this picture may be dated to 1765–6. It has been pointed out, however, that there is evidence of extensive later repainting by West.[3] With its companion of *Pylades and Orestes* it is reputed to have enjoyed a great success at the 1766 exhibition.[4] A small sketch for a *Continence of Scipio* has been recorded.[5] The subject is taken from the Roman historian Valerius Maximus, who relates how Scipio Africanus, nobly refusing to exercise his rights as a conqueror, restored a captive girl to her family and her betrothed, and provided her with a dowry, a characteristically neo-classical choice of subject as a moral example from classical antiquity.

NOTES. [1] West exhibited two paintings of this subject, one at the Society of Artists in 1766, with a companion of *Pylades and Orestes*, the second at the

R.A. in 1771 (213), with a companion of *Hector taking leave of Andromache*. The Fitzwilliam Museum *Continence of Scipio* is the only one now extant, but it may be identified as that exhibited in 1766, as the *Pylades and Orestes*, now no. 126 in the Tate Gallery, London, is also a horizontal composition, and is of almost the same dimensions (40 × 50 in, 101·6 × 127·0 cm), while the *Hector taking leave of Andromache*, belonging to the New York Historical Society, is an upright composition measuring 42 × 48 in (106·7 × 121·9 cm). [2] See G. Redford, *Art sales*, 2 vols. (1888), II, p. 128; the name is inscribed twice at the back of the picture. Perhaps Sir Thomas Dalrymple Hesketh, Bart (1777–1842), of Rufford Hall, Lancashire. [3] By Professor Helmut von Erffa, who agrees with the identification, in 1955 (Fitzwilliam Museum records). [4] John Galt, *Life, studies and works of Benjamin West Esq.* (1820), part II, p. 16, though Horace Walpole commented on all four subject paintings in the exhibition, 'hard and gaudy and little expression' (William T. Whitley, *Artists and their friends in England, 1700–1799*, 2 vols. (1928), II, p. 373). [5] Galt, *op. cit.*, part II, p. 234.

656 CHRIST HEALING THE SICK IN THE TEMPLE

Canvas, $35\frac{5}{8} \times 27\frac{1}{2}$ in (90·5 × 69·8 cm).[1] Christ stands at the left facing towards a group of people at the right in which some men restrain a maniac youth, while in front kneel a man and woman, and a young woman with a baby at her back appeals for a sick person lying at Christ's feet; among other figures behind the group and to the left of it is a blind old man. Four men stand behind Christ, and in the centre background a group of men watch the scene from a stone balcony between massive classical columns, the folds of a hanging overhead. The head of Christ is silhouetted against a cloudy sky seen through an arch. Brown chiaroscuro monochrome.

Given by Charles Fairfax Murray, 1908. Coll. West family;[2] Benjamin West posthumous sale, London, Robins, 20–5 May 1829 (128),[3] bt Wood.

Cleaned 1960. About 1780 George III formed the project of building a chapel at Windsor Castle, to be decorated with thirty-five paintings by West illustrating the history of revealed religion.[4] Among the subjects selected was *Christ healing the sick in the Temple*,[5] for which the present picture is an early design.[6] The large completed picture was exhibited at the R.A. in 1781 (80), and in it the design has been fundamentally revised, with the introduction of a different group of figures before Christ and an elaborated architectural setting.[7] This design reappears in two similar versions of the subject, which are, however, horizontal in shape instead of vertical, one in London, Tate Gallery no. 131, exhibited at the B.I. in 1812, no. 214, the other, a repetition by West with variations, at the

Pennsylvania Hospital, Philadelphia, U.S.A.[8] In 1801 further work on the paintings for the chapel was suspended, and subsequently the project was abandoned.[9] The paintings were returned by George IV to West's family, and appeared in the posthumous sale of West's works held in 1829[10] in which *Christ healing* was lot 55, dimensions 150 × 120 in (383·6 × 304·8 cm). It was there bought by 'Mr. Hicks of Bolton', but its present whereabouts are unknown.[11] A different version of the subject, in a landscape setting, is in the City Art Museum, St. Louis, Mo., U.S.A.

ENGRAVED. By Benjamin Smith, published 1813.[12]

NOTES. [1] Lined; dimensions of the painted surface. [2] See n. [6]. [3] Identifiable from the dimensions, given as '3 feet high by 2 feet 4 inches wide'. [4] John Galt, *Life, studies and works of Benjamin West Esq.* (1820), part II, pp. 53–6. [5] Galt, *op. cit.*, p. 212, no. 27. [6] It is included in a list of 'Original Designs in Chiaro Scuro for the large Pictures which were painted for his late Majesty's Chapel in Windsor Castle', in a *Letter from the sons of Benjamin West Deceased... offering to sell to the Government of the United States sundry paintings of that artist* (1826), no. 147; by what must be a confusion, since it applies equally to designs for other pictures of vertical proportions, the dimensions are given as 3 ft wide by 2 ft 4 in high. [7] A drawing by West belonging to the Department of the Environment, London, for one wall of the chapel, includes the *Christ healing in the Temple*. [8] Galt, *op. cit.*, pp. 186–7. [9] Galt, *op. cit.*, ,pp. 192, 199. [10] William T. Whitley, *Art in England, 1821–1837* (1930), p. 168. [11] Algernon Graves, *Art sales*, 3 vols. (1918–21), III, p. 329, and an annotation in a copy of the catalogue of the 1829 sale at the New York Historical Society. [12] Charles Le Blanc, *Manuel de l'amateur d'estampes*, vol. 3 (1888), p. 531, no. 1.

WHEATLEY, Francis

1747–1801. Born in London. Student at W. Shipley's drawing school; first exh., Incorporated Society of Artists, 1765; admitted R.A. schools, 1769; influenced by John Hamilton Mortimer, and later by Greuze; in Ireland, 1779–83; R.A., 1791. Painted landscape, portraits, conversation pieces, fancy subjects, genre and history pictures.

PD. 6–1953 BENJAMIN BOND HOPKINS PLATE 25

Canvas, $39\frac{7}{8} \times 49\frac{5}{8}$ in (101·3 × 126·0 cm).[1] He wears a brown coat over a white waistcoat, buff breeches, and black boots with brown tops. The horse is brown, the spaniel brown and white. The foliage and herbage are in tones of dense green, with some brown foliage interspersed; the tree-trunks are grey-green, the ground yellow-brown. Sky of grey-green clouds, with patches of light blue.[2]

Given by Lt-Col. B. E. Coke, O.B.E., in memory of Mrs Sarah Hopkins and the Rev. C. G. O. Bond, 1953. Exh. R.A., 1791 (85);[3] Nottingham, Castle Museum and Art Gallery, 1914–17, lent B. E. Coke; Aldeburgh and Leeds, City Art Gallery, 1965, 'Francis Wheatley, R.A.' (18).

Benjamin Bond Hopkins (1747–1794), of a family of London merchants named Bond, to which he added his mother's name of Hopkins upon receiving an inheritance from her in 1787.[4] The picture is said to be set in the celebrated grounds of Pains Hill in Surrey,[5] laid out early in the reign of George II by the Hon. Charles Hamilton, from whom Bond Hopkins bought the property, and there built a new house about 1790.[6] If the location of the portrait is indeed Pains Hill, there would be a natural connection with the purchase, giving a date for the painting possibly rather before its exhibition in 1791.[7]

REPRODUCED. Mary Webster, *Francis Wheatley* (1970), p. 98, fig. 142.

NOTES. [1] Lined; dimensions of the painted surface. [2] Mary Webster, *Francis Wheatley* (1970), pp. 99, 141, no. 75. [3] Algernon Graves, *The Royal Academy of Arts*, 8 vols. (1905–6), VIII, p. 244; exhibited as 'Portrait of a gentleman with a horse and spaniel', the identification, 'Mr Bond Hopkins', added by Graves from his own researches. [4] *Gentleman's Magazine* (1794), I, 183–4. [5] Information from the donor. [6] Owen Manning and William Bray, *The history and antiquities of the county of Surrey*, 3 vols. (1804–14), II, pp. 768–9. [7] Webster, *op. cit.*, p. 141, no. 75, dates it 1790–1; the date of the purchase is unknown.

WHISTLER, James Abbott McNeill

1834–1903. Born at Lowell, Mass., U.S.A. In Paris, 1855–9; entered the Académie Gleyre, 1856. From 1859 lived mainly in London, with visits to Paris and travel elsewhere on the Continent. Influenced by Courbet and other French painters, and by Japanese art. Painter, etcher, lithographer and decorator.

PD. 29–1970 PORTRAIT STUDY OF A MAN

Wood, $6\frac{5}{8} \times 4$ in (16·8 × 10·2 cm). Standing, almost whole-length, turned half right; bare-headed, fair hair and moustache. Dark coat to knees, light grey trousers. Background in tones of dark grey, brown towards the base; the folds of a lighter grey curtain upper right.

Bequeathed by the Very Rev. Eric Milner-White, C.B.E., D.S.O., Dean of York, 1963, received 1970. With the Redfern Gallery, London; bt from them by Clifford Hall, 1940 or 1941; exh. London, 96 Cheyne

Walk, Chelsea, 1948, 'Whistleriana' (63); anon. sale (= Clifford Hall), Sotheby's, 22 June 1955 (139), bt in; bt from him by Roland, Browse & Delbanco, London, who sold it to E. Milner-White 1956.

Small whole-length portraits similar to this are known in Whistler's work in the 1880s and 1890s. Compare, for example, the *George A. Lucas* of 1886 (Walters Art Gallery, Baltimore, U.S.A.), the *C. E. Holloway* of 1896–7 (Marquis de Ganay, Paris), and the *Miss Rosalind Birnie Philip* of about 1897 (University of Glasgow, Birnie Philip Bequest). It has been described as a portrait of the painter William Stott of Oldham (1857–1900),[1] at one time a friend of Whistler's, but comparison with a photograph of him of 1897[2] contradicts this identification, showing different features and dark hair and moustache.

NOTES. [1] So identified while with Roland, Browse & Delbanco; when it belonged to Mr Clifford Hall it bore its present title. [2] Rep. *Art Journal*, New Series (1900), 124.

Imitation of Whistler

PD. 17–1948 SYMPHONY IN GREY AND BROWN: LINDSEY ROW, CHELSEA

Canvas, $11\frac{7}{8} \times 10\frac{3}{8}$ in ($30{\cdot}2 \times 26{\cdot}4$ cm).[1] Across a grey, open expanse of water, a sailing barge, grey, black and green, with a brown furled sail, lies in front of other dark grey barges against the far embankment of the river, along which runs a road lined with buildings, mainly in tones of grey, with three trees to the left. Light grey sky. Lower left, damaged butterfly signature in pale blue.

Given by the Very Rev. Eric Milner-White, C.B.E., D.S.O., Dean of York, 1948. Coll. W. Quittner; bt from him by Roland, Browse & Delbanco, London, 1947; sold the same year to E. Milner-White; exh. London, Guildhall Art Gallery, 1971, 'London and the greater painters' (43).

Though formerly attributed to Whistler, the resemblance of this picture to his work is only superficial. It is based upon his atmospheric paintings of Thames subjects of the years towards the middle 1860s, such, for example, as the *Brown and silver: Old Battersea Bridge* (Addison Gallery of American Art, Andover, Mass., U.S.A.), exhibited at the R.A. in 1865, which has been dated 1863–5.[2] But, disguised in character to some extent though the picture is through damage and restoration, it is recognisable as the work of an imitator through the exaggerated extent of the river foreground and the finicky treatment of the buildings. The damaged butterfly signature appears under ultra-violet light to be an integral part of the paint. It is, however, of a form used by Whistler in the 1880s, and is thus incongruous with a painting of this type, suggesting that the picture is a deliberate deception. Whistler lived in Lindsey Row, now Cheyne Walk, for a number of years from 1863.

NOTES. [1] Dimensions of the painted surface; the lining canvas backing it measures $12\frac{1}{8} \times 10\frac{5}{8}$ in (30·8 × 27·0 cm). [2] By A. McLaren Young, catalogue of the Arts Council exhibition, 'James McNeill Whistler', 1960, p. 38, no. 9. The late Professor Young's help in cataloguing this and the following picture, no. PD. 975–1963, is gratefully acknowledged.

PD. 975–1963 WOMAN SEWING

Wood, 8 × 5 in (20·2 × 12·6 cm). She sits in an armchair by the wall of a room, turned towards a fireplace partially seen at the right. Her dress is dark grey; the chair has a brown wooden frame and grey-green upholstery; behind it are long ochre-grey curtains. The fireplace is white; the wall light grey with part of a gilt picture frame seen above. Green carpet. Butterfly signature lower right.

Bequeathed by the Very Rev. Eric Milner-White, C.B.E., D.S.O., Dean of York, 1963. Coll. Mrs D. E. Sternberg; her sale, Sotheby's, 30 March 1949 (102), bt Roland, Browse & Delbanco, London; bt from them by E. Milner-White, 1949.

This is of the type of Whistler's small, full-length portraits in an interior, of the 1880s and 1890s, such as *The gold ruff*, *Mrs Charles Whibley reading*, and *Miss Rosalind Birnie Philip standing* (all University of Glasgow). Though formerly attributed to Whistler, the picture cannot be accepted as more than an imitation, as is evident from the slippery paint of poor texture, the mechanical handling and the uncharacteristic diagonal design. The butterfly signature suggests that the picture is a deliberate deception, as it is of a linear form never used by Whistler in oil-paintings, but is revealed under ultra-violet light to be integral with the rest of the paint.

WILKIE, Sir David

1785–1841. Born at Cults, Fifeshire. Student at the Trustees' Academy of Design, Edinburgh, 1799–1804; to London, 1805, entered the R.A. schools; exh. R.A. from 1806; R.A., 1811; travelled abroad, chiefly in Spain, 1825–8; Painter in Ordinary to George IV, 1830; kt, 1836.

Attributed to Sir David Wilkie

1756 JOHN COWPER, AN EDINBURGH BEGGAR

Canvas, $29\frac{7}{8} \times 24\frac{3}{4}$ in ($75{\cdot}9 \times 62{\cdot}8$ cm).[1] Half-length, slightly right, taking snuff with the right hand from a snuff-horn held in the left. Clean-shaven; wears a grey-blue tam-o-shanter. A brown coat is open over a blue-green jacket, a pale buff garment beneath it; a light-coloured strap crosses the jacket from his right shoulder. Dark brown background.

Given by Kenneth, Lord Clark, K.C.B., O.M., C.H., F.B.A., 1935. Coll. Mrs Clarkson Stanfield, who gave it to Charles Hargitt;[2] exh. London, International Exhibition, 1874;[3] Hargitt sale by his executors, Branch & Leete, Liverpool, 15–18 March 1881 (544);[4] coll. Mazzini Stuart, Liverpool; sold to Messrs Rayner MacConnal, London; anon. sale (= Rayner MacConnal), Christie's, 2 March 1934 (157),[5] bt Meatyard; bought from Meatyard's by Lord Clark.

Ascribed to Wilkie himself when in the Hargitt collection, an ascription which goes back at least to 1874, perhaps deriving from its previous owner, Mrs Clarkson Stanfield, whose husband (1793–1867) was a painter almost contemporary with Wilkie. To be considered as Wilkie's work on stylistic grounds, it can only be thought of as belonging to his student days in Edinburgh (1799–1804), though nothing comparable is known; but by 1805, as shown by the dated *Mr Morison and Miss Beaton* (Scottish private collection), his work was far superior in accomplishment to this *John Cowper*. Timid as the latter appears by comparison, however, the two are not incompatible, and in the directness of presentation and the attention paid to the hands, there are elements of similarity between them. An inscription written at the back of the picture, now concealed by the lining canvas but quoted in the Hargitt sale catalogue, describes Cowper as 'An old soldier now a Beggar in Edinburgh. 1808. Aged 87'.[6] The catalogue assumes that it was 'evidently written' by Wilkie, but whether so or not, the 'now' indicates a date for the painting of the picture some length of time before 1808, not impossibly referring it to the period of Wilkie's student days, when he is known to have made use of local types as models. If these considerations are insufficient for the acceptance of a positive attribution to Wilkie, neither do they permit a complete rejection of Hargitt's belief in his authorship, which remains as a somewhat tenuous possibility.[7]

NOTES. [1] Lined; dimensions of the painted surface. [2] Catalogue of the Hargitt sale, 1881, see below. [3] As by Wilkie; Algernon Graves, *A century of loan exhibitions*, 5 vols. (1913–15), IV, p. 1672, lists it without an exhibition number, noting that this and five other Wilkie paintings (three of them lent by Hargitt) included in the original catalogue 'do not appear in the first (revised) edition'. [4] As by Wilkie; a cutting from the sale catalogue is at the back of the picture. [5] Catalogued as 'Wilkie'. [6] A transcription of it in a clerkly, copperplate hand, presumably made at the time of the lining, is on a label attached to the stretcher, but '1808' has been miscopied, assuming the sale catalogue to be correct, as '1805'. [7] Thanks must be expressed to Dr Lindsay Errington for her help over the problem of this attribution.

WILLIAMS, Solomon

Bef. 1771–1824. Born in Dublin. Studied at the Dublin Academy; visited Italy; in London, 1790–2 and 1796–1809; settled in Dublin; foundation member of the Royal Hibernian Academy. History and portrait painter.

12 DANIEL MESMAN

Canvas, $29\frac{5}{8} \times 24\frac{5}{8}$ in ($75{\cdot}3 \times 62{\cdot}5$ cm).[1] Nearly half-length, turned half right. Bare-headed, light hair; clean-shaven but for short, light-coloured side-whiskers; fair, warm complexion. Wears a black coat over buff waistcoat and spotted under-waistcoat, with white choker and jabot.

Bequeathed by Daniel Mesman, 1834.

Daniel Mesman, about whom very little is known, was a Londoner. Though not a member of the University of Cambridge, upon his death in 1834 he bequeathed to the Fitzwilliam Museum a collection of two hundred and forty-three paintings, with some drawings and prints, for which he is commemorated among the University's benefactors. The portrait shows him in early middle age, and from the costume it may be dated to the early years of the nineteenth century, probably towards the end of Williams's second stay in London.

REPRODUCED. Earp, p. 214.

NOTE. [1] Lined; dimensions of the painted surface.

WILLS, James

Active mid-eighteenth century, d. 1777. Well-known by 1743;[1] took orders in the earlier 1760s;[2] vicar of Canons, Middlesex. Portrait and history painter.

657 THE ANDREWS FAMILY (1749) PLATE 12

Canvas, $43\frac{1}{4} \times 56\frac{7}{8}$ in (109·8 × 144·5 cm).[3] The man seated at the right wears a maroon coat and breeches with a brown waistcoat; the boy beside him has a blue coat and breeches with a green waistcoat; the standing woman is in white; the seated woman wears a dress of shot mauve-pink; the young man beside her has a grey coat and breeches laced with silver and a brocade waistcoat of red, white and green on silver. The stonework is a brownish grey; the trees light bluish green; the sky light blue and cream. Signed and dated lower left, 'J. Wills pinxit. 1749'.

Given by Charles Fairfax Murray, 1908. Coll. Joseph Andrews (1691–1753); by inheritance from the Andrews family, Shaw House, Newbury, Berkshire, to the family of Eyre; H. J. A. Eyre (of Shaw House) sale, Christie's, 9 December 1905 (29), bt C. Fairfax Murray.

Seated at the right is Joseph Andrews (1691–1753), appointed paymaster to the forces in Scotland in 1715, who bought Shaw House, Newbury, in 1751.[4] Standing beside him is his second wife, Elizabeth, whom he married in 1736, and their son James Pettit Andrews. At the left is his elder son Joseph (1727–1800), who became a baronet in 1766. The lady who sits beside him is unidentified.

REPRODUCED. *Principal pictures* (1912 edn), p. 211, (1929 edn), p. 241; F. M. Kelly and R. Schwabe, *Historic costume* (1925), pl. LIII; Ellis Waterhouse, *Painting in Britain, 1530 to 1790* (1953), pl. 120a.

NOTES. [1] Included by George Vertue in a note of that year as among the best of 'the most promiseing young Painters', see *Walpole Society* (1934), XXII, 117. [2] He abandoned painting for lack of success. After 1761 he did not exhibit again until 1766, when he appears as 'The Rev. Mr Wills'. [3] Lined; dimensions of the painted surface. [4] C. H. Collins Baker and Muriel J. Baker, *The life and circumstances of James Brydges, first Duke of Chandos* (1949), p. 385.

WILSON, Richard

1713–1782. Born at Penegoes, Montgomeryshire. Trained and practised in London as a portrait painter; to Venice, 1750; in Rome by late 1751 or early 1752; had turned to landscape painting by 1753; probably left Italy, 1757; settled in London. Foundation member of the R.A., 1768.

PD. 2–1948 ITALIAN RIVER LANDSCAPE WITH A BROKEN BRIDGE

Wood, $16\frac{1}{4} \times 21$ in (41·3 × 53·3 cm). The river, blue-grey in colour, flows through the centre of the composition between banks covered with trees and shrubs, at the right in shadow with a circular temple, at the left in sunlight, the foliage in tones of olive-green and brown; crossing the river from the temple is a ruined bridge. On an elevated foreground, dark and light brown in colour, with tall trees at the right, is a group of three figures, in cream, pink and black, at the left beside a light brown bluff; at a lower level beyond them are two horsemen. In the background a flat, sunlit landscape, blue-grey and cream in colour, extends beyond the river, terminating in a distant hill. Light grey-blue sky with cream clouds.[1]

Given by Frederick John Nettlefold, 1948.[2] Coll. Benjamin Booth (1732–1807);[3] Rev. R. S. Booth; Lady (Richard) Ford (née Marianne Booth), London; Richard Ford, Devonshire; Sir Francis Clare Ford, Devonshire; Captain Richard Ford, London; exh. Brighton, Fine Art Galleries, 1920, 'Oil paintings and sketches by Richard Wilson, R.A.' (24); Captain Richard Ford sale, Christie's, 14 June 1929 (18), bt Thos Agnew & Sons Ltd, by whom sold to F. J. Nettlefold.

Much damaged everywhere by over-cleaning. This has been grouped with a number of paintings assigned to the second half of the 1760s.[4] Strongly resembling it both in composition and in the elements of the design, are two paintings by Wilson, very similar to one another, in the collections respectively of C. Norris (1962) and formerly Lt-Col. P. L. E. Walker, though with the bridge replaced by the broken bridge at Narni and many smaller differences. The Norris picture has been dated to the late 1760s, but the Walker example is compared with a painting of 1753, suggesting an origin for the composition during Wilson's Italian visit.[5] A possible variant of the Fitzwilliam Museum picture was in the J. H. Anderdon collection, and an enlarged version with variations, not by Wilson, belongs to the Smithsonian Institution, Washington, D.C., National Collection of Fine Arts.[6]

ENGRAVED. By T. Hastings, 1822, in *Etchings from the works of Ric. Wilson* (1825), no. 25.[7]

REPRODUCED. C. Reginald Grundy and F. Gordon Roe, *A catalogue of the pictures and drawings in the collection of Frederick John Nettlefold*, 4 vols. (1933–8), IV, p. 153 (colour); W. G. Constable, *Richard Wilson* (1953), pl. 106b.

NOTES. [1] W. G. Constable, *Richard Wilson* (1953), p. 218, pl. 106b. [2] C. Reginald Grundy and F. Gordon Roe, *A catalogue of the pictures and drawings in the collection of Frederick John Nettlefold*, 4 vols. (1933–8), IV, pp. 152–3. [3] No. 23 in Booth's list of his own collection, compiled after June 1790, see Constable, *op. cit.*, pp. 2 and 218, pl. 106b. [4] Constable, *op. cit.*, p. 92. [5] W. G. Constable,

Richard Wilson: a second addendum', *Burlington Magazine* (1962), CIV, 141, rep. p. 140, figs, 8, 9. The Walker example was in 1974 with Spink & Son Ltd, London. [6] Constable, *op. cit.*, n. [1], p. 218, pl. 106b. [7] See Constable, *op. cit.*, n. [1], p. 218, pl. 106b.

PD. 27–1952 APOLLO AND THE SEASONS PLATE 13

Canvas, $39\frac{3}{8} \times 49\frac{1}{2}$ in (100·1 × 125·7 cm). Foliage and herbage are in tones of grey-green and orange-brown; the castle is a lighter orange-brown and the light suffusing the sky from the right is in a more brilliant and still lighter tone; the lake is light indigo-blue, the distant water and hills blue-grey. The dancing figures are in warm tones of white, buff and pink, with passages of indigo; Apollo is in deep pink, with dark indigo drapery.[1]

Bought from the Fairhaven Fund, 1952. Probably exh. R.A., 1779 (352);[2] sold Sotheby's, Property of a lady ((?) Miss Turner), 6 March 1940 (25), bt Norris; Christopher Norris sale, Christie's, 4 July 1952 (20), bt Benson (for Tooth's); exh. Arthur Tooth & Sons Ltd, London, 1952, 'Recent acquisitions VII' (3); bt from Tooth's; exh. London, Goldsmiths' Hall, 1959, 'Treasures of Cambridge' (325); Hazlitt, 1974 (64).

Wilson painted this subject in two different compositions, which only relate to one another very broadly through their general scheme. The present picture represents the later. The earlier, and simpler, is known in two versions, one of them a painting belonging (1953) to Viscount Allendale, tentatively ascribed to the early 1770s.[3] The origin of this composition seems to go back to Wilson's stay in Rome, from the evidence of an etching by J. Plimmer inscribed 'Roma 1760', which uses it as part of the design.[4] The later composition, only known in the Fitzwilliam Museum painting, is of a more formalised type in the manner of Claude.[5] It is dated on grounds of style to the middle or late 1770s,[6] but the composition is virtually a repetition of the design of a *Phaeton*, datable between 1763 and 1767, at Ince Blundell Hall, Lancashire, of which there is a version with differences in reverse.[7] The temple at the right appears to be the same, from a slightly different view-point, as that in the *Temple of Clitumnus*, coll. late T. W. Bacon.[8]

REPRODUCED. Arthur Tooth & Sons Ltd, London, catalogue *Recent acquisitions VII* (1952) (3); Fitzwilliam Museum, *Annual Report* for 1952, pl. II; W. G. Constable, *Richard Wilson* (1953), pl. 26b; John Hayes, *Richard Wilson* (The Masters, no. 57) (1966), pl. XIII (colour); exhibition catalogue, Hazlitt, 1974, pl. 12.

NOTES. [1] W. G. Constable, *Richard Wilson* (1953), p. 167, pl. 26b. [2] Constable, *op. cit.*, pp. 93, 96, 167. [3] Constable, *op. cit.*, pp. 93–4, 167, pl. 26a, b. [4] Constable, *op. cit.*, pp. 140, 167, pl. 26a, b. [5] Constable, *op. cit.*, pp. 89, 96, see n. [7]. [6] Constable, *op. cit.*, pp. 96, 167, pl. 26a, b. [7] Constable, *op. cit.*, pp. 163–4, pl. 22a; for the version in reverse, see pp. 89, 163, pl. 22b. [8] Constable, *op. cit.*, rep. pl. 75b.

Attributed to Wilson

1126 LAKE AND HILLS

Canvas, $13\frac{3}{4} \times 17\frac{3}{8}$ in ($34{\cdot}9 \times 44{\cdot}2$ cm).[1] On the further side of a small lake, the water mainly grey-blue, rises a low hill, with a turreted building at its base by the edge of the water in front of a line of trees. The hill is in tones of olive-green, the building dark cream, the trees deep and lighter greens. The lake is enclosed at the right by a low shore, brown in colour, which continues across the foreground where a man sits near several boulders, in tones of brown, and a bare tree rises at the left. In the distance at the left is another low hill.

Given by the Friends of the Fitzwilliam Museum, 1924. (?) With Heinemann, Munich, 1910;[2] with D. Croal Thomson, Barbizon House, London, from whom it was bought.[3]

The whole surface much damaged in lining and by over-cleaning, the sky and the branches of the tree heavily restored. The ruined condition of the picture precludes any firm judgment as to authorship. In its general characteristics – design, pictorial motives, treatment – it has points of resemblance with many of Wilson's smaller landscapes, of which the *Llanberis Pass and Twr Padarn*, in the National Library of Wales, Aberystwyth,[4] provides a particular stylistic comparison through the similarity of its consistently fluid handling. From an impression of the original colour quality which may still be obtained from some areas, it seems not unlikely that the picture was once of some considerable merit. Though the obvious hypothesis of Wilson's authorship cannot be confirmed on the available evidence, neither can it be dismissed.[5]

REPRODUCED. Friends of the Fitzwilliam Museum, *Annual Report* for 1924; *Principal pictures* (1929), p. 243; W. G. Constable, *Richard Wilson* (1953), pl. 145b.

NOTES. [1] Lined; dimensions of the painted surface. [2] W. G. Constable, *Richard Wilson* (1953), p. 238, pl. 145b. [3] As by Richard Wilson. A manuscript label at the back of the picture, reading 'Landscape / Richard Wilson / by Mrs. E.

Davis', perhaps indicates a former owner. [4] Rep. Constable, *op. cit.*, pl. 42a. [5] Constable, *op. cit.*, p. xii, includes it in the section of 'Paintings attributed to Wilson'; he doubts Wilson's authorship (p. 238, pl. 145b) for stylistic reasons, though apparently without taking the condition of the picture into account.

Repetition after Wilson

1130 BRIDGE OF AUGUSTUS AT RIMINI

Canvas, $17\frac{1}{2} \times 28\frac{7}{8}$ in (44·4 × 73·3cm).[1] The bridge, with two buildings at its end to the left, greyish buff in colour, spans the centre of the composition, the river, mainly brown-grey, extending from it to fill most of the left foreground. Above its bank at the left, in shadow, some buildings are seen. In the right foreground, beyond a line of low dark brown rocks, is a shelving beach in sunlight, brownish cream, on which a woman and a kneeling man handle some washing, a kneeling figure to the left washing linen in the river. A dense clump of trees, dark olive-green and brown, stands at the right. Beyond the bridge rises a low ridge with a hill in the background, in tones of blue-green. Cream-coloured clouds with a pale blue sky above fill the centre, with grey clouds to left and right.[2]

Given by Charles Gerald Agnew, 1924. Coll. S. E. Kennedy, sold Christie's, 6 July 1917 (40), bt Agnew.

As with some other compositions of Wilson's, this *Bridge of Augustus* is known in a number of versions, none of which corresponds exactly with any of the others. Four of them are regarded as autograph, of which one, formerly belonging to Mrs L'Estrange Malone (d. 1951) at Scampston Hall, Yorkshire, signed with initials, is considered to be the prime original; the others are in the Dunedin Gallery, New Zealand, in the National Collection of Fine Arts, Smithsonian Institution, Washington, D.C., and in the collection of A. de Madeiros e Almeida, Lisbon. The Fitzwilliam Museum version, which has its own variations, is a repetition of only moderate quality.[3] On his Italian visit, Wilson passed through Rimini on his way from Venice to Rome, which he reached late in 1751 or early in January 1752.[4] Two sketches of portions of the bridge are known from this journey,[5] but neither is related to the painted composition, a terminal date for the origin of which is provided by the purchase in Rome of a *Pons Rimini* not later than 1754.[6] An elaborate drawing of the composition in pencil heightened with white on blue-grey paper, with its own differences of detail, is at Cambridge (Fitzwilliam Museum, no. PD. 47–1958),[7] and an etching by Joseph Farington, also with variations of detail, which occurs as one of the *Twelve original views in Italy* published by Boydell in 1776, inscribed 'R. Wilson del.', is presumably taken from another drawing.[8] The river which the bridge crosses is the Marecchia; on the hill in the background is the tiny Republic of San Marino, which is near Rimini though its introduction into the picture is a topographical invention of Wilson's.

NOTES. [1] Lined; dimensions of the painted surface. [2] W. G. Constable, *Richard Wilson* (1953), pp. 211–13, pl. 99a. [3] Constable, *op. cit.*, pp. 45, 71, 82, 211–13, pl. 99a; the Fitzwilliam Museum version is described as 'replica quality' (p. 212). The Malone picture is considered on grounds of style to have been painted in Italy (p. 82), and H. A. Buttery pointed out in 1936 that the Dunedin example, which had passed through his hands, was painted on an Italian canvas (Fitzwilliam Museum, letter of 2 November 1936). [4] Constable, *op. cit.*, p. 25. [5] Constable, *op. cit.*, p. 213. [6] Constable, *op. cit.*, pp. 34, 71, 81–2, 212. [7] Constable, *op. cit.*, p. 213, the Esdaile drawing, and 'Richard Wilson: a second addendum', *Burlington Magazine* (1962), CIV, p. 141, rep. p. 139, fig. 2. [8] Constable, *op. cit.*, pp. 108–9.

DE WINT, PETER

1784–1849. Born at Stone, Staffordshire. Pupil of J. R. Smith, 1802; entered the R.A. schools, 1809; member of the Society of Painters in Water-colours. Landscape painter, principally in water-colours, but also in oils.

PD. 12–1975 LANDSCAPE STUDY

Paper-faced cardboard, $12\frac{1}{8} \times 18\frac{3}{4}$ in ($30{\cdot}7 \times 47{\cdot}6$ cm). In a landscape, hilly at the left, flat at the right with hills in the distance, a gully in the foreground runs inwards towards the centre from the left; above the gully at the right stands a group of two trees. The hills to the left are in tones of dark grey-green, the ground to the right and the distant hills in paler tones of grey-green; across the centre are dark brown tree masses, which extend across the flat ground. Blue-grey sky with white cloud masses.

Bought from the Fairhaven Fund, 1975. Coll. Miss H. H. Tatlock (d. 1922), the artist's grand-daughter, by family inheritance; with Thos Agnew & Sons Ltd, London; bt from Agnew's, 1975.

Dating de Wint's paintings, oils even more than water-colours, is at best a tentative proceeding, there being virtually no evidence for his chronology. A particular problem is presented by paintings which are in the nature of a sketch, such as the present one.

WOOD, John Christopher

1901–1930. Born at Knowsley, near Liverpool. Educated at Malvern College; studied in Paris at the Académie Julian, 1921; travelled extensively, with frequent residence in Paris and London, and latterly in Brittany. Influenced by contemporary French painters. Painted mainly landscapes, still-life, and figure subjects.

2451 LA VILLE-CLOSE, CONCARNEAU, BRITTANY (1930)

Millboard, 22⅜ × 32⅛ in (56·8 × 81·6 cm). In a small harbour enclosed at the far side by massive buildings, surmounted by a cupola at the harbour mouth to the left, lie four boats, one of them in the foreground with a dinghy beyond it, against the quay-side, which runs diagonally across the lower left corner. The hulls of the boats are mainly black, but for one to the right which is partly deep red; the deck of the boat in the foreground, in which a man is sitting, is buff. Nets, pale blue in colour, hang from the masts of three of the boats. The masonry is in tones of brown, the cupola grey; the water is predominantly a greenish brown. Beyond the harbour mouth, spanned by a footbridge, an expanse of pale blue water leads to a point of land, ochre-brown in colour, on which are a lighthouse, buildings and trees. Pale grey sky.

Bequeathed by Edward Maurice Berkeley Ingram, C.M.G., O.B.E., 1941. With the Redfern Gallery, London, who bought it from the artist's mother, Mrs Lucius Wood; exh. London, New Burlington Galleries, 1938, 'Christopher Wood, exhibition of complete works' (101), bt E. M. B. Ingram; National Gallery, 1940, 'British painting since Whistler' (154); Redfern Gallery, 1941, 'Exhibition of the collection of paintings formed by the late Maurice Ingram' (23); Edinburgh, Scottish National Gallery of Modern Art, 1966, 'Christopher Wood' (26).

This is among the latest of Wood's pictures, painted in 1930[1] when he spent most of June and July at Tréboul in Brittany.[2] His death took place the following month. Concarneau is a small fishing port on the south coast of Brittany in the bay of La Forest, or Fouesnant, about twenty-five miles from Tréboul. The Ville-Close is the ancient quarter of the town, situated upon a small island.

REPRODUCED. Eric Newton, *Christopher Wood* (1938), p. 15 (colour), (1959 edn), pl. 3 (colour); exhibition catalogue, Scottish National Gallery of Modern Art, *Christopher Wood* (1966), pl. 2.

NOTES. [1] Eric Newton, *Christopher Wood* (1938), p. 74, no. 410. [2] Newton, *op. cit.*, pp. 25, 62, (1959 edn), p. 10.

WOOTTON, John

Bef. 1683–1765. Pupil of Jan Wyck (1690s); joined Kneller's academy in London, 1711; visited Rome (1720s). Sporting painter, particularly of horses, and painter of landscape in the tradition of Claude and Gaspard Poussin.

5 CLASSICAL LANDSCAPE PLATE 5

Canvas, 32 × 42½ in (81·3 × 107·9 cm). The nearer foliage is mainly in tones of blue-green, the remoter foliage olive-green; the tree-trunks are dark brown. The ground is brown; the buildings a lighter brown; the water indigo-blue. The urn and pedestal are light terracotta red and grey; the two figures beside it are respectively in white with a blue drapery, and in red; the seated figure has brown flesh-colour and a blue-grey drapery; the distant figure is in pale pink. The crags and distant hills are light blue; the sky pale blue with cream and grey clouds.

Given by Augustus Arthur VanSittart (1824–1882), 1876.[1]

This is a characteristic example of the landscape paintings which Wootton began producing, in addition to the sporting pictures which distinguished his whole career, after his visit to Rome in the 1720s. In their emulation of Claude and Gaspard Poussin they marked a break with the English topographical landscape tradition. This tradition continued to play its part in his sporting pictures, though usually modified to a greater or less extent in accordance with the principles of classical landscape.

REPRODUCED. M. H. Grant, *A chronological history of the old English landscape painters*, 3 vols. (1932(?)–1947), I, pl. 19, 8 vols. (1957–61 edn), II, pl. 72.

NOTE. [1] VanSittart inherited in 1850 from his great-aunt Anne Windsor, Countess of Plymouth, a number of paintings which had belonged to her uncle Edward King (d. 1807), but whether or not this was among them is unknown.

WRIGHT, Joseph

1734–1797. Born in Derby. Pupil of Thomas Hudson in London, 1751–3, 1756–7; in Italy, 1774–5; settled in Derby, 1777; A.R.A., 1781. Known as 'Wright of Derby'. Painted portraits, subject pictures and landscape.

1 THE HON. RICHARD FITZWILLIAM, 7TH VISCOUNT FITZWILLIAM OF MERRION (1764) PLATE 20

Canvas, 29½ × 24½ in (74·9 × 62·2 cm).[1] His academical gown is red with gold lace, his coat and waistcoat blue. Neutral brown hair; fresh complexion. Brown background.[2]

Given by the Rev. Robert Fitzwilliam Hallifax, 1819. Coll. Samuel Hallifax, D.D., Bishop of St Asaph, his father; exh. London, Goldsmiths' Hall, 1959, 'Treasures of Cambridge' (1).

Cleaned 1934. The Hon. Richard Fitzwilliam (1745–1816), eldest son of the 6th Viscount Fitzwilliam of Merrion, succeeded his father as 7th Viscount in 1776. The Fitzwilliam Museum was founded under the terms of his will by the bequest to his old university of his art collections and his library, and a sum of money for the erection of a building. He was admitted a nobleman at Trinity Hall in 1761, and is shown wearing the gown of an undergraduate nobleman fellow-commoner, of the kind worn on special occasions. The portrait was painted in 1764 for Samuel Hallifax,[3] fellow and tutor of Trinity Hall, and private tutor to Richard Fitzwilliam, who was godfather to his son, and although he received his M.A. degree in that year it depicts him as still an undergraduate.

REPRODUCED. Earp, p. 218; *Principal pictures* (1912 edn), p. 215, (1929 edn), p. 247; *Connoisseur* (1915), XLIII, 114; *Illustrated London News* (1948), CCXI, 452; J. W. Goodison, *Catalogue of Cambridge portraits* (1955), I, pl. XV; Carl Winter, *The Fitzwilliam Museum* (1958), frontispiece; Benedict Nicolson, *Joseph Wright of Derby*, 2 vols. (1968), II, pl. 49.

NOTES. [1] Lined; dimensions of the painted surface. [2] Benedict Nicolson, *Joseph Wright of Derby*, 2 vols. (1968), I, p. 197, no. 60. [3] Fitzwilliam Museum, Register labelled 'Fitzwilliam Museum Donation Book, 1817', p. 13.

659 MRS JOHN ASHTON

Canvas, $49\frac{5}{8} \times 39\frac{3}{4}$ in (126·1 × 101·0 cm).[1] She is seen somewhat from below at three-quarter-length, seated, turned slightly left, the head slightly right, her right hand on the wooden arm of her chair, her left hand placed on a book standing upon its edge on a table right. She wears a black silk dress, with plain white fichu and elbow frills, a black and white cap on her head. The table has a red velvet cover, the book is brown, the chair back behind her is red. Brown background with a pilaster to left.[2]

Given by Charles Fairfax Murray, 1908.[3] Coll. Nicholas Ashton, Woolton Hall, Lancashire, son of the sitter (1742–1833);[4] Joseph William Ashton; anon. sale (= J. W. Ashton), Christie's, 9 December 1905 (72), bt Murray.[5]

Lined and cleaned 1934. The sitter was identified in 1911 by Henry Yates Thompson, her great-great-grandson, as Elizabeth Ashton (1710–1778), daughter of John Brooks of Liverpool, and wife of John Ashton (1711–

1759), a prominent Liverpool merchant.[6] Wright was established in Liverpool from 1768 to 1771.[7] In his account book is a list of twenty-eight 'Sitters at Liverpool 1769', which includes the young son of Nicholas Ashton, but omits a number of other Liverpool sitters,[8] among them Mrs John Ashton, and Nicholas Ashton's wife and two sisters, of whom portraits by Wright are also extant.[9] An approximate date of about 1769–71 may thus be accepted for these portraits,[10] all doubtless commissioned by Nicholas Ashton.

REPRODUCED. *Principal pictures* (1912 edn), p. 216, (1929 edn), p. 248; Benedict Nicolson, *Joseph Wright of Derby*, 2 vols. (1968), II, p. 41, pl. 64.

NOTES. [1] Lined; dimensions of the painted surface. [2] Benedict Nicolson, *Joseph Wright of Derby*, 2 vols. (1968), listed I, p. 177, no. 6. [3] As by Wright, but unidentified. [4] Information from W. A. James, a descendant of Mrs John Ashton, who also stated that on Nicholas Ashton's death Woolton Hall was sold and its contents dispersed among the family (letter of 21 April 1916, Fitzwilliam Museum). [5] Catalogued as 'Northcote', unidentified. [6] Letter of 24 November 1911 (Fitzwilliam Museum). [7] Nicolson, *op. cit.*, I, p. 4. [8] Nicolson, *op. cit.*, I, pp. 33–4. [9] Mr James (see n. [4]) stated that Nicholas Ashton also possessed portraits by Wright of his wife, his son John, and his sister Elizabeth. [10] Nicolson, *op. cit.*, I, pp. 177–8, nos. 6–9, who dates them *c.* 1769.

PD. 8–1948 MATLOCK TOR PLATE 21

Canvas, $28\frac{1}{2} \times 38\frac{7}{8}$ in ($72{\cdot}4 \times 98{\cdot}7$ cm).[1] The grassy slopes are yellowish green; the shrubs are olive-green and brown, or blue-green; the crags are ochre and a greenish ochre. The water is light blue-grey, with warm reflections in the foreground; the foreground tree has a brown trunk and olive-green and brown foliage. The distant trees are a reduced olive-green. Light blue sky with cream clouds.[2]

Bought from the Fairhaven Fund, 1948. Coll. Haskett Smith, London; his sale, Christie's, 28 May 1864 (32), bt in;[3] Haskett Smith, Kent; bt from Roland, Browse & Delbanco, London.

Though formerly described as Dovedale, this is a view on the River Derwent near Matlock, Derbyshire. The river here runs from north to south, with limestone cliffs on the eastern side, from which rise isolated, precipitous rock masses, as in this picture, in which the view is towards the north. The best known of these is Matlock High Tor, but despite a strong resemblance to it the high rock at the right is identified as another feature known locally simply as Matlock Tor.[4] The picture is dated to the mid-1780s.[5] The same scene by moonlight, with a deeper foreground and without the tree at the left, is known in two earlier paintings, virtually identical with one another, which are assigned to *c.* 1778–80, respectively in the collection of Mr and Mrs Paul Mellon and at the Detroit Institute of Arts, U.S.A.[6]

REPRODUCED. *Illustrated London News* (1949), CCXIV, 282; *The Art Quarterly* (1955), XVIII, 269; Benedict Nicolson, *Joseph Wright of Derby*, 2 vols. (1968), II, p. 158, pl. 248 (colour).

NOTES. [1] Lined; dimensions of the painted surface. [2] Benedict Nicolson, *Joseph Wright of Derby*, 2 vols. (1968), listed I, p. 264, no. 310. [3] As 'A view in Dovedale'. [4] Nicolson, *op. cit.*, I, p. 88. [5] Nicolson, *op. cit.*, I, p. 90, II, p. 158, pl. 248. [6] Nicolson, *op. cit.*, listed I, p. 264, nos. 308, 309; dated *c.* 1778–80, II, p. 135, pls. 217, 218, but cf. I, pp. 88, 90–1.

PLATES

PLATE I

164 Holbein, Hans, after. *William Fitzwilliam, Earl of Southampton*

PD. 1–1963 Eworth, Hans. *Unknown lady, formerly called Mary I when princess*

PLATE 3

442 van Somer, Paul. *Lady Abergavenny*

PD. 60–1958 Johnson, Cornelius. *Unknown lady* (1646)

PLATE 4

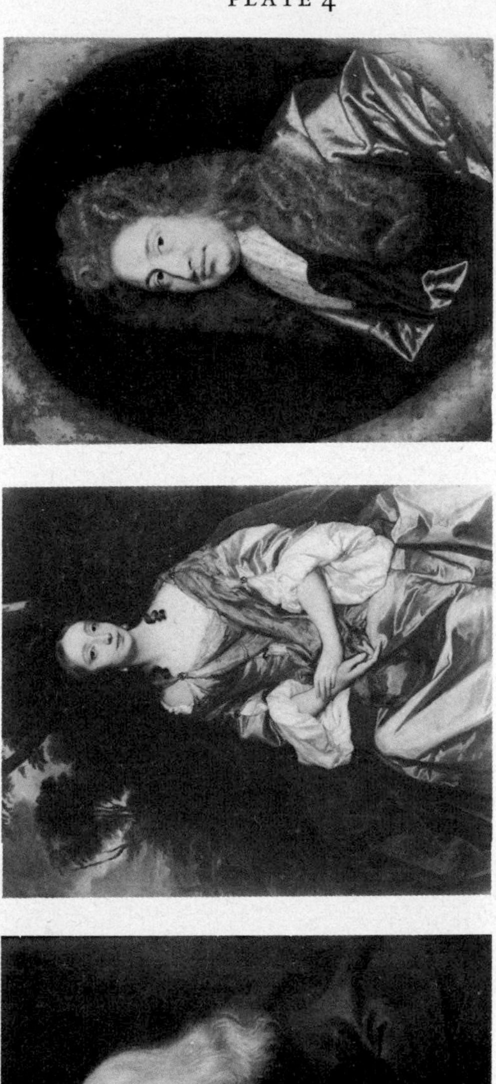

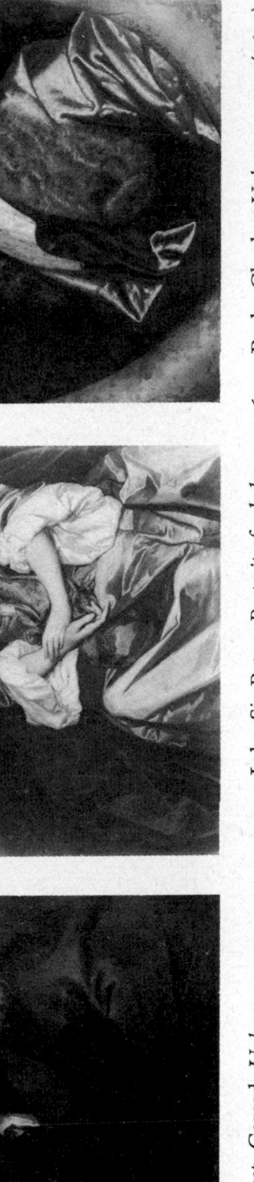

2356 Soest, Gerard. *Unknown man*

2442 Lely, Sir Peter. *Portrait of a lady*

643 Beale, Charles. *Unknown man* (1693)

361 Bogdani, Jacob. *Birds in a landscape*

5 Wootton, John. *Classical landscape*

8 Pond, Arthur, attributed to. *Thomas Gray*

16 Richardson, Jonathan, the elder. *Alexander Pope* (1742)

22 Knapton, George. *Edward Morrison*

M.Add. 6 Highmore, Joseph. *Pamela and Mr B. in the summer house*

M.Add. 9 Highmore, Joseph. *Pamela tells a nursery tale*

PLATE 8

PD. 19–1951 Highmore, Joseph. *Unknown man* (1745)

646 Highmore, Joseph. *Mrs Elizabeth Birch and her daughter* (1741)

648 Hogarth, William. *Dr Benjamin Hoadly*

PD. 11–1964 Hogarth, William. *Before*

PD. 12–1964 Hogarth, William. *After*

21 Hogarth, William. *George Arnold*

PLATE II

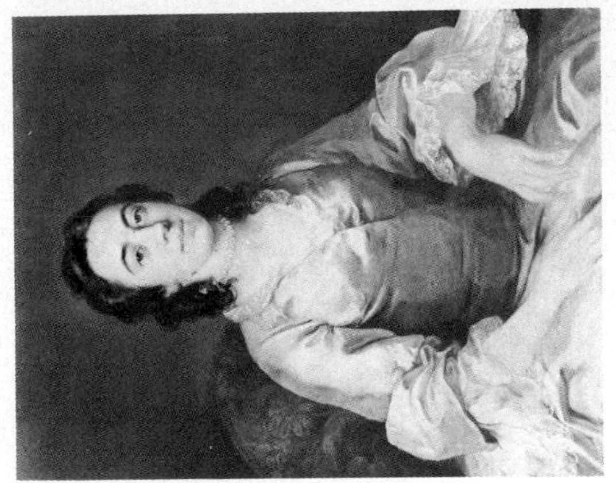

24 Hogarth, William. *Frances Arnold*

658 Dandridge, Bartholomew. *Portrait of a painter*

1642 Hogarth, William. *Unknown man*

657 Wills, James. *The Andrews family* (1749)

PD. 20–1951 Hayman, Francis. *George Dance*

1113 Devis, Arthur. *Francis Page of Newbury*

PLATE 13

PD. 27–1952 Wilson, Richard. *Apollo and the Seasons*

916 Hone, Nathaniel. *The Hon. Mrs Nathaniel Curzon* (1778)

653 Reynolds, Sir Joshua. *Lord Rockingham and Edmund Burke*

PD. 10–1955 Reynolds, Sir Joshua. *The Braddyll family*

PLATE 16

PD. 45–1971 Stubbs, George. *Isabella Saltonstall as Una in Spenser's 'Faerie Queene'* (1782)

710 Gainsborough, Thomas. *'Heneage Lloyd and his sister'*

18 Gainsborough, Thomas. *The Hon. William Fitzwilliam* (1775)

PD. 3–1966 Gainsborough, Thomas. *Landscape with a pool*

644 Gainsborough, Thomas. *John Kirby*

915 Gainsborough, Thomas. *Philip Dupont*

1 Wright, Joseph, of Derby. *The Hon. Richard Fitzwilliam, 7th Viscount Fitzwilliam of Merrion* (1764)

PD. 8–1948 Wright, Joseph, of Derby. *Matlock Tor*

655 West, Benjamin. *The continence of Scipio*

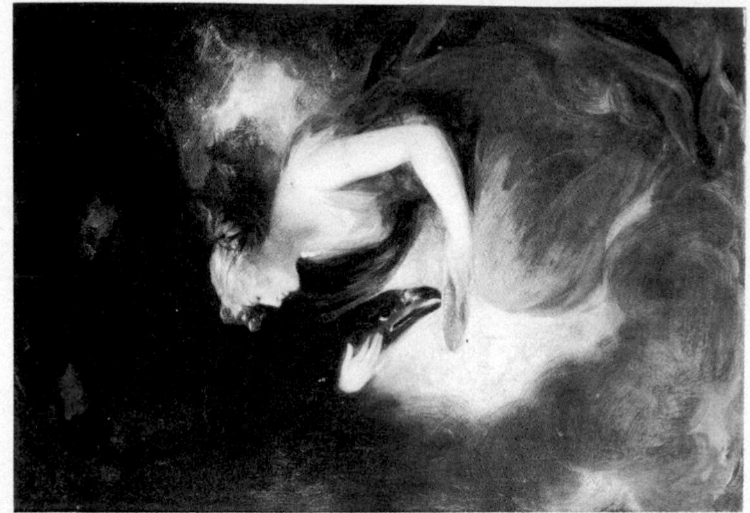

628 Beechey, Sir William. *Hebe feeding Jupiter's eagle*

PD. 21–1951 Millar, James. *Young man in red* (1769)

PD. 27–1949 Blake, William. *An allegory of the spiritual condition of man* (181(1?))

PD. 28–1949 Blake, William. *The judgment of Solomon*

7 More, Jacob. *Bonnington Linn on the River Clyde*

PD. 46–1958 de Loutherbourg, Philip James. *The River Wye at Tintern Abbey* (1805)

PD. 1–1952 Marlow, William. *View near Naples*

PLATE 25

PD. 65–1974 Reinagle, Philip. *Cupid inspiring the plants with love*

PD. 6–1953 Wheatley, Francis. *Benjamin Bond Hopkins*

220 Raeburn, Sir Henry. *William Glendonwyn*

PLATE 27

PD. 2–1974 Nasmyth, Alexander. *Loch Doon, Ayrshire*

1102 Hoppner, John. *Boy with a bird's nest*

M. 50 Ibbetson, Julius Caesar. *Ullswater from the foot of Gowbarrow Fell* (1808)

PLATE 28

1786 Morland, George. *Morning, or The benevolent sportsman* (1792)

PD. 49–1949 Crome, John. *Matlock High Tor*

60 Ward, James. *Fight between a lion and a tiger* (1797)

27 Lawrence, Sir Thomas. *Samuel Woodburn*

PLATE 31

M.Add. 17 Turner, Joseph Mallord William. *Welsh mountain landscape*

PLATE 32

PD. 207–1948 Constable, John. *Hampstead Heath*

PLATE 33

PD. 44–1972 Constable, John. *Archdeacon John Fisher*

PD. 45–1972 Constable, John. *Mrs Mary Fisher*

2291 Constable, John. *Parham's Mill, Gillingham* (1824)

2383 Constable, John. *Salisbury*

PD. 79–1959 Constable, John. *At Hampstead, looking towards Harrow*

PD. 10–1950 Cox, David. *Landscape with cattle by a pool* (1850)

1788 Cox, David. *The vale of Clwyd* (1849)

952 Mulready, William. *The farrier's shop*

630 Harlow, George Henry. *Professor Charles Hague*

641 Etty, William. *Dr John Camidge*

1797 Fielding, Anthony Vandyke Copley. *A heath near the coast*

PD. 8–1956 Nasmyth, Patrick. *View in Leigh Woods* (1830)

PD. 55–1958 Linnell, John. *The River Kennet, near Newbury* (1815)

PD. 6–1954 Stark, James. *Near Norwich*

PD. 69–1948 Stannard, Joseph. *Boats on the Yare near Bramerton, Norfolk* (1828)

PLATE 39

1104 Shayer, William, the elder. *The prawn fishers*

499 Gill, William. *Leap-frog*

PD. 11–1955 Bonington, Richard Parkes. *Landscape with a pond*

470 Goodall, Frederick. *Cottage interior* (1844)

469 Cooper, Thomas Sidney. *Cattle by a river* (1835)

490 Lance, George. *Fruit-piece*

480 Creswick, Thomas. *Crossing the stream* (1849)

492 Cooper, Thomas Sidney. *Cattle reposing* (1846)

1204 Richmond, George. *Mrs William Fothergill Robinson* (1870)

460* Lear, Edward. *The Temple of Apollo at Bassae* (1854–5)

PD. 108–1975 Elmore, Alfred. *On the brink* (1865)

503 Watts, George Frederic. *William Cavendish, 7th Duke of Devonshire* (1883)

2228 Stevens, Alfred. *Leonard W. Collmann*

PLATE 45

M.Add. 3 Brown, Ford Madox. *The last of England* (1860)

PD. 9–1950 Brown, Ford Madox. *Cordelia's portion*

676 Collins, Charles Allston. *Wilkie Collins* (1853)

774 Deverell, Walter Howell. *Self-portrait*

1760 Hunt, William Holman. *Cyril Benoni Holman Hunt* (1880)

1509 Hughes, Arthur. *The King's orchard*

728 Rossetti, Dante Gabriel. *Girl at a lattice* (1862)

1010 Millais, Sir John Everett. *Mrs Coventry Patmore* (1851)

1501 Leighton, Frederick, Lord. *Miss Laing* (1853)

PD. 2–1951 Inchbold, John William. *Anstey's Cove, Devon* (1854)

753 Sargent, John Singer. *Study of a Sicilian peasant* (1907)

1067 Sargent, John Singer. *Olives in Corfu*

PD. 17–1959 Sickert, Walter Richard. *The Lion of St Mark*

PD. 2–1955 Sickert, Walter Richard. *Mrs Swinton*

2410 Sickert, Walter Richard. *The trapeze* (1920)

PD. 18–1951 Steer, Philip Wilson. *Walberswick, children paddling* (1894)

PD. 184–1975 Steer, Philip Wilson. *The blue dress* (1892)

892 Nicholson, Sir William. *The girl with a tattered glove* (1909)

1138 Nicholson, Sir William. *A. C. Benson* (1924)

1144 McEvoy, Arthur Ambrose. *Professor James Ward* (1913)

2547 Sims, Charles. *The little faun*

851 John, Augustus Edwin. *The woman of Ower* (1914)

700 Peploe, Samuel John. *Still-life*

1641 John, Augustus Edwin. *Sir William Nicholson* (1909)

PLATE 58

1116 John, Augustus Edwin. *Thomas Hardy* (1923)

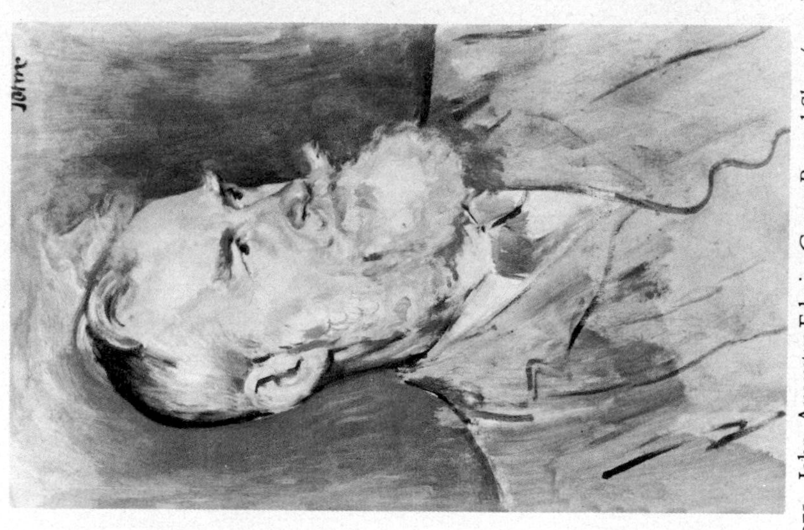

1071 John, Augustus Edwin. *George Bernard Shaw* (1915)

PD. 3–1967 Gilman, Harold. *Nude on a bed*

PD. 3–1955 Gore, Spencer Frederick. *The green dress*

PLATE 60

2453 Smith, Sir Matthew. *Landscape at Aix-en-Provence*

2450 Lees, Derwent. *Lyndra in Wales*

1121 Philpot, Glyn. *Siegfried Sassoon* (1917)

2748 Lamb, Henry. *Lytton Strachey*

PD. 6–1955 Nash, Paul. *November Moon* (1942)

1553 Spencer, Sir Stanley. *Cottages at Burghclere*

2452 Spencer, Sir Stanley. *Landscape in North Wales* (1938)

PD. 969-1963 Sutherland, Graham. *The Deposition* (1946)

INDEXES

INDEX OF PORTRAITS, SUBJECTS AND TOPOGRAPHY

INDEX OF PREVIOUS OWNERS

INDEX OF PREVIOUS OWNERS

NUMERICAL INDEX

The catalogue number is given on the left

NUMERICAL INDEX

UNIVERSITY LIBRARY
NOTTINGHAM